The Language of Law and Economics

From a historical perspective, "law and economics" constituted one of the most influential developments in legal scholarship in the twentieth century; the discipline remains today one of the dominant perspectives on the law, generating a tremendous quantity of new research and discussion. Unfortunately, one consequence of applying the analytical methods of one highly technical field to the historically layered substance of another has been the accumulation of considerable technical overhead, requiring fluency in both the language of economics and the language of the law. Further complicating matters, the field of law and economics has sometimes developed independently, creating new terms, while recasting others from their original economic or legal meanings. In this dictionary of law and economics, Francesco Parisi provides a comprehensive and concise guide to the language and key concepts underlying this fecund interdisciplinary tradition. The first reference work of its kind, it will prove to be an invaluable resource for professionals, students, and scholars.

FRANCESCO PARISI is the Oppenheimer Wolff and Donnelly Professor of Law at the University of Minnesota and Professor of Economics at the University of Bologna.

D1569168

The Language of Law and Economics

A Dictionary

Francesco Parisi

CAMBRIDGE
UNIVERSITY PRESS

CAMBRIDGE UNIVERSITY PRESS
Cambridge, New York, Melbourne, Madrid, Cape Town,
Singapore, São Paulo, Delhi, Mexico City

Cambridge University Press
The Edinburgh Building, Cambridge CB2 8RU, UK

Published in the United States of America by Cambridge University Press, New York

www.cambridge.org
Information on this title: www.cambridge.org/9780521697712

First published 2013

Printed and bound in the United Kingdom by the MPG Books Group

A catalog record for this publication is available from the British Library

Library of Congress Cataloging in Publication data
Parisi, Francesco, 1962–
The language of law and economics : a dictionary / Francesco Parisi.
   pages   cm
Includes bibliographical references and indexes.
ISBN 978-0-521-87508-0
1. Law – Economic aspects – Dictionaries.   2. Law and economics – Dictionaries.
I. Title.
K487.E3P37   2013
340.03 – dc23   2012035048

ISBN 978-0-521-87508-0 hardback
ISBN 978-0-521-69771-2 paperback

To Barbara

CONTENTS

INTRODUCTION

As an intellectual movement, the law and economics discipline has three characteristics that are at once strengths and obstacles: *first*, the vast breadth of interdisciplinary contributions, not only from lawyers and economists but also from psychologists, sociologists, political scientists, historians, mathematicians, and philosophers; *second*, the blistering pace at which new ideas emerge, develop, transform, fuse, and divide; and, *third*, the deeply technical components inherent to the law and to economics. Although these characteristics have imbued the field with scientific precision, establishing law and economics in the mainstream of legal scholarship, they have also brought about a prodigious expansion in terminology.

Communication problems plagued the early years of law and economics, as scholars from disparate disciplines struggled to find a common language to accommodate their diverse academic backgrounds. Over the years these communication problems became less pronounced, as a shared vocabulary developed. New terms were invented and established terms from specialized fields were repurposed in an interdisciplinary context. The new language has been a mixed blessing for the growth of law and economics, for, while it facilitates communication between scholars within the field, it also creates barriers for scholars working outside it. This dictionary aims at reducing those barriers.

In the age of electronic information, the idea of a dictionary, quaintly listing terms in alphabetical order, may seem anachronistic. However, the purpose of this dictionary is not merely to assemble and catalogue information, but to provide clear and concise explanations of those foundational concepts that will guide students and scholars in exploring the field of law and economics.

This project began with a handful of definitions that I wrote as a "glossary of terms," as a resource for students in my law and economics courses. The idea of developing the glossary into a comprehensive dictionary for a larger audience occurred to me after reading through Brian Bix's *A Dictionary of Legal Theory* (Oxford University Press, 2004). With such an exemplary model, it soon became clear that the work ahead of me was going to require considerably more toil, care, and nuance than I had originally anticipated. Nevertheless, I committed myself to this project, thanks to the positive feedback from my friend Chris Harrison at Cambridge University Press, who commissioned this book under the title *The Language of Law and Economics: A Dictionary*. The new direction suggested by the publisher resulted in a broadening of the scope of the project, leading to the inclusion of definitions not only for the benefit of law students but also for graduate students and professional academics.

Notwithstanding the more ambitious goals set by the publisher, I have tried to keep the entries simple; I have endeavored to provide basic definitions and foundational concepts, keeping technical details, theoretical extensions, and historical digressions to a minimum. When necessary, more formal definitions are provided in the latter portion of the entry for readers who value the additional layer of information. Whenever appropriate, I have attempted to credit the authors who first coined a new word, gave new meaning to an old term, or popularized a rarely encountered expression in the literature – though I have come to realize that the evolution of terminology in this field is quite often the result of the uncoordinated choices of several practitioners; such terms become attributable to the folk tradition of law and economics rather than any one scholar.

This book, although presented as the work of a sole author, reflects the combined expertise of many talented scholars, who suggested the inclusion of terms, corrected provisional definitions of terms, and occasionally volunteered their own definitions. I am particularly grateful to Giuseppe Dari-Mattiacci, Matteo Rizzolli, Margherita Saraceno, and several anonymous referees for identifying omissions, suggesting ideas, and volunteering their own definitions. Over the years, students from George Mason University and the University of Minnesota have helped me with research and editing. I should especially thank Johna Ohtagaki, Joshua Rusenko, Ryan Patrick, Theresa Stadheim, Chris Schmitter, Jamie Ling, and Emma Denny for their generous research assistance, providing first drafts of many definitions. Thanks must also go to Daniel Pi for his generous and valuable assistance in identifying and correcting problems in the manuscript in its final stages prior to publication. I would also like to thank the Max Schmidheiny Foundation and Anne van Aaken for the opportunity to visit the University of St. Gallen as a visiting professor in the law and economics program, during the final phase of this project. I should also thank Brian Bix for having unknowingly provided an inspiration for this dictionary, before our paths brought us together as colleagues at the University of Minnesota, as well as my uncle zio Peppino for having transmitted his interest for the multifarious use of words in modern languages and for having spent timeless hours at Starbucks with me, during my early years of work on this dictionary. As often happens with undertakings of this nature, at times I questioned the wisdom of having embarked on this project. Barbara Luppi, to whom this book is dedicated, renewed my focus and helped me to find the energy and passion for this project in those moments of doubt. I am eternally grateful to her for her support in the writing of this book, and so much more.

To aid in the use of this dictionary as a teaching and learning tool for specialized sub-fields or disciplines, I have compiled an index, which contains twelve groupings of specialized terms related to the following areas:

(1) history of law and economics;
(2) methodology and welfare analysis;
(3) preferences and choice;
(4) behavioral and experimental law and economics;

   (5) law and social norms;
   (6) the Coase theorem and remedies;
   (7) economics of contracts;
   (8) economics of torts;
   (9) economics of property;
 (10) economics of crime and deterrence;
 (11) economics of lawmaking and regulation;
 (12) economics of litigation and enforcement;
 (13) monopoly and competition;
 (14) theory of market failures;
 (15) game theory concepts;
 (16) contract theory and mechanism design;
 (17) new institutional economics;
 (18) social choice and public choice theory;
 (19) auction theory;
 (20) finance and microeconomics; and
 (21) statistics and econometrics.

Students and scholars who approach these topic areas for the first time will thus have an opportunity to focus on the specialized terms that are more relevant to their literature.

    This dictionary, as much as any other, should be viewed as a living document. To quote Carlo Dossi (1849–1910), "Dictionaries require constant updating, like geographical maps." This is especially true in a growing and fast-changing field such as law and economics. The temptation to delay the publication of this volume in the interest of greater accuracy and completeness was overcome by the desire to give life to a document that might prove useful to students and practitioners in this field. My concerns regarding any omissions in this edition are assuaged by the confidence that my many friends and colleagues in law and economics will report oversights and inaccuracies, and offer suggestions to improve future editions of this book.

A

Above-average effect: a cognitive bias, also known as the illusory superiority bias, that leads people to overestimate their positive qualities and underestimate their defects. Evidence of the above-average effect is quite robust with respect to common abilities and tasks (e.g., driving, parenting, managerial skills) but weaker with respect to unusual tasks. An above-average effect may distort one's perception of difficulties. Behavioral economists classify the above-average effect under the category of "positive illusions" (i.e., unrealistically favorable perceptions about one's self) (Taylor and Brown, 1988). As with other positive illusions, such as unrealistic optimism and illusion of control bias, the above-average effect may undermine estimations of risk and lead to a distortion of incentives. See also *optimism bias*, *illusion of control bias*, and *Hurwick optimism–pessimism index*.

Absolute advantage: a person or a firm is said to have an absolute advantage when it can produce a good or service at a lower cost than its competitors (or more quantity at the same cost). The term "absolute advantage" may be a useful descriptor when making comparisons between firms; however, being the best at producing something and having an absolute advantage over other producers does not mean that undertaking such activity is the best way to use one's productive capacity. The criterion of absolute advantage fails to take into account the opportunity cost of using one's productive capacity in a particular way. From a social efficiency perspective, the allocation of productive capacity and specialization should be determined by the concept of comparative advantage, not absolute advantage, in order to maximize all possible gains from trade. See also *comparative advantage*.

Absorptive capacity: a term used to describe the rate of learning and evaluation of outside knowledge. Absorptive capacity is determined by several factors, such as the existence of economies (or diseconomies) of scale and/or scope in the learning and processing of information, raising issues of optimal timing and sequence in the attainment of information (Cohen and Levinthal, 1990). The concept is used in both education policy and business contexts to determine the optimal pace of learning and the optimal size of knowledge-sharing institutions and firms.

Accounting profits versus economic profits: accountants and economists both define a firm's "profit" as its revenues minus costs. The difference between accounting profits and economic profits is that accounting profits count only explicit costs, ignoring implicit costs (i.e., opportunity costs), while economic profits count both explicit and implicit costs. Consequently, economic profits will tend to be represented by a smaller figure than accounting costs, although in some idiosyncratic cases, implicit benefits may offset implicit costs, in which case the measure of economic profit may be larger than accounting profit. See also *producer profit*, *producer surplus*, and *opportunity cost*.

Acoustic separation: a theoretical ideal solution to the conflict between pre-scriptive and reactive functions of legal systems. Dan-Cohen (1984) describes the analytical distinction between conduct rules (rules aimed at guiding future behavior) and decision rules (rules aimed at judging past behavior). Dan-Cohen observes that conduct rules and decision rules are often at cross-purposes, and he uses this tension to motivate the following thought experiment. Imagine a "world in which only judges and officials know the content of the decision rules and only the general public knows the content of the conduct rules." In order to sustain the separation between conduct rules and decision rules, the two groups – the general public and judges – must live in separate, insulated worlds. Dan-Cohen terms this condition "acoustic separation," and argues that the conflicting functions (i.e., prescriptive versus reactive) of a legal system would be recon-ciled in such a world. Although legal systems of the ancient past occasionally effected a selective transmission of legal information that incidentally resem-bled acoustic separation, the implementation of selective transmission would obviously raise issues of legitimacy in contemporary legal systems, as well as problems of credibility and time consistency in policymaking. Nevertheless, the concept of acoustic separation is frequently mentioned in the literature to high-light some inescapable moral dilemmas that arise when the forward-looking and the backward-looking functions of the law are in conflict with one another. See also *conduct rules versus decision rules*, *credibility*, *dynamic inconsistency*, and *ex ante versus ex post*.

Activity level externalities: in potentially tortious situations, parties impose pre-cautionary care costs upon each other. When parties increase their activity levels, they increase the cost of (non-durable) precautionary care for other parties. The residual bearers of liability do not take into account such externalities. See also *Shavell's activity level theorem* and *precaution externalities*.

Activity level versus care level: several factors affect the likelihood of an accident, including the quality and quantity of the precautions taken by tortfeasors and victims and the intensity and duration of tortfeasors' and victims' activities. Law and economics scholars group these factors under the headings of "care levels" and "activity levels." Polinsky (1980) and Shavell (1980b) independently point out the relevance of this distinction. The care level refers to the observable precautions used by courts to ascertain negligence, and indicates the extent of parties' precautionary efforts in carrying out their activities (e.g., in the case of automobiles: vehicle speed, use of headlights at night, observing road signals).

The activity level refers to the other factors that are not taken into account by courts to ascertain negligence, and indicates the intensity and duration of the parties' activities (e.g., how many miles did the tortfeasor drive, how often did the victim cross the intersection?). Dari-Mattiacci and Parisi (2005b) observe that some precautions are non-observable ex post. Investment in non-observable precautions may reduce the probability of an accident, but would not reduce the likelihood of being found negligent if an accident did occur. For this reason, the incentives to invest in non-observable precautions generally follow the activity level incentives of the parties. The distinction between care level and activity level becomes relevant when the criterion of negligence is used to establish liability. As pointed out by Shavell (1980b), negligence liability introduces a dichotomy between care-type and activity-type precaution investments. When establishing negligence, courts do not look at the "quantity" (activity level) of the parties' behavior, but only at their "quality" (care level). The distinction between care and activity level is irrelevant in regimes of strict liability and no liability. Activity level incentives (and the incentives to invest in non-observable precautions) are determined by the allocation of the residual liability (i.e., only the party who bears the cost of the accident in equilibrium has incentives to reduce his or her activity level and invest in non-observable precautions). See also *activity level externalities*, *precaution externalities*, *non-observable precautions*, and *Shavell's activity level theorem*.

Adaptive expectations: the impact of a proposed policy change depends on how consumers respond to it. The principle of adaptive expectations holds that individuals base expectations about future events on past trends and are slow to revise their expectations when trends change. The adaptive expectations model is based on the idea that individuals develop forecasts about the future value of a variable on the basis of past actual values adjusted for their own past expectations. Specifically, the expected future value of a variable is worked out by calculating a weighted average of past expected values and past actual value. Adaptive expectations models are thus based on the notion that economic actors adapt their future expectations in the light of their recent experience. The extent to which expectations change in the model depends on how individuals weight past expectations and actual experiences. Analytically, adaptive expectations are represented by the equation

$$p^e = p^e_{-1} + \lambda\left(p - p^e_{-1}\right)$$

where p^e represents the current expected value of a variable; p^e_{-1} represents the previous year's expected value; $(p - p^e_{-1})$ represents the difference between last year's expectations and the actual value; and λ designates the "lag" effect – how quickly individuals adjust to new information. According to adaptive expectations, individuals who have had a given experience in the past tend to expect a similar experience in the future. The principle of adaptive expectations, also

known as error learning because of the quantification of past error, is distinguishable from rational expectations, a notion that assumes that agents use all
and only current market data to ascertain future performance. See also ***rational
expectations***.

Adjustment dynamics: a form of dynamic analysis whereby models are subjected
to changes in parameters so that the process of convergence to a new equilibrium
can be studied. See also ***comparative dynamics*** and ***dynamic models***.

Adverse selection: adverse selection and moral hazard are the two categories of
circumstances involving asymmetric information. What distinguishes the two is
that, whereas the term "moral hazard" refers to ex post informational asymmetry, the term "adverse selection" refers to ex ante informational asymmetry. The
adverse selection problem was first analyzed by Nobel laureate George Akerlof,
in his 1970 paper entitled "The market for 'lemons,'" in which he observes that
the relationship between sellers and buyers of used cars suffers from an ex ante
information asymmetry, theoretically leading to market failure. Consequently,
adverse selection is sometimes also referred to as the "lemons problem." Adverse
selection has three elements: (a) there is a random variation in the quality of a
good; (b) parties have asymmetric information concerning the actual quality of
a specific item; and (c) sellers of poor-quality items are more willing to sell at
lower prices than sellers of high-quality items. Often cited examples of adverse
selection include insurance, labor markets, and used car markets. In these cases,
a party possesses information about quality that the other contracting party cannot easily verify. In the lemons example, sellers of used cars are in a better
position to know about the defects of their car than potential buyers. Consequently, owners of lower-quality cars would fill the market, since they would be
eager to sell their cars at market price, whereas owners of higher-quality used
cars would be selling at a loss. Therefore, the quality distribution of cars of
a given model/year offered for sale would not be representative of the overall
distribution of the quality of cars of that model/year. If buyers took such adverse
selection into account, causing the market value for cars of that model/year to
decline, the problem would simply be pushed back, since only owners of cars
that are worth less than the reduced offer price would be willing to sell. Indeed,
one can imagine the process repeating until the price were reduced to such an
extent that only the single worst car on the market would be offered. This unraveling would entail the total collapse of the used car market. Parties respond to
adverse selection problems by developing tools for screening and signaling. For
example, sellers may offer warranties for hidden defects in their products. By
offering a warranty, sellers credibly reveal private information about the quality
of their product (signaling). This induces a separating equilibrium, whereby
sellers of high-quality goods offer a warranty that sellers of a low-quality good
would be unwilling to match. Likewise, commercial records of car breakage
and car theft may reduce the cost of information for prospective buyers (screening). These signaling and screening devices facilitate the matching of sellers of

low-quality goods with those buyers who are less sensitive to defects, and sellers of high-quality goods with more sensitive or demanding buyers. Legal rules also play an important role in preventing/correcting adverse selection problems. For example, some legal rules create incentives for the voluntary disclosure of private information (e.g., penalty default rules). In other situations, legal systems create affirmative duties to disclose private information that may negatively affect the value of the transaction to the other contracting party (e.g., disclosure of hidden defects, disclosure of prior employment record, disclosure of preexisting health conditions). The question of when to impose legal rules and when to allow market forces to mitigate the effects of adverse selection has been the subject of much scholarly debate. See also *asymmetric information*, *reverse adverse selection*, and *inverse adverse selection*.

Agency problems: also known as principal–agent problems, these can be found in any relationship involving asymmetric information in which one party's conduct can produce effects on another party. Game theorists and mechanism design scholars were among the first to study agency problems systematically. The findings and the terminology of this literature have had a pervasive influence in law and economics. In a typical agency relationship, one individual (the "principal") retains another individual (the "agent") to carry out activities on his or her behalf (e.g., the owner of a company retains an individual to manage his business interest). Ab initio, principals and agents generally have misaligned incentives (e.g., a company owner wants to maximize the profits of his or her company, while the manager cares about his or her leisure time and compensation). Information is asymmetric, and the principal cannot perfectly monitor the activity of his or her agent. Hence, the agent may fail to act in the principal's best interest. The agency problem (or principal–agent problem) is to motivate the agent to adopt the interests of the principal as his or her own. Agency problems can be found in a number of situations, such as in most employer–employee relationships or in the delegation of legislative authority to bureaucratic agencies. In employment contracts, individual contracts solve the agency problem by making employee compensation a function of performance, through a variety of mechanisms, such as profit sharing, efficiency wage, discretionary bonuses, options, commissions, or contingency fees. Empirical studies have found that productivity improves when compensation is conditioned on performance. However, pay-for-performance schemes increase free-riding incentives in the jobs involving team production, characterized by large positive externalities and low returns to the individual. See also *adverse selection*, *moral hazard*, *free-riding*, *screening*, and *signaling*.

Agenda setting: policymakers face many competing challenges and have limited resources with which to address these challenges. The term "agenda setting" is generally used to describe the process by which policymakers decide the sequence of decisions and policy issues on which to focus. Kingdon (1995) distinguishes three stages that are relevant to the agenda-setting process: (a) the problem identification stage, (b) the policy formulation stage, and (c) the political deliberation stage. Public choice and social choice theorists have studied the relevance of agenda setting to determining the outcome of collective decision-making processes. They have found that the sequence of decisions does indeed often affect outcomes. For example, when collective decisions are subject to cyclicality, the setting of the voting agenda can be strategically manipulated to game the desired outcome. Empirical and theoretical literature in public choice theory further supports the proposition that agenda setters have substantial power in policymaking. See also *policy window*.

Aggregate misperception: see *pluralistic ignorance*.

Aggregate surplus: in a voluntary exchange, both sellers (producers) and buyers (consumers) benefit from a transaction. The sum of the buyers' and sellers' benefits is the aggregate surplus. In an exchange, the aggregate surplus can be easily computed as the difference between the buyer's willingness to pay and the seller's willingness to accept. The concept of aggregate surplus is important in law and economics, in which economic and competition policies are designed to maximize aggregate surplus. See also *consumer surplus* and *producer surplus*.

Aggregation problem: the need to make comparative evaluations between different rules motivates much of law and economics. Consequently, an important methodological problem in law and economics concerns the choice of criteria for carrying out such comparative analysis. In practical terms, this problem concerns the method of aggregation of individual preferences into social preferences. This problem is not unique to law and economics. It is part of a much larger methodological debate in economic philosophy and welfare economics. As early as the late nineteenth century Edgeworth (1881: 7–8) was stating the moral dilemma of social welfare analysis, observing that a moral calculus should proceed with a comparative evaluation of "the happiness of one person with the happiness of another . . . Such comparison can no longer be shirked, if there is to be any systematic morality at all." The problem obviously arises from the fact that economists do not have any reliable method for measuring individuals' utility, let alone make interpersonal comparisons of utility (Klick and Parisi, 2005). See also *Kaldor–Hicks criterion*, *Nash criterion of welfare*, *capability approach*, and *Rawlsian maximin*.

Akerlof, George Arthur (1940–): an American economist whose work has been particularly influential in the field of law and economics. He is best known for his work on markets characterized by asymmetric information. He received the Nobel Prize in economics in 2001 (shared with Michael Spence and Joseph Stiglitz) for his 1970 paper "The market for 'lemons': quality uncertainty and the market mechanism," in which he identifies the reasons for the severe problems that often afflict markets characterized by information asymmetries. Akerlof was born in New Haven, Connecticut, on June 17, 1940, and received his undergraduate degree from Yale University in 1960. He went on to receive his Ph.D. from the Massachusetts Institute of Technology in 1966. Together, he and his wife, Janet Yellen, vice chairman of the Federal Reserve System, wrote *Efficiency Wage Models of the Labor Market* (1986), in which they propose rationales for the efficiency wage hypothesis, which postulates that employers will pay above the market-clearing wage for labor for various reasons. Akerlof has also proposed, in his 1993 paper with Paul Romer "Looting: the economic underworld of bankruptcy for profit," that there may be incentives for the managers and owners of corporations to "loot" their companies rather than help them flourish, and that there should be norms embedded in macroeconomics for how corporations "should" behave in order to prevent such outcomes. In addition to his other contributions to the field of economics, Akerlof, along with Rachel Kranton, has been influential in developing the field of identity economics, which proposes that social identities and norms are as influential as monetary incentives when it comes to individual economic decision-making. See also *asymmetric information* and *adverse selection*.

ALACDE: Latin American and Iberian Law and Economics Association (originally called the Latin American and Caribbean Law and Economics Association). Founded in 1995 under the leadership of a group of scholars led by Andrés Roemer, Edgardo Buscaglia, and Robert Cooter, the association was created to promote awareness, advance, and develop legal research employing the tools of economic analysis, and to keep law schools in Latin America, the Caribbean, and Iberia abreast of the latest findings and groundbreaking work in the field. The first meeting was held in Mexico City in October 1995, organized by Andrés Roemer and Miguel de la Madrid. Since then the annual meeting has been held on a rotating basis. Presidents pro tempore of the association are elected annually, and have included Avelino Porto and Edgardo Buscaglia (1996), Julia Barragon (1997), Valeria Merino (1998), Emilio José Archila Peñalosa (1999), Rafael Mery and Ricardo Predes (2002), Alfredo Bullard (2004), Robert Cooter (2005), Juan Vicente Sola and Horacio Spector (2006), Flavia Santinoni Vera (2007), Juan Javier del Granado (2008), Pablo Salvador (2009), Rafal Barraza (2010), and Alfredo Bullard (2011). In addition to its annual meetings, the association sponsors the translation of law and economics literature into Spanish and Portuguese. Thanks to funding provided by the Microsoft Corporation, the association awards an annual ALACDE Award for Best Research in Law and Economics for both junior and senior scholars. Since 2006 the association has published the *Latin American Journal of Law and Economics*. See also *ALEA*, *CLEA*, *EALE*, and *ASLEA*.

ALEA: American Law and Economics Association. Founded in 1991 under the initiative of Henry Manne, who was then dean of George Mason University Law School in Fairfax, Virginia, the association was created to respond to the needs of the growing community of law and economics scholars and to promote and encourage research in the field. The John M. Olin Foundation provided initial funding for the development of the association. ALEA

publishes the biannual journal *American Law and Economics Review*. The first
organizational meeting occurred in January of 1990 at George Mason University and was attended by Robert Cooter (Berkeley), Charles Goetz (Virginia),
Victor Goldberg (Columbia), A. Mitchell Polinsky (Stanford), George Priest
(Yale), Steven Shavell (Harvard), Michael Trebilcock (Toronto), Thomas Ulen
(Illinois), and Richard Zerbe (Washington). The first annual meeting of the
association was held on May 24 and 25, 1991, at the University of Illinois in
Champaign-Urbana, and was attended by 200 scholars. The meeting included
a plenary session honoring Guido Calabresi (Yale), Ronald Coase (Chicago),
Henry Manne (George Mason), and Richard Posner (Chicago) as the founding
fathers of law and economics. The association has subsequently held an annual
meeting on a rotating basis. The presidents of the association are elected annu-
ally: George Priest (1991), William Landes (1992), A. Mitchell Polinsky (1993),
Robert Cooter (1994), Richard Posner (1995), Alan Schwartz (1996), Oliver
Williamson (1997), Roberta Romano (1998), Lewis Kornhauser (1999), Robert
Ellickson (2000), Steven Shavell (2001), Michael Trebilcock (2002), Frank
Easterbrook (2003), Henry Hansmann (2004), Daniel Rubinfeld (2005), Oliver
Hart (2006), Lucian Bebchuk (2007), Michelle White (2008), Orley Ashenfel-
ter (2009), Louis Kaplow (2010), John Donohue (2011), Jennifer Reinganum
(2012), and Douglas Baird (2013). See also ***American Law and Economics
Review***, ***ASLEA***, ***EALE***, ***CLEA***, and ***ALACDE***.

Allocative efficiency: resources and legal entitlements are allocated with different mechanisms, ranging from equal share distributions, first-come first-serve
allocations, random initial assignments, competitive bidding and auctions, litigation contests, etc. The concept of allocative efficiency is used to evaluate how
alternative mechanisms allocate resources and entitlements efficiently (e.g., to
the highest valuing user, to the most productive firm, etc.). Although Coase
(1959, 1960) shows that inefficient initial allocations can be corrected through
ex post (Coasean) bargaining, when ex post reallocations are costly or prohibited the efficiency of the initial allocation becomes important. See also ***Coasean
bargaining*** and ***efficiency***.

Altering rules: legal systems determine the ways in which private parties can
modify default rules. The modification of default rules can be made more or less
costly by the law, effectively turning the contractible rules versus mandatory
rules divide into a continuum. McDonnell (2007) and Ayres (2012) refer to
the rules governing the modification of default rules as "altering rules." In some
cases, altering rules aim at reducing the relative cost of opting out by encouraging
parties to negotiate explicitly and penalizing parties that fail to do so (penalty
default rules). In other cases, altering rules take a more neutral stand and leave
parties free to modify default rules without altering the relative cost of an opt-
out (majoritarian default rules). In yet other cases, altering rules allow parties to
raise the opt-out costs, creating some "stickiness" in the modification of default

rules (sticky default rules). See also *sticky default rules*, *penalty default rules*, and *default rules*.

Alternative hypothesis: see *null versus alternative hypothesis*.

Alternative versus joint care: in a bilateral accident, the probability and severity of an accident depend on both the victim's and the injurer's behavior. Law and economics scholars further distinguish between alternative care and joint care situations. In alternative care situations, the parties' care efforts are substitutable: one party's untaken precautions can effectively be overcome by an increase in the other party's precautions. At the limit, one party's care may be sufficient to avoid an accident. In joint care cases, the parties' care efforts are complementary to one another: one party's untaken precautions cannot be easily overcome by the other party's care. In this latter situation, it is desirable for both parties to take precautions in order to avoid an accident. In economic models, the sign of the cross-partial derivative describes the relationship between the two parties' efforts of care. Using the conventional notation, where x and y represent the care levels of the two parties and $p(x, y)$ represents the probability of an accident, alternative care cases will be denoted by a negative cross-partial derivative, $\partial^2 p / \partial x \partial y < 0$, while joint care cases will be denoted by a positive cross-partial derivative, $\partial^2 p / \partial x \partial y > 0$. See also *bilateral accident*, *double-edged torts*, and *hybrid precautions*.

American Law and Economics Association: see *ALEA*.

American Law and Economics Review: established in 1999 as the official journal of the American Law and Economics Association. Orley Ashenfelter and Richard Posner served as the editors of this review from its founding until 2008, followed by John Donohue (2009–present) and Steven Shavell (2009–present). The review is one of the three journals in the field of law and economics published by Oxford University Press (together with the *Journal of Law, Economics, and Organization* and the *Journal of Competition Law and Economics*). See also *law and economics journals* and *ALEA*.

American rule: see *fee shifting*.

Anchoring bias: anchoring is a cognitive bias that leads people to assess probabilities starting with an implicit reference point and then to adjust it to form their estimate. According to the anchoring heuristic, people begin with an initial approximation of the probability at which they anchor, and then make adjustments to the anchor on the basis of additional information. The anchoring bias was identified by Tversky and Kahneman (1974). One of their experimental studies asked people to estimate the percentage of African nations represented in the United Nations. Researchers asked one group of subjects whether the percentage was more or less than 10 percent and the other group whether the percentage was more or less than 65 percent. Subjects in the first group responded on average with lower values (25 percent) than the second group (45 percent). Experimental evidence suggests that the anchoring bias affects economic estimates such as fair prices and bargaining opportunities. See also *behavioral law and economics, availability bias, representativeness bias, hindsight bias, overcorrection,* and *serial position effect.*

Anchoring heuristics: see *anchoring bias.*

Anti-coordination games: see *chicken game.*

Anti-insurance: according to economic analysis, one of the objectives of imposing liability in contracts is to create optimal performance and reliance incentives for the contracting parties. By linking the promisee's compensation to the promisor's liability, standard damage provisions in contracts do not always create optimal incentives for the contracting parties. Cooter and Porat (2002) have developed the anti-insurance concept as an alternative remedy that would incentivize efficient behavior on the part of both the promisor and the promisee. In an anti-insurance system, the promisor would pay a third party in the event of a breach and the third party would not pay the promisee any damages. However, for the right to receive damages from the promisor, the third party would pay both the promisor and the promisee some smaller amount before either performance or non-performance. While traditional damages encourage the promisee to rely on the promise inefficiently and, in some cases, even to act recklessly, the promisee would have no guaranteed benefits under an anti-insurance system. While he or she would have confidence that the promisor would perform, since the promisor would need to pay damages to the third party in the event of breach, he or she would also know that he or she would receive no damages if the promisor breached. This would solve the inefficiency problems present in a traditional damages regime and force both the promisor and the promisee to internalize the risk of breach. Cooter and Porat (2002) illustrate this concept using the example of a warranty for a transmission on a new car. Under a warranty, the manufacturer would put in the optimal amount of effort to produce high-quality transmissions for each consumer. However, individual consumers, in the light of the warranty, might abuse or overwork their transmissions. Manufacturers could include an anti-insurance provision in their contracts to incentivize consumers to take precaution when using their cars, because they would know they would not receive full damages for a problem with the transmission. Instead, they would receive only what the third-party anti-insurer paid them before any problems might arise with the transmission. The logic of the anti-insurance idea is similar to the logic of "decoupling" in tort law, inasmuch as both methods disentangle (victims' and promisees') compensation from (tortfeasors' and promisors') liability. See also *decoupling, residual decoupling,* and *contributory and comparative non-negligence.*

Anti-property: the concept of anti-property rights was introduced in the law and economics literature by Bell and Parchomovsky (2003). Anti-property rights are veto rights over the use of an asset granted to a large number of private actors. The main idea is that the conservation of property creates a public good problem, leading to its undersupply in a free market economy. Anti-property regimes can be viewed as a way to create countervailing transaction costs to favor desirable conservation. As with an anticommons situation, anti-property regimes are characterized by a large number of right holders with exclusion rights, creating a holdout problem that is unlikely to be resolved through contracting because of the high transaction costs. For example, conservation easements in favor of a large number of interested individuals create a holdout problem that is unlikely to be resolved through contracting. Unlike an anticommons problem that leads to a suboptimal use of resources, anti-property regimes can be intentionally created to favor socially desirable conservation, rendering it practically impossible to have unwanted development of protected property. According to the authors, anti-property can be viewed as a quasi-private mechanism for pursuing goals that are generally reserved to the public functions. Resource conservation through anti-property relies on private enforcement by interested private actors, avoiding the capture problems that generally undermine effective governmental action in the area of conservation. See also ***anticommons***.

Anticommons: a term that is relatively new to the law and economics lexicon. The concept, first introduced by Michelman (1982) and subsequently popularized by Heller (1998, 1999) and Buchanan and Yoon (2000), is the mirror image of Hardin's (1968) well-known concept of "commons." In an anticommons problem, multiple co-owners share the right to exclude others from a scarce resource, and no one has the privilege of use without the others' consent. This is the converse of the commons problem, whereby multiple individuals can use a given resource, without a cost-effective way to monitor and constrain each other's use. However, whereas the tragedy of the commons leads to overconsumption, in an anticommons scenario the undesirable tendency is underutilization of the resource, leading to a problem known as "the tragedy of the anticommons." This effect is the opposite of the one observed in commons situations, in which the resource is vulnerable to overuse ("the tragedy of the commons"). The term "anticommons" was coined by Michelman (1982) and was discussed as if it had no counterpart in real-world property. The hypothetical example would be that of a wilderness preserve where any person has standing to enforce the wilderness conservation laws and regulations. Heller (1998) revitalized the concept, showing several real-life examples and unveiling the strong explanatory power of the concept. The definition of the anticommons as employed by Heller is "a property regime in which multiple owners hold effective rights of exclusion in a scarce resource" (Heller, 1998: 668). In the "tragedy of the anticommons," the coexistence of multiple exclusion rights creates conditions for suboptimal use of the common resource: some common resources will remain idle even in the economic region of positive marginal productivity. There is a misalignment of the private and social incentives of multiple owners in the use of a common resource. The misalignment arises from the presence of externalities that are not captured in the calculus of the interests of the excluders: multiple holders of exclusion rights do not fully internalize the cost created by the enforcement of their right to exclude others (Parisi, Schulz, and Depoorter, 2005). See also *commons*, *entropy*, and *anti-property*.

Antitrust paradox: term coined by Supreme Court nominee and Yale Law School professor Robert Bork (1927–2012) in his magnum opus, *The Antitrust Paradox* (1978). The "paradox" is that the enforcement of antitrust laws, enacted to combat the abuse of monopolistic power to the detriment of consumers, often had the effect of harming consumers, by artificially propping up uncompetitive businesses and disrupting the effects of efficient competition. The idea is that monopolies are sometimes socially efficient (e.g., natural monopolies, vertical monopolies), and that legal intervention creates inefficiencies, the costs of which ultimately fall on consumers. Bork (1978) uses this insight to motivate a clarification of the purpose of antitrust law, which he proposes to be the maximization of consumer welfare. While Bork's views have generated considerable scholarly controversy – particularly on the legislative history of the Sherman Antitrust Act and Bork's ambiguous use of the term "consumer welfare" – his influence has largely shaped the Supreme Court's approach in antitrust cases. See also *natural monopoly*, *economies of scale*, *Tullock's rectangle*, and *efficiency defense*.

Appropriator: Ostrom (1990) uses the term "appropriator" to describe a person who appropriates or takes resources from a common-pool resource. If the resource is not regenerative or if the rate of exploitation is not sustainable, the activity of the appropriator leads to the depletion of the common-pool resource. See also *common-pool resources*.

Approval voting: a voting procedure in which voters give an "approval" vote to as many candidates as they wish. Each approval vote counts one point (disapproval and lack of approval count zero) and the candidate who receives the largest number of approval votes wins. This voting procedure is often proposed in nonpartisan primary elections that draw from a large number of candidates and is used in several settings for the election of heads of governmental institutions and international organizations (e.g., the United Nations' election of its Secretary-General). Approval voting has several advantages over the traditional single-vote plurality system, including the less confrontational nature of the contest and its practicality. See also *point voting* and *Borda count method*.

Arrow–Hurwick index: see *Hurwick optimism–pessimism index*.

Arrow, Kenneth Joseph (1921–): one of the founders of social choice theory. He received the Nobel Prize in economics (with John Hicks) in 1972 for his pioneering contribution to general economic equilibrium theory and welfare theory. Arrow was born in New York on August 23, 1921. He received his undergraduate education at the City College of New York, majoring in mathematics. He received his M.A. in mathematics in 1941 at Columbia University. His subsequent graduate work was in the economics department, where, after an interruption due to the war, he completed his dissertation on the relationship between the individual and social ranking of preferences. The dissertation was subsequently published as *Social Choice and Individual Values* (1951) and became Arrow's most celebrated contribution to social choice and welfare theory. In it, Arrow shows that it is impossible to construct a social welfare function out of individual preference functions. This groundbreaking result has become a pillar of social welfare theory, as well as having significant philosophical implications. In addition to his contributions to social choice theory, Arrow has also provided foundational work in other areas of economics, including endogenous growth theory and decision theory. See also *social choice theory*, *Arrow's impossibility theorem*, and *Arrow's information paradox*.

Arrow's impossibility theorem: states that no voting rule or procedure will guarantee an outcome reflecting the combined preferences of voters under any possible set of preferences. The economist and Nobel laureate Kenneth Arrow formulated the theorem in his doctoral dissertation, published as *Social Choice and Individual Values* (1951). The theorem shows that any democratically selected policy must violate at least one of six axioms of normative political theory, commonly described by the following terms: range, universal domain, unanimity, non-dictatorship, independence of irrelevant alternatives, and rationality. The implications of the theorem concern the existence of cyclical majorities capable of repealing any resolution that has been previously adopted. The theorem further implies that the correlation between preference and choice is weaker for groups than for individuals. Among other things, there is no assurance that transitive individual preferences will lead to transitive collective choices. The intransitivity of collective outcomes can be easily manipulated by agenda setters. Arrow's negative conclusion and its various corollaries pose a dramatic threat to the legitimacy of political decisions. See also *Condorcet voting paradox*, *cycling*, and *Benholz theorem*.

Arrow's information paradox: reveals the importance of intellectual property law. The premise of the paradox (Arrow, 1971) is that a product or technology is valuable to a potential purchaser after he or she has information about that product or technology. However, paradoxically, once the purchaser has this information and could actually decide to purchase the product or technology, he or she has essentially acquired it without cost. For example, if an inventor develops a novel office organizational tool and seeks to sell it, he or she will need to tell potential purchasers in order to encourage them to buy. However, once he or she tells them about the product, they will have the knowledge they need to develop the product themselves. Intellectual property law remedies the inventor's paradox. Once the inventor acquires a patent, he or she can discuss and market the invention without fear that a purchaser will simply build the technology or product him- or herself (Takenaka, 2008). See also ***double-trust problem***.

Ascending-price auctions: see *English auctions*.

Asian Law and Economics Association: see *ASLEA*.

ASLEA: Asian Law and Economics Association. Founded in 2005, with the purpose of stimulating the study of law and economics within Asia, providing assistance to scholars researching within the field, and promoting the use of law and economics models, criteria, and analyses within the framework of political management and jurisprudence. The Korean Law and Economics Association provided the initial funding for the association's first annual meeting. The association was founded by a group of scholars led by Young Hoa Jung (Seo-Kyung University), Jeong-Yoo Kim (Kyung Hee University), Shozo Ota (University of Tokyo), and Akio Morishima (Nagoya University). The first annual meeting was held in Seoul from June 24 to 25, 2005, when almost 120 scholars presented seventy-eight scholarly papers. The meeting featured keynote addresses by Yoon-Ha Yoo, Cyrus Chu, and Robert Cooter. Since then, the association has held an annual meeting on a rotating basis. The presidents, elected to a one-year, once-renewable term, have been Ivan P'ng (2005–6), Moriki Hosoe (2006–8), Jeong-Yoo Kim (2008–9), Kong-Pin Chen (2009–10), and Chenggang Xu (2010–present). Since 2010 the association has published the *Asian Journal of Law and Economics*. See also *ALEA*, *CLEA*, *EALE*, and *ALACDE*.

Asset specificity: the lack of transferability of assets across different uses. The degree of asset specificity is determined by the difference between the value of an asset in its intended use and the value of the same asset in its second-best alternative use. High asset specificity implies that the asset has a substantially lower value outside its current use. Such difference in value represents a "sunk cost" that cannot be recouped if the asset is employed for a different purpose. The new institutional economics literature has intensely scrutinized the strategic problems associated with asset specificity. Parties who have incurred asset-specific investments for the performance of a contract are vulnerable to opportunistic behavior by the other contracting party. Consequently, scholars have suggested that contractual safeguards are necessary to combat the threat of such opportunistic behavior. See also *sunk costs*.

Assumptions: see *robustness*.

Assurance game: see *stag-hunt game*.

Asymmetric Coase theorem: a reformulation of the normative Coase theorem that is applicable to situations characterized by asymmetric transaction and strategic costs, such as when complementary fragments of property are attributed to different owners (Luppi and Parisi, 2011). The asymmetry arises from the fact that it is often harder to reunite separated property bundles than to break them apart. This variant of the Coase theorem turns on (a) an initial allocation of entitlements that minimizes the effects of the positive transaction costs, and (b) the selection of legal rules that reduce social welfare losses by facilitating optimal levels of reunification. See also ***normative Coase theorem***.

Asymmetric information: a form of market failure in which one party has access to more relevant information than the other. There are two main undesirable consequences of asymmetric information: adverse selection and moral hazard. The relevant distinction here is that adverse selection is an ex ante case of asymmetric information, whereas moral hazard is an ex post case of asymmetric information. In his 1970 article "The market for 'lemons,'" Akerlof illustrates the concept of adverse selection with the example of the used car market, in which sellers are likely to know more about the quality of their cars than buyers. Because buyers cannot ascertain the quality of a used car, uncertainty depresses prices. Owners of high-quality cars consequently become less likely to put their high-quality cars on the market at the depressed price, and the market will be predominantly populated by low-quality cars (the "lemons" in "The market for 'lemons'"). This further reduces the expected quality of cars on the market and drives yet more prospective buyers and sellers out of the market. This process of adverse selection leads to a market failure. Because of the asymmetric information, many potentially beneficial transactions do not take place in the market; consequently, the market fails to reallocate resources efficiently – the very definition of market failure. Another possible undesirable effect of asymmetric information is the moral hazard problem (Stiglitz and Rothschild, 1976). With moral hazard, asymmetric information generally takes the form of non-observable behavior or costly monitoring. A common example is the agent–principal relationship, in which the interests of the agent and the principal may not be aligned. Information asymmetries are generally "corrected" by communicating information through signaling and/or acquiring information through screening. See also ***adverse selection***, ***moral hazard***, ***signaling***, and ***screening***.

Atomistic market: see ***perfect competition***.

Attitudes toward risk: see ***risk preferences***.

Auction theory: together with market design one of the liveliest areas of economic research in recent years. Auction theory is concerned with the properties of different types of auctions and focuses on how auction mechanisms can best be designed to generate economic efficiency. In 1996 James Mirrlees and William Vickrey were awarded the Nobel Prize in economics for their contributions to this field. Their work provided important foundations to the modern analysis of complex information and incentive problems. The findings of this area of research have important implications for the design of contracts and institutions. The "auction" model is characterized by a mutual asymmetry of information between bidders and sellers. Bidders are unaware of the value of the item,

on which they are bidding, while sellers are unaware of the private valuations
of the bidders. Auction theory analyzes the properties of different kinds of
auctions in coping with such informational asymmetries. Recent contributions
to this field have concentrated on the allocative efficiency of alternative auction
or exchange mechanisms under conditions of imperfect information. See also
revenue equivalence theorem.

Auctions: see *auction theory*.

Austrian law and economics: an alternative way of looking at the field of law and
economics. The Austrian school of law and economics is grounded in methodological individualism and methodological subjectivism. Scholars who adhere
to this school emphasize the purposefulness and intentionality of human action.
Austrians view social phenomena as processes that are in constant change. Law
changes the perception, expectations, and subjective evaluations of economic
agents. This constant flux of reality and expectations makes the neoclassical
approach to law and economics ill-suited for the design of laws and legal institutions. The members of the Austrian school devote much attention to the study
of the role of knowledge and error in economic life. Austrian law and economics scholars consider freedom of contract and private property as critical
ingredients for economic prosperity. They generally hold skeptical views of the
normative use of economic analysis. They believe that, in many situations, laws
and regulations create distortions that are comparable to taxation or government intervention in the market process. Austrians are wary of the notion of
legal intervention for the correction of market failures. Although not explicitly questioning the presence of market failures they are skeptical of the idea
that governments can perform the task more efficiently than other, decentralized, institutions. In this sense, the Austrians use many of the results of public
choice theory to show the tradeoff between market failures and governmental
and political failures. Most importantly, they believe that redistribution is the
almost unavoidable consequence of democratic political decision-making. In
this respect, they emphasize the dangers of lawmaking through politics. Despite
the theoretical appeal and important philosophical underpinnings of the Austrian school, the Austrian approach has not been very influential in law and
economics, probably on account of the lack of practical guiding principles that
could direct courts and policymakers in the solution of real-life legal problems.
See also *functional law and economics*.

Availability bias: a cognitive bias according to which individuals assess the frequency of an event on the basis of how easily they can recall an instance of it.
The availability bias was discovered by Tversky and Kahneman (1974), who
should also be credited with identifying the anchoring and representativeness
bias. People tend to assess the probability of specific events (e.g., the homicide
rate) by predicting that events that appear more regularly in the media will occur
more frequently in general, since they can promptly and more easily recall an

example of that specific event from memory. Experimental research shows that people incorrectly predict death by homicide to occur more frequently than death by cancer since they recall unusual and vivid events, such as homicides and plane crashes, which are reported by the media, rather than common and unsensational causes of death, such as common diseases or car accidents. See also *hindsight bias, anchoring bias, representativeness bias*, and *serial position effect.*

Availability heuristics: see *availability bias*.

Average production cost: see *production cost*.

Axelrod's experiment: see *evolution of cooperation*.

Axiomatic theory of bargaining: bargaining models describe the process by which parties come to cooperate when a lack of cooperation would lead to inefficient outcomes. The axiomatic theory of bargaining proposed by Nash (1950b) is a frequently used model in law and economics. The model rests on two assumptions. First, bargainers are assumed to be fully rational players. Second, predictions follow from exclusive information relevant to the players. The axiomatic theory establishes the properties of bargain outcomes (bargaining will lead to the maximization of the product of the parties' utility from the bargaining). Solutions are proposed based on outcomes. Prior to the formal development of the Nash bargaining game and Nash bargaining solution, economists had postulated that the solution to a bargaining problem had to satisfy the dual criteria of individual rationality and collective rationality (Edgeworth, 1881; Hicks, 1932). In other words, when faced with a bargaining opportunity, neither party could be worse off than the status quo. See also *Nash bargaining solution*, *Coasean bargaining*, and *egalitarian bargaining solution*.

Axioms of preference: the following axioms of preference are generally cited in choice theory: (a) completeness, (b) reflexivity, (c) transitivity, (d) continuity, and (e) non-satiation. The first axiom requires preferences to be complete, in the sense that for any two goods, x and y, a consumer can establish a preference ordering (x preferred to y, y preferred to x, or x indifferent to y). Without such completeness, preferences would be undefined. The second axiom requires preferences to be reflexive, in the sense that, if $x = y$, then the consumer should be indifferent between x and y (and, likewise, if the consumer is indifferent between x and y, he or she should also be indifferent between y and x). The third axiom requires preferences to be transitive, in the sense that if x is preferred to y, and y is preferred to z, then (by transitivity) it must be that x is also preferred to z. The axioms of reflexivity and transitivity are often combined into a single axiom of consistency of choice. The fourth axiom requires preferences to be continuous. If x is preferred to y and z lies within an ε radius of y then it must be that x is also preferred to z. The requirement of continuity is instrumental to deriving well-behaved consumer demand curves. The first four axioms guarantee that utility functions can be defined. The fifth axiom applies to consumer choice with respect to desirable goods, and requires non-satiation, in the sense that consumers always place positive value on more consumption (i.e., more is preferred to less). As the term "axiom" suggests, these propositions were originally presented as self-evident and necessary features of consumer choice, requiring no further logical or empirical validation. These axioms are still widely used as starting assumptions, for the purpose of using mathematical representation of utility and to portray rational behavior and well-behaved consumer choice. Behavioral and experimental economists have recently shown several systematic departures of individual choice from these axioms.

Ayres, Ian (1959–): the William K. Townsend Professor of Law at Yale Law School. He graduated from Yale in 1981 with a B.A. (summa cum laude), majoring in Russian studies and economics. He earned his J.D. from Yale Law School in 1986, and his Ph.D. in economics from Massachusetts Institute of Technology in 1988. He clerked for Hon. James K. Logan on the Tenth Circuit Court of Appeals. Ayres is one of the most prolific authors in law and economics, having written more than 100 articles and nine books. Although he has written on a large number of subjects, he is particularly well regarded for his work in contracts, corporate law, and finance. Ayres is also known for his work in social justice, and he has a substantial media presence outside academia.

B

Background risk: certain activities or events may increase (or reduce) the probability of a given outcome. For example, exposure to a given dangerous substance may increase the risk of lung cancer. The background risk is the risk of that outcome (lung cancer) prior to the event (exposure to dangerous substance). The concept of background risk is particularly relevant in tort law. For example, if the risk materializes (the exposed individual develops lung cancer) and the background risk was sufficiently high, a causation question may arise: was cancer caused by the exposure, or would it have developed anyway due to the background risk? Similarly, when quantifying harm, should compensation be discounted by the probability that the individual would have suffered lung cancer in the absence of exposure? The legal allocation of background risk has important effects on the parties' incentives and may create adverse selection and moral hazard problems for prospective tortfeasors and victims. See also *coincidental causation*.

Backlash effect: a fundamental question addressed by the recent law and norms literature considers the critical interaction between legal and social sanctions in promoting socially desirable behavior. Kahan (1998, 2000) has pointed out that, in many situations, laws that depart from the current values of society may run against "sticky norms." This may lead to the ineffectiveness of legal intervention and, possibly, to backlash effects. Recent work in experimental and behavioral law and economics provides evidence of the backlash effects of legal intervention (Stuntz, 2000; Depoorter, Parisi, and Vanneste, 2005; Parisi and von Wangenheim, 2006; Depoorter, Van Hiel, and Vanneste, 2011). Legal sanctions and levels of enforcement may be perceived as being excessively strict and society may react to such unjust laws, undermining the intended effect of legal intervention, such as after the recent wave of copyright enforcement, which led to a backlash effect, with a resulting increase of copyright infringements (Depoorter, Van Hiel, and Vanneste, 2011). See also *inexpressive law*, *sticky norms*, *countervailing norms*, *normative overdeterrence*, and *hard shoves versus gentle nudges*.

Backward induction: a method to calculate the equilibrium solution in sequential games, requiring reasoning starting from the end of the game and working backward to its beginning to characterize the sequence of optimal actions by the players. By applying backward induction, the optimal choice of the last mover in the game is calculated for each possible situation. The process is iterated for the second-to-last player up to the first mover in the game. In a two-stage two-player game, backward induction requires the characterization of the optimal choice of the second player (i.e., the last mover) for any possible situation and then calculation of the optimal choice of the first player (i.e., the one moving first). The rationale of backward induction is that the first mover will choose by anticipating how the second mover will react. The best choice of the first mover hence incorporates the second mover's best response. An example of a game solved by backward induction is the Stackelberg oligopoly model, in which a duopolist who has a time advantage over his or her competitor will choose trying to anticipate what his or her rival will do in response to his or her action. Most legal problems involving actions that take place at different times can be analyzed through backward induction. For example, in a bilateral contract, the optimal performance investment of the party whose performance is due first can be identified through backward induction by identifying the optimal choices of the last mover. As an illustration, consider an event organizer who promises to organize a concert for a musician who promises to perform. Even though the concert needs to be organized before the music performance can take place, the optimal choice of the concert organizer (first mover) should be calculated through backward induction by considering the future choice of the singer (last mover). If the singer is expected to breach, the concert organizer's best strategy may well be to hold the organization of the concert. Zermelo (1913) used backward induction to analyze the game of chess, and this is why backward induction is also known as Zermelo's algorithm. When using backward induction, the outcome of a long-term relationship is often derived by understanding what is expected to happen in the last round of the interaction. In the jargon often used by law and economics scholars, the term "unraveling" is used to refer to situations in which a defection expected in the last round may unravel all the way back to the beginning of the relationship, as happens in the chain store paradox. Evolutionary game theory models frequently use a different approach, combining forward-looking and backward-looking techniques. See, for example, the use of tit-for-tat strategies to foster the evolution of cooperation in situations that, with backward induction, would otherwise be characterized by dominant defection strategies. See also *chain store paradox* and *Newcomb's paradox*.

Backward integration: the acquisition of ownership of a supplier (or supply chain) by a downstream firm. Backward integration is a type of vertical integration in which the firm's activities are expanded to acquire an upstream firm, such as a supplier of inputs of production (e.g., a cheese factory acquiring a milk farm). New institutional economists have studied the conditions under which backward integration may create net benefits for the merged enterprises and the conditions under which these forms of integration may also be socially efficient. Downstream firms generally pursue backward integration to reduce supplier power and to reduce input costs. Long-term firm-specific investments are also fostered by backward integration, with the improvement of the quality of inputs. There could also be anticompetitive reasons for backward integration, such as the case of acquisition of the supplier of a crucial raw material to curtail competition by other downstream firms, with relevant antitrust implications. See also *forward integration* and *vertical integration*.

Bandwagon effect: see *herding behavior*.

Bargaining in the shadow of the law: according to the Coase theorem, the law determines the initial assignment of rights but the parties' preferences and valuations ultimately determine their final allocation. Parties are said to bargain "in the shadow of the law," in the sense that the bargaining is carried out in the shadow of a legal assignment of rights, which determines the final assignment if parties fail to reach an alternative agreement (Ellickson, 2001). Law and economics scholars invoke this expression to suggest that, due to the possibility of bargaining in the shadow of the law, differences in the legal rules should have no effects on final outcomes. The term was introduced in the literature by Mnookin and Kornhauser's (1979) article on divorce settlements. Cooter, Marks, and Mnookin (1982) discuss the case of pretrial bargaining as an example of bargaining in the shadow of the law. Stevenson and Wolfers (2006) apply the idea to divorce laws, hypothesizing that marriages should dissolve only if marriage is jointly suboptimal. Spouses should bargain in the shadow of divorce laws, and the same efficient outcomes should be obtained regardless of the applicable divorce regimes (however, the hypothesis is contradicted by their data). Depoorter (2010) has used the mirror expression "law in the shadow of bargaining" to refer to the influence of novel settlement and arbitration awards on courts' case law outcomes. See also *law in the shadow of bargaining*.

Barriers to entry: both a cause and an effect of monopoly. Barriers to entry can arise from (a) the sole ownership of a resource; (b) an exclusive right to produce a class of goods (legal monopolies); and (c) the relative efficiency of a few large producers over a large number of small producers due to economies of scale (natural monopoly). Legal monopolies (i.e., those created by government action) are the most frequently encountered barrier to entry in practice. Governments may restrict entry into a market to combat other economic problems by granting a firm the exclusive right to produce or sell a good. For example, it is often thought that legal monopolies solve many intellectual property problems, when innovators would otherwise face a public goods problem. See also *strategic entry deterrence* and *contestable markets*.

Bastiat's unseen costs: the lost benefits of forgone exchanges. The concept is attributed to Frédérie Bastiat (1850), who famously illustrated the concept with the example of a shopkeeper whose window is broken by his careless son. People nearby witnessing the incident attempt to console the shopkeeper, pointing out: "Everybody has to make a living. What would become of the glaziers if no one ever broke a window?" Bastiat and subsequent economists have made the point that such folk reasoning fails to account for the alternative uses of the money paid to the glazier, and, indeed, the alternative uses of the glazier's time. In Bastiat's poetic framing, the "unseen cost" is to the shoemaker (or other manufacturer), to whom the shopkeeper would have paid the glazier's wage to mend his worn-out shoes, had the window not been broken. The point is that, while such destruction does encourage the circulation of capital, it is nevertheless a net loss to society. There is some debate about the precise interpretation of the term as Bastiat uses it; however, it is closely related to (and on some readings equivalent to) the concept of opportunity cost. See also ***opportunity cost***.

Battle of the sexes: a two-player game with a mix of coordination and conflict motives, characterized by multiple equilibria. The story associated with the game is that a couple wish to spend the evening together going to an event, but disagree on where to go. The girlfriend would prefer to go to an opera or play and the boyfriend to a football game. Consider the following matrix illustrating the battle of the sexes game in the general case, where $A > a > 0$. The couple can either choose to go to an opera (the girlfriend's preferred event) or to a football game (the boyfriend's preferred event). The two Nash equilibria are

		Boyfriend	
		Opera	Football
Girlfriend	Opera	A,a	0,0
	Football	0,0	a,A

(A,a) and (a,A). Although each player's ideal scenario would be to spend the evening together, bringing the partner to his or her favorite event, both of them would rather spend the evening together at the less favorite event than to go alone to their preferred event. The players cannot communicate with one another. In the absence of any communication between the couple, the battle of the sexes game yields two Nash equilibria in pure strategies, when both players choose the same event (either the opera or the football game). If players are allowed to have preplay communications with credible commitments, players will be able to coordinate on the outcomes of the game, with a single equilibrium. Unlike a pure coordination game, a conflict of interest remains even in the presence of communication. A first-mover advantage exists, in the sense that the first player who is able to make a credible commitment toward which strategy to adopt will be able to select the most preferred outcome. The battle of the sexes game is used as a metaphor in law and economics to describe situations of conflicts in the presence of mixed motivations. For example, states that are part of a union or federation may have interest in harmonizing their legal systems with the adoption of uniform laws. However, each state's preferred option would be to have other states adopt its legal rule, rather than having to adopt the law of another state. As a way to thwart the strategies of other states, states may precommit to retaining their own laws (e.g., raising them to the level of constitutional rules), as a way to force other states to adopt their own. Unlike the case of pure coordination problems, legal rules addressing battle of the sexes problems should take into account both the efficiency of the outcome and the social cost of the precommitment strategies undertaken by the parties in the pursuit of their competing interests. See also *Nash equilibrium.*

Bayes' theorem: provides a simple mathematical formula used for calculating conditional probabilities. Bayes' theorem estimates the conditional or posterior probability of an event (event A) after another event (event B) has been observed. It shows that the posterior probability is a function of the prior probabilities of events A and B and the conditional probability of B given A. The intuition underlying Bayes' rule is that the probability of event A given event B (e.g., the probability that a person has committed an homicide given that his or her fingerprints were found at the crime scene) depends not only on the relationship between events A and B (i.e., the accuracy of police analysis of the crime scene) but on the marginal probability of each single (disjoint) event. According to Bayes' theorem, evidence has a stronger confirming effect if it was more unlikely before being observed. So, for example, if a suspect lives in the home where the fingerprints were found, the fingerprints mean less than if they were found in a place he or she claims never to have been. See also *Bayesian updating* and *adaptive expectations.*

Bayesian updating: the updating of a prior probability estimate to produce a posterior probability estimate. Bayes' theorem provides the mathematical formulation of this updating process. See also *Bayes' theorem.*

Beccaria, Cesare (1738–94): an Italian legal scholar and philosopher of the Enlightenment era, who was a pioneer in the application of economic analysis to legal problems (in particular, to criminal punishment), and a precursor to the modern law and economics movement. Beccaria was one of the seminal proponents on the European continent of utilitarianism. His conception of utilitarianism was characterized by a uniquely contractarian element, which incorporated distributional effects in its utility maximization function. Beccaria's blending of utilitarian and contractarian principles provided the foundations for his magnum opus, *On Crimes and Punishments.* His other works also reveal economic intuitions that anticipate the application of modern economic methodology to legal problems. Beccaria held a professorship in public law and economics at Milan. See also *utilitarianism.*

Becker, Gary Stanley (1930–): received the Nobel Prize in economics in 1992 for extending the sphere of economic analysis to new areas of human behavior that are highly relevant to law and economics, including the economics of discrimination, the economics of crime and law enforcement, the economics of the family, and the economics of drug addiction. Becker was born in Pottsville, Pennsylvania, on December 2, 1930. He received his A.B. (summa cum laude) from Princeton University in 1951 and his Ph.D. from the University of Chicago in 1955. Becker taught at the University of Chicago from 1954 to 1957 and at Columbia University from 1957 to 1968. In 1968 he returned to Chicago, joining the department of economics in 1970. Becker's research has proved significant for showing how many different types of non-market human behavior follow the same rational and utility-maximizing principles of traditional market behavior. His research continues to inspire law and economics scholars and other economists to tackle new problems previously considered outside the proper domain of economic analysis. See also *Chicago school*, *rotten kid theorem*, *Becker's multiplier principle*, and *taste for discrimination*.

Becker's multiplier principle: used in the calculation of punishment or restitution to compensate for imperfect enforcement (Becker, 1968). In criminal law, fines are often used to deter undesirable behavior. If the detection rate for criminal activity were 100 percent, the fine would simply need to exceed the anticipated benefit of the activity in order to deter the risk-neutral criminal (or to compensate for the reduction in social welfare). However, detection/punishment rates are rarely 100 percent, and there may be a net private benefit to the criminal from paying the fines when caught and continuing to undertake the criminal activity. To counteract this effect, the fine needs to be equal to the anticipated benefit of the criminal activity *multiplied by* the inverse of the probability of detection. For example, if the probability of detection were 50 percent, and the potential payoff were $100, then the fine should be *at least* $200. If it were any less then the criminal could rely on imperfect enforcement, paying the fine half the time and keeping the benefit the other half of the time. Alternatively, when the payoff for the criminal is not equal to the detriment to social welfare, the multiplier can be applied to the social harm rather than the private benefit of the criminal. The idea of using a multiplier to compensate for imperfect rates of detection has a long history (Beccaria, 1764). The economic formulation in its pure form (which is often modified to account for restitutive costs, detection costs, enforcement costs, etc.) originates with Becker (1968). See also *Becker, Gary*, and *Beccaria, Cesare*.

Becker's rotten kid theorem: see *rotten kid theorem*.

Behavioral finance: the research field of behavioral finance utilizes the instruments of cognitive psychology to explain the behavior of individuals in financial markets. The research in this field has shown that, contrary to the assumptions of traditional economic and financial theory, individuals do not always act as rational maximizers, and allow their emotions to influence their economic decisions. Much of the research carried out in behavioral finance has focused on the explanation of observed market anomalies. The theory focuses on the role of cognitive biases and heuristics that may lead to irrational and unpredictable decisions (Kahneman and Tversky, 1973). Critics of behavioral finance suggest that, while capable of providing plausible explanations of past market events, it is unable to generate valuable predictions of future market development. The extensive joint work of Kahneman and Tversky, exemplified by their 1973 paper "on the psychology of prediction," is considered by many to have provided the foundations for behavioral finance. See also *behavioral law and economics*, *behavioral market failure*, and *Kahneman, Daniel*.

Behavioral law and economics: can be defined as the application of empirical behavioral evidence to the analysis of laws and legal institutions. Law and economics scholars formulate models to predict how subjects will react to any change in legal rules or institutions. In formulating these predictions, traditional law and economics scholarship has relied on the behavioral assumptions of the rational actor model. Recent empirical research reveals that the rational actor model is descriptively inaccurate. Individuals' choices exhibit behavioral regularities that systematically depart from the patterns expected from the paradigms of rational choice. The growing body of literature known as behavioral law and economics draws from the extensive findings of psychological and behavioral decision research and develops alternative paradigms of rationality built upon these empirical and experimental findings. In doing so, behavioral law and economics moves away from the theoretical abstractions of the rational actor model, providing empirically based models of human behavior for the study and design of laws and legal institutions. Early systematic attempts to formulate a behavioral approach to law and economics include those by Jolls, Sunstein, and Thaler (1998) and Sunstein (2000). Behavioral law and economics scholars consider the impact of law on humans, who are assumed to possess limited cognitive abilities and to be affected by emotion and biases (i.e., they are "boundedly rational"). Scholars in this field are also attentive to the cognitive heuristics used by humans when making judgments under uncertainty – heuristics that may lead to systematic departures from the paradigm of rational choice. See also *experimental law and economics* and *serial position effect*.

Behavioral market failure: the behavioral law and economics discipline emphasizes the limits of market interactions and competition in producing desirable equilibria. In recent literature, the term "behavioral market failure" has been used to refer to situations in which the interaction of imperfectly rational individuals in the market fails to maximize aggregate welfare. In many situations considered in the literature, competition exacerbates, rather than corrects, the problems created by cognitive biases. For example, borrowers may underestimate the true cost of a loan repayment, and competition forces lenders to exploit imperfectly rational borrowers, exacerbating their misperception. Competition will drive lenders who fail to do so out of the market. See also *behavioral law and economics* and *behavioral finance*.

Bentham, Jeremy (1748–1832): an outspoken critic of contractarianism and a proponent of using law to maximize social welfare. In his *Principles of Morals* *and Legislation* (1789), Bentham formulates one of the earliest versions of the modern utility principle, arguing that "the greatest happiness of the greatest number is the foundation of morals and legislation." Bentham's formulation proved to be problematic, since it identified both *quality* and *quantity* of happiness as maximands without specifying the relative weight of each. Bentham's utility principle was replaced ultimately by more rigorous and precise formulations of welfare maximization. Bentham was also a pioneer in the incipient field of utility theory. He identified "utility" in terms of pleasure and pain, and devised a "felicific calculus" through which the total utility of an action could be weighed, taking into account such features as the intensity, duration, certainty, and proximity of the antecedent pleasure. See also **utilitarianism** and **aggregation problem**.

Bentham's imperative: in his *Principles of Morals and Legislation*, Bentham (1789) presents his theory of value and motivation. Bentham's moral imperative, which has greatly influenced the methodological debate in law and economics, is that policymakers have an obligation to select rules that give "the greatest happiness to the greatest number." This formulation is quite problematic, since it identifies two maximands (i.e., degree of pleasure and number of individuals) without fully specifying the tradeoff between one and the other. However, Bentham's imperative. has been an important inspirational principle for policy purposes. Later economists, including Kaldor, Hicks, and Scitovsky, formulated more rigorous welfare paradigms that avoided the theoretical ambiguities of Bentham's proposition. See also **Kaldor–Hicks criterion**, **potential compensation**, **Bentham, Jeremy**, and **utilitarianism**.

Bernholz's theorem: put forward by Peter Bernholz is a 1982 article, the theorem states that the presence of externalities is a necessary condition for intransitive collective choices, as is also the case in Arrow's (1951) general impossibility theorem. For the purpose of Bernholz's theorem, externalities are defined in the Pareto sense, according to the Buchanan and Tullock (1962) definition of political externalities. As shown by Parisi (2003), to the extent that logrolling and Coasean political bargaining allow in correcting the externality problem, they will, in turn, eliminate a necessary condition for intransitive collective choices. Hence, Coasean bargaining in political markets may lead to stability. See also **Arrow's impossibility theorem**, **political Coase theorem**, and **logrolling**.

Bertrand competition: an oligopolistic market in which firms compete on prices. In the simplest setting, the Bertrand model (1883) studies the strategic choices of two firms that produce a homogeneous good at a constant marginal cost. Firms choose their respective prices simultaneously. If a firm sets a price lower than its competitor's price, all consumers switch to the cheaper seller and the low-price producer supplies the entire market; the high-price competitor loses the entire market. When the firms' prices are equal, consumers split evenly between the two firms. Because consumers are infinitely responsive to price changes, the

Bertrand model creates for each firm the incentive to undercut its competitor's price. Even a minor reduction of price allows each competitor to capture the entire market. The Bertrand model has a unique Nash equilibrium, in which each firm sets the price equal to the marginal cost, serving half the market and having a competitive market (zero) profit. Neither firm has an incentive to raise its price, since it would lose all its customers without increasing profits; and neither firm has an incentive to cut price below the marginal cost, since it would gain the entire market, but at the cost of a negative profit. In a Bertrand competition model, an oligopolistic industry generates outputs and price indistinguishable from those of a perfectly competitive market. This is in striking contrast with the outputs and prices of an industry that has an identical market structure, but in which firms behave in a Cournot-type competition. What explains the different outcome of Bertrand competition (price competition) relative to Cournot competition (quantity competition) is the idea that while consumers are infinitely responsive to a price change, prices are not infinitely responsive to a quantity change. These alternative models of competition have qualitatively different implications for competition policy. In industries in which firms are likely to compete on price rather than on quantity, market concentration does not necessarily lead to competitive outcomes. On the contrary, in industries in which firms are likely to compete on quantity, structural market tests more clearly predict the firms' behavior. When firms can choose both prices and quantities in a differentiated duopoly, the quantity (price) contract is a dominant strategy if the goods are substitutes (complements) such that firms can make only two types of binding contracts with consumers (Singh and Vives, 1984). See also *Cournot competition*.

Bertrand's duopoly model: see *Bertrand competition*.

Best response: a game-theoretic concept that identifies a player's optimal reaction to the opposing players' actions. A situation in which both players' moves are mutual best responses to each other is described as a Nash equilibrium. The set mapping a player's possible moves to the opponent's best responses is referred to as the best response function or reaction function. See also *reaction function*.

Best risk bearer: all things being equal, the law should generally allocate risks and liabilities to the individuals who can best bear them – best risk bearers. Several factors are taken into consideration when implementing the best risk bearer criterion. These factors include the risk preferences of the parties (allocating the risk to a risk-neutral party imposes a lower cost than allocating the same risk to a risk-averse party), the ability to insure the risk, and the possibility to diversify risks. The opposite logic applies when the law artificially creates new risks (e.g., fines or penalties) to promote deterrence. In these situations, risk aversion amplifies the deterrent effect of fines and penalties. All things being equal, the optimal allocation of such legally created risks may well be to the individuals who fear them the most (worst risk bearers), since they would be the most responsive to those legal threats. See also *cheapest cost avoider*, *cheapest risk avoider*, *cheapest precaution taker*, and *most effective precaution taker*.

Best response function: see *reaction function*.

Best shot problem: term used to describe situations in which the value or effectiveness of something is determined by its strongest component. Cornes and Sandler (1996) use the term to describe situations in which the largest provision of a public good determines the public good's aggregate level or quality. For example, the success of medical research into the cure for a disease is determined by the best cure found for treating the disease. The ability to study the cosmos is determined by the technology available or by the best observatory facility. Best shot situations pose problems for the provision of public goods because "less advanced" contributors free-ride on the efforts of others. The best shot problem can be seen as the opposite of the "weak link problem," in which the smallest provision level of a public good determines the aggregate level (Cornes and Sandler, 1996). See also *weak link problem*.

Bilateral accident: an accident whose occurrence is sensitive to both the victim's and the injurer's behavior, and can thus be reduced by altering the behavior of either party. For instance, the likelihood of an automobile accident between drivers A and B rests upon the level of care each takes while driving; in such bilateral situations, precautions taken by each party create positive externalities upon the other party. The development of negligence liability has been linked to the increase in litigation over bilateral accidents during the nineteenth and twentieth centuries, since a negligence rule provides optimal incentives for injurers and victims alike to take adequate precautions while engaging in risky activities. Bilateral accidents are distinguished from unilateral accidents, in which accident rates depend only upon the behavior of one party, usually the injuring party. In economic models, the specification of an accident problem as unilateral or bilateral is found in the formulation of the expected accident function. Using the conventional notation, if x and y represent the care levels of injurer and victim, and accident losses D materialize with probability p, bilateral accident problems would be modeled with an expected accident function of the form $p(x, y)D$, in which the probability of an accident negatively depends on the effort of each party $\partial p/\partial x < 0$ and $\partial p/\partial y < 0$. Law and economics scholars further distinguish two cases of bilateral care: alternative care (parties' care efforts are substitutes) and joint care (parties' care efforts are complements), distinguishable in the model by the different sign of their cross-partial derivative, $\partial^2 p/\partial x \partial y$. See also *alternative versus joint care*, *unilateral accident*, *double-edged torts*, and *hybrid precautions*.

Bilateral care: see *bilateral accident*.

Bilateral monopoly: economists have identified the problem of bilateral monopolies for over a century. A bilateral monopoly exists when one monopolistic enterprise sells to another enterprise that also operates as a monopoly (Blair, Kaserman, and Romano, 1989). For example, if only one company produced steering wheels for cars, and that company sold to the only company in the world producing and selling cars, the relationship between the two companies would represent a bilateral monopoly. In bilateral monopolies, the companies are forced to interact with each other. In the example above, the company that manufactures car steering wheels *must* sell them to the world's only car manufacturer, and that same manufacturer can purchase steering wheels *only* from the world's sole producer of steering wheels. As Judge Posner pointed out in a 1983 decision, prices in bilateral monopolies are constrained to a range "bounded by the lower end by the minimum price that the seller is willing to accept and at the upper end by the maximum price that the buyer is willing to pay" (*Milbrew, Inc. v. Commissioner of Internal Revenue*, 710 F.3d 1302, 1306–07 [7th Cir. 1983]). This range is presumably quite broad because the parties have no choice but to transact with each other.

Black's theorem: see *median voter theorem*.

Blackstonian error ratio: one of William Blackstone's most prominent maxims states: "Better that ten guilty persons escape, than that one innocent suffer" (Blackstone, 1766). All adjudicative procedures are prone to produce errors. In criminal procedure, the innocence of the defendant is presumed to be the null hypothesis that the prosecutor needs to reject before reaching a conviction. As such, type I errors (an incorrect rejection of the null hypothesis, with the conviction of an innocent individual) and type II errors (incorrect acceptance of the null hypothesis, with the acquittal of a guilty individual) may both occur. The so-called Blackstonian error ratio refers to the number of wrongful convictions (type I errors) that is justifiable for any single wrongful acquittal (a type II error). Legal systems can choose a specific Blackstonian ratio (type I/type II ratio) by deciding, among other things, the burden of proof (Dekay, 1996), the parties' right to appeal (Strazzella, 1997; Rizzolli and Saraceno, 2009), the rules on mandatory disclosure (Garoupa and Rizzolli, 2008), and the right to remain silent (Seidmann and Stein, 2000; Seidmann, 2005). Blackstone argues that the appropriate tradeoff should be set at a type I/type II ratio equal to 1/10. However, Blackstone's ratio is only one of the many ratios advocated by scholars in the course of history. Volokh (1997) finds assertions on the error ratio that date back to biblical times (Genesis 18: 23–32). The ratios range from 1/1 (as found in the sixth-century Justinian Digest 48.19.5pr., citing the second-century Roman jurist Ulpianus in book 7 of his *De Officio Proconsulis*) to 1/1000 (as found in the twelfth-century writings of Moses Maimonides interpreting the commandments of Exodus). Even more modern legal scholars do not come close to settle on any precise ratio: see, for instance, Benjamin Franklin's 1/100 ratio: "It is better one hundred guilty persons should escape than that one innocent person should suffer" (letter from Franklin to Benjamin Vaughan, March 14, 1785). It is interesting to note that, although the Blackstonian ratios advocated in the literature have varied quite a bit on the upper range (scholars disagree on exactly how many type II errors are bearable for any single type I error), scholars seem to agree on the idea that it is always preferable to have a guilty person going free instead of an innocent person being mistakenly convicted (i.e., a Blackstonian ratio below 1 would be unacceptable). The error tradeoff of criminal procedure, of which the Blackstonian ratio is the most cited exemplification, expresses the strong value that most societies (and certainly all modern Western democracies) attach to the presumption of innocence and to the avoidance of wrongful convictions of innocent defendants. See also *type I and type II errors*.

Blind spot bias: psychological studies show that people believe themselves to be less likely to be affected by cognitive biases than their average peers. The illusion to be immune from biases is known as the blind spot bias (Pronin, Lin, and Ross, 2002; Pronin and Kugler, 2007). This second-order bias gives resilience to people's inflated perceptions of themselves, rendering it particularly difficult to correct the biases of affected individuals through information and education. As hinted by Sunstein (2000) and Jolls and Sunstein (2006a), this creates a distinctive problem for policymakers when considering debiasing strategies. See also *optimism bias*, *self-serving bias*, *behavioral law and economics*, and *debiasing*.

Bliss point: in consumer theory, a bliss point is the consumption bundle that would be chosen by a consumer in the absence of the budget constraint. At the bliss point the consumer cannot increase his or her utility further by changing the consumption quantities. Formally, the bliss point is the solution of an unconstrained utility maximization problem. In the abstract world in which the property of non-satiation holds indefinitely, consumers prefer an infinite quantity of goods in the absence of a budget constraint, such that the bliss point is reached only at infinity. See also *non-satiation*.

Boilerplate: term used in the contract literature to refer to the standard terms contained in a contract. As with adhesion contracts, boilerplate terms are often drafted by one party and repeatedly used in contracts with many different parties. Generally, one party has control over the choice of contract terms, and the other party is left in the position of agreeing or rejecting the terms of the contract. Boilerplate terms, like majoritarian default rules, help reduce transaction costs, reflecting the reduced need for parties to negotiate the specific terms of a contract. Boilerplate terms are refined over time and create opportunities for learning and network externalities within an industry. Judicial rulings on past similar contracts reduce the uncertainty over the meaning and validity of boilerplate contract terms. The use of boilerplate terms in contracts can create path dependence and inertia because of the switching costs faced when firms find it necessary to change the standard language in their contracts. This inertia may allow for inefficient contract terms to be adopted. Boilerplate language may create asymmetric advantage on the party that drafted the contract. As a result of the asymmetric incentive and the ability to acquire information and to renegotiate the contract's terms, common boilerplate terms do not always reflect the content of hypothetical contracted-for terms. For these reasons, the efficiency of boilerplate terms cannot be analogized to that of majoritarian default rules. See also *default rules* and *majoritarian default rules*.

Bonding mechanisms: see *precommitment strategies*.

Borda count method: points are assigned to candidates (or alternative options) according to the ranking assigned to them by each voter. Each candidate gets one point every time he or she is ranked last by a voter, two points every time he or she is ranked next to last, and so on. In an election in which there are N candidates, N points would be assigned every time the candidate receives a first-place rank by a voter. In a Borda count contest, the candidate with the largest number of points wins the election. Borda count voting is often utilized in polling and voting situations in which the ranking of non-winners is regarded as important in addition to the selection of a winner. See also *point voting* and *preferential voting*.

Bounded rationality: refers to the fact that humans have limited cognitive abilities, limited computational skills, and flawed memory. Behavioral economists study bounded rationality and its effects on cognitive illusions and decision anomalies. In this respect, behavioral economists differ from traditional economists, who model choices made under cognitive limitations as a form of constrained optimization. The notion of ecological rationality bridges the traditional view of rational choice and these behavioral findings, hypothesizing an evolutionary selection of the observed cognitive illusions and decision heuristics. See also *cognitive bias* and *decision heuristics*.

Breach of contract: see *breach remedies*.

Breach remedies: the question of which remedy would best incentivize the optimal performance of contracts has been widely researched by law and economics scholars. Much of the traditional law and economics literature looks at the problem of optimal remedies considering a stylized contract involving two parties: a promisor (debtor of the performance) and a promisee (creditor of the performance). Each party plays a specific role: the promisor invests in performance efforts and the promisee invests in reliance. The choice of damage remedies affects the promisor's commitment to performance and the promisee's reliance on the promised performance. There is a general agreement in the law and economics literature that expectation damages are best suited for promoting optimal performance and reliance investments by the promisor and promise to a contract. A remedy of reliance damages or restitution does not produce these efficient incentives. Expectation damages link the promisor's liability to the promisee's forgone benefit from the contract, thereby restoring the promisee to the position that he or she would have achieved if the promisor had completed performance. In economic terms, expectation damages bring the promisee to the same indifference curve where he or she would have been in the event of successful performance. Although performance incentives are optimal under a remedy of expectation damages, reliance incentives may be excessive. This is because expectation damages, by compensating the promisee for the forgone benefit in the event of breach, operate as a form of implicit insurance, inducing the promisee to invest in reliance as if performance would be likely to materialize with certainty (Shavell, 1980a). Law and economics scholars have addressed the problem of optimal remedies through different analytical frameworks. Barton (1972) asks how a single, value-maximizing firm would design damage measures in order to induce two of its divisions to make optimal breach and reliance investments. Shavell (1980a) identifies a "Pareto efficient complete contingent contract," arguing that optimal contract remedies should mimic those that would have been chosen under this hypothetical framework. The issue of optimal remedies for breach of contract has also been investigated within the framework of incomplete contracts (Williamson, 1985; Hart and Moore, 1988a, 1990). More recent contributions have extended the analysis to contracts creating bilateral obligations. Schweizer (2006) has shown that bilateral expectation damages are efficient for cooperative investments (e.g., joint-venture agreements or partnerships). Parisi, Luppi, and Fon (2011) have specifically analyzed the remedies that apply to bilateral contracts, such as the defense of non-performance in unilateral breach cases and the preclusion rules in bilateral breach cases. Their results suggest that the analysis of a bilateral contract cannot be reduced to the sum of two independent unilateral contracts. See also *expectation damages* and *reliance damages*.

British rule: see *fee shifting*.

Buchanan, James McGill (1919–2013): an American economist who won the 1986 Nobel Prize in economics for his contributions to the theory of political decision-making and public choice. Buchanan graduated from the University of Chicago with a Ph.D. in economics in 1948. He subsequently held teaching positions at the University of Virginia and University of California, Los Angeles. He also served as director of the Center for the Study of Public Choice at George Mason University. Buchanan is perhaps best known for his role in the development of "public choice theory." Influenced by the voluntary exchange model of Wicksell, Buchanan's view is that individuals who behave selfishly in markets should not be expected to behave altruistically in political life. In his other research, Buchanan has posited that the outcome of a system of rules is, to a large extent, determined by the rules themselves, and that efforts to influence the outcome of specific issues are generally futile. Buchanan's view, therefore, is that the formulation of constitutional rules and reforms is critically important to the efficient functioning of society. Buchanan has written over twenty books and 300 articles, including: *The Calculus of Consent: Logical*

Foundations of Constitutional Democracy (1962) with Gordon Tullock; *Cost and Choice* (1969); *The Limits of Liberty* (1975); and *Liberty, Market, and State* (1985). See also **public choice theory** and **Tullock, Gordon**.

Bundle of sticks: in an effort to gain a better understanding of what the law means by "property," scholars and legal practitioners often use the metaphor that property is an assortment of rights of the property owner. This assortment of rights is metaphorically referred to as a "bundle of sticks." These sticks include the right to possess, the right to occupy, the right to exclude others, the right to transfer, etc. Earlier legal practitioners conceived of property as a thing (e.g., an item or a parcel of land), whereas the "bundle of sticks" metaphor acknowledges that property law is a more dynamic and composite concept. Different individuals may hold different rights, or "sticks," vis-à-vis the same "thing." Conceiving of property in this way allows the modern legal practitioner to understand the complexity of property law more fully. While no individual source has been identified as devising this metaphor, various modern scholars have thoroughly documented the meaning behind the "bundle of sticks" concept (e.g., Grey, 1980; Rose, 1994). A modern lease contract demonstrates the "bundle of sticks" metaphor in action. Although the tenant has the "sticks" of present possession and occupancy, because he or she is residing in the leased residential space, the owner retains other "sticks" that the tenant does not have. The owner, for example, retains the stick that allows him or her to sell the property. While the property in question may consist of one thing (i.e., an apartment), various actors have different property rights (i.e., sticks) vis-à-vis that physical asset. Although legal practitioners and scholars alike adopt this expression, the use of this metaphor is not without its detractors. Arnold (2002), for example, argues that the "bundle of sticks" concept is too limited, especially in the areas of environmental and natural resources law, where the "thing" incorporates diffuse interests. Arnold advocates replacing the "bundle of sticks" concept with a "web of interests" concept, which captures the "interconnectedness of humans and nature, and the value of natural objects" better (Arnold, 2002: 283–4).

Bundling: a seller's conditioning of the purchase of one product to a fixed multiple of another one. For example, cable networks offer a bundle of TV channels at a single price, instead of pricing individual channels; and software licenses bundle together multiple items, such as a word processor and a spreadsheet. Similarly, fast food restaurants offer preplanned complete meals that a consumer can order by number. Pure bundling occurs when a consumer can purchase only the entire bundle even when he or she wants to receive just the single desired good. In mixed bundling, the consumer can buy either the bundle or separate components of the bundle. Antitrust agencies interpret bundling as an anticompetitive practice and view it as a possible indicator of market power. Bundling is viewed as undesirable because it limits the choices available to the consumer (pure bundling) and can be used as an instrument of price discrimination (mixed bundling). Bundling should be distinguished from tie-ins. In a bundling arrangement, the ratios of the quantities of the tied goods are fixed, whereas, in tying arrangements, the consumer chooses the ratios of goods that are bundled together. See also *tie-ins* and *single-monopoly profit theorem*.

Business judgment rule: a substantive standard of liability that applies in corporate law in order to ascertain the liability of directors in duty of care claims, self-dealing transactions, and other related corporate law issues. There are a wide range of interpretations of this standard of conduct in state corporate law, ranging from a requirement of subjective good faith to a requirement of rational action, to a standard of due diligence. The courts' level of review under the business judgment rule is fairly limited. This is consistent with the historical origins of the business judgment rule, which emerged as a presumption against judicial review of directors' business decisions. Under the historical version of the rule, courts should abstain from reviewing the substantive merits of the directors' decisions when some minimal preconditions were satisfied.

Buyer's monopoly: see *monopsony*.

Buyer's remorse: see *winner's curse*.

C

Calabresi, Guido (1932–): considered one of the founders of the field of law and economics. He received his undergraduate education at Yale University, from which he received his B.S. in economics in 1953. He attended Magdalen College, Oxford, in 1955 as a Rhodes scholar. He received his law degree in 1958 from Yale Law School, graduating first in his class. Soon thereafter, in 1961, Calabresi published "Some thoughts on risk distributions and the law of torts" in the *Yale Law Journal*, the results of which he incorporated into his book *The Cost of Accidents: A Legal and Economic Analysis* (1970), which pioneers the economic analysis of tort law. In *The Cost of Accidents*, Calabresi argues that the minimization of the cost of accidents, rather than the compensation of victims, should be the primary objective of tort law. In his analysis he introduces the concept of the "cheapest cost avoider," which argues that liability should be the responsibility of the actor in the best position to make the cost–benefit analysis and to take cost-effective preventive measures. In 1972 he published his most influential paper, co-authored with Douglas Melamed, "Property rules, liability rules and inalienability: one view of the cathedral" in the *Harvard Law Review*. The paper develops the most important normative corollary to the Coase theorem, introducing a framework for assessing the efficiency of property rules and liability rules in the presence of transaction costs. This approach has become one of the most prominent tools for analyzing the protection of entitlements in various fields of law. In addition to his foundational work in the field of law and economics, Calabresi served as the dean of the Yale Law School from 1985 until his appointment to the United States Court of Appeals by President Bill Clinton in 1994. He is the recipient of the 2012 Ronald H. Coase medal for his lifetime work in law and economics. See also *Yale school*, *Ronald H. Coase medal*, *normative Coase theorem*, and *cathedral*.

Calibration: model calibration is a technique utilized to customize a generic model, identifying the specific values of a variable. In law and economics, models are generally formulated in implicit form to fit the broadest range of possible situations. Models that utilize implicit variables are useful to generate qualitative predictions (e.g., will crime increase or decrease?), but cannot generate quantitative predictions (e.g., how much will crime rates change?) until they are calibrated. With model calibration, data is utilized to give an explicit numerical value to an implicit variable in an attempt to generate specific quantitative predictions that match field conditions within some acceptable criteria. Model calibration generally includes comparisons between model-simulated outcomes and field observations for the given data. In policymaking, model calibration is used to predict the impact of a proposed legal change or legal innovation on human behavior. Although model calibration is generally carried out with the use of collected empirical data, experimental data becomes a valuable alternative when real-life data is unavailable. Calibrated models are developed to generate predictions in specific situations and are, by definition, calibrated to that situation. Such models and predictions are usually not useful outside the particular environment under consideration. See also *simulations*.

Call option: also called an option to buy confers the right to buy goods or shares at the sole discretion of the potential buyer at a future date within a determined time limit. A call option is generally granted through a contract between two parties, allowing one party to buy a particular quantity of a good or security at a set price, called the strike price, before an agreed-upon date in the future, labeled the expiration date. If the price of the good rises between the formation of the call contract and the expiration date, the owner of the call option makes a profit. If not, the owner is free to let it expire. In Europe, call options traditionally allow the owner to exercise the option only on the expiration date, while in the United States the owner is generally allowed to exercise it at any point. See also *put option*, *chooser's call/put option*, and *option value*.

Canadian Law and Economics Association: see *CLEA*.

Capability approach: also referred to as the capabilities approach, has emerged in recent years as an important criterion of social welfare. Initially formulated by Sen and subsequently elaborated by Nussbaum (Sen, 1985, 1989, 1993; Nussbaum 2000), this criterion of welfare stands as an alternative to the welfare criteria based on the maximization of utility or wealth. According to the proponents of this approach, the existing criteria of welfare that use utility and wealth as proxies for social welfare overlook other important factors. According to the capability approach, the freedom and ability of individuals to carry out essential activities in their life (called "functionings") are important ingredients of a more complete conception of social welfare. Nussbaum (2000) provides a listing (admittedly, tentative and subject to change) of ten such fundamental capabilities, ranging from essential freedoms to live and care for one's health to freedoms to have and express emotions and affiliations, to freedoms to have leisure and to own property. Since 1990 the United Nations Development Programme has developed various human development indexes that look at some of the "functionings" utilized in Sen's and Nussbaum's capability approach. Although it has not yet entered the standard toolbox of law and economics, the capability approach is likely to receive increasing attention in policy debates and to serve as a benchmark in the macroeconomic and economic development literature. The adoption of the capability approach for the microeconomic analysis of private law issues has less potential, inasmuch as changes in specific legal rules do not generally affect the capabilities and functionings of the relevant community. See also *welfare analysis*.

Capture theory: an industry that is regulated can benefit from its regulation by "capturing" its regulator (i.e., the controlling governmental agency). This intuition, first formulated by Stigler (1971), has given rise to a theory of regulation that considers the possible sources of influence that regulated firms or industries can exert on their regulators, such as the possibility of future positions of bureaucrats in the industry, and the agency's need for uncontested informal cooperation with the industry. In the public choice literature, whenever multiple industries or firms are competing to capture regulators, their competitive efforts are often modeled as rent-seeking games. Olson (1982) has suggested that the growth of special interest groups results in an unproductive competition to capture rents, which do not add up to social well-being. See also *rent seeking* and *Stigler, George*.

Cardinal preferences: a view of human preferences that presumes that utility is a measurable characteristic of a person, like body temperature or weight. The notion of cardinal preferences is contrasted to the notion of ordinal preferences, based on the idea that preferences over alternatives can only be ranked, not quantified or measured with numerical values along a scale. If preferences could be measured with objective cardinal values, then utility could be evaluated against an objective standard, making it possible to undertake both interpersonal and intrapersonal comparisons of utility. See also *ordinal preferences* and *interpersonal utility comparisons*.

Cardinal utility: see *cardinal preferences*.

Cardinalism: a doctrine according to which utility can be expressed in cardinal units, implying that the intensity – as well as the ordering – of preferences can be measured. See also *cardinal preferences* and *ordinalism*.

Care level: see *activity level versus care level*.

Carrots versus sticks: law and economics scholars analyze laws as a form of incentive regulation. Legal rules can affect the incentives that drive human behavior by sanctioning undesirable behavior or by rewarding desirable behavior. One metaphor often used to distinguish these two alternative ways to create incentives is that of "carrots versus sticks." "Carrots" create positive incentives by rewarding or subsidizing socially desirable activities. For example, policymakers might provide a monetary benefit to people who recycle, in order to encourage all people to engage in recycling – a behavior that society favors. "Sticks," on the contrary, create negative incentives, by sanctioning or taxing socially undesirable activities. For example, jurisdictions may impose a fine on individuals who put recyclable products in the same garbage container as non-recyclable items. From an economic perspective, carrots and sticks are in many respects equivalent: failing to receive a carrot is economically equivalent to facing a stick. On the basis of this equivalence, policymakers should be able to produce the same result using a carrot approach (e.g., giving law abiders a subsidy) rather than a stick approach (e.g., imposing a tax on law violators). Despite this equivalence, legal systems utilize sticks more frequently than carrots. Wittman (1984) explains this by pointing out that sticks carry lower transaction costs than carrots. Dari-Mattiacci and De Geest (2010) expand on this analysis to study the risk and distortion effects of both carrots and sticks and to help explain why policymakers utilize sticks more often than carrots. In addition to these practical and theoretical reasons, there are asymmetries in the effects of carrots versus sticks in the presence of enforcement errors. For example, the social cost of a wrongful sanction (i.e., a stick mistakenly used against a law-abiding individual) is generally larger than the social cost of a wrongful reward (i.e., a carrot mistakenly given to a law violator). Further, the probability of type I and type II errors in law enforcement may be different, and this may alter the effectiveness of sticks and carrots as instruments of incentive regulation. See also ***multiplication effect of sticks***.

Cartels and tacit collusion: cartels are formal agreements between competing firms in an oligopolistic market. Cartels might fix prices, total industry outputs, the allocation of customers, or the division of profits, all in order to reduce market competition and increase individual members' profits. When cartels are prohibited, firms might engage in tacit collusion by acting as cartel members without any explicit instruction. Competition laws prohibit cartels, and antitrust authorities seek to eliminate the effects of formal cartels and tacit collusion in oligopolistic markets. According to game theory, cartels are unstable, because the behavior of cartel members can be described as a prisoner's dilemma. Each cartel member has an incentive to deviate from the cartel agreement (e.g., by producing a greater quantity or selling products at a lower price) to increase its profits above the cartel profits. Nonetheless, as in the prisoner's dilemma, the cartel breaks down when all members break the agreement, and all firms will be worse off. Empirical evidence shows that achieving long-term cartel sustainability is difficult and largely depends on the ability of cartel members to monitor whether other firms are adhering to the agreement. See also ***chain store paradox***.

Cascades: see ***informational cascades***.

Cathedral: in their landmark work on protecting entitlements, Calabresi and Melamed (1972) developed the cathedral model to describe the choice a state faces in deciding which entitlements to protect and how to protect them. The cathedral model identifies three types of rules that govern the relationship between entitlement holders and those seeking to purchase or take an entitlement. Calabresi and Melamed point out that entitlements can be protected by property rules (the entitlement can be transferred only through a sale, with the consent of the right holder), liability rules (the entitlement may be taken or destroyed as long as the infringer is willing to pay damages to the right holder), or rules of inalienability (transfer of the entitlement is not permitted, even between a willing seller and a willing buyer). Courts apply the property rule by granting injunctions, apply the liability rule by awarding damages, and apply the inalienability rule by barring an entitlement holder from selling or transferring his or her entitlement. Calabresi and Melamed show that, in the choice between these remedies, a wide range of concerns need to be taken into consideration. Calabresi and Melamed outline how, given the presence of transaction costs, liability rules often achieve a combination of efficiency and distributive results that would be difficult to achieve under different remedies. This "view of the cathedral," as Calabresi and Melamed call it in their article, has also been described as a normative version of Coase's (1960) theorem (Polinsky, 1989). See also *Calabresi, Guido*, *property rules versus liability rules*, *inalienability rules*, and *normative Coase theorem*.

Causation: a concept that is ubiquitous in legal analysis. Causation generally refers to the production of an effect or result. One of the most relevant legal applications of the concept of causation is in the law of torts. Generally speaking, a party must have caused the harm in order to be held liable for it. In tort law, the most important legal standards for the assessment of causation are "causation in fact" (sometimes called "but for causation": the cause without which the event could not have occurred) and "proximate cause" (sometimes called the test of "remoteness": a cause that directly produces an event or the legally sufficient cause of the event in Anglo-American law. The difficulty with the "causation in fact" standard is that, in many cases, the evidence will point to many causes of a single event. It is with this problem in mind that the "proximate cause" standard is applied. Along the same lines, many law and economics scholars propound the idea that the law should apportion liabilities and entitlements according to what will incentivize the best long-term consequences. The main question they examine is how causation affects deterrence and the administrative costs of such a legal system. For instance, the Coase theorem turns on the idea of the "reciprocity of causation." Coase believed that accidents and nuisances should be understood as costs deriving from the intersection of activities and that causation is reciprocal (e.g., the location of crops on farmland adjacent to train tracks is responsible for a fire as much as the train is responsible for a fire on adjoining farmland). Thus, Coase asserted that both parties were at fault, and the law should allow the combination of activities (or entitlements) that would result in the greatest social wealth. Rizzo and Arnold (1980) introduced the idea of causal apportionment of the loss in tort law, as an alternative to the all-or-nothing approach used by legal systems when evaluating causation. Along similar lines, Calabresi (1996), Calabresi and Cooper (1996) and Parisi and Fon (2004) considered the idea of distributing the loss between victim and tortfeasor according to their relative causal contribution to the loss. See also *comparative causation*, *coincidental causation*, and *statistical causation*.

Causation-incorporating liability: see *Grady–Kahan rule*.

Centralized subsidiarity: according to the subsidiarity test, a given policy responsibility should be allocated to the lowest possible level of government, unless
the centralization of governmental functions brings added value over and above
what local governments could achieve locally (the so-called "subsidiarity test").
This test can be carried out in three different forms: (a) a centralized subsidiarity test; (b) a decentralized subsidiarity test; and (c) a democratic subsidiarity
test. Under a centralized subsidiarity test, centralization should take place if it
improves the aggregate well-being of all member states. Like a Kaldor–Hicks
criterion of welfare, centralized subsidiarity requires that the states that gain
from centralization gain more than what losing states would lose, such that
aggregate welfare is maximized. A centralized subsidiarity test is generally performed at the central level, and is equivalent to the case of centralized federalism
as defined by Inman and Rubinfeld (1998). See also *subsidiarity*, *decentralized
subsidiarity*, *democratic subsidiarity*, and *subsidiarity test*.

Certainty equivalence: certainty equivalence processes are used to assess the
impact of risk or uncertainty on parties' preferences. In the presence of risk or
uncertainty, a certainty-equivalent value is a value of the variable that leaves
the individual indifferent between obtaining that lower value with certainty and
obtaining a higher expected value, with some uncertainty. In the presence of
aversion to risk, the certainty-equivalent value will be lower than the mean
value of the uncertain or risky alternative. See also *risk premium*.

Chadwick–Demsetz scheme: in a natural monopoly, production can be carried
out most cheaply by a single firm. Competition can be forced through antitrust
structural remedies, but competition would lead to an increase in production
costs. In 1858 Sir Edwin Chadwick, a Victorian social reformer, proposed a
solution to the natural monopoly problem, and it was subsequently endorsed
by Harold Demsetz (1968). The idea of the Chadwick–Demsetz scheme is to
distinguish between competition "within the field" and "competition for the
field." The scheme consists of using the competition for the right to be the
natural monopolist as an alternative for the absence of competition in a natural
monopoly. For example, the right for a natural monopoly could be auctioned
off to the highest bidder, and the proceeds from the auction could be used
to compensate the consumers for their reduced welfare under the monopoly.
Even more directly, the contestants for the natural monopoly could be asked
to bid by offering more attractive terms for consumers. As pointed out by
Dnes (1995), competition under a Chadwick–Demsetz scheme would ensure
competitive pricing for the benefit of consumers, avoiding both the loss of the
scale economies that would result from structural antitrust solutions (such as
divestiture and the break-up of firms) and the shortcomings associated with
nationalization and traditional regulatory solutions (such as price regulation).
See also *Tullock's rectangle*.

Chain store paradox: formulated by Reinhard Selten (1978), this shows that, in spite of the potential benefits of cooperation, cooperation is not likely to emerge in a finitely repeated prisoner's dilemma game. Its name is derived from the main example used to formulate it: a retailer is a local monopolist through his ownership of a chain of stores, and he uses predatory pricing in order to win market share. In each local retail store, the monopolist faces a potential competitor who has to decide whether to enter into the local market and compete with the monopolist or not. If the competitor decides to enter, the monopolist can adopt either a strategy of predatory pricing, which will drive the competitor out of the market at a substantial loss, or an accommodating strategy, with a lower immediate cost to himself. Selten's chain store paradox determines which strategy the monopolist will play by proceeding with backward induction logic. The monopolist finds it irrational to play tough against the last potential entrant in the last local market, since there are no further competitors to deter. Hence, the potential entrant will find it profitable to enter the market. The same reasoning applies to the second-to-last entrant: given the expected strategy in the last round, there is no incentive to incur a loss in the second-to-last round to keep deterrence, and so on by backward induction up to the first round. The equilibrium strategies will be for all entrants to enter the market and for the monopolist not to engage in predatory pricing. Although its best-known application is with the group of games called "prisoner's dilemma" (Luce and Raiffa, 1957), the chain store paradox extends to a larger class of games, characterized by a repetition of a noncooperative game for a finite number of times. The paradox has been extended to the game-theoretic justifiability of deterrent punishment by known act-utilitarians (Hodgson, 1967; Regan, 1980). By applying a "backward induction" logic, the chain store paradox establishes that a player may find it rational to adopt actions in the beginning of the game that would otherwise look unreasonable when adopting a forward-looking logic. The experiments used to test the chain store paradox in prisoner's dilemma games reveal a discrepancy between the backward-looking (defection) logic of the game and the tendency of human subjects to utilize a forward-looking (cooperative) attitude in their initial interactions. This brings to mind what the philosopher Kierkegaard once said (1843): "Life can only be understood backwards; but it must be lived forwards." See also *prisoner's dilemma*, *folk theorem*, and *evolution of cooperation*.

Cheap talk: pre-play communication occurring between game players. Unlike signaling, which requires a costly message from the sender to the receiver and which affects the game payoffs, cheap talk takes place at no cost and does not directly change the payoffs of the game. Cheap talk can be modeled as an initial stage of the game that can be added to any game in which the players announce their strategies. Since equilibria-yielding payoffs remain unchanged, in games in which coordination is not the dominant strategy and only one dominant strategy exists for each player, cheap talk will generally be ineffective. The typical example is the "prisoner's dilemma." Players will play the dominant strategy – they will defect – regardless of the communication exchanged in the cheap talk stage, because the only Nash equilibrium of the game is for both players to defect. Cheap as it may be, cheap talk is not necessarily useless. For example, in a coordination problem in which both parties gain from coordination, cheap talk may be sufficient to facilitate coordination. See also ***costly signal***.

Cheapest cost avoider: Calabresi (1970) introduced the cheapest cost avoider principle in the context of tort liability. Applying economic analysis to the tort liability system in order to analyze the existing system and identify more efficient alternatives, Calabresi argues that the party who should bear the cost of an accident is the one who is best able to bear the cost of the accident (i.e., the one who can avoid the accident and reduce overall harm most efficiently, or cheaply). The cheapest cost avoider criterion has been used to refer to a variety of factors that may determine the optimal allocation of accident costs. These factors include the risk propensities of the parties (best risk bearer); the costs of parties' precautions (cheapest precaution taker); the value of their activities (cheapest risk avoider); and the effectiveness, or cost-effectiveness, of the parties' precautions (most effective precaution taker). Calabresi illustrates the cheapest cost avoider principle using a two-party example. Calabresi shows that, in the case of an accident between a car and bicycle that causes $3,000 in damage, if the car can avoid the accident at a cost of $1,000 and the bicycle can avoid the accident at a cost of $2,000, the car should take the precautions to avoid the accident because it can do so more efficiently than the bicycle. Taken in isolation, the cheapest cost avoider principle is at odds with the other fundamental principle: that the party that creates an externality should pay for the harm. According to the externality approach to tort law, the creators of the externality should be faced with the cost of the harm (internalization of the externality) even if their prospective victims could avoid the accident loss more cheaply (cheapest cost avoiders). Indeed, one can imagine a scenario in which the creator of the risk should not be held responsible because he or she cannot take precautions most efficiently. Despite the intuitive challenges this approach presents, Parchomovsky and Stein (2010) point out that many scholars accept the cheapest cost avoider principle. They also note that various scholars have used the principle to analyze the legal rules outside the field of tort law, including patent law, criminal law, securities law, and contract law. Indeed, the usefulness of the cheapest cost avoider principle may become most apparent when considering examples outside tort law, such as environmental policy. See also ***cheapest risk avoider***, ***cheapest precaution taker***, ***best risk bearer***, and ***most effective precaution taker***.

Cheapest precaution taker: a trivial, literal interpretation of Calabresi's (1970) cheapest cost avoider paradigm would suggest that the cost of accidents should be borne by the party who can take precautions most cheaply (cheapest precaution taker). In reality, the law and economics literature has shown that the choice of the optimal allocation of the (residual) accident loss hinges upon a variety of other factors, all of which can be viewed as ingredients of Calabresi's cheapest cost avoider paradigm. For example, a crude comparison of the parties' costs of precaution would fail to consider the effectiveness of the parties' respective precautions in reducing the probability of an accident. When the parties' effectiveness of precautions are different, the relevant factor would become the cost-effectiveness of precautions. Using Shavell's (1980b) notations, the cheapest precaution taker comparison, C_x *vs.* C_y, would therefore become the most cost-effective precaution taker, looking conjunctly at the costs and effectiveness of precautions, $\left|\frac{\partial p}{\partial x}\right| / C_x$ *vs.* $\left|\frac{\partial p}{\partial y}\right| / C_y$. In addition to the cost-effectiveness of precautions, when applying Calabresi's (1970) paradigm to determine the optimal allocation of accident costs, other factors should be taken into account, including the best risk bearer, the cheapest cost avoider, and the cheapest risk avoider. These criteria should be considered conjunctly. See *cheapest cost avoider*, *cheapest risk avoider*, *best risk bearer*, and *most effective precaution taker*.

Cheapest risk avoider: risks can be controlled by reducing activity levels, and the optimal allocation of residual liability should consider the forgone value of the relevant activities. The (social) value of the risk-creating activities is an important factor for implementing the cheaper cost avoider criterion and to allocate residual liability optimally. All things being equal, residual liability should therefore fall on the party who can reduce his or her activity level at the lowest cost (cheapest risk avoider). Following Shavell's (1980b) tort law model, consider the parties' activities with a value $Vt(w)$ and $Vv(z)$, where the value of the activity grows with the parties' activity levels, w and z. The cheapest risk avoider is the party who can avoid the risk by reducing activity level at the lowest social cost. If $\frac{\partial Vt}{\partial w} > \frac{\partial Vv}{\partial z}$, the victim is the cheapest risk avoider and should bear the residual loss (i.e., negligence-based rules should be chosen). Conversely, if $\frac{\partial Vt}{\partial w} < \frac{\partial Vv}{\partial z}$, the tortfeasor would become the cheapest risk avoider and should bear the residual loss (i.e., strict-liability-based rules should be chosen). When applying Calabresi's (1970) cheapest cost avoider paradigm, the cheapest risk avoider criterion is used in conjunction with other specific elements (including the best risk bearer, the cheapest precaution taker, and the most effective precaution taker) to determine the optimal allocation of accident costs. See also *cheapest cost avoider*, *cheapest precaution taker*, *best risk bearer*, and *most effective precaution taker*.

Chicago school: the University of Chicago Law School is identified by most scholars as the birthplace of law and economics. The first examples of application of economics to law can be traced back to the 1930s, although much of the work that laid the foundations for modern law and economics was developed in the late 1950s and 1960s. The Chicago school of law and economics, controversial as it may have been, has in many ways transformed the entire approach to legal analysis. Among the scholars that played an important role in the Chicago school, we find influential economists such as Nobel laureates Gary Becker, Ronald Coase, George Stigler, and Milton Friedman, as well as legendary figures such as Richard Posner, William Landes, Cass Sunstein, Richard Epstein, Douglas Baird, and Saul Levmore, and in more recent years younger scholars such as Eric Posner, Omri Ben-Shahar, Richard McAdams, Lisa Bernstein, and other important exponents of the law and economics movement. These scholars have played and continue to play a fundamental role in shaping the research agenda of the Chicago school and of the law and economics movement in general. The University of Chicago has been the home to two of the leading publications in the field: the *Journal of Law and Economics* and the *Journal of Legal Studies*. Over the years the Chicago school has developed a distinctive methodological approach, often referred to as Chicago-style law and economics. One of the characteristics often attributed to the Chicago methodology is the use of economics as a tool of positive analysis. The efficiency of the common law hypothesis is a frequently used example of the positive law and economics approach. The hypothesis is that common law rules, developed by judges over time, attempt to allocate resources in an efficient manner. In other words, the common law system spontaneously evolved and generated rules that create incentives for efficient behavior. Much of the early work of the Chicago school was implicitly or explicitly carried out as a testing of this hypothesis. In the positive law and economics literature, economics is used as a descriptive tool to carry out a positive analysis of the effects of law on behavior. The characterization of the Chicago-style law and economics as a purely positive approach is the result of a generalization; but most would agree that, unlike other scholars in the field, Chicago scholars, while defending efficiency as a policy objective, are generally wary of academic normative analysis. The trust in economic analysis is counterbalanced by a strong trust in the evolution of the common law toward efficiency, and Chicago scholars are fairly conservative when it comes to the use of regulatory tools to correct market failures and cognitive biases. See also *law and economics 2.0*, *positive versus normative law and economics*, *Yale school*, and *Virginia school*.

Chicken game: also known as hawk–dove game, this is a two-player non-cooperative game with multiple equilibria that describes a conflict situation among players. The story associated with the game is as follows. Two drivers meet on a one-lane bridge. Each driver should choose whether to cross the bridge before the other driver or to yield and cross afterwards. If both drivers cross the bridge simultaneously, they will crash with a negative payoff (e.g., −1). If they both choose to wait, they will get a low payoff (e.g., zero). If a driver crosses and the other waits, the one who crosses first – the "hawk," in the sense that he or she is brave – will get the highest positive payoff (e.g., 2) while the other – the "dove," or the "chicken," in the sense that he or she is a coward – will still get a positive payoff, but lower because of his or her waiting (e.g., 1). Consider

the following matrix illustrating the chicken game in the general case, where
$B > D > C > A$ and $b > d > c > a$.

		Driver 1	
		Cross	Wait
Driver 2	Cross	A,a	B,c
	Wait	C,b	D,d

In absence of any communication, the chicken game presents two Nash equilibria in pure strategies, whereby both players prefer to choose the opposite strategy (one crossing and the other waiting): (B,c) and (C,b). Each player prefers one Nash equilibrium over the other. A mixed-strategy equilibrium exists, whereby each player plays each strategy with a positive probability. The chicken game is often thought of as an *anti-coordination game*, in the sense that the Nash equilibrium requires the players to coordinate on the opposite strategy. On the contrary, in coordination games, such as the battle of the sexes, playing the same strategy Pareto-dominates. The result can be intuitively explained as follows. In coordination games, players share a resource that is non-rivalrous and that creates a positive externality for both players (e.g., in the battle of the sexes, choosing the same event provides a benefit on the payoff function of each player). In anti-coordination games, players use a shared resource that is rivalrous but non-excludable, and this creates a negative externality on the subjects, as in the case of the chicken game. The conflict situation described in the chicken game has been used in biology and in evolutionary game theory, and here it is commonly referred to as the hawk–dove game. It has been used to describe a situation in which subjects can choose either to fight or to conciliate on the distribution of a shared resource. Experimental evidence shows that, in the presence of a substantial level of reciprocity among players, different outcomes may be sustained: in the presence of positive reciprocity, both players tend to wait, while, in the opposite case of negative reciprocity, they both tend to cross. Experimental analysis on the hawk–dove game is interesting, since it allows scientists to distinguish between the motivations of equity and self-interest. The hawk–dove game introduces ideas of evolutionary biology into the context of game theory. The original game (introduced by John Mainard Smith and George Price in 1973) tells the story of two birds that should either choose to fight (behaving like a hawk) or to share the territory (behaving like a dove). If one bird behaves like a hawk and the other like a dove, the hawk will conquer the territory. If both birds choose to fight, there is a substantial risk of injury and each bird has the same probability of winning.

Chooser's call/put option: when allocating entitlements, the chooser has a choice of allocating the entitlement to the non-chooser (and receiving some payoff for doing so) or allocating the entitlement to the chooser him- or herself (if the subjective value is above the non-chooser's value). Ayres (2005) describes the second option as the "chooser's call" – the chooser's ability to allocate him- or herself an entitlement when the chooser's privately known value exceeds the non-chooser's value. When the chooser allocates the entitlement to the non- chooser for a payoff, the chooser may be said to have exercised the chooser's put option. See also *call option, put option, single-chooser rules*, and *dual-chooser rules*.

CLEA: Canadian Law and Economics Association. Founded in 1989 (and as such the second oldest association devoted to the economic analysis of law) on the initiative of Michael Trebilcock, who was at the time a professor of law and economics at the University of Toronto. The association was created to bring scholarship and research in the field of law and economics to a larger audience, via an annual conference aimed at attracting numerous scholars from various fields and countries. The association continues to be mainly funded and run by the University of Toronto. The first annual conference was held from September 22 to 23, 1989, at the University of Toronto. Unlike other associations, which have rotating locations, the annual conferences of the Canadian Law and Economics Association have always been held at the University of Toronto. The conference regularly attracts between seventy and 100 scholars, from both North America and Europe, and typically involves the presentation of between twenty and thirty scholarly papers on a variety of topics relevant to the field of law and economics. The annual meeting is preceded by the annual Olin public lecture in law and economics, which has been given by a variety of influential scholars, including Avner Greif, Ian Ayres, Robert Ellickson, Henry Manne, Guido Calabresi, John Elster, Richard Epstein, Amartya Sen, and Mancur Olson. The presidents of the association are elected biennially, and have included Christopher Bruce (1992–4), Rose Ann Devlin (1994–6), Sam Rea (1996–8), John Preston Palmer (1998–9), Gillian Hadfield (1999–2001), Douglas West (2001–3), Margaret Brinig (2003–5), Ralph Winter (2005–7), Poonam Puri (2007–9), Anita Anand (2009–11), and Benjamin Alarie (2011–13). See also *ALEA, EALE, ALACDE*, and *ASLEA*.

Close-knittedness: refers to small societies or groups in which the people are "closely knit," with personal relationships. Social scientists suggest that reci- procity, reputational constraints, and social norms are more effective in close- knit communities. Ellickson (1991), in his analysis of how neighbors and people in small communities solve disputes, argues that these groups are not hierarchical and that they must have "credible and reciprocal prospects for the application of power against one another and a good supply of information on past and present internal events." In close-knit communities, individuals have greater incentives to choose optimizing strategies. Close-knittedness fosters the emergence of opti- mal social norms and customs. In close-knit communities greater reliance can be placed on spontaneous compliance with desirable rules of conduct, even with imperfect legal enforcement (e.g., an individual takes on socially optimal levels of precaution not simply because of the law but because of the incentives created by the close-knit social network in which he or she lives). Problems such as free-riding in the voluntary contribution to a public good are less pronounced when it is part of a small, closely knit environment in which personal relationships are the glue that establish and hold together social norms. See also *embeddedness*.

Club goods: impure public goods, with mixed features of private and public goods. Similar to pure public goods, club goods are non-rival within a given range, in that the use of the club good by one person does not reduce other people's ability to use the same good. Unlike pure public goods, club goods are excludable, in the sense that it is possible to exclude non-payers from the use of a club good. Examples of club goods include museums, cinema shows, swimming pools, beaches, and gated parks. Given their non-rivalry in use, the use of a club good by a single individual is usually suboptimal. However, non-rivalry will cease when congestion occurs. The task for the theory of clubs is that of determining the optimal size of the club (which is likely to be larger than one individual but less than open access) and the optimal supply of club goods. See also *public good*.

Coase conjecture: Ronald Coase's conjecture that a monopolist selling a durable good must sell it at marginal cost. The idea behind this conjecture is the informal argument that monopolistic producers of durable goods are unable to guarantee not to lower their prices in future periods and thus cannot command higher prices in earlier periods. An additional argument that is consistent with the Coase conjecture is that, even though the monopolist has a monopoly on the primary sales of its goods, previously sold goods will eventually enter the secondary market, competing with the new units produced by the monopolist. This conjecture has been used by Edlin (2007) to explain Microsoft's need to come up with new operating systems and new generations of software on a periodical basis. See also *Schumpeter's creative destruction*.

Coase theorem: holds that, regardless of the initial allocation of rights and the choice of remedies for their protection, the market and the free bargaining of the parties will lead to their efficient final allocation. The idea is that the law creates many rights and legal entitlements, and when the initial allocation is not optimal the owners of the rights will have an incentive to transfer them to other individuals who value them more. Such an exchange will continue until there is no obtainable surplus from a potential exchange and each right is in the hands of the highest-valuing individual. This argument was first formulated by Ronald Coase in an article published in 1959 and later refined in the celebrated article "The problem of social cost," published in the *Journal of Law and Economics* in 1960. Although Coase always stressed that he never intended to convey his thoughts in the precise and analytical form of a theorem (Coase, 1988: 157), the idea he formulated has nonetheless become known as the "Coase theorem" and is widely recognized as a milestone in the legal and economic literature. The reformulation of Coase's idea in the form of a theorem is generally attributed to the work of Stigler (1966), Demsetz (1967) and Calabresi (1968). Stigler restates Coase's idea in the form of a quite powerful theorem, observing that "under perfect competition private and social costs will be equal" (113). Demsetz elaborates on Coase's insight, observing that "in a world of zero transaction costs... the output mix that results when the exchange of property rights is allowed is efficient and the mix is independent of who is assigned ownership" (349). Calabresi spells out the important legal implications of Coase's idea by observing that "if one assumes rationality, no transaction costs, and no legal impediments to bargaining, all misallocations of resources would be fully cured in the market by bargains" (68). The legal implications of Coase's idea were quite substantial. When pushed to its logical conclusions, the Coase theorem basically states that in the absence of transaction costs the law is irrelevant to overall welfare, because the parties will bargain and agree to an efficient use of legal entitlements, even in the shadow of an inefficient law. Indeed, Coase's statement triggered one of the most intense and fascinating debates in the history of legal and economic thought. The Coase theorem has served as a starting point for several important contributions to the law and economics literature. Coase formulated some positive statements on the basis of the unrealistic assumption of an absence of costs in the process of negotiation and transfer of the rights. The subsequent literature developed some normative corollaries on what should be the optimal allocation of legal rights and the optimal choice of remedies when transaction costs are instead positive. The normative corollaries to the Coase theorem were not formulated by Coase but by other scholars and are now generally referred to in the literature as the "normative Coase theorem(s)". See also *normative Coase theorem*, *asymmetric Coase theorem*, *Hobbes theorem*, and *Coase, Ronald*.

Coase, Ronald Harry (1910–): considered by most scholars the founding father of law and economics. As an economist, Coase provided important research in the areas of transaction costs and property rights. He received the 1991 Nobel Prize in economics for his work on the theory of the firm and the economics of externalities. He is best known for two articles: "The nature of the firm" (1937) and the groundbreaking "The problem of social cost" (1960). In the first, Coase explores the question of why certain economic activities were left to market exchange and others were carried out within firms. He concludes that the firm will expand to the point that the cost of conducting the activity would be the same as through a market transaction. This concept, which became known as Coase's theory of the firm, was the harbinger for the transaction costs analysis of industrial organization, specifically that the form of organization that minimizes the cost of the transaction will generally be chosen. In "The problem of social cost," Coase casts doubt on the widely accepted ideas of British economist Arthur Pigou, who believed that government taxation was the most efficient way to disincentivize a perceived wrongdoer (e.g., if a cattle rancher's cows destroy his neighboring farmer's crops, the government should stop the rancher from letting his cattle roam free or should at least tax him for doing so). Instead, Coase proposes that, in the presence of low transaction costs, the problem of externalities can be overcome simply with a system of well-defined property rights. Parties will reallocate rights until their value is maximized. This proposition, known as the Coase theorem, has been a central pillar of the economic analysis of law. In addition to his foundational work in the field of law and economics, he has made important contributions regarding public goods. See also ***Chicago school***, ***Coase theorem***, and ***Coase conjecture***.

Coasean bargaining: according to the Coase theorem, if parties are allowed to bargain in the absence of transaction costs, the optimal allocation of resources is obtained regardless of their initial allocation and remedial protection. Coasean bargaining refers to the bargaining that takes place under the Coase theorem. The term is often used in the law and economics literature as a synonym of bargaining in the absence of transaction costs. The Coasean bargaining world generally includes an assumption of no strategic costs, costless monitoring, and perfect enforcement. See also ***Coase theorem*** and ***axiomatic theory of bargaining***.

Cognitive bias: a range of observer effects that cause systematic error in an agent's assessment of contextual information. The study of cognitive bias in economics stems from Amos Tversky's and Daniel Kahneman's seminal article "Judgment under uncertainty: heuristics and biases" (1974), which examines how the use of heuristics, time-saving cognitive rules of thumb, leads sophisticated agents to systematic error in assessing the relative probabilities of certain events. The discipline of behavioral economics grew out of the recognition that cognitive bias plays a significant role in market phenomena such as prices, resource allocations, and investments. Not all bias effects are negative; some biases, called adaptive biases, may be reinforced because they improve individual or firm performance. For instance, overconfident and overoptimistic agents often outperform more realistic agents, reinforcing their biases. The study of cognitive bias has helped law and economics scholars study a wide range of phenomena at the intersection of law and decision-making, such as employer discrimination, the assessment of risk, and inconsistent applications of the precautionary principle. See also ***bounded rationality***.

Coincidental causation: in tort law, a victim recovers damages for negligence when the defendant's actions are both the actual and proximate cause of the harm. Coincidental causation describes causation that is actual, but not proximate. Shavell uses the example of a speeding bus hit by a falling tree (Shavell, 2003). The tree falls on an exact spot at a specific time and the bus is in that spot because it was speeding. However, although the bus could have missed the tree by slowing down, it also could have missed the tree by speeding more. In other words, the speeding of the bus was a "but for" cause of the accident, but it was only a coincidental cause. An action is just as likely to be the coincidental cause of harm as the coincidental cause of harm avoidance (e.g., the bus could have just as easily avoided a falling tree thanks to its speeding). Tort law would not find the bus driver liable, because of the coincidental relationship between the act of speeding and the accident. Friedman (2000) and Shavell (2003) both point out that economics justifies the coincidental causation rule. Policymakers design tort laws to stop potential tortfeasors from engaging in risky behavior that will harm others. Holding tortfeasors liable for coincidentally caused harms would not impact their behavior and would therefore impose unnecessary administrative costs. See also ***causation*** and ***background risk***.

Collateral: this term has acquired a special significance in law and economics thanks to a paper by Kronman (1985) considering contracts in the state of nature. Collateral is one of the four non-legal enforcement mechanisms (the others being hostages, hands tying, and union) considered by Kronman that can facilitate contracting in the absence of legal enforcement. Enforcement mechanisms are necessary to make most contractual promises credible. When entering into an agreement without the state's legal enforcement, parties face a trust problem. The trust problem can be particularly severe when the parties' performance and counter-performance cannot be exchanged simultaneously. A collateral can be used to transform a non-simultaneous exchange into two sequential simultaneous exchanges. Collateral is a bonding instrument characterized by the fact that the valuation of the collateral for the giver (the promisor) is generally similar to the valuation for the taker (the promisee). This characteristic distinguishes hostages from collateral (which has value for the hostage giver, but generally no value for the hostage taker). In non-simultaneous exchanges, the promisor offers collateral at the time of the promisee's performance. Upon performance by the promisor, the promisee returns the collateral. To create proper incentives, the value of the collateral should be sufficient to induce performance (i.e., the value of the collateral should be higher than the cost of performance, to avoid opportunistic defection on the part of the promisor), but it should fall below the value of performance for the promisee (i.e., if the value of the collateral is too high, the promisee may prefer to keep the collateral, forgoing the promised performance). Similar to a hostage, it is important that the collateral be simultaneously released at the time of performance. See also ***hostages***, ***hands tying***, and ***union***.

Collateral source rule: prohibits courts or juries, in tort law, from reducing a defendant tortfeasor's damages due to payments the plaintiff has received from other sources (e.g., insurance). For example, if a defendant tortfeasor negligently harms a victim by hitting him or her with a car, the tortfeasor must pay full damages to the victim, even if the victim is also fully compensated for his or her injuries by his or her own insurance. Some law and economics scholars defend this rule. Posner argues that the collateral source rule keeps in place an incentive for the tortfeasor to adjust his or her behavior to avoid harming potential victims

(Posner, 2010). When plaintiffs receive funds from collateral sources, tortfeasors' damages are not reduced in order to force tortfeasors to internalize the full external cost of their behavior and to create optimal care incentives (Posner, 2010; Marshall and Fitzgerald, 2005). Proponents of tort reform, including the American Tort Reform Association, have strongly criticized the collateral source rule (Feeley and Schap, 2006). The collateral source rule provides victims with a windfall gain. This could seriously distort prospective victims' incentives and reduce their care and activity level incentives in the face of risky behavior (Feeley and Schap, 2006). However, Posner argues that victims who receive funds from their insurance providers have paid for this benefit through insurance premiums (Posner, 2010; Feeley and Schap, 2006). One potential method for reducing the windfall to victims is subrogation, through which the insurance provider takes funds back from the victim, based on how much the victim receives from the tortfeasor. However, there is evidence that insurance companies do not always exercise this option (Feeley and Schap, 2006).

Collective action problem: the concept of collective action is used to describe situations in which a group of individuals pursues a common goal, and the pursuit of that goal requires coordination of individual efforts. Collective action problems arise when the individual choices of the members of the group fail to reach a coordinated solution that is beneficial to the group as a whole. The concept has become important in the public choice and law and economics literature since the publication of Olson's *The Logic of Collective Action* (1965), which highlights the fact that individual rationality is not a sufficient condition for collective rationality. A standard example of a collective action problem in economic theory is the provision of public goods: individuals are asked to decide the level of public good to be provided and the amount they are willing to finance (e.g., voluntary contributions for the cost of landscaping a common area). The collective action problem arises because each individual attempts to become a free rider, hoping to benefit from the contribution of others, without contributing anything of his or her own. As a result of collective action problems and free-riding, economists generally identify the provision of public goods as a market failure. Individual rationality leads to inefficient provision (underproduction) of the public good in a market economy. Economic theory has examined institutional designs and the creation of preference revelation mechanisms that reduce the inefficiencies generated by collective action problems. For example, the provision of public goods increases when the public good is offered jointly with a private good produced by a monopolist (non-contributors to the public good are excluded from the enjoyment of the private good). The notion of the collective action problem has been widely applied in law and economics to describe situations in which individual and social incentives are misaligned due to the presence of strategic behavior and opaque preferences. Dixit and Olson (2000) question whether the presence of collective action problems might undermine the workings of the Coase theorem. See also *free riding* and *public good*.

Coming to the nuisance: loosely, a nuisance is an externality imposed by a landowner on his or her neighbors, for which the aggrieved neighbors have a legal claim. However, the defendant can assert the affirmative defense of "coming to the nuisance" if the nuisance-causing activity predated the arrival of the aggrieved party. The idea is that the aggrieved party knew that the nuisance existed when he or she acquired the adjacent property, and could, most cheaply, have avoided it in the first place. Therefore, the doctrine holds that the aggrieved party cannot reasonably assert a claim against the nuisance. Contemporary courts have taken a more flexible view, recognizing that both nuisance law and the defense of "coming to the nuisance" assign the property right arbitrarily (either to the aggrieved party or to the first-comer). Consequently, efficient use of land has become an important factor in resolving nuisance issues. See also **Spur Industries *v.* Del Webb** and *cheapest cost avoider*.

Commodification: a term that has been used in the law and economics literature to describe the process of transforming rights into tradable commodities. Commodification is the process of deciding which entitlements may be the object of contracts (i.e., may be purchased, sold, etc.). For example, in a society in which every conceivable transferable object goes through commodification, everything could be the subject of a contract. Parties could traffic in body parts, legal rights, ideas, or sexual autonomy. Parties would face no alienability restrictions, and, absent market failures, the market would set prices for any of these objects. In his book on the doctrine of freedom of contract, Trebilcock (1993) describes one aspect of this doctrine: the freedom to contract for, transfer, or sell any item, service, or right (i.e., the freedom to make anything the object of one's contract). Proponents of this freedom of contract argue that the law should not stand in the way of the efficient functioning of the market. Opponents would argue that allowing unrestricted commodification would take away from the incalculable value of one's body or individual rights. Although the issue of commodification is of great relevance to law and economics, economic analysis has not shed much light on the commodification debate and has not offered much guidance in determining criteria as to what should and should not be subject to commodification. See also *inalienability rules*.

Common law: see *efficiency of the common law hypothesis*.

Common-pool resources: public resources that are accessible and that the government cannot easily stop the public from using. In many law and economics applications, the term "common-pool resources" is used interchangeably with "commons." For example, an open, abandoned field from which cows eat is a common-pool resource. Because it is difficult to control access to these resources, individuals, who have little incentive to stop using them, can easily overuse common-pool resources. Environmental scholars often use the term when discussing the excessive usage of environmental resources. Ostrom has carried out significant scholarly research into common-pool resources. Although legal regimes can govern common-pool resources and control access to them, monitoring and enforcement costs are often very high, and the protection of common-pool resources is often left to voluntary compliance. The literature points to several factors that inhibit governments from limiting access to common-pool resources, including cost–benefit analysis, ethical restraints, and constitutional/legal constraints (Ostrom, 1990; Ostrom, Gardner, and Walker, 1994). In Ostrom's terminology, a common-pool resource is a facility from which resource units are subtracted and used by individuals, called "appropriators" (Ostrom, 1990). In the cow/field example, the field is the facility and strands of grass are resource units, which the cow consumes. In this example, the resource unit is regenerative, so, if the rate of usage does not outpace the rate of regeneration, the resources will not be depleted. However, if the resource is not regenerative (e.g., oil), or if the rate of exploitation exceeds that of regeneration, the usage of the resource will not be sustainable and will eventually lead to a complete depletion of the resource (Ostrom, 1990). See also *commons*, *open-access resources*, and *Ostrom, Elinor*.

Common-value auctions: auctions at which objects are acquired for resale. Unlike private-value auctions, individual bids are not driven by subjective valuations or personal taste but by the bidder's guess on the valuation of prospective buyers. Since every bidder pursues the same potential prospects of resale on the market, these auctions are modeled as if all bidders had a common valuation of the good. However, the very nature of the process involves uncertainty and guessing about the actual resale price. Winners of a common-value auction may thus have good reasons to regret their successful bidding. Common-value models may also be applicable to situations in which bidders try to acquire goods for direct consumption but when there is significant uncertainty about the quality of the goods. See also *private-value auctions*, *direct versus indirect revelation mechanism*, *winner's curse*, and *auction theory*.

Commons: in situations in which multiple individuals can use a common resource, without a cost-effective way to monitor and constrain each other's use, the resource is vulnerable to overuse, leading to a problem known as the "tragedy of the commons." More generally, every time a depletable resource is open to access by more than one individual, incentives for overuse will emerge. As the number of individuals who enjoy free access grows larger relative to the capacity of the common resource, overuse will approach unsustainable levels and the users will risk the complete destruction of the common good. Although Hardin (1968) was the first to term this destruction the "tragedy of the commons," he credits a mathematical amateur named William Forster Lloyd (1794–1852) for formalizing it in a little-known pamphlet published in 1833 on population growth (Lloyd, 1833). Since Lloyd, other economists have identified the problems associated with the common ownership of resources exploited under conditions of individualistic competition. Most notably, Gordon (1954) has pointed out that, absent controls on entry, common resources will be exploited even at levels of negative marginal productivity. This is because external effects are not fully internalized within the choice of each individual decision-maker. The sources of externalities in a commons problem are twofold. First, there are static (or current) externalities, in that the use of the resource reduces the benefit from usage to others. Secondly, there are possible dynamic (or future) externalities, because the use of a renewable resource today bears its consequences into the future. As a result of the lack of conformity between use and exclusion rights, individuals do not have to consider the full social costs of their activities. Private and social returns diverge, and total use by all parties exceeds the social wealth maximizing point (Parisi, Schulz, and Depoorter, 2005). See also ***anticommons***, ***common-pool resources***, and ***open-access resources***.

Comparative advantage: this principle explains why it can be beneficial for two individuals, firms, or countries to specialize and trade, even though one of them has an absolute advantage in all types of production. According to the principle of comparative advantage, what matters is not the absolute advantage in production but, rather, the ratio between how efficiently two producers can produce different kinds of things. By looking at the ratio of efficiency in production, the concept excludes the possibility that a producer has no comparative advantage in anything. A producer may be the least efficient in every category of production, but would nevertheless have a comparative advantage in the sector in which it is, in relative terms, less inefficient. The principle of comparative advantage, usually attributed to David Ricardo's 1817 book *On the Principles of Political Economy and Taxation*, provides an important foundation to the theory of international trade. It underpins the economic case for free trade, showing how there can be gains from specialization and free trade even if one country is a more efficient producer in every sector. See also ***absolute advantage***.

Comparative causation: a rule that allows courts to split an accident loss between two parties, when neither of them is found negligent. This rule can be traced back to the writings of Hugo Grotius (1625), and was first considered in the law and economics literature by Calabresi and Cooper (1996), who advance the idea of loss spreading among faultless parties. The novelty introduced by comparative causation is that, if both parties are non-negligent, the loss is apportioned on the basis of the extent to which each party contributed to the harm. Parisi and Fon (2004) and Parisi and Singh (2010) find that, even though neither party faces the full accident loss in equilibrium, comparative causation does incentivize both parties to take optimal levels of care. This is because loss-sharing applies in equilibrium, after both parties have undertaken due care. The interesting effect is that, unlike other rules utilized by tort law, comparative causation incentivizes both parties to reduce their activity levels, although not to a socially efficient level. The rule of comparative causation is rarely used in modern legal systems, with only a handful of examples in court decisions, in the United States and elsewhere, in which courts applied the rule, splitting the accident loss between non-negligent tortfeasors and their non-negligent victims. See also ***causation***, *coincidental causation*, *contributory and comparative negligence*, *decoupling*, *residual decoupling*, *contributory and comparative non-negligence*, and *loss sharing*.

Comparative dynamics: a form of economic modeling in which models are subjected to changes in initial conditions and the resulting equilibria are compared. See also *adjustment dynamics*, *comparative statics*, and *dynamic models*.

Comparative law and economics: a new subfield of law and economics that utilizes economics to provide a neutral language for the comparative evaluation of legal rules adopted by various countries. Most of the founding contributions to the field of comparative law and economics come from European scholars. Comparative law and economics scholars criticize the static approach of American scholars, who often evaluate the efficiency of legal rules in a vacuum or, alternatively, assume an institutional framework modeled on the American legal process. According to comparative law and economics scholars, these limitations make it harder to generalize the results of the existing literature outside the assumed country-specific institutional context. The valuable – but, so far, not yet fully implemented – suggestion of comparative law and economics scholars is to develop models that treat the legal and institutional backgrounds as endogenous and dynamic variables, broadening the horizons of traditional research agendas.

Comparative negligence: see *contributory and comparative negligence*.

Comparative statics: these techniques are used to study the change of an equilibrium resulting from a change in some variable. Comparative statics techniques utilized in law and economics generally carry out a qualitative study of the change in the equilibrium, pointing out the direction of the change, without quantifying the measure of change from the original equilibrium. Empirical and experimental techniques, as well as mathematical simulations, can be used to "calibrate" the model and generate quantitative predictions. See also *comparative dynamics*, *calibration*, and *simulations*.

Compensatory damages: in tort law, when a tortfeasor negligently causes harm to another, courts grant damages to the victim. The most obvious type of damages is compensatory damages, which courts award to compensate the victim for the harm he or she experienced. If a driver, for example, negligently hits a pedestrian, the court might award compensatory damages equal to the cost of healing the victim plus the victim's lost wages during treatment. As Cooter and Ulen (1997) point out, compensatory damages serve to return the victim to the position he or she was in before the tortious injury and to deter negligent conduct by forcing the tortfeasor to pay a price for his or her negligence. When restoration of the harm is not possible (e.g., an irreversible loss), compensatory damages are those that would make the victim indifferent between (a) suffering harm and obtaining compensation and (b) suffering no harm. In analyzing damages, Cooter (1997) distinguishes between intentional and unintentional harm. For unintentional, but negligent, harm, Cooter argues that compensatory damages are sufficient to incentivize a potential tortfeasor to monitor his or her behavior and take an efficient level of care to avoid an accident. Forcing a tortfeasor to pay compensatory damages makes the potential tortfeasor internalize the harm he or she might cause. He or she must weigh the costs of taking precaution against the risk of liability. He or she will take a level of precaution that efficiently balances between these two considerations. However, applying extra-compensatory damages would cause the potential tortfeasor to take more caution than is socially optimal, which could reduce productive and useful behavior. For intentional harms, compensatory damages will not sufficiently deter a person who intends to harm another (Cooter, 1997). Courts should add punitive damages, beyond the cost of compensation, to deter potential injurers and punish those who commit intentional harms. See also *hedonic damages*, *expectation damages*, *reliance damages*, *punitive damages*, and *disgorgement damages*.

Competition: see *perfect competition*.

Complements: goods that should be consumed together (e.g., cars and gasoline, or shoes and shoelaces). If there is a shift in demand for a good, demand for its complements shifts in the same direction. Likewise, if the price of a good increases, demand for its complements decreases. In economic terms, this effect is described as a negative cross-price effect, $\partial j / \partial Pi < 0$, where j represents the quantity demanded of good j and Pi represents the price of its complementary good i. The economic concept of complementarity is of particular importance in legal applications. For example, when studying the effect of legal intervention on a given industry, and in order to separate the effect of the enacted policy from the effect of other environmental parameters, it is useful to look at the movement of the stock prices of producers of complementary goods and compare them against the stock prices of the regulated industries. In other contexts, legal rules may create incentives for a primary activity by taxing (or subsidizing) activities that are complementary to it. For example, in order to deter some hard-to-monitor activities, the legal system may choose to criminalize or tax complementary goods or activities. See also *substitutes* and *cross-price effect*.

Complete contracts: when parties can specify in a contract all the legal consequences relating to each party's rights and obligations for every possible outcome, the result is a "complete contract." It has no gaps in its terms; all conceivable future contingencies are specified in the contract. Far from this ideal, real-world contracts are by necessity incomplete; writing a "complete" contract would be hardly possible and prohibitively expensive. Legal systems address the incompleteness of contracts in two ways. Legal rules can be designed ex ante to provide default rules that define parties' rights and obligations in the absence of agreed-upon contract provisions. Alternatively, legal systems can tackle incompleteness ex post through a judicial gap-filling interpretation of the incomplete contract. Law and economics scholars have studied the effect of contract incompleteness on contract formation, performance, and reliance. Recent developments of contract theory by Hart (see Hart, 2009, 2011; see also Hart and Moore, 1988a, 1988b) focus on the theory of incomplete contracts. He has studied how the impossibility of writing a complete contract affects the optimal incentives of parties, with a particular attention on relationship-specific investments. See also *default rules* and *holdup problem*.

Complete information versus perfect information: in game theory, "complete information" describes each player's knowledge about the structure of the game and the players' objective functions. Each player in a game has "complete information" when he or she knows the set of strategies available to the opponents and the payoffs. Whereas "perfect information" requires knowledge of the set of actions of the other players in the game, complete information does not. Any game of incomplete information can be transformed into a game of complete but imperfect information by adding nature as a player, and conditioning each player's payoff on nature's moves. This is known as the "Harsanyi transformation." Complete information can be interpreted as an assumption of a player's rationality. Without complete information, each player cannot predict how his or her actions will affect other players' payoffs. Complete information constitutes one of the crucial theoretical assumptions of the perfect competition required for economic efficiency. See also *asymmetric information*.

Compounding: see *discounting*.

Concentration index: see *Herfindahl index*.

Concentration ratio: a measure of market concentration used to evaluate market structure. Concentration ratios measure the proportion of total activity in an industry attributable to a given number of the largest firms in the industry. A concentration ratio is calculated by summing the market shares of the largest firms in the industry, usually the four largest or eight largest. The resulting ratio is expressed as a percentage of the total relevant market controlled by those firms (e.g., the four largest firms in the market account for 68.25 percent of total sales; the eight largest firms in the market account for 81.25 percent of total sales). Concentration ratios are intuitive but not always very informative, since they include only information about the total market share of the four (or eight) largest firms, without specifying the internal split of the market among them, implicitly assuming that market control is linearly proportional to market share. Since ratios ignore how market share is internally split among the largest firms, the same concentration ratio could reflect quite different market structures (e.g., a monopoly and an oligopoly with four incumbent firms both generate the same concentration ratios). The use of concentration indexes (e.g., Herfindahl indexes), rather than ratios, can overcome these limitations, providing a more sophisticated, albeit less intuitive, measure of market concentration. See also *market concentration*, *Herfindahl index*, *market share*, and *market structure*.

Conditional fees: see *contingent versus conditional fees*.

Condorcet jury theorem: Marie-Jean-Antoine-Nicolas de Caritat (1743–94), generally known as the Marquis de Condorcet, considered the process of jury deliberation, and proved that, if individual jurors are more likely of being correct than not in their convictions, an increase in the number of jurors will increase the chance that the collective majority decision will be correct (de Caritat, 1785). This theorem, which can be seen as a consequence of the law of large numbers, has important policy implications, ranging from democratic theory to collective choice. Although the Condorcet jury theorem constitutes an important pillar of social choice theory and provides an important theoretical basis for the understanding of collective decision-making, some of the assumptions of the theorem have been criticized, including the assumption of sincere voting and costless information. Scholars have looked at the extent to which the results of the theorem are robust to strategic voting, showing that, even in the presence of strategic voting, the outcome of voting converges to the efficient outcome as the number of voters increases. The Condorcet jury theorem is, instead, less robust to the presence of information costs, and the theorem may fail to hold if the cost of information acquisition is sufficiently large (Mukhopadhaya, 2003). See also *hung jury paradox*, *social choice theory*, and *law of large numbers*.

Condorcet voting criterion: according to this, a candidate who wins in all pairwise competition contests with all other candidates should be the winner. This criterion is named after Marie Jean Antoine Nicolas de Caritat, known as the Marquis de Condorcet (1743–94). See also *Condorcet voting paradox*.

Condorcet voting paradox: shows how majoritarian voting can lead to intransitive and cyclical social preferences. This paradox, which is at the core of Arrow's impossibility theorem and of much contemporary literature in both social choice and public choice theory, was originally discovered by Marie-Jean-Antoine-Nicolas de Caritat, generally known as the Marquis de Condorcet (1743–94). The paradox is typified when, for example, three voters (voters 1, 2, and 3) have transitive preferences over three alternatives (alternatives A, B, and C). Voter 1 has ordinal preferences $A > B > C$ (where the sign ">" indicates "individually preferred to"), voter 2 prefers $C > A > B$, and voter 3 prefers $B > C > A$. Given such preferences, a majority vote in which alternatives are selected on the basis of pairwise competition would yield to $A \gg B$, and $B \gg C$ (where the sign "$\gg$" denotes "collectively preferred to"). Transitivity would imply $A \gg C$. However, if a vote is cast comparing alternatives A and C, the majority would prefer C to A, leading to intransitive and cyclical collective preferences. See also *Condorcet winner*, *Arrow's impossibility theorem*, *cycling*, and *agenda setting*.

Condorcet winner: under a majority rules vote, a Condorcet winner is the candidate who is preferred by a majority over every other candidate. For example, if there are three alternatives (alternatives A, B, and C), then A is a Condorcet winner if, for a majority of voters, $A \gg B$ and $A \gg C$ (where the sign "$\gg$" denotes "collectively preferred to"). Critically, the set of voters for whom $A > B$ need not be the same set of voters for whom $A > C$ in order for A to be a Condorcet winner. The only criteria are that the set of voters for whom $A > B$ be greater than 50 percent and that the set of voters for whom $A > C$ be greater than 50 percent. The concept owes its name to the Marquis de Condorcet, who formulated it in conjunction with his (also eponymous) voting paradox. See also *cycling*, *Condorcet voting paradox*, and *Arrow's impossibility theorem*.

Conduct rules versus decision rules: starting with Jeremy Bentham, legal philosophers have distinguished between two functions of legal rules. The first function is forward-looking and is addressed to the general public and aims at guiding its behavior. In this literature, rules of this kind are called conduct rules. The second function is backward-looking and is directed to the judges and officials who apply conduct rules. Rules of this kind are called decision rules. The distinction has been revived by Dan-Cohen (1984), who employs it to consider the purposeful use of the selective transmission of legal information to reconcile conflicting goals of the legal system. See also *acoustic separation*.

Conflict of interest: see *agency problems*.

Consistency of choice: see *axioms of preference*.

Constant-sum games: situations in which the aggregate payoff of players' interaction is constant. Analytically, a constant-sum game is a game in which players' payoffs always sum to a constant c. For two-player games, let $p_1(x, y)$ and $p_2(y, x)$ be the payoffs of players 1 and 2, given moves X and Y, respectively. The characteristic condition of a constant-sum game is simply that $p_1(x, y) + p_2(y, x) = c$. The more frequently encountered term "zero-sum game" refers to the special case in which $c = 0$. Any constant-sum game can be transformed into a zero-sum game by normalizing payoffs. The normalization (realized by subtracting the constant from the payoffs of all players in the game) leads to a zero-sum game that is strategically equivalent to the original constant-sum problem. See also *zero-sum games*, *variable-sum games*, and *inessential games*.

Constitutional political economy: a field of scholarly research that studies the rules that govern society and the impacts of those rules on the actions and interactions of individuals within society and on overall societal outcomes. Brennan and Buchanan have played an important role in the development of modern constitutional political economy, and they describe the field in their work *The Reason of Rules: Constitutional Political Economy* (Brennan and Buchanan, 1985). Instead of analyzing the actions of individual actors or firms within the existing scheme of rules, constitutional political economy studies the effects of various sets of political, social, or economic rules on individuals and their interactions with each other, and on society as a whole. While closely related to the fields of public choice theory and law and economics, constitutional political economy is focused on institutional design and the design of constitutions, rather than on conventional economic concepts of efficiency and wealth maximization, in the analysis of specific rules. Constitutional political economy might study the impacts of institutions on the actions of and interactions between individuals in society (van den Hauwe, 2005). As Buchanan (1990) has stated, the purpose of the field is to help actors within an existing system make informed decisions about changes to the governing rules and maintain positive existing rules. See also *public choice theory*, *Buchanan, James*, *Tullock, Gordon*, and *strategic constitution*.

Constitutional Political Economy: an academic journal that specializes in public choice theory and institutional design. It has published a good number of articles that are relevant to law and economics, on topics such as design of constitutions, federalism, and spontaneous law. The journal has been edited by well-known public choice scholars, including Richard Wagner (1990–7), Viktor Vanberg (1990–2001), Dennis Mueller (1997–present), Peter Ordeshook (1998–present), and Alan Hamlin (2002–present). See also *law and economics journals*.

Constrained optimization: optimization identifies the choice of the best element from available alternatives. A number of economic applications examine optimization problems under specific constraints. These types of problems are called constrained maximization problems. In many economic applications, optimization requires solving problems relating to the maximization or minimization of an objective function to identify the best available values in a defined domain. Examples of constrained optimization problems are (a) choosing between optimal consumption bundles to identify the one that maximizes the consumer's utility function given budget constraints, or (b) determining the optimal input bundles that could minimize a firm's production cost function given a level of output to be produced. Constrained optimization problems are relevant in the law and economics field. For instance, criminal sentencing and enforcement policy identifies the optimal combination of severity of punishment and level enforcement, to maximize deterrence. Similarly, many law and economics scholars attempt to determine optimal regulations that maximize social welfare, given the existing budgetary and institutional constraints. See also *corner solution versus interior solution* and *welfare analysis*.

Consumer surplus: the difference between the market price for a good and the maximum price consumers would be willing to pay for that good. In other words, the consumer surplus measures the total savings with respect to each consumer's willingness to pay. The size of the consumer surplus depends on the market structure and the degree of market power of producers. It is at its highest, and the highest efficiency is attained, in perfectly competitive markets. By contrast, the consumer surplus is zero under monopolistic first-degree price discrimination. See also *subjective value*, *producer surplus*, *aggregate surplus*, *deadweight loss*, and *fundamental theorems of welfare*.

Consumer versus producer sovereignty: Austrian law and economics scholars use the term "consumer sovereignty" to refer to the principle that the consumer is the best judge of the types and quantities of goods that should be produced by the economic system. Each consumer purchase operates as if the consumer is casting dollar votes for goods and services. These dollar votes increase companies' profits and motivate an increase in production. This concept is essential to Mises' (1966) idea of a value-free market driven by consumer demand. Many economists believe that consumer sovereignty could be undermined by several factors, such as a lack of knowledge and experience about the products, a distortion of preferences caused by advertising, and situations of monopoly or imperfect competition. These situations would be characterized as "producer sovereignty," inasmuch as producers ultimately decide what to do. See also *Austrian law and economics*.

Contestable markets: oligopolistic markets with a fairly small number of firms that operate at perfectly competitive prices. The essential feature of a contestable market is that, even if firms do not face perfect competition and operate in an oligopolistic market structure, they behave as perfectly competitive firms because of the threat posed by potential entrants. The theory of contestable markets, based on the work of Baumol, Panzar, and Willig (1983), explains the competitive outcome on the basis of a low level of entry and exit barriers that renders the threat of entry of potential competitors a sufficient deterrent. In a contestable market, the competitive pressure is caused by the ongoing threat of entry (i.e., potential competitors) rather than by the presence of a high number of incumbent firms (i.e., actual competitors). These markets are characterized by a "hit and run" type of competition. A market is said to be perfectly contestable when the entry and exit barriers are absent. According to the theory of contestable markets, therefore, even a market dominated by a single firm can exhibit highly competitive behavior. From a policy point of view, the theory of contestable markets implies that, in such markets, higher levels of market concentrations could be compatible with sustained competitive prices. One of the major critiques of the theory of contestable markets notes that very few markets are characterized by a complete absence of entry and exit barriers. An example frequently used of a contestable market is constituted by low-cost airlines, since each firm could enter the market by leasing aircraft, exploiting high positive profits, and exiting at relatively low cost. See also *barriers to entry*.

Contingent valuation: whenever possible, legal systems rely on market prices for the valuation of goods or services. However, there are situations in which the legal system needs to protect (or provide compensation for) a good that is not traded on the market and for which there is no current market price. Contingent valuation techniques are used in these cases to elicit consumer valuations. Individuals are generally asked questions related to willingness to pay or willingness to accept compensation. This approach is generally used in the area of environmental intervention, cost–benefit analysis for the protection of endangered species, and litigation for the assessment of environmental harm. The limits of contingent valuation techniques are related to the merely hypothetical nature of the choices presented and the difficulties of eliciting true preference revelation when pecuniary incentives (such as income constraints and opportunity cost) are not at work. See also *revealed preferences*, *willingness to pay versus willingness to accept*, and *endowment effect*.

Contingent versus conditional fees: in the United States, attorneys in civil cases are often compensated through contingent fee agreements. Instead of agreeing to pay an attorney a set amount, a client filing a claim may choose instead to pay his or her attorney only if the case is resolved in his or her favor. Under a contingent fee agreement, a client will commit to paying the attorney a certain percentage of the amount he or she receives from the case. Therefore, the attorney's compensation is tied to the results of the case. The attorney will receive a larger payment if he or she can secure greater compensation for his or her client, whether through trial or through a settlement agreement. Most European countries prohibit contingent fees, though some, including the United Kingdom, have allowed the use of conditional fees. A conditional fee is a fixed monetary sum an attorney will receive if the case is resolved favorably. However, unlike contingent fees, the amount of a conditional fee is set initially and is not tied to the amount of the final award in the case. For example, if a victim of an accident hires an attorney to secure a financial award for him or her from a negligent tortfeasor, he or she would be using a contingent fee arrangement if he or she agreed to pay the attorney 40 percent of the amount the attorney secures. Alternatively, if he or she agrees to pay the attorney an agreed-upon amount if the case is successfully resolved, and the amount of the conditional fee is not tied to the amount won through litigation, the victim is using a conditional fee system. In their work comparing the two types of fee structures, Emons and Garoupa (2004) argue that contingent fees are more efficient than conditional fees. Under a contingent fee agreement, an attorney has incentives to use whatever information he or she has about the case and about the likely amount he or she can secure for the client to make rational decisions about how much effort to expend on the case. Under a conditional fee agreement, the attorney has no incentive to use such information and will instead put in only an instrumental effort to secure the conditional fee. However, Emonts and Garoupa also argue that, if there is limited information available about the possible adjudicatory amount, a conditional fee structure is a better strategy to incentivize an attorney to take a "safe litigation strategy." See also *fee shifting*.

Contract as framework: see *contract as governance*.

Contract as governance: the idea of contracts as governance was introduced by Williamson in an article published in 1979, which framed long-term contracts and relational contracts as alternatives to corporate governance. Looking at alternative ways to organize production, Williamson placed the "governance of contractual relations" between the two opposite alternatives of spot markets and corporate organization, using transaction cost economics to mark the boundaries between these alternatives. Specifically, alternative governance solutions should be chosen with the goal of "economizing" (i.e., minimizing the sum of production and transaction costs). See also *governance structure*, *economizing*, *new institutional economics*, and *Williamson, Oliver*.

Contract as legal rules: see *contract as governance*.

Contract curve: given the allocation of two fixed-quantity resources between two individuals, a contract curve is the set of all Pareto-efficient allocations between those individuals. Each point on a contract curve is Pareto-efficient, inasmuch as it would be impossible to improve the well-being of one party without hurting the other. If market participants start with an allocation of rights or resources that is not on the contract curve, they have an incentive to redistribute their initial entitlements through exchange. The exact position on the curve that two individuals will settle upon will depend on their relative bargaining power; the person with superior bargaining power gets more of both. Graphically, the Pareto-efficient contract curve is depicted in an Edgeworth box, representing the line formed by the points of tangency between the two parties' indifference curves. From a policy point of view, if courts or lawmakers assign a legal entitlement inefficiently (if the initial allocation of right falls outside the hypothetical contract curve), and if the conditions for Coasean bargaining hold, the parties will have incentives to negotiate the initial allocation of rights; a Pareto-superior allocation will be chosen along the contract curve. In this example, inefficient allocations of legal rights will be corrected through private bargaining, but, under most circumstances, initial allocations may affect where legal entitlements will ultimately lie along the contract curve. See also *Coase theorem*.

Contract renegotiation: see *no ex post renegotiation assumption*.

Contract specificity: see *contract-specific investment*.

Contract theory: a subfield of economics that studies the optimal design of contractual arrangements in the presence of asymmetric information, and its main applications focus on moral hazard, adverse selection, and signaling. Contract theory attempts to design contracts that provide efficient incentives to individuals, for example to undertake the optimal level of effort and to invest optimally in reliance or to choose the optimal time structure of a contractual relationship. One important application is the design of optimal schemes of managerial compensation: finding the optimal payment schedule to align the interest of the manager (the agent) and the firm's owner (the principal). The economists' findings in the field of contract theory are of great relevance both for contract law and for the legal practice of contract drafting. However, the synergies between the economics and legal approaches to contracts have scarcely been exploited in either academic research or legal education. See also *incentives*, *incentive alignment*, *mechanism design*, *moral hazard*, *adverse selection*, and *signaling*.

Contract-specific investment: an activity that does not have much value outside a particular contract relationship. The term was introduced in the new institutional economics literature (Williamson, 1985) and has acquired a specific technical significance also in the law and economics literature (see, for example, Merges, 2005). Contract-specific investments create occasions for opportunistic behavior. Consider, for example, a firm that must produce goods and then sell them to its contracting partner; it necessarily must forgo other productive activity in order to fulfill its contractual obligations. Once the firm is in this position, the other contractual party might use its leverage to engage in opportunism and secure a more profitable arrangement. Williamson (1985) considers the role of contractual safeguards to protect against the risk of opportunistic behavior. See also *asset specificity* and *contractual safeguards*.

Contractarianism: a philosophical theory, also known as social contract theory, that justifies political authority through the rational consent of those ruled. While not describing an actual contract per se, all contractarian approaches to political authority use the idea of an enforceable agreement to characterize the obligations and entitlements of each subject or citizen vis-à-vis each other. Contractarianism has been described as a consent-based – as opposed to an outcome-based or consequentialist – theory of moral or political authority. See also *utilitarianism* and *Leviathan theory*.

Contracts as reference points: law and economics scholars study contract rules to determine the extent to which these rules encourage efficient behavior. Part of studying contracts and contract rules is developing a theoretical conception of contracts and what they provide to contracting parties. The traditional conception describes contracts as agreements that contain specific rights and obligations, but Hart and Moore (2008) propose a different conception of contracts. They argue that contracts serve as "reference points" for contracting parties as to the feelings of entitlement that exist between them. The parties' level of performance is based, in part, on the extent to which they believe they are receiving what they are entitled to under the contract. If the parties both commit themselves to performing certain services over time in exchange for the other's performance, they will likely underperform if they feel the other party is underperforming as well. They gauge whether the other party is underperforming and whether they feel entitled by looking to the contract as a reference point for what they should be receiving. Parties can avoid underperformance by being very specific in the contract, so no party has an excuse for underperforming. Hart and Moore argue that the understanding of the function of contracts as reference points should help scholars to appreciate more fully the role contracts play in a complex market economy.

Contractual safeguards: as a result of the existence of sunk costs and firm-specific or contract-specific investments, opportunistic behavior may cause conventional contract arrangements to fail (Williamson, 1985; Baumol, 1986). The protection of the weaker contractual party against the opportunistic behavior of his or her stronger counterpart may require contractual safeguards. In his work on contracts and transaction costs, Williamson (1985) uses the term "contractual safeguards" to refer to the contract practices that firms adopt so as to promote more efficient exchange when facing the risk of opportunistic behavior. Law and economics and new institutional economics scholars have further explored this concept to consider the role of alternative contractual solutions that extend beyond the standard contractual agreement. In his work on contract and property rights, Merges (2005) uses the example of when two contracting parties make an agreement under which one party has to undertake a contract-specific investment (i.e., engage in an activity that does not have much value outside a particular contracting relationship). Contractual safeguards offer the firm, exposed to the possibility of another contractual party behaving opportunistically and taking advantage of his or her economic relationship, some benefit in the case of breach and will therefore serve to limit the firm's liability. Williamson (1985) identifies three types of protective safeguards. One type is some form of "severance payment or penalty for premature termination," which incentivizes the potentially breaching party to perform. A second type is an agreement to use a "specialized governance structure," such as arbitration, instead of standard litigation, in the case of breach. Finally, expanding the relationship between the two parties is another way of guarding against breach. If one party is exposed, the two parties might reach another agreement under which the potentially breaching party is also exposed. These various methods all offer security to firms in contractual relationships as they look to mitigate opportunistic behavior and foster cooperative and efficient outcomes. See also ***contract-specific investments, hostages, collateral, union, hands tying, ugly princess***, and ***new institutional economics***.

Contributory and comparative negligence: two alternative ways to apportion liability when both tortfeasors and victims were negligent. The rule of contributory negligence bars a plaintiff's recovery if the damage suffered is in some measure the plaintiff's own fault. The rule of comparative negligence instead only reduces a plaintiff's recovery, in proportion to the plaintiff's degree of fault in causing the damage. The majority of US jurisdictions have abandoned the rule of contributory negligence in favor of a rule of comparative negligence. Under the older rule of contributory negligence, a contributorily negligent plaintiff could not recover anything from a defendant, even though the defendant was also negligent. This struck most people as exceedingly harsh and led to the gradual replacement of the principle of contributory negligence. Law and economics scholars have shown that the care and activity level incentives created by the two rules are equivalent. These findings have led scholars to question the wisdom of the move to comparative negligence, given the higher administrative costs associated with the application of the comparative negligence rule. See also *comparative causation* and *loss sharing*.

Contributory and comparative non-negligence: these use the criterion of the non-negligence of victims as a basis for assigning liability. By invoking the rule of non-negligence, a non-negligent victim can shift the loss to the tortfeasor, regardless of the care level adopted by the tortfeasor. Conversely, under a rule of comparative non-negligence, the tortfeasor pays full damages when he or she is negligent and the victim is diligent. When both parties are diligent, they share the loss. Calabresi (1970, 1996) was the first to use the term "comparative non-negligence" to refer to criteria that prevent non-negligent victims from bearing the full accident loss. See also *comparative causation, decoupling, residual decoupling, contributory and comparative non-negligence*, and *loss sharing*.

Contrived breach: in some cases, breach of contract can be induced or strategically relied upon by promisees. These cases are described in the law and economics literature as "contrived cancellation" or "contrived breach" (Williamson, 1996). Problems of contrived breach arise in conjunction with the use of liquidated damages. A promisee may have private information about the probability of breach on the part of his or her promisor and may stipulate liquidated damages higher than his or her expectation damages, strategically relying, or actively facilitating, the promisor's breach. Since situations of contrived breach are difficult to detect ex post, the new institutional economics literature has studied the possible contractual safeguards and organizational structures that can be used to mitigate these problems. See also *breach remedies, efficient breach, new institutional economics*, and *contractual safeguards*.

Contrived cancellation: see *contrived breach*.

Control group: in econometrics, regressions tell the researcher the degree of correlation between movements in exogenous variables and movements in the endogenous variable. In order to establish that variation in an exogenous variable caused a change in the endogenous variable, a control group and a treatment group can be established; a change is applied to the treatment group, but not to the control group. If the treatment group affects the endogenous variable differently from the control group, it can be implied that the treatment has an independent effect on changes in the endogenous variable. Suppose a researcher speculates that zoning agricultural land for cluster developments will raise the value of homes built there more than if the land is zoned for normal residential developments. First, the researcher could compare the change in housing prices over time in neighborhoods built on land that is newly zoned for cluster development. This is the treatment group. In order to isolate the effect of cluster zoning, the researcher will have to examine the changes in housing prices over the same time period of neighborhoods built on land that is newly zoned for normal residential development. This is the control group. If housing prices go up in the cluster zones more than in the normal zones, the researcher can infer that the additional increase is due to the cluster zoning. If the prices go up by the same amount, the price increases are attributable to some other factor (say, inflation) than the cluster zoning. See also *controlled experiment* and *treatment conditions*.

Controlled experiment: scientists, economists, lawyers, policymakers, and the public all use different types of experiments to discover truths about the world. Through an experiment, one can test and prove hypotheses. Most experiments try to reach conclusions by observing how actors behave under various pressures and circumstances. In a controlled experiment, the designer of the experiment will designate some actors to experience certain pressures and circumstances. The designer will designate other actors to be part of a control group. This control group will often experience no unusual pressures or circumstances, showing the experimenter what happens under the status quo. Kaye *et al.* (2010) distinguish controlled experiments from observational studies, in which the subjects of the experiment themselves choose the pressures and circumstances to which they are exposed. Self-selection into groups can create biases. For this reason, controlled experiments are generally more reliable and are therefore more useful for establishing chains of causation as a part of trial strategy (Kaye *et al.*, 2010). See also *control group* and *treatment conditions*.

Cooperation problems: these arise in games in which there is a surplus from cooperation. Several games (e.g., prisoner's dilemma) show that individuals may fail to cooperate if individual rationality is not consistent with aggregate rationality. Cooperation problems can be more easily solved when the players can enter into a binding agreement with one another (cooperative games), although cooperation can also be achieved in the absence of such binding agreements (non-cooperative games). See also *prisoner's dilemma*, *cooperative games*, *non-cooperative games*, and *evolution of cooperation*.

Cooperative games: in these, the parties can enter into binding agreements. This distinguishes them from non-cooperative games, in which binding agreements are not feasible. Legal enforcement mechanisms, such as contract law, as well as non-legal enforcement mechanisms, such as hostages, collateral, hands tying, and union (Kronman, 1985), provide the conditions for cooperative games. See also *non-cooperative games*, *self-enforcing contracts*, *hostages*, *collateral*, *hands tying*, *union*, and *relational contracts*.

Coordination games: these are typified by the presence of multiple Nash equilibria, in which both players must choose the same equilibrium in order to realize the expected surplus. Game theory formalizes the problem of coordination, of which there are four subspecies: (a) "common interest," (b) "stag hunt," (c) "choosing sides," and (d) "battle of the sexes" games. In the common interest games and stag hunt games, one of the equilibria is Pareto-dominant over the other, providing players a method of selecting between competing equilibria. With the choosing sides and battle of the sexes games, the selection of equilibrium may occur through the use of information that is not present in the analytical formalization of the game. According to the theory of focal points (Schelling, 1960), players may naturally converge toward equilibria that are focal (e.g., have higher payoffs, are more salient, are perceived as fairer, are perceived as safer). See also *cooperative games, focal point, multiple equilibria, equilibrium selection, cheap talk*, and *stag hunt game*.

Cooter, Robert D. (1945–): a pioneer in the field of law and economics. Cooter was born on May 2, 1945, and received his undergraduate education at Swarthmore College in Pennsylvania, where he graduated in 1967 with a degree of Bachelor of Arts, majoring in psychology. He also received a Bachelor of Arts from Oxford University in 1969, majoring in philosophy, economics and politics. He carried out his graduate work in economics at Harvard University, receiving his Ph.D. in 1975. Cooter is the author (with Thomas Ulen) of one of the leading textbooks in the field of law and economics, which has been translated into several languages. Cooter's research has been wide-ranging, touching fields as diverse as private law and constitutional law and economics. In his book *The Strategic Constitution* (2000a), Cooter draws upon principles of constitutional political economy and social choice theory to explain how constitutions should be designed to create optimal incentives for citizens, lawmakers and officials alike. See also *strategic constitution*.

Corner solution versus interior solution: in standard optimization problems the optimal value is generally an interior solution in the range of available values. However, in some cases, the solution lies at one extreme or the other of the available range; such a solution is called a corner solution. Mathematically, a corner solution occurs alternatively when the first-order condition cannot be satisfied (e.g., the tangency point occurs outside the feasible range) or when the second-order condition of the optimization problem is not satisfied (e.g., the point identified with the first-order condition represents a minimum (maximum) in a maximization (minimization) problem). In these cases, the optimal solution is a corner solution, at one of the two extremes of the range of available values. In consumer theory, a corner solution is the optimal solution when consumer preferences are linear or when the goods in the consumption bundle are perfect substitutes. In the case of a bundle composed of two goods, the corner solution occurs when the consumer finds it optimal to buy zero of one good and to spend all income on the other good. In law and economics, the terms "interior solution" and "corner solution" are occasionally used to describe policy objectives. Socially optimal levels of tort accidents are described as an interior solution (i.e., a positive number of accidents are viewed as socially optimal), because a world without accidents (the corner solution) would create excessive constraints on valuable human activities. In other situations, a corner solution is deemed desirable. For example, according to the sixth amendment to the US constitution, all criminal defendants should be entitled to legal defense. The chosen objective is a corner solution (every defendant). Similarly, a legal policy that sets the optimal level of genocide in US territory to zero chooses a corner solution. See also *constrained optimization*.

Correlated-values claim: comparing property rules and liability rules, Kaplow and Shavell (1996) argue that liability rules cannot harness private information when the parties' valuations are correlated. With the use of numerical examples, Kaplow and Shavell show that property rules are preferable when correlated-value entitlements are involved. With correlated values, the taker's willingness to pay damages (based on average valuation) does not imply that the taking is efficient, since the current owner's valuation is also likely to be above average. The efficient allocative effect of liability rules is therefore undermined by the presence of correlated values. Consider the example of an art expert, who is willing to pay high damages to obtain a piece of art. His or her willingness to pay may be an indication of a higher common value of the piece of art itself, rather than reflecting a higher idiosyncratic value. If the current owner is also an art expert, their valuations of the piece of art are likely to be correlated. A non-consensual taking under a liability rule cannot be trusted to lead to an efficient reallocation, because the current owner also has a high valuation of the piece. Ayres and Goldbart (2003) have criticized the validity of the argument put forth by Kaplow and Shavell (1996). See also *property rules versus liability rules* and *information harnessing*.

Cost of accidents: published in 1970, Calabresi's *The Cost of Accidents: A Legal of Economic Analysis* is one of the foundational works in the field of law and economics. Along with early publications by Coase, Calabresi's work is widely credited with helping to create the now expansive field of law and economics. Calabresi thoroughly analyzed accident, or tort, law, providing the first comprehensive economic analysis and comparisons of various common law tort remedies. Calabresi challenged the conventional legal wisdom that tort law is merely designed to deter tortfeasors from taking inadequate precautions. Calabresi argued that the goal of tort law is to minimize the cost of accidents (i.e., minimize both the occurrence of accidents and the costs associated with taking precautions and limiting one's activity level to avoid accidents). Calabresi wrestled with the critical questions of how costs of accidents should be allocated and how accidents should be valued. He analyzed and critiqued the traditional tort law doctrines and introduced the concept of the cheapest cost avoider. In explaining this concept, Calabresi argued that the party who should bear the cost of an accident is the one who is best able to bear the cost (i.e., the one who can avoid the accident and reduce overall harm most efficiently, or cheaply). Calabresi illustrated this principle using a two-party example. Calabresi demonstrated the cheapest cost avoider principle in the case of an accident between a car and bicycle that causes $3,000 in damage. If the car can avoid the accident at a cost of $1,000 and the bicycle can avoid the accident at a cost of $2,000, it should be the car that takes the precautions to avoid the accident, because it can do so more efficiently than the bicycle. Calabresi's concept runs counter to an assumption that the party who should pay to avoid the harm is the one most likely to be at fault for the harm. Calabresi's book shifted the discussion about tort law from one of fault and deterrence to one focused on efficiency and cost reduction. His work is widely credited for making the economic analysis of law an accepted method for discussing and debating the effectiveness of law and policy in non-market-based legal issues. See also **Calabresi, Guido**, and **cheapest cost avoider**.

Cost–benefit analysis: this weighs the expected benefits of a choice or policy against its expected costs. The difference between the anticipated benefits and the anticipated costs is then used to choose among competing alternatives. Benefits are often approximated by a willingness to pay, while costs are usually formalized either as a willingness to pay to avoid or, alternatively, as opportunity cost. Cost–benefit analysis requires the expression of benefits and costs in money terms and the calculation of their present value. When costs and benefits materialize at different times, a critical element of cost–benefit analysis is the choice of discount rates. See also **cost-effectiveness analysis** and **precautionary principle**.

Cost-effective precautions: see **most effective precaution taker**.

Cost-effectiveness analysis: a technique aimed at identifying the least costly way of achieving a given objective. Unlike cost–benefit analysis, cost-effectiveness analysis provides a choice among alternative "means," and does not address the preliminary question of whether the "end" is worth pursuing, or which among alternative goals should be pursued. This technique is appropriately utilized when an administrative or governmental agency needs to implement a given policy with sole discretion as to the choice of means and no discretion as to the choice or extent of implementation of the goal. Cost-effectiveness analysis is also used when the policy goal cannot be easily quantified along a monetary dimension or, as a pragmatic expedient, when comparing the costs and benefits of a given policy would be politically inappropriate or undesirable. See also **cost–benefit analysis**.

Costly signal: through signaling, an informed party reveals private information to an uninformed party. In most instances, a signal needs to be costly to avoid a cheap talk problem and to become credible. When the cost of signaling information differs according to the content of the information, a separating equilibrium can be observed such that only a subset of individuals credibly signals their private information. So, for example, a seller of good-quality products may be able to offer an extended warranty more cheaply than a seller of defective products. Hence the offer of an extended warranty may be a credible (and costly) signal of the seller's private information regarding the quality of the goods. See also **signaling**, **cheap talk**, and **credibility**.

Countervailing norms: recent contributions to the law and economics literature have pointed out that the effects of law further depend on the "social response" triggered by the enactment and enforcement of a new rule (Tyler, 1990; Parisi and von Wangenheim, 2006). Social reaction may boost or weaken the effects of legal intervention. A legal rule may be perceived as unfair in two alternative ways: excess or defect. A law fails in excess when it punishes conduct perceived as harmless or socially desirable; it fails in defect when it fails to provide adequate punishment for harmful and undesirable behavior. Legitimacy is undermined when the content of the law departs from social norms, be they based on moral, ethical, or merely cultural values. According to countervailing norms theories, absent such initial alignment between legal rules and social values, expressed social opinion and reaction to unjust laws may undermine the effect of legal incentives. A high number of people opposing the law may reinforce or weaken its deterrent effect, depending on whether the law falls short or in excess of current social values. See also *inexpressive law*, *sticky norms*, *backlash effect*, *normative overdeterrence*, and *hard shoves versus gentle nudges*.

Cournot competition: this term describes an oligopolistic market in which firms compete on quantities. In its simplest form, the model of Antoine-Augustin Cournot (1838) studies the strategic choices of two firms that produce a homogeneous good at a constant marginal cost and face a linear demand function. Each firm chooses its quantity simultaneously. In the Cournot model, each firm chooses its level of output on the assumption that the competitor's behavior is fixed (i.e., given the output quantity chosen by the rival firm). Each firm acts on the market as a monopolist on the so-called "residual demand," equal to the total market demand net of the quantity produced by the rival firm. The Cournot model has a unique Nash equilibrium, in which each firm sets the price above the marginal cost, earning positive profits. In the Cournot model, firms have a positive level of market power, which is lower than in the case of monopoly. Cournot firms produce lower quantities at a higher price than perfectly competitive firms, but produce higher quantities at a lower price than a monopolistic firm. This is in contrast with the outputs and prices of an industry that has an identical market structure, but in which firms behave in a Bertrand-type competition, generating outputs and price similar to a perfectly competitive market. What explains the different outcomes of Cournot competition (quantity competition) and Bertrand competition (price competition) is the fact that, while consumers are infinitely responsive to a price change, prices are not infinitely responsive to a change in production quantity. These alternative models provide different predictions on the effects of market concentration on prices and welfare and therefore yield qualitatively different implications for competition policy. See also *Bertrand competition*.

Cournot's duopoly model: see *Cournot competition*.

Creative destruction: see *Schumpeter's creative destruction*.

Credence goods: see *experience goods versus search goods*.

Credibility: in formulating and implementing macroeconomic policy, policymakers need to consider various factors, including which policies have the best record of achieving growth and reducing inflation and which policies have an actual chance of being supported by a majority of relevant stakeholders. Rational expectations theory suggests that actors shape their behavior on the basis of their expectations on future events and policy changes. Policymakers must therefore consider whether their announced short-term policies, decisions, actions, and pronouncements will be credible in the eyes of economic actors. Alesina (1987) notes that the political cycle in the United States can leave different parties in power that have dramatically different policy goals for the country. This, in turn, can lead to policy volatility, reducing the long-term stability and credibility of any announced policy agenda. Alesina uses the example of the United States, in which Democratic presidential administrations tend to be more focused on reducing unemployment and Republican presidential administrations tend to be more focused on reducing inflation. Alesina argues that, if the two political parties are focused on short-term electoral gains and fail to work together, it can lead to greater policy fluctuations, credibility problems, and inefficiency. He argues that political parties should adopt common policy goals for the sake of the country's long-term economic well-being. Parties can do this through binding commitments or, they might do so due to "reputational forces arising from the repeated interaction of the two parties" (Alesina, 1987). Alesina's model rests on the assumption of "rational expectations," unlike some of the older "political business cycle" theories. See also *costly signal*, *rational expectations*, *dynamic inconsistency*, and *precommitment strategies*.

Credible commitments: see *credibility*.

Credible threat: see *credibility*.

Cross-price effect: this measures the change in the consumption of a good when the price of another good changes. In economic terms, the cross-price effect is defined as $\partial j / \partial P_i$, where j represents the quantity demanded of good j and P_i represents the price of good i. The cross-price effect is positive for substitute goods and negative for complementary goods. See also *substitutes* and *complements*.

Crowding out versus crowding in effects: "crowding out" and "crowding in" are terms used in the law and economics literature to describe the effect of a legal rule or a governmental policy on private behavior. Crowding out occurs when legally created incentives reduce and displace other private and social incentives. For example, by creating legal incentives to undertake Good Samaritan actions, altruistic motives and other social incentives may be crowded out. Crowding in, by contrast, occurs when legally created incentives reinforce other private and social incentives. For example, legal sanctions against drunk driving may reinforce social norms against that behavior and lead to a crowding in of private and social sanctions against violators. The terms are also used to describe the effects of government's fiscal policy on private investment. Crowding out occurs when government spending crowds out private investment. Crowding in, instead, occurs when government spending encourages private investment (Baumol and Blinder, 2011). In economic analysis, the presence of crowding out and crowding in effects hinges upon the empirical question of whether the legal (or governmental) activities and the private (or social) activities are substitutes or complements. For example, consider the effect of public enforcement on private enforcement. If the two types of enforcement were "substitutes," an increase in public enforcement would dilute (crowd out) private enforcement; if they were complements, an increase in public enforcement would reinforce (crowd in) private enforcement. See also *incentives*.

Customary law: the term "custom" describes practices between individuals and organizations that emerge outside the law but that acquire the character of legal obligation over time. When legal systems enforce the preexisting customs, they are referred to as "customary law." Because customary rules acquire the force of law without necessarily being formally incorporated into any written body of law, they are usually classified as "immaterial" sources of law. An enforceable custom emerges from two formative elements: (a) a quantitative element consisting of a general practice; and (b) a qualitative element consisting in the belief that the practice is socially desirable or even necessary and possibly reflects an underlying obligation (opinion *iuris ac necessitatis*). Modern legal systems generally recognize customary rules that have emerged either within the confines of positive legislation (*consuetudo secundum legem*) or in areas that are not disciplined by positive law (*consuetudo praeter legem*). When custom is in direct conflict with legislation (custom *contra legem*), the latter normally prevails. However, in some instances a custom supersedes prior legislation (abrogative custom), and some arguments have been made in support of emerging practices that conflict with obsolete provisions of public international law (*desuetudo*, or abrogative practice). In a "social contract" framework, customary rules can be regarded as an implied and often non-verbalized exercise of direct legislation by the members of society (Parisi, 2000). See also *expressive law* and *descriptive versus prescriptive norms*.

Cycling: the possibility that a majority vote could lead to cyclical deliberations was first identified by the Marquis de Condorcet, in 1785. The problem was subsequently studied by Dodgson (1876) and Black (1948), and became the core of Arrow's (1951) impossibility theorem. Looking specifically at majority rule systems in which the choice that receives the majority of the votes wins, Arrow shows that, when multiple people are voting for multiple options, it is possible to imagine a scenario in which the vote of individuals leads to cyclical deliberations. The important idea is that collective decision-making can lead to intransitive collective choices even when individual voters' preferences are transitive. In the absence of a Condorcet winner, a majority rule cannot select any winner, and the reshuffling of majority coalitions can lead to cycling, unless the cycling is arbitrarily interrupted. See also ***Arrow's impossibility theorem***, ***Condorcet winner***, and ***Condorcet voting paradox***.

D

Damage compensation: see **indifference criterion of perfect compensation**.

Damages: see *compensatory damages*.

Danger in numbers: see *safety in numbers versus danger in numbers*.

Deadweight loss: this identifies the loss of economic surplus that occurs when the market equilibrium is not Pareto-optimal. The deadweight loss can entail a loss of both consumer surplus and producer surplus. In other words, it can occur when some consumers are willing to pay higher than the marginal cost of producing the good and would benefit from the consumption of the good. It can also occur when firms have a marginal cost lower than the quoted price on the market and would benefit from selling additional units of the good. A deadweight loss may arise from conditions such as monopoly pricing (in which case the deadweight loss is measured by Harberger's triangle), oligopoly pricing, price discrimination, government intervention in the form of taxes, subsidies, binding price ceilings or floors, and externalities. See also *Harberger's triangle*, *producer surplus*, *consumer surplus*, and *fundamental theorems of welfare*.

Debiasing: the study of behavioral law and economics shows that people display psychological biases that affect their many everyday decisions. The presence of psychological biases affects the ability to estimate the likelihood of events, to perceive risk, or to process information correctly. This creates a distinctive problem for legal policymakers: in the presence of behavioral biases, people tend to react inadequately to legal threats and incentives in a number of areas of law. Law and economics scholars view issues of behavioral biases as a problem caused by imperfect information which can be appropriately corrected through the provision of additional information, such as accurate information about average risks in the population. Debiasing consists, therefore, of the attempt to reduce or eliminate these behavioral biases through the dissemination of additional information. Evidence suggests that debiasing strategies through risk education and information are only partially effective. Legal scholars have introduced the concept of debiasing through law, both with reference to procedural rules governing adjudication (Babcock *et al.*, 1995; Babcock, Loewenstein, and Issacharoff, 1997) and substantive law (Jolls and Sunstein, 2006b). Debiasing through law, as most notably presented by Jolls and Sunstein (2006b), suggests that substantive law should take into account the need to correct the systematic judgment errors of individuals. See also ***behavioral law and economics*** and ***debiasing versus insulating strategies***.

Debiasing versus insulating strategies: behavioral law and economics scholars focus on the departures of human behavior from full rationality in order to take into account the shortcomings in human behavior when structuring the law. Jolls and Sunstein (2006b) introduce the distinction between debiasing strategies (which they also refer to as "debiasing through law") and insulating strategies (which they also refer to as "debiasing law"). Debiasing strategies aim at developing legal solutions that reduce or eliminate boundedly rational behavior. Insulating strategies, in contrast, aim at developing legal instruments that insulate legal outcomes from boundedly rational behavior. Take the example of an individual biased by unrealistic optimism regarding his or her future ability to repay a loan with high interest rates. A "debiasing through law" approach (debiasing strategy) would attempt to correct the bias, for example by educating the individual about the financial risk he or she is undertaking. A "debiasing law" approach (insulating strategy) would, instead, try to insulate the effects of bounded rationality, for example by imposing restrictions on high-interest lending or setting borrowing limits. See also ***debiasing*** and ***behavioral law and economics***.

Decentralization theorem: according to Oates' (1972) "decentralization theorem," when the cost of providing a public good is the same for central government as it is for local government, and the benefits of the public goods depend on geography, it is more efficient to provide public goods through the local than the central government. See also *federalism*.

Decentralized subsidiarity: one of the three forms of subsidiarity, the other two being centralized subsidiarity and democratic subsidiarity. According to decentralized subsidiarity, a decision to centralize should be made at the local level, and the unanimous consent of all member states is required for centralization. Like a Pareto test, a decentralized subsidiarity test requires that each individual state benefits (or, at least, is not harmed) from a proposed reallocation of governmental functions. This is equivalent to the case of decentralized federalism as defined by Inman and Rubinfeld (1997). Given that states often have diverse preferences, centralization is generally easier to carry out in a regime of centralized subsidiarity than under a regime of decentralized or democratic subsidiarity. It has been shown in the literature that, when the decentralized subsidiarity test is satisfied for all member states, the centralized and democratic subsidiarity tests would also be satisfied (Carbonara, Luppi and Parisi, 2009). This result is rather intuitive: if all member states benefit from centralization, then the aggregate benefits must outweigh the aggregate costs of centralization (i.e., the "centralized subsidiarity test" would be satisfied) and the median state would likewise benefit from centralization (i.e., the "democratic subsidiarity test" would be satisfied). However, the opposite is not necessarily true.

Satisfaction of the centralized or democratic subsidiarity tests does not necessarily imply satisfaction of the decentralized subsidiarity test for all member states. See also *subsidiarity*, *subsidiarity test*, *centralized subsidiarity*, and *democratic subsidiarity*.

Decision heuristics: the term "heuristics" is often invoked to account for many behaviors that are inconsistent with rational choice theory. Scholars have distinguished between a descriptive and a prescriptive heuristic. Descriptive heuristic is an explanation for a bias or error in decision-making. Behavioral economists use the phrase "ecological rationality of heuristics" to refer to the evolutionary nature of decision heuristics and the ways in which decision processes have evolved to cope with humans' limited cognitive abilities. Prescriptive heuristic can offer guidance in the formulation of standards and decision rules that minimize the overall cost of imperfect decision-making. See also *bounded rationality*, *ecological rationality*, and *behavioral law and economics*.

Decision rules: see *conduct rules versus decision rules*.

Decision theory: the study of how actors make choices to produce desired outcomes. In its broadest sense, decision theory encompasses many fields, including moral philosophy, cognitive psychology, mathematics, and economics. The standard economic approach in decision theory is known as "normative" decision theory, since the methodology focuses on providing optimal solutions to strategic choice problems. The normative approach is built upon three axioms. First, agents are presumed to be rational, in some sense of the term. Second, rational agents maximize their utility (or some other form of subjective well-being); they select among alternatives so as to secure the greatest possible benefit from their decision. Third, since rational agents are rarely certain of the actual consequences of their decisions, agents rank alternatives with respect to expected utility. Economists formally articulate the substance of concepts such as rationality, maximization, and expected utility differently. The alternative to normative decision theory is "descriptive" decision theory. The goal of descriptive decision theory is to illuminate how real agents, as opposed to ideally rational agents, make decisions in concrete situations. Descriptive decision theory has gained increasing influence in the recent law and economics literature, studying the influence of factors such as socialization, habit, and cognitive bias, which lead actual agents to systematic errors in decision-making. See also *behavioral law and economics*.

Decoupling: this disentangles the plaintiff's award/compensation from the defendant's liability/penalty. The concept was motivated by the double-edged sword that increasing liability on defendants has the unintended consequence of incentivizing undesirable behavior for plaintiffs. Decoupling the plaintiff's award from the defendant's liability opens the possibility of setting optimal care for both parties. The idea of decoupling has been used in the tort law literature, but can easily be applied to any system of liability and compensation (contract damages, takings compensation, etc.). The concept of decoupling has been particularly popular in the tort law literature. When analyzing the efficiency of alternative liability rules in tort law, scholars have looked at the incentives created on tortfeasors and victims to take efficient levels of care and activity. Although there are some liability rules (e.g., negligence-based rules) that induce both tortfeasors and victims to take optimal care levels, there are no liability rules that induce both parties to take optimal activity levels. The idea of decoupling was introduced by Polinsky and Che (1991) as a solution to the activity level problem. By disentangling liability from compensation, decoupling can produce optimal care and activity level incentives for both parties. In practical terms, decoupling would occur when, after an accident, a court or adjudicative body forces a tortfeasor to pay for his or her actions without giving any of the proceeds to the victim (e.g., the payment collected from the defendant could be given to charity or to the state). By decoupling the tortfeasor's liability from the victim's compensation, both parties would face the full loss in the event of an accident, ultimately incentivizing both parties to take efficient precaution and activity levels. Despite the fact that decoupling efficiently achieves the deterrence goals of tort law, no jurisdiction has adopted it. Besides the limited political viability of the decoupling rule on fairness grounds, decoupling would be a difficult rule to implement. By eliminating the victim's right to obtain compensation, decoupling would also eliminate the victim's interest to initiate litigation against the tortfeasor, hence eliminating the deterrent effect of the threat of liability. It should be noted that lawyers' fees create a wedge between the damages paid by defendants and the compensation effectively received by plaintiffs; real-life tort law may be closer to decoupling than one may think. See also ***anti-insurance***, ***activity level versus care level***, ***non-observable precautions***, and ***Shavell's activity level theorem***.

Default rules: in negotiating the terms of a contract, parties often include detailed and specific terms to govern the actions of both parties in the face of changing external conditions. Although the parties are free to negotiate many of the terms that govern their contractual relationship, two key principles impact their ability to contract. First, certain immutable rules exist in contract law that contracting parties cannot negotiate away. Second, default rules exist that apply if the parties leave gaps in their negotiated terms. These default rules apply only in the absence of contrary provision by the parties (i.e., parties can change or alter them in their contractual language). The law and economics literature has identified two main functions of default rules. First, default rules are provided by legal systems to reduce the need for specific bargaining and to reduce transaction costs. The law and economics literature refers to this category of rules as "majoritarian default rules." Second, default rules can be designed to correct for information asymmetries and other market failures. The law and economics literature refers to these rules as "penalty default rules." Unlike majoritarian default rules, penalty default rules incentivize the parties to contract explicitly (Ayres and Gertner,

1989). They do so by placing a penalty on one or both of the parties in the event of a dispute. The possibility of being penalized under a penalty default rule will generally spur the parties to draft explicit contract terms that eliminate any gaps. See also *transaction costs*, *altering rules*, *sticky default rules*, *penalty default rules*, *majoritarian default rules*, and *boilerplate*.

Defendant choice rules: these provide defendants with the option to allocate a title to themselves when their subjective valuation exceeds the costs of damages or to grant the entitlement to the plaintiff to avoid damages (Ayres, 2005). Depending on how damages are assessed, this may require the defendant to choose on the basis of imperfect information (i.e., how much the plaintiff subjectively values the entitlement at). When damages are fixed, the defendant allocates the entitlement solely on the basis of the valuation of the entitlement relative to the fixed damages. See also *single chooser rules*, *dual chooser rules*, *chooser's call/put option*, *first-order rules*, and *property rules versus liability rules*.

Demand-revealing process: a term used in public choice theory and mechanism design that refers to mechanisms for inducing agents to reveal their true preferences over alternatives. For example, a demand-revealing voting process would induce voters to reveal their expected gains from various policy choices, in order to select the policy that achieves the highest aggregate benefit (Mueller, 2003). The process encourages each potential voter to reveal the specific financial gains he or she expects to receive from his or her preferred policy. Once each voter has revealed this information, the amounts for each policy are added together and the policy with the highest level of potential benefit wins. Mueller uses the example of voters A, B, and C, and policies P and S. Voter A expects $30 and voter C expects $20 from policy P. Voter B expects $40 from policy S. In Mueller's example, policy P wins because the expected benefit from the policy totals $50. This process reveals honest policy preferences and makes it possible to select the policy that will result in the highest aggregate benefit to voters. In order to encourage voters to reveal their preferences, the process utilizes a tax. A voter pays a tax if his or her vote affects the ultimate selection of the winning policy. The tax is equal to the net gains the other voters would expect to receive if the voter in question did not vote. In Mueller's example, voter A's vote does impact the outcome. Without his vote, policy S would win. C would not gain $20 and B would gain $40. The net benefit would be $20, which is A's tax. B's vote does not affect the outcome, so he or she owes no tax. C's vote does impact the outcome, and his or her tax is $10. The tax ensures that voters reveal their true preferences. As Mueller points out, if A chose policy S, he or she would owe no tax, but he or she would also lose his or her expected benefits of $30 and his or her net gain, after the tax of $10. See also *revealed preferences*.

Demand-side versus supply-side economics: the core question of the demand-side versus supply-side economics debate is whether changes in demand are responsible for changes in supply (demand-side theories) or whether it is, instead, supply that drives demand (supply-side theories). The term "demand-side economics" refers to the group of theories that suggest that economic change is driven by consumer demand. In its application to macroeconomic phenomena, demand-side economics finds an important expression in the work of John Maynard Keynes. For this reason, demand-side economics is often referred to as Keynesian economics. According to demand-side theories, economic stimulus should be directed toward consumers (e.g., a tax stimulus spread across consumers). The term "supply-side economics" refers, instead, to the group of theories that suggest that economic growth can be most effectively generated by stimulating supply. In its application to macroeconomic and fiscal policy, supply-side economics finds important expression in the work of Robert Mundell and Arthur Laffer. According to supply-side theories, policymakers should stimulate the supply side by adopting appropriate fiscal policies (e.g., by lowering marginal tax rates and capital gains taxes), and by reducing regulation to facilitate the creation of new businesses and to foster a greater supply of goods and services. In the law and economics literature, the demand side versus supply side debate has implications for a large number of issues. For example, in areas such as drug or prostitution enforcement policy, the question arises as to whether changes in supply are mainly responsible for changes in consumption, or vice versa. The answer to these questions has important implications for enforcement policy. If demand-side theories are correct and consumers' demand is what drives changes in supply, enforcement efforts should be more effectively directed toward demand (e.g., by deterring drug users and consumers of prostitution). The opposite enforcement policy would be warranted under supply-side theories. It should be noted that, in the law and economics literature, these questions are often tackled with microeconomic instruments (e.g., by studying the elasticity of the demand and supply of drugs and prostitution). See also *consumer versus producer sovereignty*.

Democratic subsidiarity: one of the three forms of subsidiarity, the other two being centralized subsidiarity and decentralized subsidiarity. According to democratic subsidiarity, a decision to centralize requires the approval of the majority of the member states. Applying the terminology of Inman and Rubinfeld (1997), this case is germane to the case of "democratic federalism," in which the allocation of power among the various levels of government is decided on the basis of a majority rule. In order to obtain a majority vote in favor of centralization, a proposed reallocation of governmental functions should improve the aggregate well-being of the majority of member states. In an application of the median voter theorem (Black, 1948; Downs, 1957), centralization should occur if the subsidiarity test is satisfied for the median state. It has been shown in the literature that we can find situations in which the satisfaction of the centralized subsidiarity test does not imply satisfaction of the democratic subsidiarity test. Given that, under democratic subsidiarity, centralization occurs if the test is satisfied for the median state, manipulation of the cost and benefit of centralization for the median state can have important effects (Carbonara, Luppi, and Parisi, 2009). See also *subsidiarity, subsidiarity test, centralized subsidiarity*, and *decentralized subsidiarity*.

Demsetz scheme: see *Chadwick–Demsetz scheme*.

Demsetz, Harold (1930–): an American economist whose work has been most influential in the field of law and economics. Demsetz's research focuses on property rights, the business firm, and problems of monopoly, competition, and antitrust. Harold Demsetz received his MBA (1954) and Ph.D. (1959) degrees from Northwestern University. Demsetz was among the first to begin applying Coase's theory of property rights to a variety of contexts. In his 1967 paper "Toward a theory of property rights," he argues that the allocation of property rights is necessary for the efficient functioning of markets. His work also identified the emergence of institutions such as property rights, contracts, firms, and oligopolistic behavior in transaction costs and information problems. In addition, a paper co-authored with Armen Alchian, "Production, information costs and economic organization" (Alchian and Demsetz, 1972), was one of the earliest analyses of the principal–agent problem. Among his other contributions to law and economics, Demsetz has also refined the method used to review the desirability of antitrust legislation. Up until the 1950s it was common for economists and courts to infer a lack of competition in markets simply from the fact that a high percentage of sales was accounted for by the four largest firms in an industry. However, along with Yale Brozen, Demsetz's ideas contributed to the growing body of work that established that these correlations between concentration and profits could be either transitory or due to superior efficiency rather than to anticompetitive conduct. See also *Chadwick–Demsetz scheme*.

Dependency theory: the product of a United Nations study of the relationship between economic growth in industrialized countries and developing countries. Contrary to the predictions of neoclassical economic theory, the data suggested that economic activity in the richer countries often exacerbated the economic problems of poorer countries. The initial explanation for this was found in the relationship between the value of primary inputs exported by poor countries and the value added by manufacturing in industrialized countries. Dependency theory has since evolved with a wealth of nuanced methodological differences among its various exponents, but it remains focused on the study of economic inequalities between two sets of states (generally described by scholars in this field as dominant/dependent, center/periphery, or metropolitan/satellite) – inequalities that are often seen as dynamic and self-reinforcing. See also *import substitution industrialization*.

Deregulation: see **regulation and deregulation**.

Descending-price auctions: see *Dutch auctions*.

Descriptive decision theory: see *decision theory* and *behavioral law and economics*.

Descriptive norms: see **conventions**.

Descriptive versus prescriptive norms: descriptive norms depict practices and behavioral regularities within a group that are not driven by an underlying sense of obligation. Prescriptive norms, on the contrary, are norms that reflect an "ought to" sense of obligation. The two types of norms share a common element: the quantitative element of practice. The same observed practice may therefore reflect a descriptive norm or a prescriptive norm, and an investigation of the qualitative element of obligation is necessary in order to distinguish between the two. So, for example, we can observe a behavioral regularity in the fact that individuals turn off their outdoor lights at night. This may be a descriptive norm, inasmuch as people may do so out of a sense of personal preference or convenience. The practice of turning off lights following a campaign for energy conservation may instead reflect a prescriptive norm. Individual deviations from descriptive (prescriptive) norms usually do not (do) carry consequences in terms of social sanctions and social stigma. See also *reputation tax*.

Destructive competition: see *rent seeking*.

Deterrence: a fundamental concept in law, and economic analysis has played an important role in shedding light on the use of law as an instrument of optimal deterrence. Legal systems seek to deter harmful and undesirable acts and to incentivize socially desirable acts. Criminal law, for example, attaches penalties to various illegal acts in order to deter individuals from engaging in criminal activities (Becker, 1968; Stigler 1970). Likewise, tort law attaches liability to tortious acts to deter tortious behavior and incentivize the adoption of efficient precautions (Posner, 1981; Landes and Posner, 1987; Shavell, 1987). Straightforward as they may appear, the choice of legal instruments to produce optimal deterrence is far from obvious. As Polinsky and Shavell (2007) point out, policymakers often have to consider the deterrence effects of criminal sanctions before making decisions to increase penalties to reduce enforcement costs. Although policymakers might intuitively believe that raising the penalties on lower-level crimes will decrease the need to employ law enforcement officers, this reduction in the probability of detection will also affect high-level crimes, which already carry high penalties. Since these crimes also tend to carry higher levels of benefits, the increase in penalties for lower-level offenses and the resulting decrease in law enforcement may reduce the law's deterrent effect on high-level offenses. Becker (1968) has pointed out that, when actors consider multiple harmful acts, legal penalties should be designed to provide marginal deterrence for each harmful act. If the law attaches the most severe penalty to less severe crimes, there may not be anything left to deter the commission of more severe crimes. As Polinsky and Shavell (2007) point out, marginal deterrence can sometimes affect deterrence generally. In order to increase penalties enough on severe crimes to have a meaningful marginal deterrence effect, the penalties on lower-level crimes might be so low that they serve no deterrent effect. See also *incentives* and *marginal deterrence*.

Dictator game: a simple game with two players: a proponent and a responder. It is sometimes used to show the existence of an altruism motive and other non-self-interested motives in economic behavior. In this game, the proponent chooses an allocation of a monetary endowment. In contrast to the ultimatum game, the responder plays only a passive role, in the sense that he or she receives the part of the endowment allocated to him or her by the proponent and has no actions. Economic theory says that the outcome of the dictator game is an allocation of the entire endowment to the proponent and zero to the responder. Because the outcome of the game depends only on the proponent's choice (the responder has no actions), there is no interdependence between the players' decisions. Therefore, the dictator game falls outside the proper game theory field. Instead of being considered a game theory problem, it should be viewed as a decision theory problem. Experimental economists have frequently studied the dictator game, together with the ultimatum game and other games. Experimental evidence has shown a systematic departure from the equilibrium behavior predicted for the proponent: according to Forsythe *et al.* (1994), and contrary to economic theory predictions, proponents tend to allocate a positive amount to responders, thereby reducing the amount allocated to themselves. Results show that proponents tend to offer an amount between 0 percent and 50 percent of the total endowment, but never more than 50 percent. Additionally, only a small number of proponents (fewer than 20 percent) offer zero. These results are interpreted as a refutation of the assumption of self-interested economic behavior, since a self-interested proponent would rationally allocate no money to the responder. This suggests that economic behavior may be driven by other motivations, such as altruism, inequity aversion, a taste for fairness, and similar other-regarding motivations. See also *ultimatum game*, *experimental law and economics*, *inequity aversion*, *taste for fairness*, and *kindness function*.

Difference principle: an important pillar of Rawls' theory of justice is what he calls the "difference principle." This captures the difficult tradeoff between efficiency and fairness in distribution. In his landmark work on distributive justice, Rawls articulates his own guiding principles for the allocation of resources in society (Rawls, 1971). Rawls' principles offer an alternative to other allocation principles, such as utilitarianism. According to Rawls' view of social welfare, inequalities are acceptable only to the extent that they are instrumental in creating incentives to work and produce. Rawls' difference principle states that any inequality between members of society must be part of an allocation scheme that is the best possible scheme for the least advantaged in society. Rawls is not arguing for perfect or absolute equality between members of society; instead, he merely argues for the allocation scheme that is best for the least advantaged. If a system containing pervasive inequality is the best possible scheme for the least advantaged, Rawls' difference principle would argue for that scheme over perfect equality. Any change in an allocation scheme must therefore be better for the least advantaged than the existing scheme. For instance, if policymakers considered a change in the law, such as a tax reform measure, that would positively impact most members of society but would leave the least advantaged worse off (e.g., a regressive sales tax increase on low-cost food), the difference principle would hold that the policymakers should not ultimately adopt that measure. Rawls' difference principle differs from utilitarianism, because it would reject an allocation scheme that maximizes total societal wealth, unless that scheme also was the best possible scheme for the least advantaged in society. Rawls' difference principle offers scholars a different welfare maximization tool for use in analyzing laws, regulations, or public policies. The law and economics discipline has traditionally analyzed existing laws by comparing their effects on aggregate social welfare. Those results could be revisited using the difference principle as a benchmark of evaluation, by analyzing how alternative laws would impact the well-being of the least advantaged in society. The difference principle can be formally represented in terms of maximin (maximizing the minimum possible payoff) objective functions. See also *veil of ignorance*, *Rawlsian justice*, *maximin strategy*, *Nash criterion of welfare*, and *Rawlsian maximin*.

Diminishing marginal product: this describes a condition in which each addition of a unit of labor yields progressively less production capability. The concept of diminishing marginal product has relevant applications in virtually all areas of legal analysis. For example, in the context of jury decision, as the number of jurors grows larger, the accuracy of verdicts increases, but at a decreasing rate. When undertaking precautions to avoid an accident, it is reasonable to assume that, as more precautions are taken, each additional unit of precaution contributes to reduce the probability of an accident, but at a decreasing rate. Likewise, in law enforcement, as more police power is deployed, each additional police unit contributes to reduce crime, but at a decreasing rate; and so on. See also *marginal product* and *production function*.

Diminishing marginal utility: in consumer theory, the law of diminishing marginal utility hypothesizes that consumers experience diminishing returns from their consumption: a consumer's utility from his or her first unit of consumption of a good or service is greater than the utility of each subsequent unit. Diminishing marginal utility implies that consumers' marginal satisfaction decreases with the amount of the good they consume. This concept is expressed analytically by the negative second derivative of the utility function. Economists generally rely on the principle of non-satiation to ensure that the marginal utility of a good remains positive, although decreasing for each subsequent unit. If a point of satiation is reached, the marginal utility of a good can go to zero (for freely disposable goods) or can actually become negative (when disposing of excess goods is costly). At that point, an economic good would become an economic "bad." Diminishing marginal utility also applies to wealth. The diminishing marginal utility of wealth is generally axiomatically derived as a result of consumer rationality. We use the first unit of wealth to acquire the goods that give us the greatest utility and use successive units of wealth to acquire increasingly less desirable goods; hence, each successive unit of wealth yields lower increments of utility (diminishing marginal utility). Risk aversion is usually shown as the natural consequence of the diminishing marginal utility of wealth. See also *risk aversion* and *non-satiation*.

Direct revelation mechanism: see *direct versus indirect revelation mechanisms*.

Direct versus indirect revelation mechanisms: an important distinction in auction theory is whether the auction protocol utilizes a direct or an indirect revelation mechanism. In a direct revelation mechanism, agents submit bids without receiving feedback, such as price signals, from the auction. This is the case for first-price sealed-bid auctions. In mediation, direct revelation mechanisms can be used, allowing the mediator to develop recommendations based on the collected private information. In an indirect revelation mechanism, agents can instead acquire information during the bidding process. These mechanisms permit the incremental revelation of preference information and allow participants to refine their bids in response to information feedback and price signals received from the auction. This is the case for ascending-price auctions. In auction design, the choice between direct and indirect revelation mechanisms depends on the nature of the auction (e.g., private-value versus common-value auctions) and on the likely need of preference information to achieve the desired allocative efficiency. See also *auction theory*, *common-value auctions*, and *mediation (contract design)*.

Director, Aaron (1901–2004): played an important role in the development and rise of the Chicago school of law and economics, and was noted for his pioneering views on the importance of free market analysis in antitrust law. He was born in Staryi Chortoryisk in what is now Ukraine in 1901. His family emigrated to the United States in 1913, and he received his undergraduate degree from Yale University in 1924. He then worked in a number of jobs related to his communist and radical beliefs before attending the University of Chicago, at which he studied labor economics, and where his views were transformed from left-wing radicalism to a free market conservative ideology. He published only two books, both in 1931 and both co-written with Paul Douglas. *Unemployment* (1931a) and *The Problem of Unemployment* (1931b). He was influenced by the work of Friedrich Hayek, particularly *The Road to Serfdom,* and, together with Hayek, his brother-in-law Milton Friedman, Ludwig von Mises, George Stigler, and others, he was a founding member of the Mont Pelerin Society, which was dedicated to the proposition that government interference with market activities is harmful.

In 1958 he founded the *Journal of Law and Economics*, which provided a valuable platform during the early development of law and economics. Director co-edited the journal with Ronald Coase. Numerous influential jurists have named him as an important influence on their judicial philosophy, including Robert Bork, William Rehnquist, Richard Posner, and Antonin Scalia. See also *Chicago school*.

Disagreement point: the default solution or arrangement that applies if the parties fail to reach an agreement (disagreement point). According to the Coase theorem, the choice of one disagreement point or another should not affect the parties' incentives to reach a more efficient arrangement. However, the disagreement point does affect the distribution of the surplus between the parties, and may affect the eventual bargaining solution in the presence of wealth effects. The concept of the disagreement point is germane to the concept of the threat point, used by game theorists in bargaining situations. In some settings, the disagreement point is given by the status quo (e.g., the payoff obtained if the parties choose not to enter the game). In other settings, the second best alternative (i.e., opportunity cost) provides the disagreement point of the parties when they are deciding whether to enter into a contract. In litigation contexts, the expected net judicial award in the event of litigation often represents the disagreement point. See also *Nash bargaining solution*.

Disappearing defendant problem: the incentives created with the use of a threat of liability hinge upon the legal system's ability to identify and impose liability on the responsible individuals. When the responsible party can successfully avoid being identified or avoids the enforcement of a liability judgment, the threat of liability becomes ineffective against him or her. The law and economics literature refers to this as the disappearing defendant problem. Like the judgment proof problem, the disappearing defendant problem undermines the incentive effects of legal rules. The fact that the legal process is not always successful at identifying and imposing liability on the responsible parties may lead to excessive risky behavior and suboptimal levels of precaution. Disappearing defendants also have reduced incentives to purchase liability insurance. The disappearing defendant problem may justify the adoption of mandatory insurance, ex ante safety regulations, and the use of criminal sanctions for disappearing defendants (e.g., hit-and-run accidents). See also *judgment proof problem*.

Disappointment prevention principle: Bentham's (1830) disappointment prevention principle follows from the idea that individuals draw direct utility from their expectations, even before their expectations actually materialize. Put in modern terms, in Bentham's view expectations become an argument of the utility function, just like other goods that generate utility. This concept, described in the literature as "expectation utility," is thus different from the modern concept of "expected utility," whereby utility is obtained only if the uncertain future event materializes (Postema, 1986). Bentham elaborates various normative corollaries of his principle. Expectations are worthy of per se protection, and policies should aim at preventing the disappointment of individuals' expectations. Common law adjudication, unlike statutory lawmaking, is by its nature retrospective and should be particularly attentive to the protection of individual expectations. Judicial innovations driven by the desire to improve justice may conflict with the protection of prior expectations and thus create instability and ultimately injustice. See also *expected utility* and *Bentham, Jeremy*.

Discounting: the calculation of future income in present value terms. The present value of future income is lower than present income for a number of reasons. First, money in hand now can earn interest over time. Second, there is risk involved in waiting. Third, all other things equal, people prefer to have things now rather than later. Discounting is used for cost–benefit analysis and for debt instruments. Compounding is the opposite of discounting. The calculation is performed thus: at discount rate r, a dollar invested for t years will be worth $(1 + r)^t$. Consequently, the present value of a dollar available t years in the future is $(1 + r)^{-t}$. In law and economics, the concept of discounting has been applied in a variety of different contexts. For example, discounting is used to determine the present value of a pending lawsuit – a value that becomes the threat point in settlement negotiations. The choice of appropriate discount rates to compute the net present value of legal intervention also raises important issues. Legal intervention imposes present costs and creates benefits that materialize over time, and policymakers often disagree on the choice of social discount rates that appropriately capture the time preference of society. The problem becomes even more complex when benefits or costs materialize over very long periods of time that involve overlapping generations. See also *discounting cost effect*, *exponential discounting*, *hyperbolic discounting*, and *present value*.

Discounting cost effect: first identified by Porat and Tabbach (2011), the idea is that, in establishing how much people would be willing to spend to save their life, humans tend to discount the costs of reducing their risk of death by the probability that they will die anyway. The discounting cost effect follows from the fact that, after one's death, the utility of unspent wealth goes to zero. This private cost–benefit calculation leads to a divergence of private and social incentives and to overinvestment in precautions. The discounting cost effect, together with the inflating benefit effect (also identified by Porat and Tabbach, 2011), may lead to a widening of the willingness to pay versus willingness to accept gap. See also *discounting*, *inflating benefit effect* and *willingness to pay versus willingness to accept*.

Discrimination: see *statistical discrimination*.

Discrimination coefficient: see *taste for discrimination*.

Discriminatory pricing: see *price discrimination*.

Diseconomies of scale: these are the mirror image of economies of scale. In the presence of diseconomies of scale, the unit cost of production increases as the scale of production increases. See also *economies of scale*.

Diseconomies of scope: these occur when the firm's average cost increases, as product diversification increases, and play the opposite role to economies of scope. See also *economies of scope*.

Disgorgement damages: a measure of liability when damages are imposed to offset a wrongdoer's expected gain from making the wrong choice. In order to serve as a deterrent, disgorgement damages should be (at least) as large as the incremental gain that might induce a potential tortfeasor to choose the wrong course of action. By taking expected disgorgement damages into account, potential tortfeasors might realize that committing a tort does not pay. See also *disgorgement liability*, *compensatory damages* and *punitive damages*.

Disgorgement liability: following the same rationale of disgorgement damages, disgorgement liability in torts is aimed at offsetting the precaution savings of negligent tortfeasors. Disgorgement damages are computed on the basis of the savings for a tortfeasor's untaken precautions multiplied by the inverse of the probability of detection. The imposition of disgorgement liability is useful to produce deterrence when standard damages based on the actual accident loss are ineffective due to tortfeasor's insolvency. See also *disgorgement damages* and *punitive damages*.

Dispositive takings principle: this principle (Ayres, 2005) states that an optimal regime should avoid the reciprocal takings problem by focusing on facilitating takings that will be final and dispositive. Alternatively stated, damages should be set to induce a litigant to take whenever the taker's private value is greater than the expected valuation of the original owner of the entitlement/good. This results in efficient takings; the takers will take when their valuation is higher than damages and the takee's subjective valuation. See also *reciprocal takings problem* and *property rules versus liability rules*.

Disruption costs: a firm is subject to these if it suffers a substantial financial loss that compels a downsizing of its operations. In the presence of disruption costs, a firm that faced a loss faces a reduction in value greater than the direct loss that it suffered. The reason for disruption costs are the forgone economies of scale and scope brought about by the resizing of the firm in the face of a large and unexpected loss. A firm can reduce the risk of disruption costs through insurance and access to a perfect capital market. Diversification does not easily eliminate disruption costs for individual firms. The concept of disruption costs was introduced into the law and economics literature by Trimarchi (2003), and it has important implications on the appropriate economic modeling of firms. Firms are usually modeled as risk-neutral entities, since investors can diversify through portfolios. However, in the face of disruption costs, firms should be modeled as risk-averse entities with respect to potential losses (although they would remain neutral with respect to potential windfall gains). See also *risk premium* and *risk preferences*.

Distributive reciprocity: see *kindness function* and *procedural preferences*.

Disutility monster: see *utility monster*.

Diversifiable risk: see *systematic versus unsystematic risk*.

Diversification: a method of mitigating risk by spreading it out over numerous small and independent instances, rather than concentrating it in one large gamble. Unlike hedging, diversification does not shield against systematic or market risk (i.e., the risk associated with the entire economy that affects all economic actors at once). Portfolio theory specifies the techniques to minimize the variance in the return of a portfolio by balancing investments that face inversely correlated risks. When a diversification of risk is possible, legal policymakers can set aside concerns for the optimal allocation of risk between alternative parties and focus on the creation of optimal behavioral incentives. See also *portfolio theory*, *risk management*, *hedging*, and *systematic versus unsystematic risk*.

Divestiture aversion: see *endowment effect*.

Dominant firm: in markets with high levels of concentration, measured by concentration ratios and concentration indexes, firms that have larger market shares in the industry and exert a higher market power are referred to as dominant. See also *Herfindahl index*, *concentration ratio*, *market share*, and *market structure*.

Dominant strategies: in game theory, players must make choices about their own actions. Their choices are sometimes impacted by the choices, or the anticipated choices, of other players in the game. When making interdependent choices, players choose the best response to the opponent's expected strategy. A Nash strategy is the conditionally best response to the opponent's strategy choice. Although players often have best strategies that depend upon the opponent's choices, in some situations players have a strategy that offers the highest payoff, no matter what the other player chooses to do. This strategy is an unconditionally best response to the opponent's choice, and is called a dominant strategy. When a player has a dominant strategy available to him or her, he or she will always make the dominant strategy choice. When both players have dominant strategies, they will both play their dominant strategies. This will lead to a dominant strategy equilibrium. For example, in the prisoner's dilemma, if both co-conspirators can secure a better payoff by confessing, regardless of what the other co-conspirator does, both will choose to confess. In the classical prisoner's dilemma, each player has a dominant strategy, and the game has a dominant strategy equilibrium. See also *dominant strategy equilibrium* and *dominated strategies*.

Dominant strategy equilibrium: a Nash equilibrium in which all players play a dominant strategy (i.e., a strategy that is always optimal regardless of the strategies and preferences of other agents). By applying the iterated process of the elimination of dominated strategies, each player is left with one single strategy, and the set of the players' strategies constitute the equilibrium of the game. An example of such equilibrium is the prisoner's dilemma equilibrium, in which all players follow dominant defection strategies. See also *Nash equilibrium*, *dominant strategies*, *subgame-perfect strategy and equilibrium*, and *prisoner's dilemma*.

Dominated strategies: a pure strategy is strictly dominated for a player in a game if there is at least one available strategy that offers a higher payoff to the player, for any strategy played by all the other players in the game. Intuitively, a strictly dominated strategy is an undesirable one, because there will always exist, by definition, at least one alternative strategy that yields a higher payoff regardless of the opponent's moves. Clearly, strictly dominated strategies can never be equilibrium strategies. When choices are strictly dominated by alternative strategies, which are themselves dominated by alternative strategies, rational players rule them out by a process of elimination called iterated dominance (Luce and Raiffa, 1957). Analytically, denote with s_i the strategy of player i in the game and S_i the set of strategies available to player i, where $s_i \in S_i$. In an analogous way, denote with s_{-i} the strategy selection of all the other players other than i in the game, where $s_{-i} \in S_{-i}$, the set of strategies available to all the other players in the game. The strategy s_i is strictly dominated if there exists a strategy s_i' such that $u_i(s_i', s_{-i}) > u_i(s_i, s_1)$ for all $s_{-i} \in S_{-i}$. The process of eliminating dominated strategies may help to reduce the set of strategies in order to determine the equilibria of the games or to identify the equilibrium of the game, in the case that each player is left with one single strategy after applying iterated dominance. However, note that most games studied in economic analysis cannot be solved by iterated dominance, and other equilibrium concepts, among which the Nash equilibrium is the best known, should be used to identify a proper solution. See also *dominant strategies*.

Dominated strategy equilibrium: see *dominant strategy equilibrium*.

Double auctions: a method of clearing a market with multiple buyers and sellers. In a double auction, buyers and sellers submit their bids and asks respectively to an auctioneer, who determines a market price p. Buyers offering a bid higher than p and sellers offering an ask lower than p all exchange at price p, leaving all sellers and buyers with a margin, and clearing the market. See also *auction theory*, *Dutch auctions*, and *English auctions*.

Double marginalization: a double marginalization problem arises in a vertical market when the upstream firm and the downstream firm both enjoy market or monopoly power. In order to maximize its profit, the downstream firm prices above marginal cost and restricts its output (or sales). The choice of the downstream firm further restricts the market for the upstream supplier, with a double price marginalization, and a resulting increase in social deadweight loss. The problem of double marginalization can be solved by allowing the upstream firm to set (maximum) resale prices for the downstream firm (e.g., newspaper and book pricing). Price setting becomes less viable when the vertical market involves an upstream input producer and a downstream producer of final goods. Vertical mergers and other forms of upstream or downstream integration may also reduce the problems of vertical monopolistic markets. See also *monopoly*, *vertical integration*, *backward integration*, and *forward integration*.

Double trust problem: this arises when two complementary inputs of production (e.g., ideas and capital) are owned by different parties. In the absence of complete contracting and effective enforcement, both inputs are subject to appropriation by the other party. Cooter and Schaefer (2011) use the following narrative to illustrate the double trust problem. Imagine "an economist who works at a Boston investment bank received a letter that read, 'I know how your bank can make $10 million. If you give me $1 million, I will tell you.'" In this example, the parties face a double trust problem, assuming that the author of the letter has legitimate money-making knowledge. If the money-making secret is disclosed first, the bank could appropriate it without payment. If the payment is made first, the sum could be appropriated without the disclosure of the valuable information. Legal systems may offer instruments for the solution to this problem. The double trust problem and its solutions (or lack thereof) provide a relevant explanatory variable to understand the different rates of growth in developing countries. See also *Arrow's information paradox*.

Double-edged torts: these are characterized by the condition that parties are exposed to the risk of being tortfeasors and victims simultaneously. Luppi, Parisi, and Pi (2012) have introduced the term "double-edged torts," providing a systematic analysis of the incentives created by tort liability in such double-edged activities. In double-edged tort situations, some subset of the available precautions has the effect of reducing both the probability that the precaution taker is a tortfeasor and the probability that he or she is a victim. This category of precautions is referred to as "hybrid precautions." A modification of the common negligence standard is desirable to promote optimal care incentives in double-edged tort situations. See also *hybrid precautions*, *precaution externalities*, *alternative versus joint care*, and *bilateral accident*.

Double-peaked preferences: see *single-peaked versus double-peaked preferences*.

Dual chooser rules: those that give both the plaintiff and the defendant control over the ultimate allocation of an entitlement. Since the defendant and plaintiff must both choose where the entitlement is allocated, they can identify when the defendant values the entitlement more than the plaintiff without resorting to adjudication. Ayres (2005) studies the role of dual chooser rules with an interesting set of extensions and applications. Plaintiff-centered dual chooser rules initially allocate an entitlement to the plaintiff but then give the defendant the option to negotiate with the plaintiff to shift the entitlement. The entitlement will shift to the defendant only when the plaintiff values the entitlement less than the damages and when the defendant values the entitlement more than the cost of paying damages. Alternatively, rights could be allocated to a defendant in a "defendant presumption" scenario, unless both parties agree to shift entitlement to the plaintiff. This gives either party veto power over the allocation of the entitlement to the plaintiff. See also *single chooser rules*, *chooser's call/put option*, *first-order rules*, *single price allocation*, *property rules versus liability rules*, and *Coasean bargaining*.

Dummy variable: a variable widely used in statistical analysis, and also known as an indicator variable, that takes either value 0 or 1 to indicate the absence or the presence of an effect of interest. A dummy variable can be used, for example, to proxy the phase of the economic cycle (e.g., 0 = recession, and 1 = growth) and test its empirical effects on the dependent variable in the regression analysis (e.g., the probability of default by firms, or the level of criminality). See also *proxy variable*.

Duopoly: an oligopolistic market in which only two sellers compete in the production of a good. As with an oligopoly with N firms, the actions of each firm affect the structure of the other firm's demand and costs. In game-theoretical language, firms' actions are interdependent. When firms compete over prices according to the Bertrand model, the equilibrium outcome coincides in the duopoly and in the N-firm oligopoly, and the price is set equal to the marginal cost. When firms compete over quantity according to the Cournot model, the equilibrium of a duopoly does not coincide with the N-firm oligopoly: competition becomes more intense as the number of firms increases, leading to a higher price and lower aggregate output in the duopoly case. Duopoly is frequently studied in economic theory because of the simplicity and tractability of its model. See also *oligopoly*, *Bertrand competition*, *Cournot competition*, and *market structure*.

Duopsony: an oligopsony characterized by the presence of two buyers in the presence of multiple sellers. See also *oligopsony* and *market structure*.

Durable versus non-durable precautions: tort law encourages potential tortfeasors to invest in precautions to avoid harming others. When one individual causes harm to another person, he or she is a negligent tortfeasor if he or she failed to take the precautions a reasonable person should take to avoid such harm. Grady (1988), in his work on tort law, identifies two types of precautions. Durable precautions are precautions that are long-lasting and that one need not remember to take on a frequent basis. Non-durable precautions are precautions that one must frequently remember to take. Difficulties arise when applying the negligence test to these two types of precautions. Let us consider a non-durable precaution that needs to be undertaken for every unit of activity (e.g., stopping and looking every time one reaches an intersection). If such a precaution is useful, it should be undertaken every time, regardless of the number of times an intersection is crossed. However, the desirability of durable precautions may depend on the level of activity. Investing in some precaution technology (e.g., a radar to help identify approaching cars at an intersection) may be desirable for those who undertake high levels of activity, but not for occasional users. The two types of precautions could be closely tied together because of cross-price effects. For example, the cost of non-durable precautions might be lower if durable precautions are undertaken (e.g., checking for cars at the intersection might be easier and faster with a radar on board). A lower cost for non-durable precautions might raise the standard of due care, paradoxically imposing a higher standard on those who had already invested in durable precautions. This, in turn, may discourage the investment in durable precautions. Grady (1988) points to another cross-effect, observing that the use of a durable precaution might require taking other associated non-durable precautions to maintain or make proper use of the durable precaution. Grady uses the example of a dialysis machine. While the dialysis machine itself is a durable technology that allows individuals to survive and avoid kidney failure, the maintenance associated with properly using the dialysis machine requires one to remember frequently to do numerous tasks. These tasks are non-durable precautions. Grady argues that, although a person might simply have died before the invention of dialysis machines, their creation presents numerous new opportunities for a medical professional to fail to take one of the non-durable precautions. Grady attributes the rise in medical malpractice claims in the late twentieth century to the increase in technology, the accompanying increase in the number of non-durable precautions a medical professional must take to maintain technology, and the resulting increase in the number of medical professionals who fail to take non-durable precautions and therefore act negligently (Grady, 1988). See also *Learned Hand formula* and *activity level versus care level*.

Dutch auctions: unlike traditional auctions, at which the price rises with sequential bidding until one bidder is left, a Dutch auction is a descending-price auction, at which the auctioneer sets a price that is substantially higher than any bidder is likely to pay and then gradually lowers it until someone bids on the item. The Dutch auction is a type of first-price auction, since the bidder pays the price corresponding to his or her own bid. These auctions are named after a mechanism utilized in wholesale flower markets in the Netherlands, where a "clock" indicated the descending offer price for the object for sale. The price would keep descending until a bidder indicated his or her willingness to take it at the going price. Dutch auctions are adopted for goods that must be sold quickly and in private-value environments (hence their use in flower, fish, and tobacco markets). Dutch auctions could also be utilized in procurement auctions, in which case the clock would mark the ascending offer of the auctioneer for the procurement. See also *first-price auctions*, *second-price auctions*, *English auctions*, *common-value auctions*, and *auction theory*.

Duty to rescue: see *Good Samaritan rule*.

Dynamic consistency: see *dynamic inconsistency*.

Dynamic inconsistency: when an economic agent's preferences change over time, it is possible for his or her preferences at one time to be incompatible with his or her preferences at another. For example, an agent may prefer pretzels to peanuts one year, then peanuts to pretzels the next year. This incompatibility of preferences over time is known as dynamic inconsistency, or time inconsistency. In decision theory, dynamic inconsistency implies that people make only imperfect plans, since an agent's best plan for the future may not be optimal when his or her future preferences differ in relevant respects from his or her preferences when he or she initially made plans. Dynamic inconsistency often creates problems of credibility. Hands tying and precommitment strategies are key issues in mitigating the mischief that dynamic inconsistency creates. See also *precommitment strategies* and *intergenerational equity*.

Dynamic models: these explicitly and centrally consider changes that occur over the passage of time. Dynamic models are common in macroeconomic analyses, when they are used to analyze inherently dynamic phenomena such as economic growth, inflation, and business cycles. In the economic analysis of law, dynamic models have useful potential applications for explaining the evolution of law and the evolution of regulated environments over time. In setting up a dynamic model of law, the current legal system should be built into the initial conditions of a dynamic model. How people or resources respond to changes in the legal structure is present in the parameters of the model. When a law changes, a parameter may also change, and the model progresses along a different dynamic path. For example, if a law is enacted and individuals internalize the values expressed by a law, their preferences or propensities to engage in certain behavior may also change. The original environment changes as an effect of legal intervention. Researchers can alter the parameters (or variables) in dynamic models to predict how society will respond to legal changes over time and what new equilibrium paths will look like. See also *comparative dynamics* and *adjustment dynamics*.

E

EALE: European Association of Law and Economics. Founded in 1984, and the oldest of the several academic associations devoted to the economic analysis of law. The European Association of Law and Economics was founded under the initiative of Göran Skogh, who developed the idea while he was a visiting professor of law and economics at the University of California at Santa Barbara. The association was created to respond to the increasing institutional importance of the economic analysis of law in Europe and to provide assistance to law and economics scholars and bring their scholarship to a wider audience, including policymakers, legislators, and judges. The Marianne and Marcus Wallenberg Foundation provided the initial funding for the development of the association. The first annual conference of the association was held from March 19 to 21, 1984, in Lund, Sweden. Since 1985 the conferences have become an important forum for the exchange of research findings and ideas, and have been held on an annually rotating basis. The presidents of the association are elected periodically, and have been Göran Skogh (1984–7), Roger Van den Bergh (1987–2001), Gerrit De Geest (2001–4), Hans-Bernd Schäfer (2004–7), Roger Bowles (2007–8), Eli Salzberger (2008–2011), and Bruno Deffains (2011–14). Since 2004 the association has published the *Review of Law and Economics*. See also **Review of Law and Economics**, *ALEA*, *CLEA*, *ASLEA*, and *ALACDE*.

Ecological rationality: economists and law and economics scholars routinely assume that the relevant actors in a model are rational and self-interested. However, it is tacitly understood that supernumerary psychological factors will often exert countervailing influences. One such non-rational influence is the cost of rational deliberation itself. Ecological rationality explains less than perfectly rational behavior as an evolutionarily selected mechanism for coping with the cost of rational deliberation, drawing from psychology, neuroscience, evolutionary biology, and behavioral economics. On this view, the allocation of cognitive resources conforms to evolutionarily determined second-order "rationality," resulting in apparently irrational first-order behavior. In other words, while the decisions of the economic actor may not always represent efficient choices, this may nevertheless be the result of an efficient allocation of decision-making resources. See also *decision heuristics*, *behavioral law and economics*, *experimental law and economics*, *Smith, Vernon*, and *bounded rationality*.

Econometric models: econometrics is a field of applied statistics used to estimate the relationships between economic variables. Econometrics produces these estimates through the use of econometric models. For example, economic theory suggests that the quantity demanded (Q_d) of a good depends on the good's price (P), prices of substitute goods (P_{sub}), prices of complement goods (P_{comp}), consumer incomes (INC), and expectations about future prices (P_{exp}) and income (INC_{exp}). This relationship can be described algebraically:

$$Q_d = \beta_0(P) + \beta_1(P_{sub}) + \beta_2(P_{comp}) + \beta_3(INC) + \beta_4(P_{exp}) + \beta_5(INC_{exp})$$

Q_d is an endogenous variable, because its value is determined within the model. P, P_{sub}, P_{comp}, INC, and INC_{exp} are exogenous variables. Their values are determined outside the model and used as input for the model. Regressing the quantity demanded on the exogenous variables results in estimations for the β parameters. Each estimate of β represents the strength and direction of the relationship between the endogenous variable and the corresponding exogenous variable. For example, the estimate of β_1 might be –0.5, indicating that, for each unit increase in price, the quantity demanded decreases by 0.5 of a unit. Econometric models can have many variables connected by many equations. This is common when the model is intended to describe large-scale and complex relationships, such as macroeconomic models or models attempting to explain the operation of the criminal justice system as a whole. One recent law and economics paper examined the effect of parental notification laws on abortion rates among teenagers. Exogenous differences in state abortion laws and several control variables were compared to state abortion rates. The corresponding estimates (like the βs above) indicate the presence and magnitude of reduction in teenage abortions that lawmakers can expect from enacting parental notification laws.

Economic constitution: governments frequently adopt constitutions to establish the central rules by which they govern. These constitutions can establish rules and principles that govern a host of activities and concepts, from politics to individual rights. Scholars have used the term "economic constitution" to refer to "the rules of the game under which economic activities can be carried out in the respective jurisdictions" (Grundmann, Kerber, and Weatherill, 2001). Through an economic constitution, governments can either establish general economic principles or establish rules for intra-state trade, labor standards, and antitrust regulations, among others. Trade agreements are also examples of economic constitutions, because they provide the "rules of the game" under which two states can engage in economic activity.

Economic institutes for judges: economic programs for judges have played an important role in bringing economic thinking into the courtroom. There are several programs that offer training to judges to aid their use of economic methods in the analysis of law. Historically, Henry G. Manne has been a pioneer in the establishment of such judicial programs. A number of top US law schools currently host economic institutes for judicial training, including Northwestern University, the Law and Economics Center at George Mason University, the

Institute for Law and Economics at the University of Chicago. Outside the United States, the Jevons Institute at University College London and the Institut d'Economie Industrielle at the Université des Sciences Sociales de Toulouse run a joint judicial training program specializing in law and economics. See also *Manne, Henry*.

Economic profits: see *accounting profits versus economic profits*.

Economic rent: see *rent*.

Economic theory of politics: see *public choice theory*.

Economies of scale: with these present, the unit cost of production decreases as the scale of production increases. More precisely, the term "economies of scale" describes the property such that long-run average total cost decreases with an increase in output (in a single product context). Economies of scale can arise in the presence of large fixed costs of production, which are better utilized when production takes place on a large scale. Alternatively, economies of scale can be found when the variable inputs of production (e.g., physical inputs, human capital, financial resources) have decreasing marginal costs. The presence of economies of scale acts as an entry barrier, and is one of the possible causes of natural monopoly. The economies of scale concept is relevant to a number of legal areas, ranging from antitrust to tort law and federalism. In a well-known article, Williamson (1968) considers the role of economies of scale as an antitrust defense, identifying the tradeoff between the economies of scale (Tullock's rectangle) obtainable in a concentrated market and the deadweight loss (Harberger's triangle) caused by imperfect competition. In tort law, costs of precaution may be characterized by decreasing marginal costs. This result implies that, in situations of alternative care, precaution incentives may be better concentrated on one party or the other (the so-called cheapest cost avoider), rather than being spread evenly between the parties. Economies of scale are also relevant in issues of federalism and subsidiarity, informing much of the debate on the allocation of federal and state powers. See also *returns to scale, diseconomies of scale, economies of scope, ray economies, cheapest cost avoider, Tullock's rectangle*, and *network effects*.

Economies of scale as an antitrust defense: see *Tullock's rectangle*.

Economies of scope: these – first studied by Panzar and Willig (1977) – occur when the firm's average cost decreases, as product diversification increases, when the firm produces more than one product. The relevance of economies of scope in legal analysis spans fields ranging from competition policy to constitutional design. For example, in merger policy, economies of scope become relevant and may legitimize requests for horizontal integration in concentrated markets. In constitutional design, economies of scope, together with economies of scale, inform much of the debate on the allocation of powers in a federal setting. See also *diseconomies of scope, economies of scale*, and *ray economies*.

Economizing: one of the core insights of the new institutional economics literature is that firms and organizations develop to "economize" production. The idea was already present in Coase's (1937) theory of the firm, but was greatly developed and popularized by Williamson (1979), who suggests that alternative governance structures (ranging from markets to contract governance and corporate organization) are chosen with the goal of "economizing" – a term that in this literature means minimizing the sum of production costs and transaction costs. See also *governance structure* and *contract as governance*.

Edgeworth box: see *contract curve*.

EDLE: European Doctorate in Law and Economics. A Ph.D.-level degree jointly offered by the Universities of Bologna, Hamburg, and Rotterdam, the program is sponsored by the European Commission under the Erasmus Mundus excellence program. Students in this doctoral program are given the unique opportunity to study law and economics at a doctoral level, attending courses in (at least) three different countries. See also *Erasmus program in law and economics*, *EMLE*, and *Vanderbilt Ph.D. in law and economics*.

Efficiency: much of the economic analysis of law is informed by the goal of promoting efficiency. Several competing definitions of efficiency are utilized, including the notions of Pareto efficiency, Kaldor–Hicks efficiency, Nash efficiency, and Rawlsian maximin efficiency. Although in some situations these alternative criteria of efficiency lead to similar normative results, in most applications the choice of a specific criterion of efficiency drives most of the prescriptive results. Hence, the methodological choice in efficiency analysis carries important ideological significance. The concept of efficiency as a normative criterion should be distinguished from the concept of cost-effectiveness as an instrumental criterion. When used normatively, the efficiency criterion guides policy choices. Cost-effectiveness analysis takes the policy goal as given and is used as an instrument of cost minimization in the implementation of the policy objectives. The instrumental use of cost-effectiveness is therefore less controversial, and is accepted even by scholars who do not endorse the normative use of economic analysis. See also *allocative efficiency*, *welfare analysis*, *wealth maximization*, *utility maximization*, *Kaldor–Hicks criterion*, *Nash criterion of welfare*, *Rawlsian maximin*, *Pareto efficiency*, *two-step optimization*, and *capability approach*.

Efficiency defense: antitrust law bars companies from securing excessive market power and driving out competitors. Corporate mergers often raise antitrust concerns. In fighting an allegation that a merger violates antitrust law, Williamson (1968) argues that, in some cases, companies can claim an efficiency defense. To assert an efficiency defense, merging companies would need to argue that the economies of scale gained through the merger, and the resulting decrease in the prices of the companies' goods or services, outweigh the increase in price that might accompany increased market power. Williamson states that most mergers do not result in increased market power or significant new economies of scale. However, in cases when a merger does generate such results, he argues that governmental authorities should consider the efficiency defense, weighing the economies obtainable through the merger against the deadweight loss and increase in prices that might result from an increase in market power. If the benefits of a merger outweigh its costs, the government should not attempt to prevent a merger. Williamson believes that the onus is on the government not to challenge a merger when a valid efficiency defense exists, largely because the courts lack the resources to assess an efficiency defense accurately. See also *Tullock's rectangle*, *Harberger's triangle*, *concentration index*, and *market power*.

Efficiency of democracy: some economic scholars have argued that democracy is economically efficient; more precisely, that the preferences of some majority, coalition, or plurality will yield a socially optimal set of policies. This view has been challenged on a number of fronts – notably the rationality of voters and the high information cost of rational voting, among others. In addition, the view runs into technical problems (e.g., the voting paradoxes, the median voter theorem, incumbent's advantage theorem, etc.). The efficiency (or relative efficiency) of democratic policymaking remains a subject of lively scholarly debate. See also *political markets*, *logrolling*, *vote trading*, *voting paradoxes*, *median voter theorem*, *Condorcet voting paradox*, and *Arrow's impossibility theorem*.

Efficiency of the common law hypothesis: according to the efficiency of the common law hypothesis, the common law (i.e., judge-made law) is the result of an effort – conscious or not – to induce efficient outcomes. This hypothesis provided an important premise of the positive law and economics of the Chicago school. According to the hypothesis, first intimated by Coase (1960) and later systematized and greatly extended by other scholars (Ehrlich and Posner, 1974; Rubin, 1977; Priest, 1977; Posner, 1994), common law rules attempt to allocate resources efficiently, typically in a Pareto- or Kaldor–Hicks-efficient manner. Common law rules are said to enjoy a comparative advantage over legislation in fulfilling this task because of the evolutionary selection of common law rules through adjudication and the gradual accretion of precedent (Fon and Parisi, 2003). The several important contributions that provide the foundations for this claim are often in disagreement as to their conceptual basis. While most of the early theories focused on the role of litigants and the selection of legal disputes (demand-side theories), subsequent work concentrated on the role of judges and their motivation to create efficient precedents (supply-side theories) and the combined effect of litigants' case selection and judges' incentives. See also *survivor theory of efficiency*, *Chicago school*, and *positive versus normative law and economics*.

Efficiency wage theory: this helps to explain why labor markets do not clear: wages might remain high in countries or regions with high unemployment. Stiglitz (2002) recalls that his efficiency wage theory was developed while he was working in Kenya during the early 1970s. Urban Kenya faced high unemployment and high wages, despite the fact that falling wages would allow unemployed workers to secure jobs. In its original formulation, efficiency wage theory (Stiglitz, 1974, 1976) acknowledges that, absent perfect information about the productivity of each employee, firms might pay more than the wages they would need to recruit workers. While employers might pay less if they could cheaply and thoroughly monitor the performance of their employees, reality requires them to pay more in the hopes of motivating workers and recruiting high-quality workers who are productive. The fact that high unemployment exists serves as a threat against shirking employees. Even with imperfect monitoring, shirking employees face a higher probability of dismissal. If there was no unemployment, employees could shirk their duties and could easily find another job paying the same wage. Where high unemployment exists, however, shirking employees would risk longer-term unemployment. Any employer attempting to undercut the efficiency wage would face an adverse selection, with a higher incidence of low-quality and shirking employees. Stiglitz's (1974, 1976) efficiency wage theory shows the effect of "information imperfections" on labor markets, and can be read to imply that the unemployment wedge may be higher in industries in which monitoring is more costly and in societies with weak work ethics. See also ***asymmetric information*** and ***adverse selection***.

Efficient breach: contract law imposes liability on parties who breach their contractual obligations. Liability encourages parties to invest in effort to fulfill their contractual promises. The theory of efficient breach was introduced in the law and economics literature by Goetz and Scott in their 1977 article "Liquidated damages, penalties, and the just compensation principle. According to the theory of efficient breach, not all breaches should be deterred. In some instances, society as a whole may be better off with a breach of contract. There are two reasons why a breach may be deemed efficient: (a) an increase in performance costs for the promisor that makes performance more expensive than the benefit it creates; and (b) a decrease in the benefits of performance for the promisee, which brings the benefit below the performance cost faced by the promisor. In both these situations, the performance of the contract would lead to a net social loss (i.e., in both instances, the costs are larger than the benefits). According to the theory of efficient breach, contract remedies (and contract damages in particular) should incentivize performance when performance is efficient but allow for breach to take place when performance is not efficient. The theory of efficient breach has attracted criticism from some scholars, who have argued that performance is the fulfillment of a moral obligation and that giving room to breaches of contract on the grounds of efficiency undermines the reliability of contractual promises (see, for example, Fried, 1981). The law and economics literature has identified the measure of expectation damages (i.e., damages equivalent to the expected benefit of the promisee) as those that would encourage optimal performance and allow for efficient breach. Viewed in this way, the theory of efficient breach can be seen as an economic explanation of the existing measures of contract damages, rather than being normative in content. Besides the two situations considered above, there are other more problematic situations under which parties might prefer to pay expectation damages for breach of contract rather than to perform. These situations might involve (a) the rise of new opportunities for the promisor to deploy his or her performance with greater gains or (b) the rise of cheaper opportunities for the promisee to obtain performance from others at a lower price. In these situations, the concept of efficient breach would not necessarily support a breach of contract. In both cases, expectation damages would induce one or the other party to breach the contract, even though performance might still be socially efficient. Although the possibility of inefficient breach exists in these cases, if transaction costs are low the parties could renegotiate the original agreement to avoid a – privately rational, but socially inefficient – breach. See also *breach remedies*, *expectation damages*, and *contrived breach*.

Efficient market hypothesis: this holds that the free flow of information in markets causes prices to adjust rapidly, and efficiently, as new information becomes available. Because prices change quickly as new information spreads, opportunities for investors to seize on inefficiencies and take advantage of prices that are too low or too high rarely exist. The hypothesis is generally attributed to Fama (1965), a Chicago economist, although prior scholars expressed similar ideas with respect to financial markets. The efficient market hypothesis, in its three variants (weak form, semi-strong form, and strong form), was developed with respect to equity markets. The expression has subsequently been adopted by the general economics literature to invoke the idea that markets operate efficiently, and that prices reflect available information and expectations about future events. After the collapse of the US housing market in 2008 and the recent financial crisis, scholars have developed a considerable degree of skepticism about the efficiency hypothesis, pointing the finger at its believers for ignoring the issues identified in behavioral finance and the dynamics of price expectations. See also *fundamental theorem of welfare*.

Efficient scale: in production theory, the efficient scale of a firm is defined as the scale of production (quantity) that minimizes average total cost. When the firm operates at the efficient scale of production, the marginal cost equals the average total cost. See also *production cost* and *economies of scale*.

Egalitarian bargaining solution: most theories of bargaining propose solutions based on outcomes. The egalitarian bargaining solution (Kalai, 1977) identifies a solution to bargaining that grants equal gains to both parties. By doing so, the distribution of payoffs follows a maximin pattern, maximizing the minimum payoff among players. See also *axiomatic theory of bargaining*.

Embeddedness: social scientists debate the extent to which human behavior is driven by economic rather than social incentives. The term "embeddedness" is used in this literature to describe the extent to which human behavior is influenced by social relations and informal norms. The concept of embeddedness refers to the idea "that the behavior and institutions to be analyzed are so constrained by ongoing social relations that to construe them as independent is a grievous misunderstanding" (Granovetter, 1985). As Granovetter points out, anthropologists and sociologists, among others, believe that humans' economic behavior was once heavily embedded in social relations. However, in the wake of industrialization and modernization there has been a radical shift, and humans are no longer so constrained. Many economists, on the other hand, hold to the belief that human beings are rational actors, that their economic behavior has rarely been heavily impacted by social relations, and that modernization has had little impact on the extent to which humans are embedded within social relations. Granovetter subscribes to a middle ground, arguing that humans' economic behavior has been more embedded and less impacted by modernization than traditional social scientists believe, and that embeddedness is more influential than economists give it credit for. The law and economics literature has considered this important question in a variety of contexts. Experimental law and economics has considered the extent to which anonymity may undermine the role of trust and compliance with social norms in contractual relationships. The findings support the idea that human business interactions are embedded in the social context in which they take place. Relevant differences in parties' behavior can be, at least partially, explained by the social relationships and desires within which human actions are embedded. This theory is also consistent with the empirical findings that spontaneous compliance with cooperative social norms is more easily sustained in close-knitted communities (Ellickson, 1991). The theoretical and empirical findings of the law and social norms literature can be enlightened by a greater acknowledgement of the relevance of embeddedness in human choice. See also *close-knittedness*.

EMLE: European Master in Law and Economics. A graduate degree offered by a network of European and international universities that are members of the Erasmus program in law and economics. This degree program offers students a unique opportunity for the interdisciplinary study of law and economics, allowing them to attend courses at two or even three European and non-European universities. A large number of European law and economics scholars obtained their training through the EMLE degree. Several graduates of the EMLE program continue their academic training through the European Doctorate in Law and Economics (EDLE) or other Ph.D. programs. See also *Erasmus program in law and economics* and *EDLE*.

Endogenous variables: ones that are decided within an economic system (as opposed to exogenous variables). Endogenous variables are determined in the model on the basis of the other, exogenous variables that are determined outside the model and taken as a given. In consumer theory, consumption levels are determined endogenously as the result of equilibrium choices, given the exogenous level of prices and individual income. In production theory, output levels are determined as the optimal production choices given the exogenous input prices. The classification of a variable as endogenous as opposed to exogenous often depends on the objective of the analysis, the time frame being considered, and the other assumptions of the model. For example, in conventional economic models, laws and legal institutions are generally specified as exogenous variables. Other variables in the model are endogenously determined, given those exogenous factors. When economic analysis is used in legal policymaking, laws (and often legal institutions as well) are instead modeled as endogenous variables that can be chosen and changed over time in response to other exogenous factors. In econometric models, the use of the term has similar implications. Suppose that an econometric model wants to investigate whether the marital status of the felon, the local rate of unemployment, and the felon's average consumption of alcohol affect the likelihood of criminal recidivism. In this econometric model, the likelihood of recidivism will be the endogenous variable. It will be decided in the model on the basis of the inputs of the other variables, whose values are exogenously determined outside the model. See also ***exogenous variables***.

Endogenous versus exogenous preferences: in many economic contexts, preferences are assumed to be exogenous – that the surrounding legal, economic, or social environment does not modify individual preferences. However, in many real-life situations, preferences cannot be taken as given, but are affected by the external environment. In these cases, preferences are said to be endogenous – that external factors, such as law, social institutions, experience, or education, affect individual preferences. In the law and economics literature, preferences are modeled as exogenous or endogenous according to the problem at hand. For most legal problems, the assumption is that individuals optimize in response to their preferences and to the external legal and financial constraints that they face: preferences are treated as exogenous. In other applications, preferences are instead treated as endogenous; in these cases, the law "shapes" individual preferences through the expression and internalization of the values expressed by the law. Recently the law and economics literature has studied the expressive effects of law, considering the way in which legal rules can affect individual preferences and social norms. See also ***expressive law***.

Endowment effect: also known as divestiture aversion, this refers to the finding that people tend to assign more value to their own goods than to comparable goods that they have not owned or possessed. Empirical and experimental research has shown that individuals systematically ask for higher prices for goods assigned to their possession, while they name a lower price for goods they do not possess. The endowment effect widens the distance between the willingness to accept (WTA) and the willingness to pay (WTP): a person may refuse to sell a good he or she possesses even though the offered price is higher than what he or she would be willing to pay to acquire the same good in the first place. Thaler identified this departure from rational choice in 1980, in an article on consumer choice involving the allocation of fungible goods, such as coffee mugs and chocolate bars. The endowment effect constitutes a specific form of status quo bias. The endowment effect can reinforce the loss aversion bias in the presence of market downturns, which push market prices below buying prices. Empirical research shows the presence of the endowment effect both on the real estate market and the financial market. See also *endowment effect theory, willingness to pay versus willingness to accept, reference points, indifference criterion of perfect compensation, contingent valuation, behavioral law and economics*, and *legal endowment effect*.

Endowment effect theory: one of the most common explanations of the so-called endowment effect (i.e., of the observed gaps between an individual's willingness to pay [WTP] and his or her willingness to accept [WTA]. Endowment effect theory is an application of prospect theory. In behavioral law and economics, endowment effect theories have been used in both descriptive and prescriptive analyses. Plott and Zeiler (2007) have suggested that many asymmetries in consumer behavior have been mistakenly interpreted as evidence of endowment effect theory and prospect theory, but are instead attributable to other problems of consumer choice. See also *prospect theory, endowment effect, loss aversion, willingness to pay versus willingness to accept, settlement versus trial, behavioral law and economics*, and *legal endowment effect*.

Enforcement costs: a form of transaction cost (also called "policing costs") associated with ensuring that the other party to an agreement abides by the terms of the agreement. Enforcement costs may be further analyzed as being composed of detection costs and litigation costs, for which the enforcement mechanism is the courts. See also *marginal deterrence* and *litigation costs*.

English auctions: ascending-price auctions in which an auctioneer begins with the lowest acceptable price (the reserve price) and takes successively higher bids until no one is willing to increase the bid. The highest bidder is then the winner of the auction and pays a price corresponding to his or her winning bid (first-price auctions) or a price corresponding to the second highest bid (second-price auctions). English auctions can also be utilized in procurement auctions, in which case the English auction operates with sequential descending prices and the procurement is adjudicated to the lowest bidder. See also *first-price auctions, second-price auctions, Dutch auctions, common-value auctions*, and *auction theory*.

English rule: see *fee shifting*.

Entitlement principle: a central tenet of the libertarian theory of distributive justice, and a justification for "minimal state" governance. According to the entitlement principle, an allocation of resources is just so long as those who possess holdings are entitled to those holdings either through an initial acquisition of the title or through the legitimate transfer of title. In *Anarchy, State, and Utopia* (1974), Nozick illustrates the entitlement principle by asking the reader to envision a perfectly just distribution of resources at time T_0. Between T_0 and T_1, Nozick stipulates that every citizen willingly pays $0.25 directly to Wilt Chamberlain in exchange for his appearance in basketball games. At T_1, the distribution of resources will be unbalanced, since Chamberlain will have significantly more resources, and each spectator slightly less. Nozick argues that, while many principles of distributive justice obligate the state to redistribute wealth to correct for the imbalance (for instance, the Rawlsian state), under the entitlement principle the general allocation of resources at T_1 would be just so long as each of the $0.25 transactions were voluntary and legitimate. See also ***Rawls, John***.

Entropy: building upon the literature on property fragmentation (Heller, 1998; Buchanan and Yoon, 2000), Parisi (2002) and Schulz, Parisi, and Depoorter (2002) suggest that property is subject to a fundamental law of entropy. In the property context, entropy induces a one-directional bias toward increasing fragmentation. This bias is driven by asymmetric transaction costs: it is often harder to reunite separated property bundles than to break them apart. Parisi hypothesizes that courts and legislators account for the presence of asymmetric transaction costs and correct for the problem through the selective use of remedies and by selecting default rules designed to minimize the total deadweight losses of property fragmentation. See also ***anticommons***, ***asymmetric Coase theorem***, and ***holdout problem***.

Entry barriers: see ***barriers to entry***.

Entry deterrence: see ***strategic entry deterrence***.

Epstein, Richard Allen (1943–): a very influential legal scholar, who has written widely on a large number of subjects; he may be best known for his controversial advocacy and economic analyses of personal property rights. Epstein earned a B.A. (summa cum laude) from Columbia University in 1964, and a B.A. in jurisprudence from Oxford University (first-class honours) in 1966. He received his LL.B. from Yale Law School in 1968. Epstein taught at the University of Southern California Law School from 1968 to 1972. He then moved to the University of Chicago Law School, where he spent most of his career. He is currently the Laurence A. Tisch Professor of Law at New York University School of Law, although he continues to teach for part of the year in Chicago. One of the most prolific and frequently cited legal scholars, his most influential works include *Takings: Private Property and the Power of Eminent Domain* (1985), which was the locus of much debate during the confirmation hearings of Justice Clarence Thomas, and which has subsequently been cited by the US Supreme Court on a number of occasions, and *Simple Rules for a Complex World* (1995a), in which he gives a systematic presentation of his perspective on the law. Although he is often considered a "conservative," his views hew more closely to "libertarian." His work is strongly influenced by philosophers John Locke and Robert Nozick, and economists Adam Smith and Friedrich Hayek.

Equilibrium: see *Nash equilibrium*.

Equilibrium selection: this process identifies reasons for the players of a game to select a certain equilibrium over another in the presence of multiple equilibria. This concept appears to be especially relevant in the evolutionary game theory. In this branch of game theory, different methods of equilibrium selection are used depending on what a player values in the different equilibria, even if other players deviate. Economic theory has proposed refinements of the equilibrium concept in order to identify a way to select between multiple equilibria. In some real-life situations, the selection of equilibrium may occur through the use of information that is not present in the analytical formalization of the game. According to the theory of focal points (Schelling, 1960), players may naturally converge toward those equilibria that are focal, for example because they offer higher payoffs, or appear to be naturally more salient, or more fair, or safer. Legal systems, social norms, and conventions serve as important focal points, and in some cases can be used to facilitate convergence toward socially desirable equilibria. Another criterion is represented by Pareto-dominance (payoff dominant): a Nash equilibrium that Pareto-dominates the other will be preferred by players in the game if they are able to talk before the game is played. Another criterion is represented by risk dominance: a Nash equilibrium characterized by a lower payoff variance with respect to any opponent's strategy will be preferred. Different criteria may lead players to choose different equilibria. In the stag hunt game, "stag, stag" is the Pareto-dominant equilibrium, while "rabbit, rabbit" is the risk-dominant one. See also *multiple equilibria, focal point, subgame-perfect strategy equilibrium*, and *Pareto-dominant equilibrium*.

Equity motivation: see *inequity aversion*.

Erasmus Mundus: see *Erasmus program in law and economics*.

Erasmus program in law and economics: this consists of a network of universities to promote the study and teaching of law and economics. In 2004 the Erasmus program in law and economics received recognition by the European Union as an Erasmus Mundus program, which allowed the expansion of the European Master in Law and Economics (EMLE) degree to an international level. The membership of the Erasmus program has changed over the years. Current members include the universities of Aix-en-Provence, Bologna, Ghent, Haifa, Hamburg, Manchester, Mumbai, Rotterdam, Vienna, and Warsaw, with the external participation of George Mason University and the University of California at Berkeley, through an exchange program. See also *Vanderbilt Ph.D. in law and economics, EMLE*, and *EDLE*.

Error learning: see *adaptive expectations*.

ESS: see *evolutionary stable strategy*.

Euclidean preferences: Euclidean preference profiles are used to represent individual preferences over alternatives in a multidimensional space: an individual prefers alternatives closer to his or her ideal point more than alternatives farther away. Euclidean preferences are often used in spatial voting models, in which policy alternatives are represented as points in a multidimensional policy space. See also *spatial voting*.

European Association of Law and Economics: see *EALE*.

*European Journal of Law and Economics***:** established in 1994 under the joint editorship of Jürgen Backhaus and Frank Stephen; Backhaus is currently the editor-in-chief. The journal has given particular attention to the intellectual history of law and economics, with occasional articles on the precursors and founding fathers of the discipline. See also *law and economics journals*.

Evolution of cooperation: the traditional prisoner's dilemma demonstrates how rational agents will choose not to cooperate, even though mutual cooperation is both socially and personally preferable to mutual defection. Traditional "solutions" to the prisoner's dilemma generally rely upon Hobbesian governments to restructure the expected payoffs of agents, thereby transforming the dilemma into a game with equilibrium at cooperation. In 1981 Axelrod and Hamilton presented an alternative solution that demonstrated how cooperation can become established among rational individuals without government intervention. In *The Evolution of Cooperation*, Axelrod (1984) expanded on the earlier paper and showed that, when cooperative and defecting strategies were conceptualized as properties of populations that interact through iterated prisoner's dilemmas with different individuals, mixed cooperative strategies provide greater average returns for players than perpetual defectors. Axelrod conducted a computerized tournament of iterated prisoner's dilemmas using as the input a number of potential pure and mixed strategies from scholars around the world. Axelrod's tournament indicated that the highest-yielding strategy was "tit for tat," a strategy of initial and continuous cooperation until the other party defects, at which point the first party reciprocates with defection. Tit for tat is a forgiving strategy, which means that, after one defection and as soon as the opponent resumes cooperation, the first player also returns to cooperation. Lauded for describing the origins of positive and negative reciprocity, and altruism, Axelrod's work illuminates how conditional cooperation can be justified. Axelrod's experiment provides an early example of the extensive and growing literature characterized as evolutionary game theory. Like Axelrod's experiment, this literature shows that the choice of optimal strategies often depends on the environment – an environment that, in turn, is affected by the individual players' decisions. See also *evolutionary game theory*, *tit for tat strategies*, *grim strategies*, *chain store paradox*, and *folk theorem*.

Evolution of property rights: see *origins of property*.

Evolutionary game theory: this developed as a method for analyzing strategic behavior when interactions are repeated indefinitely between large sets of players, and when persistently successful strategies displace unsuccessful strategies. Evolutionary game theory differs from traditional game theory in that it characterizes strategies as traits or meta-strategies rather than as choice alternatives – traits that either thrive or perish depending on the outcomes of iterated interactions. In evolutionary game theory, the choice of optimal strategies depends on the environment – an environment that is, in turn, affected by the individual players' decisions. As such, evolutionary game theorists stress that no assumptions about rationality are implicit in evolutionary games; strategies that perform poorly over time "die off," while high-performing strategies grow within the population (Maynard Smith and Price, 1973). Since strategies are not selected through rational optimization, evaluative concepts such as dominance and the Nash equilibrium are inapplicable to evolutionary games. However, the evolutionary analogue to the Nash equilibrium is the evolutionary stable strategy (ESS). If a strategy that predominates in a population strategy cannot be "invaded" by alternative strategies, that strategy is an ESS. For instance, driving on the right-hand side of the road in the United States is an ESS, since the "mutant genotype" of left-side drivers will not perform as well as right-side drivers when there are disproportionately more right-side drivers than left-side drivers. Evolutionary game theory was a central tool in Axelrod's *The Evolution of Cooperation* (1984), which explains how the cooperative strategy "tit for tat" emerges as the highest-return strategy in iterated prisoner's dilemmas. However, notwithstanding the success of tit for tat, it is not an evolutionary stable strategy, since persistent defectors or cooperators can successfully invade. The findings of this literature are of great relevance for law and legal policy, identifying conditions for the emergence and sustainability of social cooperation. The findings of evolutionary game theory provide a valuable criterion for the choice of legal instruments and for the optimal timing of legal intervention. See also *evolution of cooperation*, *evolutionary stable strategy*, *tit for tat strategies*, and *strategic complexity*.

Evolutionary stable strategy: a fundamental concept in evolutionary game theory, and also known as an ESS. An ESS is a strategy that, if adopted by most of a population, cannot be "invaded" by mutant strategies – in other words, strategies that are unfavorable to alternatives. As such, an ESS, unlike game theory concepts such as the Nash strategy, dominant strategy or the Nash equilibrium, is highly sensitive to the initial distribution of strategies in the overall population. An ESS is called a "pure" ESS if one strategy is played by all individuals all the time. An ESS may be a "mixed" ESS if either (a) individuals play mixed strategies asynchronously (e.g., 60 percent chance of cooperation, 40 percent chance of defection) or (b) discrete populations play pure strategies against one another such that no alternative strategy can invade. For instance, driving on the right-hand side of the road in the United States is a pure ESS, since no alternative will do as well as right-side driving when the American population consists predominantly of right-side drivers. Evolutionary game theory was a central tool in Axelrod's 1984 book *The Evolution of Cooperation*, which explains how the cooperative strategy "tit for tat" emerges as the highest-return strategy in iterated prisoner's dilemmas. However, notwithstanding the success of tit for tat, it is not an ESS, since persistent defectors can successfully invade. See also ***Nash equilibrium***, ***dominant strategy equilibrium***, and ***evolutionary game theory***.

Ex ante versus ex post: "Ex ante" and "ex post" are terms commonly used in legal discourse to describe conditions prior to an event and subsequent to an event, respectively. In designing legal rules, policymakers are generally concerned with the ex ante effects of the rule (i.e., the incentives created by the rule on the relevant parties). In the application of legal rules, ex post considerations are also relevant. These may include ex post considerations about equity and the distributive effects of the decision. Because specific legal remedies are meant to incentivize ex ante conduct, but typically have an ex post application to heterogeneous cases, the distinction takes on heightened significance in the economic analysis of law. See also ***acoustic separation***.

Ex post renegotiation: see ***no ex post renegotiation assumption***.

Excludable: economic theory identifies two essential elements of private goods: excludability and rivalry in use. The term "excludability" refers to the fact that the owner or possessor of a private good can exclude others from using, entering, or enjoying it. Unlike common goods and public goods, which would often be too costly to protect from outsiders (non-excludable), private goods are relatively easy to protect. For example, using a password to protect one's home internet service is an easy and affordable way to protect the internet service – a private good – from outsiders. Similarly, a person could easily fence in a yard or lock a tool shed, in order to exclude others. Cooter and Ulen (2008) argue that efficiency dictates the distinction between public and private goods. Because it is easy to enforce ownership rights over private goods, it is efficient that they be privately owned. The community as a whole should own public goods, which cannot be so easily protected by individuals.

Exit/voice model: the concepts of "exit" and "voice" were introduced into the organizational theory literature by Hirschman's (1970) book *Exit, Voice, and Loyalty: Responses to Decline in Firms, Organizations, and States*. The terms refer to different ways to express dissatisfaction within an organization. With "exit," a dissatisfied member of an organization leaves the organization. Alternatively, a dissatisfied individual can continue to work within the organization and "voice" his discontent, in an attempt to change the dissatisfying situation. The concepts have been used in the public choice and law and economics literature to refer to different ways to express views in a collective decision-making context. Voting through voice may be relatively ineffective in large groups and organizations, and "voting with one's feet" by exiting an unsatisfactory organization may at times be more practical and effective. The exit/voice models have been used to provide a theoretical explanation for certain phenomena in the labor market. For example, some studies indicate that, counter-intuitively, unionized workers are less satisfied with their employment than non-unionized workers. Bender and Sloane (1998) consider the hypothesis that this may be explained on the basis of the exit/voice model. Dissatisfied non-unionized workers are less likely to appear on surveys because they will quit after reaching a certain level of dissatisfaction. Unionized workers, on the contrary, will be more likely to stay on and express their dissatisfaction through the various mechanisms that unions provide for voicing complaints. Put differently, the dissatisfied and non-unionized workers exited, while the unionized and dissatisfied workers voiced their dissatisfaction through the union. Therefore, the dissatisfaction of unionized workers was more conspicuously present on worker surveys, while dissatisfied non-union workers were no longer available to respond to the survey. See also *voting with your feet*.

Exogenous preferences: see *endogenous versus exogenous preferences*.

Exogenous variables: a variable is exogenous in an economic model when the value of the variable is determined outside the economic system (as opposed to an endogenous variable). In consumer theory, the prices of the consumption goods are determined exogenously. Similarly, input prices are exogenous variables in production theory. In a law and economic setting, the care level choices of a tortfeasor or a prospective victim are affected by the applicable liability rule. With respect to that choice, the liability rule is exogenously determined by the legal system. The care choices of the parties are (endogenously) influenced by the liability rule, but the legal system's choice of liability rule is exogenous and is not affected by the specific choice of the parties involved. See also *endogenous variables*.

Expectation damages: contract law provides remedies for breach of contract. In the majority of cases, contract law redresses a breach of contract by ordering the payment of contract damages, although under certain conditions the promisee can obtain specific performance of the obligation. One way to calculate damages for breach of contract is to pay the non-breaching party an amount equivalent to the benefit expected from the contract. Scholars and courts refer to this type of damages as expectation damages. These are the amount of damages necessary to make the non-breaching party indifferent between performance and breach. In economic terms, expectation damages bring the promisee on the same indifference curve he or she would have been in the case of performance. By linking damages to the forgone benefit of the contract, expectation damages produce a full internalization of the externality caused by the breach. The law and economics literature has shown that expectation damages create optimal incentives for performance and breach, encouraging performance when performance is efficient, and allowing for breach when performance is inefficient (efficient breach). Facing expectation damages, the promisor will perform unless his or her benefit from breaching exceeds the expected benefit of the promisee. In that case, the promisor will breach and pay the promisee expectation damages, leaving both parties in the same position as, or better off than, they would have been absent the breach. However, expectation damages can create an excessive level of reliance for the promisee. Courts correct this problem by liquidating expectation damages based on reasonable reliance; losses that are attributable to unreasonable reliance are not compensated. See also *incentives*, *perfect expectation damages*, *reliance*, *reliance damages*, *efficient breach*, and *zero marginal damages*.

Expectation utility: see *disappointment prevention principle*.

Expectations: see *rational expectations*.

Expected utility: expected utility theory is a rational choice model under uncertainty. The theory was first introduced by Bernoulli (1954 [1738]) and subsequently formalized by von Neumann and Morgenstern (1944). According to expected utility theory, rational agents evaluate risky outcomes on the basis of a utility function of the payouts, the probability of each uncertain outcome, and the attitude toward risk. The expected utility framework takes into account individual risk preferences. For a risk-averse individual, the expected utility of a gamble is lower than the utility associated with the expected payoff, $U^e < U(w^e)$. Expected utility theory has been introduced as an alternative criterion to the expected value criterion, solving the well-known St. Petersburg paradox. See also *risk preferences* and *St. Petersburg paradox*.

Experience goods versus search goods: consumers (and buyers, in general) are generally less informed than producers (and sellers) about the qualities of products and services in the market. Nelson (1970) introduced the distinction between what he calls "search goods" and "experience goods," based on the different ways with which consumers can acquire information about the product or service. For search goods, the quality can be observed in advance, prior to acquiring and consuming the good. With experience goods, the quality can be ascertained only through the use or consumption of the product or service (e.g., vintage wine, legal services, therapeutic treatments). Experience goods pose greater difficulties in terms of correcting asymmetric information problems, because the information can be acquired only after the purchase of the product or service. Economists have also pointed out that, in the absence of ex ante information, consumers tend to infer information about quality from price. This may create some price inelasticity: consumers may think that a cheaper good must be of lower quality, and consequently not be attracted by lower prices. The low price elasticity of experience goods relative to search goods may undermine competition in the respective market. Consumers of experience goods cope with asymmetric information by trying to obtain third-party information (e.g., consumer ratings, reputation). Producers of experience goods try to mitigate the asymmetric information though signaling (e.g., offering a right to return the good, or providing satisfaction warranties). A special category of experience goods is known as credence goods (also referred to as "post-experience goods"). With credence goods, consumers cannot even acquire information about the quality after consumption. The quality may be revealed after some extensive period of time, or it may never be ascertained (e.g., life-extending food supplements, medical treatments, education). These goods are called credence goods because the value of these goods often hinges upon the consumer's belief or credence. Like experience goods, credence goods may exhibit an inverse relationship between price and the value attributed by the consumer, with a resulting low price elasticity. See also *asymmetric information*, *adverse selection*, and *inverse adverse selection*.

Experimental law and economics: scholars in the field of law and economics study the effect of law on human behavior both theoretically and empirically. The empirical approach to law and economics includes the use of experiments. The use of experiments to test law and economics theories has become particularly important during the last two decades, and is known as experimental law and economics. The work of Smith and Thaler has played an important role in laying the methodological foundations for experimental law and economics, and experimental economics in general. In law and economics, experiments have been used to test existing theories, but they have also led to the development of new theories. Much of the literature on behavioral law and economics developed at the interface of the experimental literature. Experiments are used to test and to calibrate existing theoretical models: for example, a theoretical model can predict that the adoption of strict liability versus simple negligence should not affect the level of care, but may affect the activity level adopted by prospective tortfeasors. Empirical data and experimental methods can be used to test and calibrate this theory. Experiments can test whether the care level of tortfeasors is not affected by the choice of liability rule, and can provide information to calibrate the effect of liability rules on the activity level. The theoretical model provides qualitative predictions (e.g., telling us that the activity level should be lower under strict liability), while the empirical and experimental findings could help us develop quantitative predictions (e.g., telling us how much lower activity levels will actually be). Arlen and Talley (2008) point out that many law and economics theories, as well known as the Coase theorem, have been tested using experiments. The experimental testing and calibration of a theoretical model is a fundamental step to validate and to give predictive value to a theory used to inform future legal policy. See also *behavioral law and economics*, *neuroeconomics*, *Smith, Vernon*, *Kahneman, Daniel*, *laboratory experiment*, *salience and dominance in experiments*, and *calibration*.

Exponential discounting: the present value of an anticipated future good is ordinarily thought to be less than the value of the same good consumed currently.

Economists calculate the difference between the present value of a future good and the value of an equivalent present good by multiplying the value of the future good by a discount factor. The discounting effect is "exponential" when the discount function is $\sum_{t_A}^{t_B} \delta^{t_B - t_A}$. Traditionally, economists have favored exponential discounting, because it is time-consistent (e.g., the discount effect is equal as between t_m and t_{m+1} versus t_n and t_{n+1}) and therefore theoretically convenient. However, empirical evidence suggests that humans and animals both use hyperbolic discounting rather than exponential discounting in assessing future consumption (Chung and Herrnstein, 1961; Ainslie, 1992). See also ***hyperbolic discounting*** and ***discounting***.

Expressive law: expressive law theories revisit the traditional price theory conceptions of law as an incentive mechanism, developing a richer theory of how legal rules can affect human behavior. According to expressive law theories, the expression of values is an important function played by the law (Cooter, 1998, 2000b). Through expression the law can trigger the emergence of other incentives by the internalization of the values it embodies. Expressive laws affect behavior, not by threatening sanctions or promising rewards but by changing individual preferences and tastes and, in some cases, by affecting social norms and values. This distinguishes expressive law theories from traditional theories, focused as they are on the role of law as an instrument for creating external incentives, such as taxes, sanctions, and rewards. According to expressive law theories, internalized rules may trigger private enforcement mechanisms and change observed patterns of behavior even in the absence of other external incentives. According to this literature, private enforcement mechanisms include three main interrelated situations, known as first-party, second-party, and third-party enforcement. These three interrelated mechanisms are important ingredients of the expressive effects of law. Expressive law theories, by shedding light on the role of law in shaping social values and norms, point to the relevance of legal intervention and the important responsibility of lawmakers as prospective norm entrepreneurs. See also ***expressive theory of punishment, focal point theory of law, private enforcement, first-party enforcement, second-party-enforcement, third-party enforcement, incentives***, and ***dynamic models***.

Expressive theory of punishment: scholars have long debated the justifications for and purposes of criminal punishment. One such explanation for punishment is the expressive theory of punishment. This holds that punishment holds a largely communicative purpose (Davis, 1991). Criminal punishment serves to condemn a criminal morally for his or her acts. This moral condemnation happens in plain sight of the rest of the world (Bennett, 2011) and produces effects that exceed the cost imposed by the sanction. Legal sanctions no longer operate as a "price" attached to a given behavior, but produce additional effects through expression and internalization (Cooter, 1998, 2000b). Punishment rebukes the criminal for his or her actions in the eyes of society at large. Scholars disagree about whether this communicative function is right in and of itself and is focused backward on the crime and the criminal (Bennett, 2011), or whether it is focused toward the future and results in desirable consequences (Duff and Green, 2011). Other scholars argue that a democratic state lacks the type of political and moral authority needed to justify condemnatory punishment (Bennett, 2011). See also *expressive law*.

Expressive voting: the rational abstention paradox notes that voters incur costs to participate in elections, even though their vote will almost certainly not impact the outcome of the election. One of the ways with which the rational abstention paradox has been explained is by saying that voting has an expressive function: voters receive direct utility from the act of voting, making it rational to vote even when their vote is not decisive. An important implication of the expressive theory of voting, first proposed by Buchanan (1954), and further developed by Tullock (1971a) and Brennan and Lomasky (1993), is that, if individuals choose to vote as an act of expressive behavior, their vote will be more likely to reflect their true values or moral beliefs than the pursuit of their own narrow self-interest. In other words, a voter can vote for a policy or candidate in order to make an expressive statement about his or her preferences, even if that policy or candidate is harmful to his or her rational economic interests (Brennan, Kliemt, and Tollison, 2002). Buchanan (1954) uses the example of a voter who votes for policies or candidates who support the poor, even if that means he or she will face higher taxation as a result. As public choice theorists put it, thanks to expressive voting individuals will "vote with their heart, not with their wallet." In the midst of the widespread skepticism of public choice scholars about voting, expressive voting theory emerges as a note of positive wisdom. See also *rational abstention* and *rational ignorance*.

Extensive-form games: see *normal-form versus extensive-form games*.

External diseconomies: see *externalities*.

External economies: see *externalities*.

External preferences: a term used in legal theory to describe preferences regarding the well-being of others. These types of preferences are generally studied by economists with the use of interdependent utility functions. Utilitarian models generally aim at maximizing aggregate utility by taking into account all individual preferences – be they internal or external – without questioning their content. Dworkin (1977) poses an important critique to this conception of utilitarianism. Utilitarian welfare functions that indiscriminately take into account all external preferences might lead to highly undesirable policy outcomes. Imagine a case in which envy, group prejudice, or even malice are involved. If the utilitarian calculus takes into account such external preferences, quite undesirable policies could follow. Even allocations of wealth that might appear Pareto-superior could be excluded to satisfy unsavory external preferences. See also *interdependent utility functions*, *meddlesome preferences*, and *utilitarianism*.

Externalities: a form of market failure. An externality is either a cost (a negative externality) or a benefit (a positive externality) imposed on a third party outside the voluntary mechanism of the marketplace. The creator of the externality neither pays nor receives any compensation for the "external effect". The externality is the value of the uncompensated effect to a third party. In the presence of externalities, the market equilibrium fails to maximize the sum of the producer surplus and the consumer surplus. Externalities create a divergence between privately optimal and socially optimal equilibria. The intersection of the demand curve and the social cost curve determines the optimal output level. However, in the presence of externalities, the market equilibrium quantity differs from the socially optimal output level. More specifically, negative externalities lead markets to produce a larger quantity than is socially desirable, while positive externalities lead markets to produce a smaller quantity than is socially desirable. Relevant examples of negative externalities include accident losses, the effects of crime on victims and society, and environmental pollution. Relevant examples of positive externalities include private policing, immunizations, and spillover effects in research or technology. The "internalization of an externality" is the term used to refer to the set of instruments used to induce people to take account of the external effects of their actions. The economic literature has identified several ways through which externality-based problems can be corrected, including private solutions (such as mergers and integration), Coasean bargaining and contracting, Pigouvian taxes and subsidies (such as environmental pollution taxes for negative externalities, and industrial policy subsidies for industries creating positive externalities), regulatory solutions (such as safety regulations and controls on dangerous activities), and mixed solutions. See also *spillovers*, *market failures*, *internalization*, *Coase theorem*, *Pigouvian taxes*, *reverse liability rule*, and *harm principle*.

Extralegal means of enforcement: see *private enforcement*.

F

Fads: see *herding behavior*.

Fairness: see *taste for fairness*.

Fairness equilibrium: a Nash equilibrium in the presence of a degree of reciprocity, either positive or negative, in the objective function of the players. This equilibrium notion was introduced by Rabin (1993), who studied the role of procedural reciprocity by introducing the kindness function in the context of psychological games, a concept introduced by Geanakoplos, Pearce, and Stacchetti (1989). Psychological games are distinguished from traditional games, in that they account for beliefs as well as choices in terms of the determination of players' motivations. The idea behind the fairness equilibrium is that beliefs regarding the actions of the other players in the game and the way in which those actions affect each individual player's payoff play a crucial role in the definition of the equilibrium strategy. See also *reciprocity*, *kindness function*, *procedural preferences*, and *reciprocity-induced cooperation*.

False consensus bias: this describes an individual's tendency to regard his or her own opinions as normal and to assume that others think and behave in a similar manner. Individuals who exhibit a false consensus bias tend to believe that their opinions, beliefs, and behavior are more popular and widely accepted than they are in fact. This bias leads people to overestimate the amount that others agree with them, imagining a "consensus" that is absent in reality. False consensus bias is common among overconfident individuals. See also *social projection bias*, *self-serving bias*, *false uniqueness bias*, and *optimism bias*.

False negative: see *type I and type II errors*.

False positive: see *type I and type II errors*.

False uniqueness bias: a term describing the tendency to regard oneself as better than most other people. This bias leads people to believe that they have greater abilities and can make better decisions than others. False uniqueness bias is common among individuals who tend to be overconfident and those who exhibit unrealistic optimism. See also *optimism bias*, *false consensus bias*, *social projection bias*, *self-serving bias*, and *behavioral law and economics*.

Falsifiability: a concept generally associated with Popper's (1959) critique of the scientific method. The falsifiability of an hypothesis identifies the logical possibility of contradicting an assertion on the basis of an observation or the outcome of an experiment. In many fields of human inquiry, the concept of falsifiability has triggered a paradigmatic shift in scientific research. Several theories and methodologies in economics have undergone the strict scrutiny of the falsifiability test. Allegations of non-falsifiability have been raised against some of the core results of economics, ranging from the essential theorems of game theory to the propositions of the Coase theorem – none of which were originally formulated as falsifiable and testable hypotheses. Kuhn (1962) has criticized Popper's paradigm of theory testing through falsification, warning against the risk that the incompleteness or imperfection of the existing data could lead to the rejection of otherwise sound theories. See also ***assumptions***, ***robustness***, and ***Ockham's razor***.

Fee shifting: in litigation, parties spend significant amounts of resources to pay for this representation, in the hope of achieving some sort of victory, either through trial, adjudication, or settlement. The term "fee shifting" refers to the allocation of these costs between the parties involved in the litigation. Legal systems adopt different rules with respect to fee shifting. The United States uses what is often called the "American rule," which bars the winner from shifting significant amounts of his or her attorney's fees on to the loser. The "English rule," on the other hand, does allow the winner to engage in fee shifting, transferring his or her attorney's fees on to the loser. Many scholars regard fee shifting as a desirable instrument for discouraging frivolous litigation. Law and economics scholars have studied the effect of fee shifting on the selection of disputes for litigation and on the parties' total expenditures in litigation. Katz and Sanchirico (2010) challenge the theoretical findings of the law and economics literature with a substantial review of empirical analyses of the two rules, and find that scholars and policymakers cannot reliably conclude that adopting the English rule and allowing fee shifting in the United States would actually lead to less frivolous litigation and lower costs. See ***contingent versus conditional fees***.

Field experiment: a popular tool for testing economic theories and hypotheses under controlled real-world conditions. Like natural experiments, field experiments take place in the real world, as opposed to the laboratory. Unlike natural experiments, field experiments usefully combine controlled and naturally occurring events. The main difference between a field experiment and a natural experiment is the fact that, in a field experiment, the independent variable is endogenously determined as part of the experiment. For example, a field experiment in legal policymaking could be used to evaluate the effectiveness of proposed laws or legal programs, by implementing some pilot programs in some communities but not in others. After the implementation of these programs, data is collected to study their effects and unintended consequences. Field experiments deliver valuable information for determining the effectiveness of alternative policies, without requiring a full scale implementation of new laws or policies. By necessity, field experiments take place in a particular economic, geographic, or political environment, and their findings should be used with caution prior to extrapolating general conclusions. The use of field experiments becomes particularly important in areas in which instances of natural experiments are not available. See also *natural experiment*, *laboratory experiment*, and *calibration*.

Filtering effect: many legal rules allow for a sharing of accident losses between the parties. Dari-Mattiacci and De Geest (2005) point out that, in situations in which only one of the parties could have avoided the loss but the court cannot readily establish that party, sharing rules help create ex ante incentives that filter out the most harmful violations. In other words, sharing rules help filter out those violations that created the greatest harm compared to the cost of avoiding them. If the court fully burdened one party, the other party would have no incentives to take precaution, and hence all accidents that that party could have prevented would occur (say 50 percent of the accidents). By sharing the loss (say, fifty-fifty), both parties have some incentives to take precaution and will prevent all accidents that can be prevented at relatively low costs (in the example, at a cost equal to or less than 50 percent of the accident loss). These are precisely the most harmful accidents, because they entail a large net social loss (the harm minus the cost of prevention). See also *activity level versus care level*.

Firm: see *theory of the firm*.

Firm-specific assets: see *asset specificity*.

First theorem of welfare: see *fundamental theorems of welfare*.

First best versus second best: "first best" identifies the efficient equilibrium in the economy (i.e., the solution that maximizes social welfare). The law and economics discipline focuses on regulations that provide first best incentives to agents. The solution of the social objective function identifies the first best outcome. In law and economics, this solution characterizes the ideal behavior of agents. It is frequently the case that such ideal behavior cannot be effectively induced by legal rules. This is often the case when a tradeoff arises between alternative policy objectives. The solutions that provide optimal incentives for attaining such alternative goals are generally referred to in the literature as second best efficient solutions. While there is generally only one first best outcome, multiple "second best" solutions often exist. The weight that policymakers attach to competing policy objectives guides their choice between alternative second best efficient outcomes. In law and economics, Markovits (2008) has been critical of the general theory of second best, given the difficult tradeoffs involved in implementing second best policy choices. See also *efficiency*.

First-degree price discrimination: see *price discrimination*.

First-mover advantage: the advantage obtained by a player who is able to make the first move in a one-shot sequential game or in a repeated game. Legal problems are often characterized by the presence of a first-mover advantage. For example, plaintiffs control the filing of a suit. At times, this opportunity gives them an advantage in choosing between alternative jurisdictions (forum shopping). First-mover advantages may lead to competition between players for appropriating the first move in the game. In the forum shopping example, the race to steal the first move from the other player may consist in a "race to the courthouse." This may be seen when would-be defendants take the initiative to file first as plaintiffs (e.g., by asking for a declaratory judgment or filing for a counterclaim). This race to the courthouse might lead to the filing of cases that might never have been filed, with a possible increase in litigation rates. Procedural rules tend to mitigate the plaintiff's advantages with procedural safeguards, such as the *forum non conveniens*. In the competition literature, it is often observed that firms compete to enter a new market before their competitors, in the hope of securing a first-mover advantage. Empirical evidence shows that the first-mover advantage does not guarantee success but does give firms a competitive short-term, and long-term, advantage. Economists have attempted to explain the first-mover advantage by pointing out that a new entrant in a market faces significant entry barriers; since the first mover has already entered the market, that firm has already faced and, presumably, overcome these barriers (Kerin, Varadarajan, and Peterson, 1992). The study of the social consequences of an individual's first-mover advantage is important in deciding the response of legal systems. A first-mover advantage has distributive effects between the players, but there is not necessarily a deadweight loss for society associated with that advantage. See also ***last-mover advantage***.

First-order assignment: see *first-order rules*.

First-order rules: legal rules determine the initial assignment of rights and the form of legal protection. Ayres (2005) refers to first-order rules as the rules that determine the initial assignment of legal entitlements. For example, a prospective polluter may be granted the first-order entitlement to pollute, giving its neighbors no remedy against its pollution. Alternatively, the neighbors could be granted the first-order entitlement, requiring the factory to compensate the loss caused by pollution (liability rule) or to bargain with the neighbors beforehand to acquire the right to pollute (property rule). The *Restatement (Second) of Torts* directs courts to establish first-order rules that allocate entitlements to those who value them the most. See also ***Coasean bargaining***, ***defendant choice rules***, ***dual chooser rules***, and ***chooser's call/put option***.

First-party enforcement: a concept based on the idea that laws may affect behavior not only through external incentives, such as sanctions or rewards, but also by changing individual preferences and tastes. Social psychological research shows that people have an intrinsic taste for obeying the law, and that citizens tend to internalize the values expressed by the law and obey out of internal respect for the law in general (Tyler, 1990). This intrinsic taste for law abidance triggers first-party enforcement mechanisms, meaning that, independently of the content of the law, violations of legal commands become subjectively more costly. A sense of guilt and shame at committing illegal actions are examples of first-party enforcement. Laws that reflect internalized values can be very effective, inasmuch as first-party enforcement mechanisms require no outlays of resources for monitoring and enforcement. See also *second-party enforcement, third-party-enforcement, social sanctions, private enforcement*, and *expressive law*.

First-price auctions: in these, the highest bidder wins the auction and is awarded the object at a price equal to the amount bid. First-price auctions can also be used in procurement auctions. In this case, the lowest bidder wins the procurement and is paid an amount equal to its bid. Unlike second-price auctions, in first-price auctions bidding one's full private valuation is not a dominant strategy, and bidders tend to bid below their true value. See also *second-price auctions, Dutch auctions, English auctions, common-value auctions*, and *auction theory*.

Fiscal delusion: redistributive fiscal policy is often utilized to provide economic stimulus. However, recent experience has revealed that promoting economic stimulus though redistributive fiscal policy can be highly ineffective. The term "fiscal delusion" has been used to describe the failed attempts to stimulate consumption through redistributive taxation. A possible explanation for the fiscal delusion can be found in the asymmetric wealth effects produced when transferring wealth from one individual to another. Behavioral and experimental economists have observed that people feel differently about gaining wealth from how they feel about losing it. The magnitude of the wealth effects depends on the reference point. Hence, zero-sum redistributions of wealth provokes wealth effects of different magnitude according to whether they involve gains or losses of wealth. Because of loss aversion, those who lose wealth may have a negative wealth effect that is greater than the positive wealth effect of those who receive the transfer. Hence, more is lost than is gained in terms of consumption. Furthermore, reflecting political instability, tax benefits are perceived as transitory, and in line with the permanent income hypothesis (Friedman, 1958), are mostly used toward savings and investments, rather than consumption spending. See also *fiscal illusion* and *wealth effect versus income effect*.

Fiscal federalism: a concept of public finance according to which constituent jurisdictions or states are given discretion on how to spend, distribute, or allocate expenditures. This is usually effected through some form of fiscal autonomy or through federal grants awarded to states, with a corresponding freedom on the part of the local units to determine how to spend the funds. Ordinarily, the local tax revenues and the federal grants are subject to conditions, which direct the objectives or manner in which the funding may permissibly be used. See also *Tiebout competition*.

Fiscal illusion: although public expenditures lead to tangible results and benefit a clearly identifiable group of recipients (e.g., the construction of a new public library or a new highway), the costs are dispersed across a much wider taxpaying community, and the fiscal burden of any individual project is hidden among other government spending programs. This creates a fiscal illusion, with visible benefits and less visible costs, which may lead to excessive public spending and unwise fiscal policy. See also *fiscal delusion* and *capture theory*.

Fitting a regression line: see *regression analysis*.

Flat tax: see *flat tax versus lump-sum tax*.

Flat tax versus lump-sum tax: a flat tax is a tax imposed with a constant marginal rate of taxation, whereas a lump-sum tax is a tax imposed in fixed amount (not *rate*). For example, requiring that everyone pay 25 percent of their income in taxes, regardless of total wealth or income level, is a flat tax. By contrast, requiring that everyone owning a car pay $500 to the government is an example of a lump-sum tax. See also *progressive taxation* and *marginal tax rates*.

Focal point: in game theory, multiple equilibria may arise when applying the Nash equilibrium solution concept. The presence of multiple equilibria generates coordination problems among the players, who may fail to select the equilibrium on which to converge. Communication between the players may overcome these coordination problems. Experimental analysis shows that cheap talk can help players converge on the same equilibrium. In the absence of pre-play communication, players can coordinate tacitly on an equilibrium, guessing how the other players might solve the coordination problem. The concept of focal points, introduced into economic analysis by Schelling (1960), refers to equilibrium solutions that players frequently select because they are recognized as more salient, natural, or relevant. Focal points help players coordinate tacitly on an equilibrium solution. Focal points depend on empirical evidence and not only on a priori reasoning. Experimental studies show that the focal point for meeting in New York in the absence of any communication among parties is the Grand Central Station at noon. According to the focal point theory of law, introduced by McAdams (2000), law is a means of creating focal points that might foster coordination and legal compliance, even in the absence of any enforceable legal sanction. See also *multiple equilibria, coordination games, Pareto-dominant equilibrium, focal point theory of law*, and *cheap talk*.

Focal point theory of law: the idea that law may operate as a focal point was introduced by McAdams (2000), who argues that law acts as a means of creating focal points in the presence of coordination problems. The conventional wisdom in economic analysis suggests that legal rules affect incentives and solve cooperation problems by changing payoffs through the use of sanctions and rewards. The focal point theory of law suggests that law helps individuals coordinate around a solution, even in the absence of any sanction. In the presence of coordination problems, law changes individual expectations as to the equilibrium solution that will be selected by the other persons independently of payoffs. Law influences behavior by providing salience to the chosen solution and making it a focal point. In this way, law helps individuals coordinate on the focal equilibrium, by creating expectations that others will act accordingly. The basic mechanism at play is that expectations, once formed, are self-fulfilling. Individuals prefer to utilize the focal point strategy, even without a payoff change. Law identifies focal points according to the same mechanism associated with third-party communication. However, law often has a comparative advantage. It facilitates coordination on account of the wider publicity, the uniqueness of the message contained within the law, and the higher reputation of government officials selecting the equilibrium solution. In the presence of coordination problems, focal points exist even when individuals have conflicting objectives. Focal points exist in the presence of iterated interactions over time. Legal focal points can substitute for existing conventions. Examples range from traffic regulation to unenforced anti-smoking law, sanctionless rules setting the rights and obligations of users of public spaces (e.g., bike trails, dog parks, sailing waterways), and tenant–landlord relationships. See also *expressive law*, *focal point*, and *multiple equilibria*.

Folk theorem: this characterizes the solution to infinitely repeated games. Since no specific scholar has been attributed the paternity of this theorem, it has been called the "folk" theorem, as being part of the tradition of game theory. The best-known application of the theorem considers the sustainability of cooperation in a prisoner's dilemma game with an infinite number of iterations. In its most general form, the folk theorem states that, for most repeated games, parties who agree upon an equilibrium will maintain that equilibrium if the discounted rate of future returns is roughly equal to the rate of present returns (the discount factor). Hence, parties who can agree upon an equilibrium in a repeat game scenario can have a sustained outcome. Put differently, the folk theorem demonstrates that any feasible and individually rational payoffs can be sustained as an equilibrium outcome in infinitely repeated games if the players are sufficiently "patient" (i.e., if they exhibit a sufficiently low time preference or discount rate). The folk theorem is criticized for merely being descriptive without having any real predictive power. It does not describe or predict what equilibrium parties might agree upon, which is often just a function of bargaining. The folk theorem for an infinitely repeated prisoner's dilemma game may be illustrated with an industrial organization example. Economic analysis shows that, in the absence of a binding commitment, monopolistic cartels cannot be sustained as an equilibrium of a duopoly if firms interact for only one period (in analytical terms, in a static model). The folk theorem demonstrates that, if firms interact for an infinite number of periods and, under some conditions, if they are assumed not to know their final period of activity (as may often be the case in real-life conditions), monopolistic profits can be sustained as an equilibrium outcome of the game, if firms are sufficiently patient (i.e., if they do not heavily discount their future profits). In this simple example, collusion through a monopolistic cartel can be sustained through the following strategy (assume two firms in the market for this example): each firm produces a half of the monopolistic quantity in each period if the other firm has produced half the monopolistic quantity in the previous period, and each firm produces the Bertrand quantity for the rest of the game if the other firm has produced any other quantity in the previous period. This strategy is called the "grim trigger" strategy, in the sense that, if the other player deviates from the desired outcome, the player punishes the opponent with retaliatory defection, starting from the period after the deviation and continuing for all subsequent periods. See also *prisoner's dilemma, chain store paradox, evolution of cooperation, evolutionary game theory*, and *grim strategies*.

Forward auctions: see *double auctions*.

Forward contracts: see *spot contracts versus forward contracts*.

Forward integration: this refers to the acquisition of the ownership of a down-stream firm by an upstream firm in the supply chain. Forward integration is a type of vertical integration in which the firm's activities are expanded to integrate downstream firms, such as the distributors of products in the supply chain. A farming firm acquiring a distributing or retail company to sell its agricultural products constitutes an example of forward integration. Long-term firm-specific investments are fostered by forward integration, with the improvement of distribution or retail quality. See also *backward integration, vertical integration*, and *double marginalization*.

Forward price: see *spot contracts versus forward contracts*.

Free riding: in economic theory, an individual acts as a "free rider" when he or she contributes to a public good less than his or her share of the good's production cost. Free-riding behavior causes underprovision – or, in the worst cases, no provision – of the public good. Free riding thereby creates a market failure. The term "free rider" originates with the example of an individual who uses public transportation without paying the fare, taking advantage of the public good without contributing to its cost. In the case of public goods, provision by the government with financing through taxation constitutes the main mechanism for addressing the free-riding problem. Free rider problems are pervasive and are not limited to situations of the voluntary provisions of public goods, and generally occur in bargaining situations in which individuals have opaque preferences and there are no mechanisms in place to induce them to reveal their true preferences. See also *collective action problem* and *public good*.

Freiburg school of law and economics: see *Ordoliberalism*.

Friedman, Milton (1912–2006): an important figure in the Chicago school of economics. Although his main body of work was in monetary theory and

consumption analysis, his occasional incursions into the field of law and economics have made him a reference point for several scholars within law and
economics. Milton Friedman was awarded the Nobel Prize in economics in
1976 for his research in the fields of consumption analysis, monetary history,
and theory and for his demonstration of the complexity of stabilization policy.
He was born in Brooklyn, New York, on July 31, 1912. He received his undergraduate degree from Rutgers University in 1932, his Masters degree from the
University of Chicago in 1933, and his Ph.D. from Columbia University in 1946.
Friedman is widely regarded as the leader of the Chicago school of monetary
economics. He advocated the belief that the business cycle is determined primarily by money supply and interest rates rather than by government fiscal policy
(Keynesian theory). In *Capitalism and Freedom* (1962), written in collaboration
with Rose D. Friedman, his wife, Friedman argues that bureaucratized social
welfare services are abhorrent to the traditional values of individualism and
useful work. He proposes that they should be replaced with a negative income
tax or guaranteed income system. More generally, he is known as a leading
advocate of education vouchers and of a free market economy. Milton Friedman
has published many books and articles in economics, most notably *Essays in
Positive Economics* (1953), *The Theory of the Consumption Factor* (1957), *A
Monetary History of the United States* (1963, with Anna Jacobson Schwartz)
Price Theory (1976), and *Monetary Trends in the United States and the United
Kingdom* (1981, again with Anna Schwartz). Milton Friedman's son, David
Friedman, is a physicist by training, but is also an active scholar in the field of
law and economics, and teaches law and economics at the University of Santa
Clara. See also ***Chicago school***.

Frivolous suit: a claim that has no legal basis or merit. Economics scholars often
define these claims as those that plaintiffs bring even though they are aware
that the probability of success at trial does not justify the cost of bringing
the suit. The exact parameters of this definition depend, necessarily, on the
viability of a suit in the context of the existing law and procedure in any
given jurisdiction. Law and economics scholars have shown that a party in a
frivolous suit is not necessarily irrational or misinformed. Frivolous litigation
does not necessarily yield negative expected returns. Parties may engage in
frivolous litigation because they value the delay that litigation brings, or may
want to establish a reputation for carrying out threats, or may derive utility
from the defendant's disutility or from the vindication of their cause. Some
scholars propose that court error incentivizes frivolous suits, in that suits that
appear ridiculous often do prevail. Additionally, frivolous suits are sometimes
attributed to a plaintiff's desire to extract a monetary settlement from a defendant
because the plaintiff knows that the defendant incurs greater costs in going to
trial. However, this type of extortion would be successful only if the plaintiff's
threat to go to trial is credible. For example, in the case in which a plaintiff has
sunk most of the costs up-front (e.g., the plaintiff pays a flat salary to in-house

counsel, and has no other use for the counsel's time), his or her threat to go to trial would be particularly credible and improve his or her bargaining position. A defendant's ignorance of fact or law may likewise impact bargaining; as long as the defendant does not know that the plaintiff's threat is not credible, the plaintiff may be able to extort a settlement.

Functional analysis: see *functional law and economics*.

Functional law and economics: in the 1990s a new generation of literature, known as "functional law and economics," developed at the interface of law, economics, and public choice theory. This literature focuses on the origins and formative mechanisms of legal rules. The resulting approach is quite skeptical of both the normative and the positive schools of law and economics. The functional approach is wary of the generalized efficiency hypotheses espoused by the positive school. In this respect, the functionalists share some of the skepticism of the normative school. Nothing supports a generalized trust in the efficiency of the law in all areas of the law. The functional approach is also critical of the normative extensions and corrective policies that are often carried out by the normative schools. Economic models are a simplified depiction of reality, and normative economic analysis often risks overlooking the many unintended consequences of legal intervention. In this respect, the functionalists are aligned with the positive school in their criticism of the normative approach. Public choice theory provides strong methodological foundations for the functional school of law and economics. According to the functionalist approach, courts and policymakers should thus undertake a functional analysis, investigating the "market conditions" that generated the law (or set of laws) rather than undertaking a cost–benefit analysis of the laws themselves. The functionalist view assumes a certain degree of opacity, which prevents courts and policymakers from usefully determining whether a law is efficient by looking at the law itself. Instead, the functionalist view is that one can infer efficiency if the mechanisms generating the law constitute a sound market. In this way, the functionalist approach to law and economics extends the inquiry to consider the influence of market and non-market institutions (other than politics) on legal regimes, and the comparative advantages of alternative sources of centralized or decentralized lawmaking in supplying efficient rules. See also *Virginia school*, *positive versus normative law and economics*, *Chicago school*, and *Yale school*.

Functional property: in functional property regimes, property rights are assigned on the basis of specific uses of the land (e.g., farming, fishing, hunting, etc.) rather than physical partitions of the property. In these regimes, common in early societies, property is divided along horizontal functional partitions, with different individuals or families owning specific rights over the land related to specific uses, rather than along physical boundaries. Such functional conceptions of property were the natural consequence of the derivation of property from past use and possession of the land: the way in which the land had been used in the past determined the content and scope of functional property rights. For example, those who had used the land to hunt would acquire hunting rights, and those who had raised livestock would have grazing rights in the same geographic area. This system often resulted in multiple property claims coexisting on the same land. Customary rules then regulated the possession, use, and transfer of such functional rights. Such functional divisions often made good sense, because different owners could undertake specialized activities over the same territory with little encroachment on one another. In an economy characterized by low population density and a limited rate of exploitation of natural resources, functional partitions of property were often sustainable, providing an opportunity to allocate the same land toward multiple privately held use rights, allowing an efficient use of the territory, as all parts of the property could be used. Detailed customs, based on past usage and historic rights, determined what was considered acceptable conduct with respect to the interaction (natural externalities) between the various activities. As time progressed, agricultural societies developed a more complex conception of property in which functional partitions of rights survived as exceptions to a regime of unified ownership. This paradigmatic shift is understandable, given that in an agricultural economy the coexistence of multiple rights over the same land created conflicts and increased opportunities for wasteful externalities. Furthermore, functional partitioning of land, while efficient in a stable economy, became unsustainable, creating anticommons problems in conditions of rapid economic change. Moving from pastoral to agricultural economies, many societies thus changed their property systems, abandoning functional property in favor of spatial property (i.e., making their property systems more similar to those we are accustomed to observing in the modern Western world). This transition has a plausible economic explanation. With a rapidly changing economy, optimal uses of land are also subject to rapid flux. The division of property along functional lines, while allowing the optimization of property with respect to all its potential uses, did not provide sufficient flexibility to accommodate structural transformations over time. See also ***bundle of sticks***, ***origins of property***, and ***anticommons***.

Functionings: see ***capability approach***.

Fundamental theorems of welfare: the first and second fundamental theorems of welfare (also simply called theorems of welfare) state that, under competitive conditions, the price system leads to Pareto-optimal allocation (first theorem) and that any efficient allocation can be sustained under competition (second theorem). The first theorem of welfare can be viewed as a mathematical restatement of the ideas expressed by Bernard Mandeville's (1714) *Fable of the Bees: or, Private Vices, Publick Benefits* and Adam Smith's (1776) "invisible hand" conclusion. In a competitive market, self-interested individuals who independently maximize their private well-being will bring about a Pareto-optimal allocation of resources, maximizing the welfare of society. Under fairly standard assumptions, the theorems relate competitive equilibria and Pareto optimality, stating that prices adjust efficiently in response to changes in demand and supply. See also ***Pareto efficiency***.

Futures: contracts whereby goods are sold for a "future price" – a rate that is determined at the time of the agreement, but for which the exchange occurs at some subsequent date. Traders generally utilize futures to hedge market risks. Traders who are holding a good sometimes use futures contracts to protect themselves against a lower price. Those who know they are going to have to buy a good also use futures contracts to protect against a higher price. These types of contracts can also be used to speculate by buyers or sellers who believe that they have better information than the market about the future prices of a good. These types of contracts are considered derivative securities, because their value is derived from some other asset or index. See also ***hedging*** and ***risk management***.

G

Game theory: a field of microeconomics for the study of strategic or interdependent decision-making. A strategic situation arises whenever an agent, seeking to maximize the returns to his or her actions, is placed in a context in which his or her returns may be influenced by the actions of others. The "game" is thus created by the interaction of players, their possible strategies, and the payoffs for each strategy. Virtually every legal problem involves a strategic component (e.g., the precautions of a prospective tortfeasor depend on the expected behavior of his or her victim, and vice versa; the reliance of a promisee in a contract depends on the expected behavior of the promisor; and so on). The analytical tools of game theory become particularly valuable in understanding how human beings make such interdependent decisions. Game theory is used to predict how rational players will behave in strategic situations, or at least to explain how idealized rational players should behave under such circumstances. The representation of strategic situations under the form of games is educational. In games, players devise strategies on the basis of expected countermoves from the other player(s). Many real-life economic situations are characterized by similar strategic interactions, and game theory thus provides a very useful set of tools for strategic decision-making. The foundations of game theory were laid by the monumental work by John von Neumann and Oskar Morgenstern entitled *Theory of Games and Economic Behavior* (1944). See also *Nash equilibrium*, *prisoner's dilemma*, *battle of the sexes*, *chicken game*, and *assurance game*.

Gap-filling rules: see *default rules*.

Gaps in contracts: see *complete contracts*.

Gender gap: the presence of gender differences in social and economic contexts. Empirical evidence shows the presence of a substantial gender wage gap (i.e., an income disparity between the genders and lower female labor force participation and political representativeness). The debate around this concept generally centers on the extent to which this phenomenon is the result of gender differences or discrimination. Industrialization has been accompanied by a narrowing of this gap in highly industrialized countries, but wage disparities are still pervasive in less industrialized countries. Public policy is often designed to reduce the gender gap by introducing regulation that requires equal opportunities for both genders, such as equal pay or political representation.

Gentle nudges: see *hard shoves versus gentle nudges*.

Giffen good: an inferior good characterized by an increasing demand function. In Alfred Marshall's influential treatise *Principles of Economics* (1890), the most widely used economics textbook at the start of the twentieth century, the concept is attributed to the Scottish financial economist Robert Giffen (1837–1910). Interestingly, no mention has been found of the concept in any of Giffen's writings; nevertheless, the appellation is now well established (Taylor, 2011). Giffen goods contradict the law of demand: an increase in the price of a Giffen good leads to an increase in the quantity demanded. The reason for the positive relationship between price and quantity is that the wealth effect created by an increase in the price of a Giffen good dominates the substitution effect. See also ***normal good***, ***inferior good***, ***substitution effect***, and ***wealth effect versus income effect***.

Good Samaritan rule: term used to describe legal rules that govern the obligations of bystanders in situations in which a person is in danger. The legal duties of bystanders to provide rescue to a third party vary greatly across legal systems. Some legal systems adopt a strong Good Samaritan rule, imposing an affirmative duty to rescue when the bystander is in a position to offer rescue without serious risk to him- or herself or to his or her property. Other legal systems adopt a weak Good Samaritan rule, which leaves the bystander free to provide rescue, but incentivizes bystanders to provide rescue by giving them some financial compensation (ranging from simple reimbursement of the reasonable costs incurred during the rescue to higher financial rewards). While several European legal systems adopt some combination of strong and weak Good Samaritan rules, Anglo-American systems do not impose a duty to rescue and do not require the imperiled person to reward the rescuer for his or her activity. Law and economics scholars have examined the incentive effects of the European and Anglo-American solutions. According to standard economic thinking, the European rules are better able to incentivize efficient rescue. First, by compensating the rescuer for low-cost rescues and making a would-be rescuer liable for inaction, the rules incentivize rescue when it is economically efficient to do so (when the cost is relatively low). Second, by requiring that the imperiled person pay for his or her rescue, the European rule incentivizes that person to take the appropriate level of care to avoid the danger in the first place. Economic arguments have also been used in support of the Anglo-American rule. According to these arguments, altruistic motives and social norms, rather than legal or financial incentives, are those that effectively drive bystanders to become rescuers. By making rescue a duty or incentivizing it monetarily, strong and weak Good Samaritan rules corrode the altruistic and social incentives that might induce people to offer voluntary rescue.

Governance structure: a term that has acquired a particular significance in the new institutional economics literature through the work of Oliver Williamson. Williamson (1979, 1991) distinguishes three main types of alternative governance structures: markets, long-term contracts, and corporate organizations.

Like Ronald Coase's (1937) theory of the firm, Williamson uses transaction costs (broadly intended, to include opportunistic behavior) to explain the respective domains of these three forms of organization. The criterion of choice between alternative governance structures is that of "economizing" costs – a concept that Williamson (1979) uses to refer to the sum of production and transaction costs. So, for example, at one end of the spectrum, when transaction costs are negligible, spot markets would be the most cost-effective means of procurement. As transaction costs increase, other governance structures, ranging from relational contracts to corporate governance, may provide preferable alternatives. The law and economics literature has adopted these concepts and terminology to refer to complex relationships between alternative governance structures. See also *contract as governance* and *economizing*.

Graduated consent theory: consent is an important element of the law, from contract to criminal law. Intuition might lead one to believe that the concept of consent is as simple as a person saying either "Yes" or "No" to a visitor who wishes to cross the person's land. However, graduated consent theory holds that consent is a much more complex concept. Bell (2010) argues that there are different grades of consent and unconsent: consent and unconsent can be express, implied, or hypothetical. Bell points out that the existence of different shades of consent can have important consequences for courts and legislatures, which seek to enforce legal documents, laws, and, most importantly, constitutions. Graduated consent theory suggests that courts, scholars, and practitioners should consider the level of consent in any agreement, as well as the nature and the context within which the parties have consented.

Grady's uncertainty theorem: see *Grady–Kahan rule*.

Grady–Kahan rule: traditional tort law held that a negligent tortfeasor was liable for the entire cost of the harm resulting from his or her actions, even if that harm was partially caused by the negligence of the victim. According to the Grady–Kahan rule (Grady, 1983; Kahan, 1989), a victim should receive compensation for only that harm that would *not* have occurred had the tortfeasor taken due care. Put differently, in the event of accidents due to negligence, the amount of liability should not cover the full harm, but should compensate only for the incremental harm caused by the tortfeasor's negligence. This form of causation-incorporating liability shifts to the tortfeasor only the marginal harm caused by his or her negligence, effectively leaving the background risk of non-negligent harm with the victim. The example commonly associated with the Grady–Kahan rule is that of an owner of a baseball field who fails to erect a fence of appropriate height around the field. As an example, imagine that due care would require a ten-foot tall fence, but the owner instead builds a nine-foot tall fence. According to the Grady–Kahan rule, the owner should be liable only for accidents caused by balls that fly over the fence between nine and ten feet above the ground (Faure, 2009). In other words, the owner is liable only for the harms, or portions of harms, caused by his or her negligence. The risk of non-negligent harms rests with the victim. The reduced liability of the Grady–Kahan rule is sufficient to encourage tortfeasors to take due care. Furthermore, given the fact that the risk of non-negligent harms lies with the victim, incentives are also present for victim's precautions. The extent to which the Grady–Kahan rule is descriptive of actual tort law, rather than being prescriptive of an alternative approach in the assessment of liability, is open to debate. See also ***comparative causation***.

Granger causality: regression analysis is useful for establishing correlations but is not useful for establishing causal relationships. The Granger causality is a statistical notion introduced by Clive Granger (1969), according to which a time series of variable X "Granger-causes" a time series of variable Y, when lagged values of X contain information that contributes to predicting Y more than the lagged values of Y itself. Put simply, a Granger test allows the extrapolation of causality information from correlations that have a systematic time lag. Granger causality provides a causality based on the predictive ability of time series but is not sufficient to establish true causality. If both X and Y are the result of a third process with different time lags (e.g., lightning and thunder caused by a storm), one might establish Granger causality, even though the lightning is not the true cause of the thunder. See also ***time series***, ***regression analysis***, and ***instrumental variable approach***.

Grim strategies: these (also known as grim trigger strategies) are used by players to punish other players' deviation from the desired strategy with retaliatory defection, starting from the period after the initial defection and continuing for all subsequent periods. Basically, a grim strategy puts an end to cooperation after a single defection. Grim strategies are much more unforgiving than tit for tat strategies, when retaliatory defection follows for only one period, allowing for cooperation to resume after a round of tit for tat retaliation. In terms of incentives, grim strategies provide maximal ex ante deterrence, but they could prove problematic in case of involuntary deviations due to human error. See also ***tit for tat strategies*** and ***trembling hand***.

Grim trigger strategies: see ***grim strategies***.

Group polarization: in group deliberations, when expressions of belief or voting decisions are made sequentially, late movers may be influenced by the statements of others, discounting their own information signals. Members of the group who hold extremist views or have strong feelings about the issue being deliberated may influence the view of other members of the group. This may lead to a polarization of beliefs. Schkade, Sunstein, and Kahneman (2000) consider the group polarization of jurors who are asked to deliberate on punitive damages. By comparing ex ante valuations and ex post deliberation, the stylized fact is that a jury tends to impose punitive damages in a measure that exceeds the median ex ante valuation, and often approaches the highest ex ante assessment by individual jurors. When faced with a continuum of choices, consensus tends to form toward the extremes rather than at intermediate levels. Sunstein (2000) explores the possible causes of this polarization effect in the jury deliberation process. He identifies a number of plausible explanations for group polarization, including the effect of social influence and the limited "argument pools" within any group. There are several policy implications of these findings. For example, in situations in which polarization is deemed undesirable, procedural rules may be used to randomize the sequence of decisions, preventing extremist members of the group from jump-starting the deliberation process and triggering polarization effects. Alternatively, the polarization associated with sequential decision-making may be avoided by introducing simultaneous decisions or closed-ballot voting by the members of the group. See also *herding behavior* and *informational cascades*.

Group-serving bias: see *self-serving bias*.

H

Hand formula: see *Learned Hand formula*.

Hands tying: a promisor can increase the credibility of his or her promise by cutting off some of its options. Hands tying refers to precommitment strategies that parties can undertake to cut off defection options and to foster cooperative outcomes. The term was introduced into the law and economics literature by Kronman (1985), in an article considering non-legal enforcement mechanisms. Kronman includes hands tying in the list of non-legal enforcement mechanisms, which also features hostages, collateral, and union. Hands tying strategies are defined as self-imposed conditional costs that make performance more appealing than breach for the promisor. For example, by publicly announcing and publicizing the completion date of a public work, a building contractor can credibly precommit to finishing the construction project by the due date. Hands tying generally involves some commitment by the promisor that will force him or her to take on additional losses or costs if he or she fails to perform. When the promisor ties his or her hands, the additional losses will automatically follow his or her breach, without need of action by the promisee. In our example, in the event of late completion, the contractor will face a reputational cost. This conditional cost can create incentives for timely completion even in the absence of legal penalties for late performance. Recent law and economics literature builds upon the findings of new institutional economics for the study of the effects and limits of hands tying as an instrument of contract enforcement. Even though the term was first used in the context of credible promises, its use in the recent literature has become virtually undistinguishable from the term "precommitment strategies" as introduced by Schelling (1966) in the context of credible threats. See also *precommitment strategies*, *self-enforcing contracts*, *hostages*, *collateral*, *union*, *relational contracts*, *cooperative games*, and *non-cooperative games*.

Happiness economics: see *happiness research*.

Happiness research: much of economics relies on notions of utility or happiness, though, until recently, happiness has not been the subject of analytical scrutiny. However, in the past decade interdisciplinary work in psychology, neuroscience, and economics has made substantial progress in measuring happiness in quantitative terms – though the project of reducing happiness to a metric has been seriously questioned by skeptics on a number of fronts. Nevertheless, happiness remains a fertile area of new research and interdisciplinary cooperation. Economists working in happiness research have tended to focus on the relationship between wealth and happiness, but Frey and Stutzer (2008) argue that democracy and social participation play at least as effective a role in determining a person's well-being. See also *neuroeconomics* and *utility maximization*.

Harberger's triangle: in the case of monopoly without price discrimination, monopoly pricing creates a social deadweight loss. The area that represents the social deadweight loss is known as Harberger's triangle. However, in the case of natural monopoly, the existence of a single producer is due to economies of scale in production. By permitting monopolistic production, economies of scale are obtained and production costs are minimized. The area representing these savings in production costs is known as Tullock's rectangle. When doing a welfare analysis of monopoly, it is important to consider the tradeoff between Harberger's triangle and Tullock's rectangle, choosing the appropriate remedies to minimize monopoly deadweight losses without forgoing economies of scale. This argument has been used in antitrust cases when economies of scale have been invoked as an antitrust defense. See also *Tullock's rectangle*, *efficiency defense*, *natural monopoly*, and *Chadwick–Demsetz scheme*.

Hard shoves versus gentle nudges: Kahan (2000) has highlighted the problem presented by sticky social norms. Social norms sometimes reflect troublesome values or views that governments intend to change, by enacting statutes. However, communities will often cling to social norms and refuse to change. These "sticky" social norms resist the efforts of legislators to implement change using new statues. Kahan, acknowledging the need to change some sticky social norms, argues that governments enact statutes that are too strict or that too aggressively penalize the targeted norm. Statutes that depart too much from existing social norms leave a decision-maker (e.g., a police officer enforcing the law, or a juror considering criminal allegations) less comfortable with the law and less likely to apply it. These types of statutes are an attempt by government to give the existing social norms a "hard shove," and they often move too far beyond the existing moral views of society. Kahan argues that governments should instead use "gentle nudges." Instead of trying to push a community too far beyond its own conceptions of right and wrong, governments should take small steps by enacting statutes that only marginally change how the law treats the sticky social norms in question. Decision-makers will be more comfortable with these marginal shifts and will be more likely to apply the new law. See also *backlash effect*, *sticky norms*, and *countervailing norms*.

Harm principle: a basic tenet of both criminal and tort law, governing ordinary human behavior, from the playground to the roadway. The harm principle divides the actions of individuals between those actions that cause harm and those that do not. If a person goes about his or her business and causes no harm to others, his or her actions are upheld and present no problem. However, if a person harms another through his or her actions, the victim of that harm may, or society at large should, be entitled to a legal remedy. Simple as it may appear, the harm principle is a problematic criterion to implement. Virtually all behavior results in positive and negative externalities, and regulating all externalities may be difficult and at times undesirable. Epstein (1995b) points out that the harm principle is widely accepted by governments and citizens. He observes that, in modern times, governments and courts have undertaken an expansive interpretation of the harm principle, and have become more likely to regulate behavior because of that fact. Epstein is critical of this modern approach, which tries to control for too many externalities and could lead to excessive regulation of human behavior. See also *externalities*.

Harsanyi transformation: in game theory, a game of incomplete information can be transformed into a game of complete (but imperfect) information by adding a non-strategic player (called nature), and conditioning each player's payoff on nature's moves. See also *complete versus perfect information*.

Harsanyi's impartial observer theorem: see *impartial observer theorem*.

Hawk–dove game: see *chicken game*.

Hayek, Friedrich August von (1899–1992): is considered to be the most eminent of the modern Austrian economists. His work has been particularly influential for the development of the Austrian approach to law and economics. Hayek received the Nobel Prize in economics in 1974 (shared with Gunnar Myrdal) for his work in the theory of monetary and economic fluctuations and his analysis of the interdependence of social, economic, and institutional phenomena. He was born in Vienna, Austria, on May 8, 1899. Hayek received doctorates in law and political science from the University of Vienna in 1921 and 1923. Most of his work from the 1920s to the 1930s was on the connection between business cycles, capital investment, and monetary policy, concluding that artificially low interest rates lead to overinvestment, which in turn leads to economic "busts." Later he turned to analyzing the role of government in the economy, and, building on the work of his mentor, Ludwig von Mises, he published *The Road to Serfdom* in 1944, probably his most widely known work. In it, he argues that socialism can be maintained only by central economic planning, which ultimately leads to tyranny of a kind no different from that under fascist rule. Hayek's views that the government should intervene as little as possible in the functioning of the free market were fundamental to the founding of the University of Chicago's department of economics, where he was a professor from 1950 to 1962. His large body of work in the various fields of economics, political science, law, philosophy, and psychology are still hugely influential today, and he is seen as one of the most important contributors to the Austrian school of economics, as well as an influential defender of classical liberalism and free market capitalism. See also *Austrian law and economics*.

HDI: see *Human Development Index*.

Hedging: a form of risk management. Unlike diversification, which reduces unsystematic risk in a portfolio, hedging is a form of management of systematic or market risk. Hedging identifies a risk minimization strategy that consists of taking a position in one market to offset a financial exposure in another. Typically, this offset is accomplished with the use of financial instruments, including forward contracts, swaps, options, and futures, or other derivative market instruments. Hedging can be used to defend against a number of market risks, such as commodity risk, which arises from fluctuations of the value of commodity contracts (e.g., agricultural products, metals, and energy products). Other typical "hedgeable" risks are credit risk (e.g., the risk that borrowers fail to pay back the amount of the loan because of changes in the real estate market), currency risk, interest rate risk or equity risk, arising from unforeseen fluctuations of exchange rates, interest rates (in the short or long term) and stock market prices. See also *futures*, *risk management*, *diversification*, and *systematic versus unsystematic risk*.

Hedonic damages: under tort law, when a tortfeasor negligently harms another person, he or she may be liable to that victim for some amount of damages. These damages help compensate the victim, or, in the case of a wrongful death case, the victim's family, for the harm caused. Damages can encompass loss of income, medical costs, and loss of potential earnings if one's ability to work or develop has been permanently impacted. Damages can also reflect intangible factors, such as some valuation of the pain and suffering suffered by the victim. Many jurisdictions also award a victim or a victim's family hedonic damages. Hedonic damages are meant to capture the loss of the pleasure of living life (Berla, Brookshire, and Smith, 1990). Although court recognition of hedonic damages is a recent trend, its aim is to extend damages beyond one's economic productivity and the pain one has suffered. Hedonic damages try to capture what one loses if one is no longer able to live life, or to live life to the fullest. Hedonic damages present several issues, including how best to calculate a concept as amorphous as the value of the pleasure of life. Berla, Brookshire, and Smith also raise difficult questions, including whether the benefit of not experiencing further pain in life should also be calculated. They have proposed a lost pleasure of life scale, but courts continue to differ on how best to calculate hedonic damages. See also *compensatory damages*.

Herding behavior: a situation in which individuals act as a group without planning their course of action. The terminology refers to the behavior of animals in herds or flocks. Economic analysis has extended the term to human behavior in the context of stock market bubbles, sporting and religious events, and, in general, decision-making and judgment formation when the actions of the other individuals in the group are contemporaneously observable. Herding behavior has been analyzed in economic contexts as a mechanism of transmitting behavior between individuals in the form of informational cascades. An early reference to this concept in the field of economics is that by Grossman and Stiglitz (1976), who show that uninformed traders in a market context can infer information from the choice of others in the marketplace. The price becomes a vehicle for the transmission of private information that efficiently aggregates individual preferences into collective valuations. More recent models of herding behavior have focused on the problems associated with this mechanism of information transmission. Banerjee (1992) and Bikhchandani, Hirshleifer, and Welch (1992) show that behavioral cascades and herd behavior can result from the tendency of uninformed individuals to believe that other individuals may possess better information than they do. When uninformed individuals act sequentially on the basis of both their private information and the information they infer from the behavior of others, fads and herding behavior may amplify the errors of the first movers and lead to socially undesirable outcomes. The aggregation of information through the price system in market contexts may therefore be biased. These models have been tested experimentally, and the findings suggest that, although the conditions for inefficient herding behavior may rarely be satisfied in real markets, the consequences of herding behavior in financial markets could be quite severe. See also *informational cascades*, *group polarization*, and *path dependence*.

Heresthetics: the art of structuring and framing alternatives within a choice situation so that people will act rationally in a desired way. William Riker (1986) introduced the concept of heresthetics to bridge the gap between rational choice models of decision-making, in which strategies and payoffs are fixed, and legislative decision-making, in which policy alternatives are dynamic and revisable. In *The Art of Political Manipulation* (1986), Riker notes that "the distinguishing feature of a heresthetic is that voters are induced to change sides, not by persuasion, but by reinterpretation of the issue." Research highlights three major heresthetic strategies: agenda control, manipulation of issue dimensions, and strategic voting. For example, to support a policy replacing homeless shelters with condominiums, a politician can reframe the debate by offering alternative solutions for voting blocks that oppose the condominiums for different reasons (agenda control); by introducing new issues such as environmental sustainability, traffic congestion, and tourism revenue (dimension manipulation), or by strategically controlling decision-making procedures such as voting times (strategic voting).

Herfindahl index: the most common concentration index used to study market structure. The Herfindahl concentration index is calculated by adding the square of the market shares of all firms in the industries. Unlike concentration ratios (expressed in percentage terms), concentration indexes generate less intuitive values but provide a better insight into market structure. The Herfindahl index, by using square values, gives greater weight to larger firms, assuming that market control is an exponential function of market share. Herfindahl indexes can generate values as high as 10,000 for the case of a monopoly and can approach zero for the limit case of an atomistic market. Markets with a Herfindahl index of below 1,000 are generally considered as having low concentration, while those over 2,000 are generally considered as having high concentration. Indexes ranging from 1,000 to 2,000 denote markets with medium concentration. See also *concentration ratio*, *market share*, and *market structure*.

Hierarchies: see *governance structure*.

Hindsight bias: a term used by behavioral economists and psychologists to describe the tendency by people to overestimate the likelihood of an event after they observe its occurrence. Hindsight bias leads individuals to overestimate the accuracy of their predictions of future events if one of their previous predictions turns out to be correct. As an example, consider an individual's ability to predict the final result of a sports game or a political elections: a person might observe that "it is likely that the New York Yankees will win the major league," given his or her general knowledge of tournaments or players' ability. If the New York Yankees win after this statement is made, the person might feel that the prediction was stronger than it really was. The hindsight bias can be explained by the availability heuristic: people tend to give more weight to events that occurred than to other possible events that did not occur. The effects of the hindsight bias can be reduced if the individual is asked to examine a list of possible alternatives to the outcome he or she predicted. Hindsight bias can also affect the accuracy of witnesses in criminal cases, and should be taken into account appropriately, since it may affect witnesses' ability to restore and recall information. See also *availability bias*, *hindsight bias*, *anchoring bias*, *representativeness bias*, *behavioral law and economics*, and *bounded rationality*.

Hobbes theorem: Cooter (1982) introduced the Hobbes theorem as the ideal counterpart to the Coase theorem. If the Coase theorem takes an optimistic view of the ability of private parties to bargain in the absence of government and seeks a government that will eliminate transaction costs and then fade away, the Hobbes theorem takes an entirely different approach. The Hobbes theorem, drawing on Thomas Hobbes' cynical view of humanity, holds that a Leviathan-like government is necessary to reduce the inefficiencies that occur when private bargaining breaks down (Cooter, 1982). Under the Hobbes theorem, government is a necessary institution to foster cooperation and watch over the private bargaining process. Cooter uses the Hobbes theorem as a theoretical counterpart to the Coase theorem. Cooter explicitly states that the Hobbes theorem is a false, but nevertheless useful, concept. The Hobbes theorem should be understood as a metaphor to encourage government to eliminate the "most destructive non-cooperative outcomes" (Cooter, 1982). In other words, government need not be as cynical as Hobbes, but it must do the bare minimum to forestall a complete breakdown of private negotiation and agreement. See also *Coase theorem* and *game theory*.

Holdout problem: these often occur in the presence of complements. For example, a holdout problem often occurs when ownership of a resource is widely scattered and fragmented among a number of agents. The presence of shared property gives to each owner powers over all the other owners, thereby creating an externality. In the presence of fragmented property, consider an agent willing to unify the ownership buying all the properties from the actual owners. Each individual property owner has an incentive to hide his or her true willingness to accept payment to sell his or her property, and he or she will try to be the last seller and attempt to "squeeze" the buyer for nearly all the surplus he or she stands to gain. Holdout problems may lead to failures in negotiations and to suboptimal allocations of resources. The problem of entropy in property associated with the tragedy of the anticommons is an example of an holdout problem, preventing the optimal level of reunification of the fragmented property. Another example of this problem occurs in the case of a bond issuer close to default who launches an offer to restructure the debt. In the presence of a dispersed bond ownership, some bondholders have an incentive to reject the restructuring offer and seek full payment. This will likely disrupt the restructuring process. See also *holdup problem*, *anticommons*, and *entropy*.

Holdup problem: in economic literature, the holdup problem describes a situation in which a Pareto-efficient transaction, involving an asset-specific investment by only one of the parties, fails to occur because of the parties' conflict of interest. Consider, for example, the case of a supplier and a manufacturer, who may cooperate in the production of a certain good. This requires the supplier to make a firm-specific investment (e.g., buy a specific piece of equipment needed for joint production with the manufacturer) that would also benefit the other party. After the parties have entered the contract, the investment is a sunk cost, and the manufacturer has incentive to renegotiate the contract, asking for a higher share of profits from the supplier, who could then make a loss on the investment. In a holdup situation, parties may fail to cooperate and achieve the Pareto-efficient solution, as a result of concerns that they might give the other party increased bargaining power, thereby reducing their own profits. The holdup problem may occur with labor (and not only with investment), as long as labor displays an asset specificity (or firm specificity) for the economic relationship under scrutiny. Like other transaction costs, the holdup problem is one of the economic reasons for the existence of firms and one fundamental determinant of the optimal boundaries of a firm. Williamson (1979, 1983) argues that firms emerge because of asset specificity in the production process as a viable solution to minimize the transaction costs. When different firms that are in a long-term economic relationship own assets that are critical to one another's activity, they may have the incentive to enter in recurring renegotiation of the contracts to appropriate a higher portion of profits, leading to a sharp increase in transaction costs. The most efficient way to overcome the conflict of interest between two parties in a holdup problem may be to realign the parties' incentives through merger or vertical integration, or to enter into other renegotiation-proof vertical agreements. See also *holdout problem*, *theory of the firm*, and *vertical integration*.

Horizontal integration: this occurs when a firm acquires or merges with another company that produces in the same industry or at the same stage of production of similar goods and services. Horizontal integration often materializes through the acquisition of a firm by a competitor (e.g., takeovers or buyouts). Horizontal mergers can be driven by the firms' wish to exploit economies of scale and scope (welfare-enhancing), or by the attempt to reduce competition and monopolize an industry (welfare-reducing). Given the difficulties in establishing the welfare effects of a proposed horizontal merger, competition authorities generally follow a set of guidelines and procedures to assess the prospective competitive effects of proposed mergers. See also *union*, *Herfindahl index*, *concentration ratio*, *vertical integration*, *forward integration*, and *backward integration*.

Hostages: hostage giving is an enforcement mechanism that can promote contracting in the absence of legal enforcement (Williamson, 1983). Kronman (1985) explores the concept in comparison with other non-legal enforcement mechanisms, such as collateral, hands tying, and union. In the absence of enforcement, parties' promises are not credible, and a trust problem arises. The trust problem is particularly severe when the parties' performance and counter-performance cannot be exchanged simultaneously. In these situations, one party can create or increase the other party's incentives to perform by accepting what is called a "hostage." A hostage is a bonding instrument characterized by the fact that it is of value to the promisor (the hostage giver) but of little or no value to the promisee (the hostage taker) or to society in general. This characteristic distinguishes hostages from collateral (which is generally equally valued by the two parties). Hostages can be used to foster cooperative exchanges when the parties are trapped in a prisoner's dilemma because of the non-simultaneity of the exchange. The use of a hostage can transform a non-simultaneous exchange into two simultaneous exchanges. In the first exchange, the parties would trade one's performance for the hostage. In the second exchange, the parties would trade the hostage back in exchange for the counter-performance. Consider, for example, an individual who owns a 120-gram piece of gold and who would like to have the gold forged into a bracelet by an artisan. The artisan agrees to make a 100-gram gold bracelet with the gold, keeping the remaining twenty grams as compensation for his or her labor. Absent an enforcement mechanism, the parties are faced with a prisoner's dilemma: if the individual trusts the artisan and gives him or her the gold, there is no assurance that he or she will actually deliver the bracelet. If the individual does not trust the artisan, the artisan will not be able to build the bracelet. A hostage could be used to transform this non-simultaneous exchange problem into two sequential simultaneous exchanges. Any object that is of sufficient value to the artisan and of little value to the owner of the gold could serve as a hostage (e.g., a hostage could be anything, ranging from the artisan's favorite pet to a portrait of his or her grandmother). In the first round, the parties would exchange the gold for the hostage; in the subsequent round, the parties could exchange the hostage back in return for the bracelet. It is important that the hostage be simultaneously released at the time of performance. The interesting characteristic of hostages lies in the fact that they avoid promisee's opportunism: unlike the instrument of collateral, the promisee does not value the hostage and has no interest in keeping the hostage and forgoing the sought-after contractual performance. One of the difficulties in the use of hostages is that, absent a market value for the hostage, it may be difficult for the promisee to ascertain the actual value of the hostage to the promisor. See also ***ugly princess***, ***self-enforcing contracts***, ***collateral***, ***hands tying***, ***union***, ***relational contracts***, ***cooperative games***, and ***non-cooperative games***.

Hostile takeovers: see **takeovers**.

Hotelling competition: Harold Hotelling's (1929) model of spatial competition shows that when firms sell identical products they try to locate in the market such that they are near as many customers as possible. Hotelling's model of spatial competition hinges upon the assumption that customers buy from the nearest seller. If customers were evenly distributed along a five-mile stretch of beach, the optimal location for two competing sellers would be in the center of that space. Hotelling's model provides the foundations for models of spatial competition used in public choice theory, and is the basis of the median voter theorem. See also ***median voter theorem***.

Hotelling's rule: as finite resources are used, they increase in scarcity. Scarcity in turn drives up the price of the resource, decreasing quantity demanded. According to Harold Hotelling's (1931) rule, the optimal rate for the extraction of non-renewable natural resources is the one that yields a net return (price minus extraction cost) that rises over time at the same rate as the rate of interest. The rule follows the intuition according to which the depletion of finite resources leads to higher prices and lower demand for those resources, with suppliers then reducing accordingly the rate at which resources are harvested. A rational owner should adjust extraction rates of a natural resource until the following two alternatives yield equal expected returns: (a) conservation of the natural resource for future exploitation, and (b) extraction and investment of the revenue at the market interest rate. When Hotelling's rule is followed, the net present value of the natural resource should be the same regardless of when the resource is actually extracted. This rule has played an important role in conservation and environmental policy. Hotelling's rule is at the center of the debate about allocating property rights to resources between generations. Proponents of the rule insist that the price system results in efficient allocations of resources over time. For example, an owner of an oil well will exhaust the oil in his or her well in such a way as to maximize the net present value of the resource if he or she responds only to signals from the market. Critics of Hotelling's rule point out that reliance on current market interest rates ignores the value of the resources to future generations. See also *intergenerational equity* and *dynamic inconsistency*.

Human Development Index (HDI): this provides a normalized measurement of development by combining indicators of life expectancy, educational attainment, and income into a composite index. The index, which has been widely utilized by academics since its introduction by the United Nations in the early 1990s, provides a single statistic that serves as a frame of reference for both social and economic development. For each measured category, the HDI sets a minimum and a maximum and then assigns a normalized score between zero and one to each country according to where it stands in relation to these extreme values. The HDI has become a standard means of measuring well-being, and is used to classify countries as developed, developing, or underdeveloped. In law and economics, the HDI has been used to measure the impact of legal and economic policies on the quality of life.

Human error: see *trembling hand*.

Hung jury paradox: since the 1970 US Supreme Court decision *Williams v. Florida* (399 U.S. 78), the minimum number of jurors required under US constitutional law has been reduced from twelve to six. Few jurisdictions have exercised the opportunity to change the size of juries. Those that did provided scholars with a great natural experiment on jury decision-making. The expectation was that smaller juries would lead to a lower mistrial rate (a lower probability that a dissenting juror could "hang" the jury). According to probability theory, a jury comprised of n jurors, each of which deliberates accurately with an error rate of $1 - p$, should have a probability of mistrial increasing in n at a rate of $p^n(1 - p) + (1 - p)^n p$. Empirical analysis shows that the probability of a hung jury in US criminal cases is around 5.5 percent for a jury of twelve. This implies that independent jurors deliberate with an error rate of 0.4 percent (i.e., a 99.6 percent probability that each juror deliberates correctly). A jury of six people should, therefore, be expected to deliver a mistrial 1.3 percent of the time. However, current evidence shows that changes in jury size have not had much of an impact on the probability of hung juries and conviction rates. Luppi and Parisi (2012b) have attempted to explain the hung jury paradox by revisiting some of the main results of Condorcet's jury theorem, suggesting that informational cascades may provide an explanation for the paradox. See also *Condorcet jury theorem* and *informational cascades*.

Hurwicz optimism–pessimism index: psychologists and social scientists have used a variety of tools to study human decisions made under uncertainty, and have shown that optimism and pessimism can both make a great difference in a person's attitude toward uncertainty. The Hurwicz optimism–pessimism index was developed in the appendix of a book published in 1977 that consisted of papers that had been individually or jointly authored by Nobel laureates

Kenneth Arrow and Leonid Hurwicz (Arrow and Hurwicz, 1977). The index provides a measure of the decision-maker's optimism or pessimism, attaching an index value, α, to the result of a calculation that incorporates both the value of the worst possible outcome of a decision and the best possible outcome. The coefficient of the Hurwicz equation lies between zero and one (with a value of one being the most optimistic and a value of zero being most pessimistic). In practice, the index generates a decision rule that maximizes the weighted sum of the maximin and maximax decision rules. The index has been widely used to identify the effect of optimistic or pessimistic attitudes when decisions are taken with little knowledge about what outcomes are most likely to follow (Etner, Jeleva, and Tallon, 2009). See also *optimism bias*, *risk aversion*, and *loss aversion*.

Hybrid precautions: a subset of precautionary measures, they simultaneously reduce the risks posed to others and the risks posed to oneself. For example, in the context of automobile accidents, driving sober is generally regarded as a tortfeasor precaution, since it reduces the probability that the driver will cause an accident. Likewise, the use of a seat belt may be regarded as a victim precaution, since it reduces the probability of being harmed in an accident. However, the use of headlights at night simultaneously improves visibility for the driver and makes it easier to be seen by other drivers, reducing both the probability of being a tortfeasor and the probability of being a victim. The dual purpose of these non-role-specific precautions has received only limited recognition in traditional legal theory. Simons (1995) provides an early recognition of the category, albeit without using the term "hybrid precaution." Cooter and Porat (2000) consider the case of precautions when there is a risk of harm to the self, suggesting that optimal standards of care should be raised when some of the precautions undertaken are instrumental to the tortfeasor's self-protection. The most recent revision of the Restatement (Third) of Torts (2005) reflects these recent studies. Luppi, Parisi, and Pi (2012) provide a systematic analysis of hybrid precautions in situations of role uncertainty. See also *double-edged torts*, *precaution externalities*, *alternative versus joint care*, and *bilateral accident*.

Hyperbolic discounting: the present value of anticipated future goods is ordinarily modeled by multiplying the value of the good by a discount factor. The discount function conventionally preferred by economists is referred to as exponential discounting (Samuelson, 1937; Frederick, Loewenstein, and O'Donoghue, 2002). However, empirical studies suggest that human (and animal) appreciation of future values consistently and systematically diverge from the predictions of the exponential discounting model (Chung and Herrnstein, 1961; Ainslie, 1992; Loewenstein and Prelec, 1992). An alternative model of discounting was subsequently developed, called hyperbolic discounting, which is characterized by a *declining* discount rate $\frac{\gamma}{1+\alpha\tau}$, where τ is the period and α is the degree of discounting; this contrasts with the *constant* discount rate in exponential discounting. In other words, the marginal effect of discounting decreases the further off the future realization. Clearly, this will create dynamic inconsistency, since proximity to the present distorts the magnitude of the discounting effect (Laibson, 1997) – that is, the effect of discounting is greater between t_1 and t_2 versus t_n and t_{n+1}. Hyperbolic discounting has been used to explain addiction, crime, and procrastination. See also *exponential discounting* and *discounting*.

Hypothesis testing: see *null versus alternative hypothesis*.

$$\boxed{I}$$

Idiosyncratic risk: see *systematic versus unsystematic risk*.

Illusion of control bias: term used in the behavioral literature to describe people's tendency to overestimate their ability to control certain outcomes, even when it can be shown that human actions have little or no control over certain events. Behavioral scholars classify the illusion of control bias in the category "positive illusions" (i.e., unrealistically favorable perceptions about one's self) identified by Taylor and Brown (1988). Like other positive illusions, such as the optimism bias and the above-average effect, the illusion of control bias acquires relevance in a variety of legal contexts. The illusion of control leads individuals to believe that their actions can achieve desirable outcomes (such as the performance of a contract under an unrealistically tight deadline), or can help them avoid undesirable outcomes (such as the avoidance of an accident under very risky conditions). To study the effect of the illusion of control bias in legal contexts, the bias can be modeled as a false perception on the effectiveness of one's actions in changing the probability of certain events. Consider the probability p of an accident (or of a breach of contract) and x as the precautions taken by the tortfeasor (or promisor). Illusion of control can be denoted as an inflated perception of the effectiveness of one's actions, $\left|\frac{\partial p}{\partial x}\right| > \left|\frac{\partial p^*}{\partial x}\right|$. See also *optimism bias*, *above-average effect*, and *Hurwicz optimism–pessimism index*.

Illusory superiority bias: see *above-average effect*.

Impact analysis: see *regulatory impact analysis*.

Impartial observer theorem: this has no universally agreed-upon formulation, but states, fundamentally, that when choosing between alternative income distributions (the theorem equally applies to alternative allocations of legal entitlements) the policymaker should evaluate the alternatives from the viewpoint of an impartial observer. In the context of this theorem, an impartial observer is an individual who does not know which position he or she would occupy, and gives an equal chance to receiving each possible allocation. Vickrey (1945) and Harsanyi (1953) are credited with having independently introduced this concept, providing an important foundation for rule utilitarianism. Rawls' (1971) "veil of ignorance" is in several ways similar to the impartial observer theorem, though Rawls does not fully recognize the work of his predecessors when formulating his theory of justice. See also *veil of ignorance*.

Imperfect competition: this defines competitive markets in which one or more of the conditions identifying perfect competition are violated. Imperfectly competitive markets include monopoly, monopsony, duopoly and oligopoly, duopsony and oligopsony, and monopolistic competition. See also *perfect competition, monopoly, natural monopoly, monopolistic competition, oligopoly, monopolistic competition, oligopsony, duopsony,* and *market structure*.

Implicit cost: see *shadow price*.

Import substitution industrialization: contrary to the predictions of neoclassical economic theory, empirical data seems to suggest that, under certain conditions, economic inequalities between rich and poor countries increase as a result of economic activity. One explanation for this phenomenon, initially known as dependency theory, was fairly straightforward. When poor countries are exporters of primary inputs to rich countries and the value added by manufacturing countries exceeds the value of the primary inputs, poor exporting countries do not earn enough from their export to pay for their imports. Economic activity thus leads to an increase in economic inequality. A possible solution to this form of dependency was seen in the opportunity to adopt "import substitution" industrialization programs: developing countries would be encouraged to export primary inputs to industrialized countries without purchasing back the manufactured goods. See also *dependency theory*.

Impossibility of a Paretian liberal: see *Paretian liberal*.

Inalienability rules: Calabresi and Melamed (1972) identify three types of rules governing the relationship between entitlement holders and those seeking to purchase or take an entitlement: property rules, liability rules, and inalienability rules. Inalienability rules bar the entitlement holder from selling or transferring his or her entitlement. Courts and legislatures apply the inalienability rule by barring an entitlement holder from selling or transferring his or her entitlement. Examples of inalienable entitlements include the traditional legal prohibition on selling one's body parts or blood. While this prohibition may have a variety of moral and philosophical justifications, Cooter and Ulen (2008) point out that attempts to justify inalienability rules on economic grounds largely fail. Barring individuals from being able to transfer their entitlements will not make such transfers more efficient. Although some scholars point to the fact that markets can destroy the incentives to give freely, Cooter and Ulen argue that this is not a compelling argument for the use of inalienability rules. See also *cathedral* and *property rules versus liability rules*.

Incentive alignment: a term that is widely used in the law and economics literature. The concept of incentive alignment originates from mechanism design and contract theory. In an agency problem, the objective function of the principal differs from the objective function of the agent. The principal faces the problem of aligning the agent's incentives to his or her own. This is usually done with the design of a contract that, with the use of conditional rewards or sanctions, will induce the agent to behave the way his or her principal would like him or her to behave. Analytically, any solution to the agency problem entails characterizing the optimal incentive scheme to realign the principal's and the agent's objectives. In the law and economics literature, the notion of incentive alignment is applied more broadly to describe the problem faced by a lawmaker and to consider the incentives created by the law. Law and economics theorists start from the premise that the objective functions of the subjects of the law differ from the objective pursued by the lawmaker. Like an agency problem, when designing laws the lawmaker faces the problem of aligning the incentives of individuals subject to the law (agents) to those of society (principal). This is usually achieved with the design of laws that will induce the subjects of the law to behave consistently with the social objectives. See also *incentives, incentive compatibility constraint, mechanism design, contract theory*, and *carrots versus sticks*.

Incentive compatibility: Nobel laureate Leonid Hurwicz (1972) introduced the idea of incentive compatibility to describe a process whereby participants arrive at the best outcome by not concealing private information or violating the rules of the mechanism. The concept of incentive compatibility can be found as early as 1759, in the writings of Adam Smith in *The Theory of Moral Sentiments*. In incentive-compatible scenarios, parties follow the rules according to their true characteristics regardless of the actions of the other party. Alternatively, it could be stated that an incentive-compatible mechanism is one such that no individual can achieve greater success by violating the rules of the mechanism or by concealing private information. The concept of incentive compatibility is relevant to auctions, voting mechanisms, and central planning. See also *incentive alignment, incentive compatibility constraint*, and *direct versus indirect revelation mechanism*.

Incentive compatibility constraint: in agency problems, the principal introduces incentive-compatible mechanisms so as to align the agent's objectives with his own. A mechanism is incentive-compatible if all participants derive the most benefit from interaction when they truthfully reveal any private information relevant to the mechanism. Incentive-compatible mechanisms, therefore, eliminate the withholding of strategic information and do not suffer problems associated with asymmetric information. When modeling the agency problem, the incentive compatibility "constraint" requires that agents act coherently with the contract offered by the principal. If the incentive compatibility constraint is violated, the solution of the agency problem could be meaningless, as long as the agent chooses not to act in accordance with the optimizing solution proposed by the principal. Any solution to an agency problem should satisfy simultaneously the incentive compatibility and the participation constraint. See also *incentive compatibility, mechanism design, agency problem, participation constraint*, and *strategy proofness*.

Incentive-compatible mechanism: see *incentive compatibility constraint.*

incentive constraint: see *incentive compatibility constraint.*

incentives: the concept of incentives is central to virtually any study in law and economics. The field of law and economics could indeed be described as the "theory of incentives." The economic analysis of law builds on the premise that law affects human choice by creating external incentives and promoting the individual internalization of the values expressed by the law. According to the literature on the economics of deterrence, legal rules can create incentives by affecting the relative cost of alternative behavioral choices. For example, by imposing a fine for a given illegal activity, the law raises the "price" of this activity relative to others, which may lead to a substitution effect. Price theory models of deterrence focus on the role of law as an instrument for creating external incentives, such as taxes, sanctions, and rewards. When these incentives are at work, the law may modify observed patterns of behavior while leaving individual preferences and "tastes" undisturbed. Recent work in experimental and behavioral law and economics has brought to light situations in which the observed effects of legal intervention are at odds with the predictions of the price theory models. The recent literature has addressed these anomalies, emphasizing other important functions played by the law in the creation of incentives. Two trends in the literature can be identified in this respect: expressive law theories and countervailing norms theories. According to expressive law theories (Cooter, 1998, 2000b), law plays an expressive function. Through expression, the law can facilitate the emergence and operation of other incentives by the internalization of the values it embodies. Expressive laws affect behavior, not by threatening sanctions or promising rewards but by changing individual preferences and tastes and by affecting social norms and values. Internalized rules may change observed patterns of behavior even in the absence of legal sanctions and other external incentives. Countervailing norms theories point out that the effects of law further depend on the "social response" triggered by the enactment and enforcement of a new rule (Tyler, 1990; Parisi and von Wangenheim, 2006). Social reaction may reinforce or undermine the effect of legal intervention. A law that reflects prior social values is likely to enjoy immediate acceptance, internalization, and support. However, a law that departs too visibly from prior values is not likely to enjoy immediate acceptance and internalization. In some cases, laws that are inconsistent with shared values may actually trigger opposition. Expressive law, countervailing norms, and social response theories are important ingredients of a richer theory of legal incentives and a more complete understanding of the role (and limits) of law in affecting human behavior. See also *deterrence, incentive compatibility constraint, incentive alignment, mechanism design, contract theory, carrots versus sticks, expressive law, countervailing norms,* and *private enforcement.*

Income effect: see *wealth effect versus income effect.*

Incomplete contracts: see *complete contracts*.

Incomplete information: see *complete information versus perfect information*.

Inconsistent time preference: see *dynamic inconsistency*.

Incremental risk: see *background risk*.

Incumbent's advantage theorem: in public choice theory, the incumbent's advantage theorem follows as a corollary to Black's (1948) median voter theorem. Statistics indicate that, in bipartisan presidential elections in the United States, incumbents have a sizeable advantage over challengers. Although several theories have been put forth to explain the incumbent's advantage (ranging from voters' risk aversion to the structure of campaign financing), the so-called incumbent's advantage theorem provides an explanation that follows as a corollary to the median voter theorem. According to the median voter theorem, a successful challenger facing a primary election needs to present a policy bundle capable of attracting the vote of the median voter of his or her party. However, capturing the vote of the median voter in a primary election is a double-edged sword. Targeting the median voter of one party increases the chances of winning the primaries, but undermines the chances of winning the final presidential race. In order to win the final presidential race, the challenger will in fact have to relocate him- or herself in an attempt to capture the vote of the median voter of the general electorate (which is unlikely to coincide with the median voter of his or her party). This political "relocation" needs to take place in the short period of time between the primaries and the final election. Incumbents in office who do not need to run for primaries have had a much longer span of time to identify and secure the optimal spot in the political spectrum and are more likely to attract the decisive median vote. The incumbent's advantage theorem explains why challengers are often willing to reconsider positions taken during the campaign for primaries, in the hope of moving closer to the new target location in the political spectrum. This also explains why, in an attempt to prevent last-minute relocations, candidates pay so much attention to statements that seem to contradict the position taken by their opponents during primaries. See also *median voter theorem*.

Independence of irrelevant alternatives: according to the criterion of the independence of irrelevant alternatives, the winner of an election should remain the winner in any recalculation of votes if one or more of the losing candidates drop out of the electoral contest. Although this criterion seems a rather self-evident axiom of collective decision-making, social choice theorists have shown that there are several situations in which this criterion is either violated or incompatible with other equally important criteria of social choice. See also *axioms of preferences* and *social choice theory*.

Indicator variable: see *dummy variable*.

Indifference criterion of compensation: according to the indifference criterion of perfect compensation, damage compensation should make the victim of an accident indifferent between (a) a state of the world in which an accident occurred and damage compensation was paid and (b) a state of the world in which no accident occurred. Several problems arise when implementing the indifference criterion in practice. Endowment effects create difficulties in achieving the indifference result. Should compensation be linked to the victim's hypothetical willingness to accept to disturb the status quo, or should compensation be based on the victim's willingness to pay to avoid disturbance of the status quo in the first place? In implementing the indifference criterion of compensation for cases of irreparable harm, additional problems emerge. When an accident creates irreparable harm, it will not be possible to take the victim back to the same *point* of the indifference curve on which he or she was prior to the accident. The indifference criterion, in this case, can only take the victim to the same indifference *curve* on which he or she was prior to the accident, which may necessitate (over)compensating the victim for his or her actual financial loss. See *endowment effect*, *willingness to pay versus willingness to accept*, and *contingent valuation*.

Indirect revelation mechanism: see *direct versus indirect revelation mechanism*.

Inequity aversion: in recent decades the empirical and experimental literature has brought to light numerous examples of human behavior that departs from the paradigm of self-interested rational choice. Humans tend to be less selfish and more concerned about fairness than one would expect on the basis of a crude rational choice model. Further, the same individuals can be very selfish in some cases and not in others. Fehr and Schmidt (1999) have used the idea of inequity aversion to explain some of this evidence. They argue that certain actors can be intensely concerned with cooperation and averse to inequity. The existence of (even a minority of) actors who, in addition to being self-focused, are also inequity averse can explain some counter-intuitive phenomena. Examples of behavior that has been explained on the basis of inequity aversion include customers' concern over the fairness of the pricing decisions of firms, firms' decisions not to lay off workers during a recession, evidence of players in bilateral negotiations who do not care only about material payoff, and evidence of economic actors who are more cooperative than the rational self-interest model would predict. See also *kindness function*, *taste for fairness*, *ultimatum game*, *dictator game*, and *experimental law and economics*.

Inessential games: term used by political scientists and public policy scholars to describe situations in which all obtainable equilibria are characterized by the same total payoffs. Inessential games differ from zero-sum and constant-sum games because the payoffs of the parties are not constant in all outcomes, but only in those outcomes that can be observed in equilibrium. These games are labeled "inessential" because, from a welfare point of view, policymakers should be indifferent between the choice of one equilibrium over the other.

Given that equilibrium payoffs yield the same level of aggregate welfare for the players, these situations generally fall outside the concerns of policymakers and, absent other policy considerations, do not warrant any form of legal intervention. See also *pure conflict games*, *zero-sum games*, and *constant-sum games*.

Inexpressive law: according to expressive law theories, the expression of values is an important function played by the law (Cooter, 1998, 2000b). However, new laws can run up against sticky social norms, which may undermine their expressive effects (Kahan, 2000). The term "inexpressive law" has recently been introduced in the literature to describe laws that incorporate a value that is not shared by the community and that fail to change current social norms and values. Dynamic models in the literature have considered the effects of inexpressive laws on the values shared by members of society, studying the possible feedback effects between laws and social norms. Inexpressive laws may not simply be ineffective in affecting behavior; they may actually push the norms and values of society away from those expressed by the law. Additionally, unlike expressive laws, which can foster consensus even in heterogeneous groups, inexpressive laws can create a social divide, even in previously homogeneous societies. See also *sticky norms*, *expressive law*, *countervailing norms*, *backlash effect*, and *normative overdeterrence*.

Inferior good: in economic terminology, this term refers to a good that reacts negatively to changes in consumers' income. An increase in income leads to a decrease in the consumption of inferior goods: wealthier people buy less of it. A decrease in income leads, instead, to an increase in the consumption of an inferior good. For inferior goods, the income elasticity of demand is negative. Giffen goods are a special case of inferior goods that react positively to changes in the goods price. See also *normal good* and *Giffen good*.

Inflating benefit effect: people are unwilling to accept a risk of death in exchange for money, not only because they ascribe a high value to their lives as such but also because they can draw value from the consumption of their wealth only while they are alive. When considering whether to accept a high risk in exchange for a large sum of money, individuals will consider two factors: (a) life is valuable, and (b) money received becomes useless if one dies. Porat and Tabbach (2011) call this latter effect the inflating benefit effect. An individual's willingness to accept a risk of death therefore fails to be an accurate metric for computing the value of the individual's life. The inflating benefit effect also leads to a divergence between private and social incentives. Consuming one's wealth while alive is privately valuable. However, this private value is not necessarily a social value, because other people would consume that wealth if the particular individual died. The inflating benefit effect, together with the discounting cost effect (also identified by Porat and Tabbach, 2011), may lead to overinvestment in precautions and to a widening of the observed gap between willingness to pay and willingness to accept. See also *discounting cost effect* and *willingness to pay versus willingness to accept*.

Information costs: a form of transaction cost, also known as search costs. They are the value of the resources spent or effort expended in gathering, processing, or communicating information involved in effecting an exchange. Generally, the term is understood broadly also to include those ex ante computational costs involved in determining whether a potential exchange will be beneficial or in determining which exchange among many alternatives to pursue. When information costs are high and resources are limited, rational agents often rely on heuristic decision-making mechanisms rather than calculating costs and benefits on a case-by-case basis. See also *transaction costs*.

Information harnessing: a concept used in the law and economics literature by a number of scholars. Kaplow and Shavell (1996: 725) use the concept of information harnessing in the context of liability rules: "The virtue of the liability rule is that it allows the state to harness the information that the injurer naturally possesses about his prevention cost." The idea is that, when courts set damages equal to the owner's estimated valuation, they induce prospective takers to reveal information about their own valuation. Liability rules allow courts to harness information and so promote value-enhancing takings: a prospective taker will choose to appropriate an entitlement protected by a liability rule only if his or her benefits are greater than the estimated damages, and hence greater than the current owner's value. The term "information harnessing" has been used in the literature in a variety of related contexts. Ayres and Goldbart (2003) have shown that, in many situations, the information-harnessing effects of liability rules dominate and compensate for other shortcomings of liability rules. Ayres (2005) relates information harnessing to internalization, in that it describes the process by which an adjudicator is forced to take into account all relevant information in order to allocate entitlements or damages. Courts must consider the implications, both positive and negative, of granting an entitlement to a party, the process of which Ayres (2005) calls information harnessing. The idea of information harnessing is in many ways germane to the idea of information-forcing effects of penalty default rules, discussed in the literature by Goetz and Scott (1980) and Ayres and Gertner (1989). See also *penalty default rules*.

Information paradox: see *Arrow's information paradox*.

Information-forcing default rules: see *penalty default rules*.

Informational cascades: these occur when individuals make a decision on the basis of the observation of others disregarding their own private information. Informational cascades result from a psychological tendency of imperfectly informed individuals to believe that surrounding people possess better knowledge about a given situation than they do. Information is inferred from the behavior of others, and the actions of first movers, informed or uninformed though they may be, have a self-reinforcing effect. When decisions are made sequentially, late movers imitate the actions of others regardless of their own information signals. This may trigger fads, herding behavior, or bandwagon effects. The standard reference is that by Bikhchandani, Hirshleifer, and Welch (1992), who show that herding behavior may result from private information that is not publicly available and that is inferred from the observation of others' choices. Informational cascades are modeled as a rational choice on the part of the person in the group, even though they may lead to suboptimal decisions or irrational herding behavior. A special kind of informational cascade is the reputational cascade, according to which individuals who act later in a sequence tend to adopt the same decision as those who acted earlier, in order to avoid dissenting from the previous actors. The concept of informational cascades has gained relevance in the behavioral law and economics literature and has been used to explain a wide range of observed phenomena, including financial bubbles, consumer trends, bias in jury deliberation, opinion leadership, and social norms formation. See also *herding behavior*, *group polarization*, *hung jury paradox*, and *signaling*.

Informational social influence: see *informational cascades*.

Initial assignment of rights: see *first-order rules*.

Input–output analysis: in real-world markets, the inputs and outputs of industries are closely interrelated: the output of one industry serves as the input of another, and so on. Input–output analysis considers these interrelations, measuring how one industry depends on another as supplier of its inputs and/or consumer of its outputs. Although input–output models are mathematically quite straightforward, the data requirements are quite burdensome. When sufficient data is available, input–output models can be used as a tool for national and regional economic planning, and more generally as instruments for the study of the structure of economies.

Instrumental variable approach: developed in econometrics to deal with the problem of endogeneity and possible reverse causation between the dependent variable and the explanatory variables in a regression. For example, delinquency in peer groups may be affected by multiple factors, such as education, income, place of residence, etc. However, criminally inclined individuals are more likely to drop out of school (lower education), or to perform poorly in their job (lower income), or to live in areas with greater rates of criminality. This constitutes an endogeneity problem, which may indicate possible reverse causation. In regression analysis, endogeneity arises when there are omitted variables in the regression. The omitted variables are explanatory factors that affect both the dependent variable and the explanatory variables. For example, the "family history" of the individual (e.g., divorced parents, substance abuse, etc.) may affect both the dependent (e.g., the delinquency rate) and the explanatory variables (e.g., education, income, place of residence) in a regression. The family history of the individual would be the omitted variable in our example. Endogeneity undermines the validity of the regression estimation. The association we make between the dependent and explanatory variables is not the result of a causal effect. Over the past several decades econometric techniques have been developed to disentangle these effects and to achieve a better identification of relationships and causal links between variables. The consistency of regression estimators requires exogeneity (i.e., the regressors X should be uncorrelated with the unobservable determinants of the dependent variable Y). This implies that the error terms in the regression should be uncorrelated with the regressors X. Omitted variables cause endogeneity and may be corrected using the instrumental variable approach. Instruments are correlated with the regressors X but are uncorrelated with the dependent variable Y. Instruments affect Y only through the correlation with Xs. One way of implementing the instrumental variable approach is the so-called "two-stage least-squares" technique (often written as 2SLS). See also *regression analysis*, *Granger causality*, and *causation*.

Intensity of preferences: see *cardinal preferences*.

Interdependent utility functions: these model individual preferences that are not purely self-interested. A person's utility depends not only on his or her leisure or consumption but also on the well-being of another person. In formal terms, consider two agents, i and j. Individual i has interdependent preferences if his or her utility function, U_i, depends on j's utility function, U_j. Individual i's interdependent utility function can take the following functional form, $U_i = u(x) + \lambda U_j$, where u is the material utility component that depends positively on i's consumption x and λU_j is the interdependent utility component, modeled as a function of agent j's utility, U_j. In this formulation, λ is the weight that individual i attaches to agent j's utility (i.e., the weight assigned to the interdependent component). The interdependent utility function reduces to the self-interested case if $\lambda = 0$. Positive values of the parameter, $\lambda > 0$, capture positive level of altruism, while negative values, $\lambda < 0$, can be used to denote envy. More general characterizations of interdependent utility functions model fairness on income distribution, group identity, and psychological considerations based on intentionality. See also *relative preferences*, *other-regarding preferences*, *Paretian liberal*, and *interpersonal utility comparisons*.

Interest groups: see *capture theory*.

Intergenerational equity: issues of intergenerational equity and economic justice are gaining exponential importance in today's political discourse. The concept of intergenerational equity was made popular in the economics literature thanks to the work of the winner of the 1981 Nobel Prize for economics, James Tobin. Tobin (1974) elaborates the concept of intergenerational equity in conjunction with the possible overexploitation of common resources by present generations, at the expense of future generations. Intergenerational equity requires that spending and exploitation rates should be sustainable in the long run and therefore should not exceed the inflation-adjusted rate of return or natural yield. Intergenerational equity thus requires that gains and natural resources be equally enjoyed by current and future generations. Issues of intergenerational equity are ubiquitous in modern-day public policy, ranging from the exploitation of natural resources to the control of public debt, social security and governmentally managed pension funds, environmental quality, and urban policy. Problems of intergenerational equity are complicated by the fact that essential facts about the future are often uncertain. Uncertainties regarding population growth, innovation and technological advancement, environmental shocks, etc. render it difficult to implement intergenerational economic models, leaving too much room for political discretion. As Sandler (2001) has pointed out, one of the main difficulties in carrying out intergenerationally equitable policies lies in the fact that long-run thinking is alien to modern-day political institutions and that much institutional change is necessary to ensure the protection of future generations against the actions of present generations. The economic analysis of issues of intergenerational equity moves the analysis beyond the dogmatic legal debate of intergenerational justice (i.e., the question of what duties, if any, currently living individuals owe to those who will live in the future). See also *social discount rate*, *Hotelling's rule*, and *dynamic inconsistency*.

Interior solution: see *corner solution versus interior solution*.

Internalization: the "internalization of an externality" is the term used to refer to the set of instruments used to induce people to take account of the external effects of their actions. There are several ways in which externality-based problems can be corrected, including Coasean bargaining and other private solutions, Pigouvian taxes and subsidies, regulatory solutions, and mixed solutions. Each of these instruments will either properly internalize the externality or induce outcomes that mimic those that could be obtained through proper internalization. Legal systems play a fundamental role in providing instruments for the internalization of externalities. For example, in the absence of product liability, the production of a dangerous product would create a negative externality, leading to a discrepancy between the private and social costs of production. The social cost of the product would in fact include not only the private cost of the producer but also the external cost to third parties adversely affected by the product. Product liability forces the producer to internalize the full social cost of his or her product. Opposite solutions are adopted to correct positive externalities. For example, when a firm's innovation or design benefits society as a whole, by increasing society's pool of technological knowledge, the social value of the firm's activity exceeds the private value captured by the firm. The market therefore produces a smaller quantity than is socially desirable. Patents allow the firm to internalize the positive value of the externality that it created. Patent laws can in fact be viewed as a form of subsidy (the monopoly profit paid by consumers) to incentivize socially valuable research and discovery. See also *externalities*.

International Review of Law and Economics: established in 1981 under the editorship of Anthony Ogus and Charles Rowley. Subsequent editors have been Robert Cooter (1988–2002), Daniel Rubinfeld (1988–2002), Claus Ott (1997–2011), Hans-Bernd Schafer (1997–2011), Avery Katz (2003–present), Giuseppe Dari-Mattiacci (2012–present), Nuno Garoupa (2012–present), Eric Helland (2012–present), Jonathan Klick (2012–present), and Eric Talley (2012–present). For many years, until 2006, the *International Review of Law and Economics* published a symposium issue with a selection of the papers presented at the annual conference of the European Association of Law and Economics (EALE). See also *law and economics journals*.

Interpersonal utility comparisons: utilitarian welfare calculations generally assume that utilities are measurable and can be summed to build an aggregate measure of welfare. In the estimation of aggregate welfare, comparisons of utility across different individuals (interpersonal utility comparisons) play a crucial role. The idea that utility can be measured and compared across different individuals has been heavily criticized. According to Robbins (1935), individual utility cannot be objectively measured. The non-measurability of individual utility makes interpersonal utility comparisons impossible and undermines any attempt to construct a utilitarian paradigm of welfare maximization. This implies that the desirability of a wealth transfer, for example, from a rich individual to a poor individual in society cannot be evaluated, since the utility gain of the poor and the utility loss of the rich cannot be objectively compared. Other authors, such as Harsanyi (1955) and Sen (1970a), argue that utility comparisons are partially possible in some states of the world, because of a common culture, habits, and experience backgrounds that allow the comparability of individual utilities. Sen (1970a) exemplifies the point by observing that it should not be difficult to say that Emperor Nero's gain from burning Rome was smaller than the Romans' loss. He argues that interpersonal utility comparisons may lead to suboptimal social choices because emotions and mental states can be manipulated. In the theory of informational broadening, Sen proposed minimizing the problems associated with interpersonal comparisons of utility by grounding social choice decisions on objective variables that cannot be manipulated, including primary goods that satisfy basic needs, freedoms, and capabilities. See also *cardinalism, ordinalism, aggregation problem, utility maximization*, and *interdependent utility functions*.

Interpersonal utility functions: see *interdependent utility functions*.

Inventor's paradox: see *Arrow's information paradox*.

Inverse adverse selection: in the standard "market for lemons" scenario, adverse selection takes place when uninformed buyers purchase goods from informed sellers. The inverse case of adverse selection is characterized by uninformed sellers who contract with informed buyers. This might be the case for goods of uncertain value, such as artworks, or for sales between an expert buyer and a one-time seller, such as a real estate investor and a homeowner, or a diamond expert and an individual seller. The recent literature has referred to this scenario as the "market for gems," to mirror the "market for lemons" nomenclature (Dari Mattiacci, Onderstal, and Parisi, 2011). When buyers, rather than sellers, possess private information, sellers may withdraw from the market suspecting that, if an (informed) buyer shows interest in what they are selling, the good that is being sold must have some hidden quality of which they are not aware. These two variants of adverse selection are dual to one another and are both detrimental to social welfare compared to the ideal world, in which both sellers and buyers are informed and prices reflect actual quality. See also *adverse selection* and *reverse adverse selection*.

Investment theories of lawmaking: lawmaking and financial investing share a number of salient structural similarities. Like making an investment, the decision to legislate involves an initial cost, which is expected to generate long-term benefits. However, like an investment, the decision to legislate is also fraught with risks and uncertainties. Recognizing this similarity, legal scholars have redeployed the tools of modern investment theory to the problems of lawmaking. When uncertainty exists, lawmakers may use techniques analogous to diversification, options, and hedging to determine the territorial scope, timing, and specificity of legislative intervention (Parisi and Fon, 2009). The analytical framework of investment theory gives legal scholars a robust set of methods for assessing these decisions and their consequences. See also *option value*, *diversification*, *portfolio theory*, *risk management*, *hedging*, and *systematic versus unsystematic risk*.

Invisible hand: term coined by Adam Smith in *The Wealth of Nations* (1776) to describe the way the unregulated price system, or the market mechanism, coordinates the decisions of individual buyers and sellers to direct resources to their highest valued uses. According to Smith, markets work automatically, as if directed by an invisible hand, to promote economic efficiency and maximize individual welfare of participants in a market economy. See also *efficient market hypothesis*.

ISNIE: International Society of New Institutional Economics. Founded in 1997, primarily through the efforts of Lee and Alexandra Benham of Washington University in St. Louis, Missouri. The society was created in response to a rising awareness of the worldwide interest in new institutional economics, an economic perspective that focuses on the social and legal norms that underlie economic activity. Washington University and the Bradley Foundation provided the initial funding for the development of the society. The first annual meeting was held from September 19 to 21, 1997, in St. Louis and attracted 215 attendees from twenty-four countries. The meeting included an address by Ronald Coase (Chicago), the founding president. Since then the society has held an annual meeting on a rotating basis. Subsequent presidents of the society, who are elected annually, have been Douglass North (1997–9), Oliver Williamson (1999–2001), Claude Ménard (2001–2), Paul Joskow (2002–3), Mary Shirley (2003–4), Gary Libecap (2004–5), Benito Arruñada (2005–6), Lee Alston (2006–7), Thrain Eggertsson (2007–8), Scott Masten (2008–9), Pablo Spiller (2009–10), Frank Stephen (2010–11), Barry Weingast (2011–12), and Lee Epstein (2012–13). Since 1997 the society has published a regular *Newsletter of the International Society of New Institutional Economics*. In addition, the society sponsors the New Institutional Economics eJournal on the Social Science Research Network. See also *new institutional economics*.

Iterated dominance: see *dominated strategies*.

Iterated prisoner's dilemma: a repeated game in which the constituent game is the prisoner's dilemma. When the prisoner's dilemma is played repeatedly, each player has the opportunity to punish the other players when they defect from cooperation. When the game is repeated a finite number of times, cooperation cannot arise as a subgame-perfect Nash equilibrium. This can be explained by using backward induction (applying a similar argument to the chain store paradox). When players play an infinite or a random number of times, cooperation may arise as a solution to the game. The incentive to defect can be overcome by the threat of punishment. Experimental economics has studied the iterated prisoner's dilemma game to investigate cooperative behavior and trust. See also *prisoner's dilemma*, *chain store paradox*, *folk theorem*, and *evolution of cooperation*.

J

JARing: term referring to the behavior whereby one tends to "jeopardize assets that are remote." This behavior is characterized by current decisions that greatly discount their long-term effects. This behavior is found to be particularly frequent in decisions involving land use and the environment. See also *cognitive bias*.

Joint care: see *alternative versus joint care*.

Joint maximization: see *Kaldor–Hicks criterion*.

Journal of Law and Economics: the oldest journal specializing in the economic analysis of law. It was established in 1958 at the University of Chicago, and since then has published many influential articles in law and economics, including Ronald Coase's (1960) widely cited article "The problem of social cost". Aaron Director served as the first editor of the journal from 1958 to 1963, followed by Coase, who served as editor from 1964 to 1982. He was joined by William Landes from 1974 until 1991. In more recent years the journal's editors have been Dennis Carlton (1981–present), Frank Easterbrook (1982–9), Sam Peltzman (1990–present), Alan Sykes (1992–2000), Richard Epstein (1992–2002), George Triantis (2001–4), Austan Goolsby (2003–4), Edward Snyder (2003–9), Randall Kroszner (2005–6), Douglas Lichtman (2005–6), John Gould (2007–present), and Anup Malani (2007–present). *The Journal of Law and Economics* is one of the three journals in the field of law and economics published by the University of Chicago Press (together with *The Journal of Legal Studies* and the *Supreme Court Economic Review*). The journal continues to provide a valuable resource for academic economists and law and economics scholars, although its scope and prominence have been reduced by the creation of other journals in the field of law and economics. See also *law and economics journals*.

Journal of Competition Law and Economics: established in 2005 under the editorship of Damien Geradin and Gregory Sidak. The *Journal of Competition Law and Economics* is one of the three journals in the field of law and economics published by Oxford University Press (together with the *American Law and Economics Review* and *The Journal of Law, Economics, and Organization*). See also *law and economics journals*.

Journal of Empirical Legal Studies: established in 2004 under the joint editorship of Theodore Eisenberg, Jeffrey Rachlinski, Stewart Schwab, and Martin Wells, who were subsequently joined by Michael Heise (2005–present). The *Journal of Empirical Legal Studies* is devoted to empirical studies, both experimental and non-experimental, of the legal system, and it has emerged as a leading journal in this growing area of research. See also *law and economics journals*.

***Journal of Law, Economics, and Organization*:** established in 1985 under the editorship of Jerry Mashaw and Oliver Williamson, who served as editors respectively until 1988 and 1992. Subsequent editors have been Roberta Romano (1989–92), Alan Schwartz (1993–2001), Ian Ayres (2002–9), and Pablo Spiller (2010–present). *The Journal of Law, Economics, and Organization* is one of the three journals in the field of law and economics published by Oxford University Press (together with the *American Law and Economics Review* and the *Journal of Competition Law and Economics*). See also *law and economics journals*.

***Journal of Legal Analysis*:** established in 2009, under the editorship of J. Mark Ramseyer. The co-editors are drawn from other universities as well as Harvard Law School, and include several law and economics scholars, such as Richard Craswell from Stanford University, Mathew McCubbins from the University of Southern California, Daniel Rubinfeld from the University of California, Berkeley, and Steven Shavell from Harvard Law School. The journal has entered the landscape of academic journals with a strong emphasis on interdisciplinary work, and it is likely to become a new reference point for law and economics scholarship. Since 2011 the journal has been published by Oxford University Press. See also *law and economics journals*.

***Journal of Legal Studies*:** founded in 1972 at the University of Chicago. Richard Posner served as the sole editor during the first decade of the journal's publication, establishing its reputation as a leading journal in both economic and legal theory. Subsequent editors have been Richard Epstein (1984–91), Geoffrey Miller (1990–5), William Landes (1992–2000), J. Mark Ramseyer (1996–8), Eric Posner (1999–2010), Alan Sykes (2001–6), Thomas Miles (2006–present), and Omri Ben-Shahar (2009–present). *The Journal of Legal Studies* is a journal of interdisciplinary legal research, emphasizing economic analysis, but with a balanced representation of other social sciences, ranging from political science to psychology, history, and political philosophy. *The Journal of Legal Studies* is one of the three journals in the field of law and economics published by the University of Chicago Press (together with *The Journal of Law and Economics* and the *Supreme Court Economic Review*). See also *law and economics journals*.

Judgment proof problem: in many situations, the law creates incentives using a threat of liability. So, for example, in tort law a tortfeasor who negligently or intentionally causes an injury to another is liable to compensate his or her victim. In certain circumstances, tortfeasors may not have enough resources to compensate the victim. In these cases, the threat of liability is partially or entirely ineffective. The law and economics literature refers to this problem as the judgment proof problem. This problem is similar to the disappearing defendant problem, which is related to imperfect enforcement and to the fact that the legal process is not always successful in identifying and imposing liability on the responsible parties. Shavell (1986) analyzes this situation, showing that the judgment proof problem results in potential tortfeasors excessively engaging in risky activity and taking fewer precautions than they should. This is because the potential tortfeasor knows the value of his or her assets and his or her insurance policy, and knows he or she will not face any loss that exceeds the total of those two amounts. The problem is aggravated by the fact that the judgment proof problem reduces the incentive to purchase appropriate amounts of liability insurance. The judgment proof problem provides an explanation for policy solutions, including the requirement of liability insurance, ex ante safety regulations, and the joint use of criminal and civil liability for certain types of risky behavior. See also *disappearing defendant problem*.

jury polarization: see *group polarization*.

K

Kahneman, Daniel (1934–): considered to be one of the founders of behavioral economics. Kahneman received the Nobel Prize in economics in 2002 (jointly with Vernon Smith), for his work in behavioral and experimental economics. Kahneman was born in Tel Aviv, in what was then Palestine, on March 5, 1934. He received his undergraduate education at the Hebrew University of Jerusalem, where he graduated in 1954 with a degree of Bachelor of Science with a major in psychology and a minor in mathematics. He then served in the Israeli Defense Forces, first as a platoon leader and later in their Psychology Branch, until 1956. He then moved to the United States, where he received his Ph.D. in psychology from the University of California, Berkeley, in 1961. He completed his dissertation "on a statistical and experimental analysis of the relations between adjectives in the semantic differential" (Kahneman, 2002). Daniel Kahneman is best known for his work with Amos Tversky in the field of behavioral economics on what they termed "prospect theory." Their idea was first put forward in the paper "Prospect theory: an analysis of decision under risk," published in 1979 in *Econometrica*. Kahneman describes the "core idea" of prospect theory as one in which "changes and differences are much more accessible than absolute levels of stimulation" (Kahneman, 2002). This research critiques the expected utility model as a descriptive model of economic decision-making, and instead shows that decision-makers are risk-averse, and underweight the probability of certain events occurring. His alternative theory of economic decision-making, based more on psychological research and real-world behavior, laid the groundwork for the field of behavioral economics. In addition to his contributions to prospect theory, Kahneman is also well known for his work on the psychology of judgment, framing and mental accounting, and cognitive bias. See also *prospect theory*, *behavioral finance*, *experimental law and economics*, and *Smith, Vernon*.

Kaldor–Hicks compensation: see *Kaldor–Hicks criterion*.

Kaldor–Hicks criterion: this criterion of welfare should be attributed to the independent work of three economists: Nicholas Kaldor (1939), John Hicks (1939), and Tibor Scitovsky (1941). These economists formulated a welfare paradigm that formalized the wisdom of the utilitarian Benthamite tradition. The core idea of the Kaldor–Hicks approach is that state A is to be preferred to state B if those who gain from the move to A gain enough to compensate those who lose. The test is also generally known as the Kaldor–Hicks test of potential compensation.

It is one of "potential" compensation because the compensation of the losers is only hypothetical and does not actually need to take place. In practical terms, the Kaldor–Hicks criterion requires a comparison of the gains of one group and the losses of the other group. As long as the gainers gain more than the losers lose, the move is deemed efficient. Mathematically, both the Bentham and the Kaldor–Hicks versions of efficiency are carried out by comparing the aggregate payoffs of the various alternatives and selecting the option that maximizes such summation. See also ***Bentham's imperative, potential compensation, wealth maximization, utility maximization, Nash criterion of welfare, Rawlsian maximin, Pareto efficiency, utilitarianism, welfare analysis, joint maximization, capability approach***, and ***transferable utility***.

Keynesian economics: see ***demand-side versus supply-side economics***.

Kindness function: constructed by Rabin (1993) by noting that individuals are willing to sacrifice their well-being to be "fair" toward those individuals who behave nicely and to punish those who behave in an "unfair" way. Experimental studies suggest that an individual's behavior is often contingent on the behavior of others, and the magnitude of the individual's reactions tend to be inversely proportional to the cost of modifying his or her behavior. The kindness function is used to introduce procedural reciprocity in a game-theoretical model of fairness. See also ***inequity aversion, taste for fairness, distributive reciprocity***, and ***procedural preferences***.

Knowledge spillover: see ***spillover***.

$$\boxed{\text{L}}$$

Laboratory experiment: used since the 1960s in the field of experimental economics (and, in more recent years, in experimental law and economics), to test theories and hypotheses. A laboratory experiment is conducted by an experimenter in a controlled setting, such as a classroom or computer lab, where the economic decisions of the participants (often college students recruited by the experimenter) are observed under a variety of conditions. The acceptance of laboratory experiments by mainstream scholarship necessitated the establishment of a well-defined set of methods and protocols for carrying out experimental work. For example, salience and dominance have become essential requirements for the validity of a laboratory experiment. The most common method used to guarantee salience is to incentivize study participants by using a monetary payoff. The payoffs are affected by the participant's choices and actions in the experiment. The concept of salience distinguishes economic experiments from other forms of experiments used in the social sciences. Although experimental methods are now widely accepted for testing theories and policies, some concerns remain about their use. One such concern is that the typical group of subjects used in experiments may not be representative of the relevant population. Representativeness may be further undermined by a self-selection problem. Another common criticism is that it is not possible to replicate several important real-life conditions in the context of a laboratory. See also *salience and dominance in experiments*, *experimental law and economics*, *natural experiment*, *field experiment*, and *calibration*.

Laffer curve: this postulates that, if the marginal tax rate rises above a certain threshold, there is a negative relationship between taxable income and the marginal tax rate. Beyond a certain level, higher tax rates may actually lead to a reduction in total tax revenue. Wanniski (1978) dubbed the concept the Laffer curve after Arthur Laffer, who sketched the tradeoff between tax rates and revenues on a napkin during a dinner meeting in 1974 with Wanniski, Donald Rumsfeld, and Dick Cheney. However, Laffer does not claim credit for the idea, attributing its origins to Ibn Khaldun, a fourteenth-century Muslim philosopher (Laffer, 2004). See also *marginal tax rates*.

Laissez-faire: literally, "let do"; denotes a bundle of closely related ideas. Foundationally, a laissez-faire market is one free from government interference, in which individuals and firms are allowed unfettered voluntary exchange. A laissez-faire economic theory claims that the market, left to evolve naturally, will tend toward efficiency. Some public officials and economists also use the label to describe themselves as advocates (or opponents) of deregulation and/or decreased taxation.

Landes, William M. (1939–): an economist who taught at the University of Chicago Law School from 1974 to 2009. He was one of the early pioneers of the law and economics movement. Along with Richard Posner, with whom he co-wrote several dozens of papers, Landes was very active in the field of tort law and economics, and was an outspoken proponent of the efficiency of the common law hypothesis. Several of his models have become standard in the economic modeling of law. He received his B.A. in 1960 and his Ph.D. in economics in 1966, both from Columbia University. He taught economics at a number of schools – Stanford University from 1965 to 1966, the University of Chicago from 1966 to 1969, Columbia University from 1969 to 1972, City University of New York from 1972 to 1974 – before finally settling at the University of Chicago Law School, where he was the Clifton R. Musser Professor of Law and Economics from 1980 to 2009. Together with Richard Posner and Andrew Rosenfield he founded Lexecon, a law and economics consulting firm. Landes was an editor of *The Journal of Law and Economics* from 1974 to 1991 and *The Journal of Legal Studies* from 1992 to 2000. Landes served as president of the American Law and Economics Association in 1992. He was inducted as a fellow of the American Academy of Arts and Sciences in 2008. See also *efficiency of the common law hypothesis*.

Last-mover advantage: the advantage obtained by a player who is able to make the last move in a one-shot sequential game or in a repeated game. Examples of the last-mover advantage are generally less frequent than, but equally difficult to solve as, problems characterized by a last-mover advantage. Last-mover advantages may trigger strategies between the players for appropriating the last move in the game. This may lead to holdup and free-riding problems. For example, when trying to reunite fragmented property, prospective sellers perceive that there might be an advantage in being the last ones to sell, inasmuch as they can have a better opportunity to exploit the prospective value of the reunified property. Markets and legal systems have both developed solutions to mitigate the deadweight losses that might be caused by last-mover advantage strategies. See also *first-mover advantage*.

Latin American and Caribbean Law and Economics Association: see *ALACDE*.

Law and economics: expression used to refer to the application of economic methods in the analysis of law. The similar role that market forces and laws play in incentivizing conduct naturally led to a repurposing of the methods of the one field within the other – a cross-pollination that has borne much fruit. As a coherent interdisciplinary movement, the roots of law and economics extend back to the mid-twentieth-century work of Ronald Coase. The movement gained prominence in the 1970s and 1980s through the work of Richard Posner and Guido Calabresi, and it is today the most influential methodology in legal scholarship, other than standard doctrinal law. Historically, there were three "styles" of law and economics scholarship, each associated with a top law school and economics department: the Chicago school, Yale school, and Virginia school, identifying loosely with positivist, normative, and functionalist methodologies, respectively. The three schools were characterized less by any affirmative program than by a methodological flavor. Today these historical distinctions have become increasingly blurred. Critics of law and economics sometimes attribute agendas or positive theses to the movement (e.g., the efficiency of the common law hypothesis or the rational actor hypothesis). Although progress in the field owes much to research supporting and refuting these claims, and much can be learned about the methodology and history of the field from the literature on these topics, it is a mistake to identify law and economics with an endorsement of a particular agenda. Rather, to the extent that it forms a coherent intellectual movement, the term "law and economics" refers to the application of economic methods to the field of law. See also *Chicago school*, *Yale school*, *Virginia school*, *efficiency of the common law hypothesis*, *rational actor model*, and *rational choice theory*.

Law and economics 2.0: the University of Chicago Law School has played an important role in the development of law and economics. In 2011, a half-century after the publication of "the problem of social cost" (Coase, 1960), the Law School launched a new initiative, called Law and Economics 2.0, to build on its tradition and to expand the influence of law and economics, nationally and internationally. The initiative comes at a critical moment in the Law School's history, and is likely to ensure the preeminent role of the Chicago research program for the next generation of scholars. According to the official announcement, the new program intends to provide a platform for a broad range of national and international programs, with the establishment of a new Institute for Law and Economics, and a new J.D./Ph.D. program in law and economics, aimed at forming new scholars and professors in the discipline. Omri Ben-Shahar is serving as the first director of the newly established institute. See also *Chicago school*.

Law and economics journals: an important ingredient in the success of law and economics research has come from the establishment of specialized journals. The first such journal, *The Journal of Law and Economics*, appeared in 1958 at the University of Chicago. Its first editor, Aaron Director, should be credited for this important initiative, successfully continued by Ronald Coase. Other journals emerged in the following years: in 1972 *The Journal of Legal Studies*, also housed at the University of Chicago, under the editorship of Richard Posner; in 1979 *Research in Law and Economics*, under the editorship of Richard Zerbe, Jr.; in 1981 the *International Review of Law and Economics* was established in the United Kingdom under the editorship of Charles Rowley and Anthony

Ogus (later joined by Robert Cooter and Daniel Rubinfeld); in 1982 the *Supreme Court Economic Review*, under the editorship of Peter Aranson (later joined by Harold Demsetz and Ernest Gellhorn); in 1985 *The Journal of Law, Economics, and Organization*, under the editorship of Jerry Mashaw and Oliver Williamson (later joined by Roberta Romano); in 1994 the *European Journal of Law and Economics*, under the editorial direction of Jürgen Backhaus and Frank Stephen; in 1999 the *American Law and Economics Review,* under the editorship of Orley Ashenfelter and Richard Posner; in 2004 the *Journal of Empirical Legal Studies*, under the editorship of Theodore Eisenberg, Jeffrey Rachlinski, Stewart Schwab, and Martin Wells; the same year the *Journal of Competition Law and Economics,* under the editorship of Damien Geradin and Gregory Sidak; in 2005 the *Review of Law and Economics*, under the editorship of Robert Cooter, Ben Depoorter, Lewis Kornhauser, Gerrit De Geest, Nuno Garoupa, and Francesco Parisi; and in 2009 the *Journal of Legal Analysis*, established at Harvard Law School, under the initial editorship of J. Mark Ramseyer. These specialized journals provide an extremely valuable forum for the study of the economic structure of law. Several journals in related disciplines have been increasingly open to the methodology of law and economics, including *Public Choice* and *Constitutional Political Economy*. See also **Journal of Law and Economics, Journal of Legal Studies, International Review of Law and Economics, Journal of Law, Economics, and Organization, European Journal of Law and Economics, Public Choice, Constitutional Political Economy, Review of Law and Economics, Journal of Empirical Legal Studies, American Law and Economics Review, Supreme Court Economic Review, Journal of Competition Law and Economics**, and **Journal of Legal Analysis**.

Law in the shadow of bargaining: expression used by Ben Depoorter (2010) to refer to the influence of novel settlement and arbitration awards on courts' case law outcomes. The expression mirrors the more popular idea of bargaining in the shadow of the law. See also ***bargaining in the shadow of the law***.

Law of large numbers: this characterizes the results of an experiment repeated a large number of times. According to the law, the average result of a large number of trials (observations) tends to be closer to the expected value of the theoretical probability distribution and becomes closer for each experiment performed. Consider the repeat tossing of a fair coin. The theoretical probability of the coin coming up heads is one-half (or $p = 0.5$). If the coin is flipped several times, it is unlikely that heads will appear exactly half the time. However, according to the law of large numbers, the frequency of getting heads will approach one-half ($p = 0.5$) in a large number of trials. The law of large numbers does not apply to a small set of observations, as small sets do not necessarily approximate the expected value. The law of large numbers is relevant in economic analysis, since it provides a long-term stability result for random events. See also ***Condorcet jury theorem***.

Law of small numbers: term used by Matthew Rabin (2002) for the tendency of people to extract too much inference from small samples or personal experience. The law of small numbers is one of the implications of the representativeness bias identified by Tversky and Kahneman (1974). As a result of this tendency, individuals neglect the relevance of base rates in assessing the probability of an event. See also *representativeness bias*.

Learned Hand formula: this represents one of the earliest attempts to apply principles of economics in the form of an algebraic formula to tort law. The formula was written by Learned Hand, a judge from the United States Court of Appeals for the Second Circuit, in the case *United States* v. *Carroll Towing*, 159 F.2d. 169 (2d. Cir. 1947). The formula states that negligence should be assessed on the basis of three factors: the probability of an accident, the gravity of an injury resulting from the accident, and the burden of taking precautions. An act will be held negligent if the cost of the burden of taking precautions, B, is less than the product of the probability of the loss, p, and the cost of the loss, L. In mathematical terms, negligence in torts will be found when $B < pL$. The boundary between negligence and diligence is therefore drawn where $B = pL$. The formula is still used in tort law and remains an important early example of practical law and economics. However, in spite of its popularity and widespread legal adoption, it should be noted that the original formula contains a fundamental economic error, inasmuch as it sets the optimal level of care where costs equal benefits. Economically, optimization instead requires equating marginal costs and benefits. The restatement of the Learned Hand formula in marginal terms is known as the marginal Learned Hand formula. See also *marginal Learned Hand formula*, *optimal scope of negligence*, *durable versus non-durable precautions*, and *alternative versus joint care*.

Least-squares analysis: see *regression analysis*.

Least cost avoider: see *cheapest cost avoider*.

Legal endowment effect: it is widely accepted that, when the costs or benefits of performance change, the potential for an efficient breach will materialize, regardless of whether the available remedy is one of damages or specific performance. However, recent research has hypothesized that legal remedies may create a legal endowment effect. The idea is that, psychologically, the parties to a contract may perceive (efficient) breaches differently depending on the remedy that is available to them. Even though, prior to performance, a promisee has not yet had physical possession of the object of the contract, the availability of a strong remedy such as specific performance may create an entitlement effect on the promisee. The hypothesis currently under consideration is that the legal entitlement effect may influence the parties' willingness to forgo a promised performance, and in turn affect the rates of successful renegotiation and the frequency of efficient breach. These hypotheses are the subject of ongoing experimental research. See also *Coase theorem*, *endowment effect*, and *endowment effect theory*.

Legal origins: modern developed countries often have dramatically different social, political, and economic systems, rules, and outcomes. Since the late 1990s economists have carried out extensive research to study whether the legal origins of a country's legal system have had any effect on economic outcomes. The term "legal origins" has been used in this literature to refer to the "type" and historical origins of legal systems. This important development in the law and economics literature has been particularly noted for linking observed differences in economic performance to the common law versus civil law origin of the legal system. These results have been, at one and the same time, interesting and controversial. Among several others in this growing literature, Glaeser and Shleifer (2002) have identified a correlation between the legal origins of a state's legal system and its economic performance. The theory behind the legal origins effect is that decentralized sources of law, such as judge-made law and common law rules in general, enjoy greater protection from undue pressure or influence. Centralized sources of law, such as legislation and civil law rules in general, are more vulnerable to special interest conflicts. Over time these competing legal systems have generated different political, social, and economic realities. Civil law countries, which are more comfortable with heavy-handed government control, tend to have more regulation, "less secure property rights, more corrupt and less efficient governments, and even less political freedom" (Glaeser and Shleifer, 2002). Common law countries, on the other hand, have less regulation, more efficient governments, and more political and economic freedom. On the basis of this stylized premise, the hypothesis – tested and fairly uniformly confirmed by empirical literature – is that common law systems should have a comparative advantage in fostering economic and social development.

Legal standards: see *rules versus standards*.

Lemons problem: see *adverse selection*.

Level of significance: when testing a hypothesis, researchers identify a critical value against which to compare the test results. For example, in a regression, a parameter estimate is significantly different from zero at the 1 percent level, if the value has a 99 percent chance of being non-zero. See also *null versus alternative hypothesis*.

Leviathan theory: *Leviathan* is the title of Thomas Hobbes' 1651 work on the social contract and the appointment of a benevolent dictator. Public choice theorists often refer to the Leviathan as a metaphor for government – though not necessarily a benevolent one. Leviathan theory views the central government as a tax-maximizing monopolist constrained by the possibility that individuals will withhold their supply of labor (Brennan and Buchanan, 1980). Empirical tests of the Leviathan hypothesis have generated mixed results, with little evidence of a correlation between the degree of centralization and the size of government (Oates, 1985). See also ***contractarianism***.

Liability rules: see ***property rules versus liability rules***.

Liberal paradox: see ***Sen's liberal paradox***.

Lighthouse in economics: see ***public good***.

Litigation costs: those costs incurred in the pursuit of a remedy in a dispute, usually in courts. Although litigation costs may be categorized as a transaction cost, law and economics scholars have historically found it analytically useful to distinguish litigation costs from other transaction costs – particularly when contrasting property and liability rules. See also ***enforcement costs*** and ***property rules versus liability rules***.

Local public good: a good that has the general features of public goods but that generates benefits to a local community, such as street landscaping or public lighting. The local nature of these public goods allows the tailoring of their supply to the preferences and needs of the local population. Tiebout's (1956) model suggests that local communities will compete in the supply of different bundles of local public goods and that individuals will reveal their preferences by choosing in which community to live. This will result in the matching of the differing needs of the population with a diverse offering of local public good bundles. See also ***public good***, ***Tiebout competition***, and ***voting with your feet***.

Logrolling: a practice of vote trading in which legislators agree to trade votes for issues on which they hold weak preferences in exchange for votes on issues that they value more highly. Logrolling is a widespread practice in legislative bodies around the world. Public choice theorists have emphasized the negative effects of logrolling, which are often associated with the pursuit of special interest legislation. Law and economics scholars look at logrolling with less skepticism. The undesirable illustrations of logrolling used by public choice scholars are the consequence of agency problems in representation and a lack of political accountability, not of logrolling as such. Absent a mechanism to force the revelation of the intensity of voters' preferences, democracy generally gives equal weight to all votes regardless of how strongly voters feel about an issue. Logrolling introduces market-type mechanisms (i.e., bargaining, vote trading) in the political process, allowing for the intensity of preferences to be reflected in the decision-making process. With logrolling, legislators have an opportunity to reveal their preferences through the vote-trading process. Bargaining will continue until the marginal utility of gaining one vote on a certain issue equals the marginal cost of giving up one vote for another issue. Constitutional scholars are generally hostile to a rationalization of politics as a market for consensus. Ordinary citizens with little information about legislative bargains would resist any institutionalization of political bargaining, objecting to their representatives participating in open logrolling. See also ***triangulation***, *political markets, political Coase theorem, Bernholz theorem, pork barrel legislation,* and *prodigal son's effect.*

Loser pays all: see *fee shifting.*

Loss aversion: human beings make decisions on a daily basis, some of which can result in significant gains or significant losses. Economists have explored how individuals make decisions in the face of potential gains and losses. In addition to the fact that humans are risk-averse, Kahneman and Tversky (1979) and Tversky and Kahneman (1991) in their prospect theory have observed that people have a strong tendency to prefer avoiding losses to acquiring gains. Loss aversion impacts how humans make decisions. Cooter and Ulen (2008) use a helpful hypothetical that helps illustrate the relevance of loss aversion in the legal context. Consider an individual's decision about whether to initiate a dispute or accept a settlement. If a person must choose between a sure gain of fifty units (settlement offer) and a 50 percent chance at 100 or nothing, the person will choose the sure gain of fifty, settling the dispute. However, if roles are reversed, and an individual must choose between a sure loss of fifty units or a 50 percent chance at a loss of 100 or a loss of nothing, he or she will choose the gamble and proceed to litigation. In other words, the person is averse to loss and will therefore be more willing to take the litigation gamble in order to avoid the certainty of a loss of fifty. Hence, in spite of the apparent symmetry between the positions of plaintiffs and defendants, a plaintiff might be more apt to settle, in order to secure certain benefits, while a defendant may be more likely to proceed to trial, in lieu of settling and accepting a certain loss. Prospect theory, and understanding how reference points can affect risk aversion and loss aversion, are helpful in understanding how individuals behave in a variety of legal contexts. See also *risk preferences, endowment effect theory, willingness to pay versus willingness to accept,* and *Hurwicz optimism–pessimism index.*

Loss leader pricing: firms occasionally offer some portion of their products at prices below cost, in the hope of attracting customers and facilitating sales of other products with a higher profit margin. The products sold at prices below cost are called loss leaders.

Loss sharing: in negligence-based torts, loss sharing refers to a division of the loss between the tortfeasor and victim – when both or neither parties are negligent. Examples of loss-sharing rules are comparative negligence, comparative non-negligence, and comparative causation. At present, comparative negligence is the only variety of loss sharing commonly adopted by legal systems. See also *contributory and comparative negligence, contributory and comparative non-negligence,* and *comparative causation.*

Lost treasure effect: Tullock's (1980) rent-seeking paradox shows that, in the presence of strong contestants, aggregate expenditures can exceed the value of a contested prize. This could lead to negative expected returns for the players.

If given an exit option, rational players should exit the rent-seeking contest; but this would leave valuable rents unexploited. Dari-Mattiacci and Parisi (2005a) have shown that this lost treasure effect is also present when players are allowed to use mixed-participation strategies: the treasure might remain unclaimed when none of the players joins the contest, thinking that others would do so. Understanding the lost treasure effect is relevant for the design of optimal competition and industrial policy, in which the presence of strong competitors and/or large number of prospective competitors may discourage participation by companies in valuable but costly research. See also *rent seeking* and *Tullock's paradox*.

Lump-sum tax: see *flat tax versus lump-sum tax*.

M

Majoritarian default rules: legal systems provide default rules to fill gaps in incomplete contracts. The existence of default rules allows parties to enter into a binding contractual relationship without having to specify all contingencies in the contract. A reduction in transaction costs is an important function of default rules. The term "majoritarian default rules" has been used in the law and economics literature to identify default rules that aim at reducing transaction costs. The term derives from the fact that, in choosing default rules, lawmakers and courts ask what the majority of parties in a similar contractual situation would have contracted for if they had had the opportunity to write a complete contract (Ayres and Gertner, 1999). By filling contractual gaps with majoritarian default rules, the largest possible number of parties avoid the need to draft their own contractual terms (Scott and Krauss, 2007). However, Ayres and Gertner (1989), in their work on default rules, have criticized a blind adherence to majoritarian default rules. They argue that, because of the costs and challenges of forcing a court to pick majoritarian default rules, there are instances when it would be preferable to select rules, whether accepted by the majority of contracting parties or not, that incentivize the parties to contract explicitly. They introduce the concept of penalty default rules as one alternative to majoritarian default rules. Penalty default rules are rules that would not be accepted by the majority of contracting parties and that place a penalty on one or both of the parties in the event of a dispute. The possibility of being penalized under a penalty default rule will generally spur the parties to draft explicit contract terms that eliminate any gaps. See also *boilerplate*, *default rules*, *minoritarian default rules*, *penalty default rules*, *transaction costs*, and *normative Coase theorem*.

Manne, Henry G. (1928–): generally considered to be one of the founders of the field of law and economics. He was born on May 10, 1928, in New Orleans, Louisiana. He received his undergraduate degree from Vanderbilt University in 1950, his law degree from the University of Chicago Law School in 1952, and his S.J.D. from Yale Law School in 1966. His predominant areas of research are insider trading, legal education, university governance, and law and economics. His article "Mergers and the market for corporate control" (1965) is credited with the introduction of economic analysis to corporate law, and his 1966 book *Insider Trading and the Stock Market* continues to stir considerable controversy on that subject. In addition to his research in the field of economics, he has also

researched and published work on legal education and intellectual history. See
also *Virginia school*.

Marginal: term referring to the incremental effect (e.g., in terms of cost, benefit,
utility) induced by one additional unit. In every optimization problem in economic applications, the optimum is found when marginal cost equals marginal
benefit. This is true, for example, in producer theory, when the optimum is
reached when the price (i.e., the marginal benefit of selling one additional unit
of the good) equals the marginal cost of production. When applied to legal
choice, optimization similarly requires a balancing of marginal costs and benefits. For example, an additional unit of enforcement is justified when the impact
of that unit in terms of deterrence (benefit) outweighs the incremental cost of
enforcement. Additional units of enforcement will generate a net social benefit up to the point at which marginal cost and marginal benefits are equal and
no longer generate a net benefit from enforcement. This concept can be found
in the application of the Learned Hand formula of negligence, which draws a
boundary between diligence and negligence when the marginal burden of precaution (marginal cost) equals the marginal decrease in expected accident costs
(marginal benefit). An important application in criminal law relates to the concept of marginal deterrence. This idea is that small crimes cannot be punished
with the maximal penalty because there would be nothing left to deter more serious crimes for individuals who have already committed the lesser crimes (e.g.,
by punishing rape with the death penalty, there would be no instruments left
to deter murder of the rape victims). See also *marginal-cost pricing*, *marginal
product*, *marginal utility*, *marginalism*, *marginal Learned Hand formula*, and
marginal deterrence.

Marginal analysis: see *marginalism*.

Marginal deterrence: when actors consider multiple harmful acts and are likely
to choose one, legal penalties should be structured in such a way as to provide
deterrence for all harmful acts. Becker (1968) introduced the concept of marginal
deterrence, in his study of optimal penalties for multiple harmful acts. The law
attaches maximal penalties to the most severe harms and attaches lower levels
of penalties to less severe harms. If maximal penalties were used for less severe
crimes, there would be nothing left to deter more severe crimes. As Polinsky and
Shavell (2007) point out, marginal deterrence can sometimes affect deterrence
generally. In order to increase penalties enough on severe crimes to have a
meaningful marginal deterrence effect, the penalties on lower-level crimes might
be so low that they serve no deterrent effect. See also *deterrence*.

Marginal Learned Hand formula: this is a restatement of the formula written
by judge Learned Hand in the case *United States* v. *Carroll Towing*, 159 F.2d.
169 (2d. Cir. 1947). The marginal Learned Hand formula restates the notion of
negligence in marginal terms, setting the boundary between negligence and

diligence such that the marginal costs of care equal the marginal benefits (marginal reduction in expected accident costs). The original Learned Hand formula defined optimal care as the point at which the burden of precaution, *B*, equaled the expected accident loss, *pL* (i.e., where $B = pL$). The original formulation contained a fundamental economic error, inasmuch as it set optimal levels of care where costs equal benefits, rather than equating marginal costs and marginal benefits. The reformulation in marginal terms instead requires $B' = p'L$. See also ***Learned Hand formula*** and ***optimal scope of negligence***.

Marginal product: a measure of the additional unit of output produced by increasing one unit of a given input, keeping constant the level of all other inputs employed in the production of the good. Analytically, marginal product is calculated by dividing the change in total product by the change in the variable input. A standard assumption in economics is the so-called law of diminishing marginal returns, according to which marginal product declines as additional units of a given input are used in the production, holding all other inputs fixed. For example, the product produced by each hour of work declines, even to the point that it reaches zero. Judge Learned Hand used the concept of marginal product in a famous calculation regarding negligence. According to the Learned Hand formula, a reasonable person would take a safety precaution if the marginal product (or additional benefit) that the precaution produced outweighed the additional cost of the precaution. The court case in which Hand stated his formula involved boat harbor accidents. For example, the marginal cost of providing a watchman to make sure a barge does not float away is low. The marginal product of providing the watchman is the value of a lower incidence of accidents that results from the watchman's presence (the probability of accident times the damage). If the marginal product exceeds the marginal cost, a reasonable person would hire the watchman, according to the Learned Hand formula. See also ***marginal***, ***diminishing marginal product***, and ***production function***.

Marginal production cost: see ***production cost***.

Marginal rate of substitution: the ratio between the marginal utility of two goods in the consumption bundle. In economic theory, the marginal rate of substitution can be interpreted as the subjective valuation of the two goods implied by the consumer's utility function. In consumer theory, the optimal consumption bundle is characterized by the equilibrium condition, when the marginal rate of substitution is equal to the relative price of the good. Off equilibrium, when the marginal rate of substitution is different from the relative price of the goods on the market, the consumer should adjust the consumption bundle, increasing the consumption of the cheaper good, until the subjective valuation (the marginal rate of substitution) equals the market valuation (the relative price). See also ***relative price***.

Marginal tax rate: the rate charged on the last taxable unit of income. Many countries have a progressive taxation system, according to which income taxes are subject to increasing marginal tax rates. Altering marginal tax rates allows the taxing authorities to change the effects of taxation on different social groups. The increasing marginal income tax rates are progressive: average tax rates go up as a proportion of a person's income as his or her income rises. Marginal tax rates affect the individual's optimal incentive to increase income. Much of the distortionary effect of taxation is linked to marginal tax rates. The Laffer curve postulates that, once the marginal tax rate rises above a certain threshold, there is a negative relationship between taxable income and marginal tax rate, thereby reducing total tax revenue. In a pure flat tax system, each unit of income is taxed at the same rate, so the marginal tax rate is constant. Most popular flat tax proposals retain progressive outcomes because low income levels are still exempt from taxation entirely. Under lump-sum taxation, the marginal tax rate is equal to zero, so it is not distortionary. See also ***marginal***, ***Laffer curve***, ***progressive taxation***, and *flat tax versus lump-sum tax*.

Marginal utility: the increment in total utility drawn from an increase of one unit in the consumption of a good. It is typically assumed that the marginal utility of consuming a commodity declines as consumption increases, holding consumption of all other goods constant. This is called the law of diminishing marginal utility. See also ***diminishing marginal utility*** and ***utility monster***.

Marginal value product: term describing the increase in the value of output value per each additional unit of input. Production theory shows that a producer maximizes profit when the marginal value product is equal to the marginal cost of production. In the case of a one-input production function (e.g., labor) the producer chooses the optimal level of output when the marginal value product equals the wage (which is the marginal cost of hiring one additional worker). When the marginal value product is lower than the minimum wage, the producer will not hire the worker. This fundamental optimization rule often finds impediments and frictions in real markets. For example, the regulation of the minimum wage may prevent employers from paying a wage equal to the marginal value product of their employees. In turn, this may affect unemployment rates, with a higher minimum wage leading to higher unemployment rates. See also ***minimum wages***.

Marginal-cost pricing: this describes a firm's policy if it sets the price equal to the marginal cost of producing the last unit of output, for any given level of output. Under perfect competition, profit-maximizing firms produce an output level at which marginal cost equals price and earn positive profits on all units of output except for the last one (at which they break even). Under imperfect competition, when one or few firms in an industry have market power, profit-maximizing firms restrict output and sell at a price higher than the marginal cost. Market regulation can require that firms set the price at marginal cost in order to induce firms to expand output up to the socially efficient level. This is called first best regulation. However, in the case of a natural monopoly, first best regulation may not be attainable, because the marginal cost is lower than the average cost of production and marginal-cost pricing would cause a loss to the monopolist. In these cases, the second best solution requires that the firm set its price equal to average cost, attaining zero profits. See also *two-part tariffs* and *perfect competition*.

Marginalism: the predominant schools of thought in economics focus their analysis on small, incremental changes in variables. These incremental changes are known as marginal changes. "Marginalism" is the term used to refer to this type of analysis. Many economic decisions are made using marginal analysis. A rational consumer decides whether to buy one more unit of a good by comparing his or her marginal benefit derived from it to the marginal cost of acquiring it. A rational producer decides whether to hire another worker by comparing the worker's wage (the marginal cost) with the value of the output he or she will produce (the marginal revenue product). Law and economics scholars apply marginal analysis to people's interactions with the legal system. A thief will decide to steal a car by comparing his or her expected prison term if he or she is caught (the marginal cost) with the resale value of the car in the black market (the marginal benefit). Marginal analysis is commonly used because it is amenable to rigorous formal modeling. By focusing on small, incremental changes, mathematical techniques can be used in marginal analysis to determine maximum, minimum, or optimum levels of an activity under certain ideal conditions. The logic of marginalism suggests that there is an optimal level for most activities (such as crime, pollution, tortious behavior). By identifying these optimal levels, policy analysis can be used to determine where social resources should be directed. An important limit of marginalism is given by the presence of discontinuities. Critics of marginalism point to the fact that marginal analysis cannot be used to explain large social changes. It is alleged that major social changes, such as those that accompanied economic reform in the former Soviet Union, are inherently discontinuous and therefore not susceptible to marginal analysis. See also *marginal*.

Market concentration: a concept used to characterize the level of fragmentation and competitiveness of an industry. Market concentration is measured as a function of the number of firms active in the industry and their market shares. Standard market concentration indexes are the industry four-firm concentration ratio (measuring the market share of the four largest firms in an industry) and the Herfindahl index. Under both measures, higher values of market concentration suggest that firms have higher levels of market power. Although there is no deterministic correspondence between market concentration and the competitive behavior of firms, competition authorities often look at concentration indexes as a proxy for the competitiveness of an industry. See also *concentration ratio*, *Herfindahl index*, and *contestable markets*.

Market failures: economic situations in which the market equilibrium is not Pareto-efficient. Economic rationality leads self-interested agents to optimize their objective functions, but it fails to achieve social optimality at equilibrium. The main sources of market failure are asymmetric information, monopoly and imperfect competition, public goods, and externalities. According to economic analysis, the need for legal intervention is justified by the presence of market failure: the government intervenes to restore Pareto efficiency when markets fail to do so. According to laissez-faire economic analysis, market failures also serve to define the proper scope of legal intervention: regulation is unwarranted when markets work efficiently. Economic analysis shows that governmental policies, such as legal sanctions, safety regulations, taxes, subsidies, and price controls, should be optimally calibrated to correct market failure, warning against the risk of the distortionary effects of regulation. See also *monopoly*, *asymmetric information*, *public good*, and *externalities*.

Market for gems: see *inverse adverse selection*.

Market for lemons: see *adverse selection*.

Market for votes: see *logrolling*.

Market power: this results when a market system is not perfectly competitive. In the presence of market power, firms and other economic actors are able to influence prices. While competitive firms are price takers, firms with market power are, to different degrees, price makers. The degree of market power depends on the market concentration, and it will be higher for monopoly than for duopoly or oligopoly. In all such cases, market power can cause markets to supply inefficiently low quantities of goods, with a resulting social deadweight loss. See also *monopoly*, *duopoly*, *oligopoly*, *monopsony*, *concentration index*, and *market structure*.

Market risk: see *systematic versus unsystematic risk*.

Market share: the percentage or fraction of total activity in an industry controlled by one or more firms. The analysis of market shares is relevant for the study of market structure. Market structure is generally assessed with the use of concentration ratios and concentration indexes. Concentration ratios are calculated by summing the market shares of the largest firms in the industry (usually the four largest or eight largest firms) and generating a ratio, which is expressed as a percentage of the total relevant market. Concentration ratios can range from one (i.e., 100 percent) for the case of a monopolistic market and to approaching zero in the case of an atomistic market. Concentration indexes are calculated with the squares of the market share of individual firms. The most common concentration index is the Herfindahl index, which generates concentration values that range from 10,000 for the case of a monopoly to values approaching zero for the case of atomistic competition. Although these latter measures of market concentration are expressed through less intuitive numbers, they provide a better insight into market structure. See also *concentration ratio*, *Herfindahl index*, and *market structure*.

Market structure: economists broadly define "markets" as structures that facilitate the exchange of goods or services. The main elements of such structures are: the number of buyers and sellers, barriers to entry, product differentiation, and costs (Baumol, 1982). This abstraction of the most general salient features of markets has resulted in a taxonomy of four types: (a) perfect competition, (b) monopolistic competition, (c) oligopoly, and (d) monopoly. See also *perfect competition*, *oligopoly*, *monopoly*, *monopolistic competition*, *market share*, *concentration ratio*, and *Herfindahl index*.

Market share liability: in tort law, a defendant who negligently causes harm is liable to the victim of that harm. The twentieth century saw a rise in the number of cases in which a product or activity carried out by multiple individuals or firms caused harm to a victim. For example, many pregnant women in the 1950s took the mass-produced drug DES (diethylstilbestrol). This drug was manufactured and distributed by several pharmaceutical companies. The drug caused genital disease, including cervical cancer, in the daughters of mothers who had taken it. In many cases, although there was no doubt that DES caused the harm in question, it was impossible to determine which company had produced the drug that harmed each individual victim. The California Supreme Court applied the principle of market share liability (Cooter and Ulen, 2008). Under market share liability, defendants would bear liability in proportion to the market share their company had at the time of the tort. While market share liability provides a venue for compensating victims in the absence of an identifiable tortfeasor, the incentives it creates are less than optimal. If operating under market share liability, precautions impose a private cost on the firm that adopts them but create a benefit (positive externality) for all firms in the industry. This positive externality leads to a suboptimal level of precautions. For this reason, market share liability should be applied only in situations in which prospective tortfeasors face activity level decisions (e.g., how many units to sell) but no care level decisions. Priest (2010) observes that market share liability amounts to a tax imposed on current consumers to provide compensation to consumers from an earlier era. As such, market share liability does little to impact present and future behavior. See also *statistical causation*, *proportional liability*, and *comparative causation*.

Markets versus hierarchies: see *governance structure*.

Markovian strategies: game theory uses a variety of models to study interactions between parties over an extended period of time. Players can use information from a variety of sources under most strategies, including information based on past interactions between the players. When players adopt Markovian strategies (also called Markov strategies) they undertake strategies that depend only on the current state of the game and not on the history of the game or the past interactions between the players. A player who is playing a Markovian strategy will therefore condition his or her action solely on the basis of the state of the game at that point, and not on the history of the game. The use of Markovian strategies may hinder the emergence and sustainability of cooperation in repeated games. See also ***normal-form versus extensive-form games***.

Maximand: in optimization problems, this term identifies the object of the maximization. In the law and economics literature, the term is used to define the policy objective (e.g., two sets of rules can be compared in light of the policy objective pursued through such instruments). The choice of the appropriate maximand for legal analysis has been the subject of methodological debates within law and economics: what should the legal system try to maximize? In this debate, even strict adherents to the instrumentalist view of the law may question whether the objective of the law should be the maximization of aggregate wealth or, rather, the maximization of aggregate utility, or freedoms and capabilities. Although there seems to be consensus on the idea that the human dimension cannot be bypassed in policy evaluation, the choice of the maximand is often determined by pragmatic considerations and looks at proxies such as wealth (or quantities of physical resources) that can be objectively measured. Furthermore, the choice of an objectively measurable maximand avoids difficult interpersonal comparisons, which would render any balancing or redistributions across groups or individuals largely arbitrary. Given these reasons, law and economics scholars have distanced themselves from the nineteenth-century utilitarian ideal of utility maximization, and have increasingly used the paradigm of wealth maximization. Posner is the most notable exponent of the wealth maximization paradigm. Under wealth maximization principles, a transaction is desirable if it increases the sum of wealth for the relevant parties (with "wealth" defined as including all tangible and intangible goods and services). However, several scholars in law and economics manifest some uneasiness in accepting the notion of wealth maximization as an ancillary paradigm of justice, raising two fundamental objections. The first relates to the need for specifying an initial set of individual entitlements or rights as a necessary prerequisite for operationalizing wealth maximization. Here, property right advocates criticize the instrumentalist view of wealth maximization: the protection of property rights has a value in itself that must be taken into account, beyond the instrumental value of those rights for the accumulation of wealth (Buchanan, 1974; Rowley, 1989). The second objection comes from the opposite end in the ideological spectrum, and springs from the theoretical difficulty of defining the proper role of efficiency as an ingredient of justice vis-à-vis other social goals. Legal scholars within the law and economics tradition (see, for example, Calabresi, 1980; Sen, 1985; Nussbaum and Sen, 1993; Nussbaum, 2000) have claimed that an increase in wealth cannot constitute social improvement unless it furthers some other social goal, such as utility, equality, or freedom to exercise human capabilities. Denying that one can trade off wealth-based efficiency against these other goals, these scholars advocate the inclusion of different maximands in the formulation of a social welfare function. See also *utility maximization*, *wealth maximization*, *capability approach*, *welfare analysis*, and *utility monster*.

Maximin strategy: such a strategy, also known as a minimax strategy, favors choices that maximize the minimum possible gain. These strategies have been studied in the context of weak link problems, such as those discussed by Cornes and Sandler (1996) and Sandler (2006). See also *minimax strategy*, *zero-sum game*, and *weak link problem*.

Maximize the pie: in the law and economics literature, the term "size of the pie" is often used as a metaphor for aggregate wealth, distinguishing it from "splitting the pie" (a metaphor for distribution). These metaphors have been often used in the debate regarding the competing goals of efficiency and distributive justice. Should the legal system and the courts create and enforce rules that maximize the aggregate welfare of society (maximizing the size of the pie) or should they be concerned with the equitable redistribution of wealth (splitting the pie)? Although the idea of a two-step optimization (i.e., maximizing wealth through law and redistributing wealth through taxation and public spending) has dispelled some of the controversy regarding equitable redistribution through law, this remains a debated question in the field of law and economics, as evidenced by the contributions to this debate by Kaplow and Shavell (1994) and Sanchirico (2000). See also *two-step optimization*, *welfare analysis*, and *capability approach*.

Mechanism design: this studies the optimal structure of Bayesian games in the presence of private information. What distinguishes mechanism design from standard problems in game theory is that the designer can choose the structure of the game, rather than just playing the game. The structure of the game is chosen according to the desired outcome by the designer. Leonid Hurwicz, Eric Maskin, and Roger Myerson won the Nobel Prize in economics in 2007 for founding mechanism design theory. In the subset of agency problems called mechanism design problems, a principal aims to condition his or her own actions on the private information of agents. However, the principal cannot get the private information by asking the agents directly; they have an incentive to act in their own self-interest by distorting information. For example, an individual interested in buying a used car can ask the salesman about the true quality of the car, but the seller has no incentive to reveal truthful information. The principal chooses optimally designed game rules in order to offer the agents incentives to reveal truthful information. Auction design and monopolistic price discrimination constitute examples of mechanism design games. The seller in an auction would like to extract information about the buyers' valuation, and the auction can be designed to induce buyers to reveal their private evaluation of the good truthfully via a bidding structure. Similarly, a monopolist may be unable to identify consumer groups characterized by different valuations of the good.

The monopolist can offer a menu of contracts in order to induce each consumer to self-select the contract revealing his or her true valuation. Mechanism design theory, based on the revelation principle, shows that the principal should choose only games in which agents truthfully report their private information. See also *contract theory*, *agency problems*, *revelation principle*, and *optimal versus efficient mechanism design*.

Meddlesome preferences: within a libertarian free market economic system, individuals can take risks and engage in harmful behavior, so long as they pay for the costs associated with that behavior. However, individuals sometimes develop preferences about the way others behave. Public choice scholars use the term "meddlesome preferences" to refer to preferences about other people's behavior, such as preference about other people's drinking or living habits. Sen's (1970) well-known paradox provides an example of meddlesome preferences, with one of the characters preferring that other people not read *Lady Chatterley's Lover*. Public choice theorists point out that meddlesome preferences are more likely to arise in collective economies in which the behavior of one member of the community invariably affects the costs incurred by others. Meddlesome preferences may lead a state with a strong government to enact policies or use litigation to regulate the behavior of people engaging in unsupported behavior. When the intensity of meddlesome preferences is weaker than the intensity of personal preferences, majoritarian outcomes can impose an externality on the minority and a deadweight loss to society. Buchanan (1988) illustrates the interaction between meddlesome preferences and rent extraction. According to him, sin taxes (e.g., taxes on cigarettes, alcoholic beverages, bullets, and, more recently, soft drinks and fatty snacks) can be viewed as a form of rent extraction based on meddlesome preferences. Wagner (2004) observes that these taxes exceed the value of any externality created by the sins, and illustrate the problematic interaction between meddlesome preferences and rent extraction. See also *external preferences*, *interdependent utility functions*, and *Sen's liberal paradox*.

Median voter theorem: this theorem, also known as Black's theorem, was first articulated by Duncan Black (1948) and later popularized by Anthony Downs (1957). Downs analyzes how the desires of political candidates to win affect the policy positions they take as candidates. In a two-party system in which a candidate wins by obtaining the majority of the votes, candidates will take on the policy preferences of the median voter. The support of the median voter will bring with it the support of the largest possible number of voters, making victory more likely for the candidate adopting the median voter's position. The median voter theorem builds upon Harold Hotelling's (1929) model of spatial competition, in which competing firms sell identical products and try to locate in the market to be near as many customers as possible. Like firms in market competition, political contestants try to locate themselves in the ideological spectrum to be close to as many voters as possible. In a two-party competition in a one-dimensional space, this will lead to the formulation of policies that reflect the median voter's preferences. The assumptions of the median voter theorem include the following: (a) two-party competition; (b) unidimensional issue space; (c) no voter abstention or alienation; (d) full spatial mobility of candidates in the policy spectrum; (e) single-peaked preferences by voters; (f) uniform or unimodal distribution; and (g) voters' full information about the policy platforms of the candidates. In game theory terms, the targeting of the median voter amounts to a Nash strategy for both political contestants. The median voter outcome is therefore derived as a Nash equilibrium. The median voter theorem has been shown to be a useful concept with both explanatory and predictive value in real-life politics. The median voter theorem offers some helpful insights and may help explain the tendency of political candidates, and elected officials, to take moderate stances that anger their political base. The main implication of the median voter theorem is that policy bundles proposed by candidates in a bipartisan race are likely to be centrist and moderate, and much closer to one another, than one would expect given the different ideological backgrounds of the candidates. The median voter theorem also poses a challenge to the efficiency theories of politics, inasmuch as the maximization of the median voter's preferences is not necessarily equivalent to the maximization of aggregate welfare. Rowley (1984) notes that the theorem makes a number of assumptions. The sheer number of assumptions reduces the usefulness of the median voter theorem. Voters, for example, are frequently not fully informed regarding the policy positions of political candidates and are often influenced significantly by carefully crafted political attack ads. By relaxing some of the assumptions, the predictions of the theorem change, and a possible differentiation of policy proposals can be observed in equilibrium. Likewise, the targeting of modal voters, instead of median voters, can be observed under certain conditions. The median voter theorem has implications for the so-called incumbent's advantage theorem. See also *single-peaked versus double-peaked preferences*, *public choice theory*, and *incumbent's advantage theorem*.

Mediation (contract design): there are situations in which the availability of a neutral mediator enlarges the set of incentive-compatible mechanisms. When two individuals are forced to interact face to face or through noiseless channels, they may strategically withhold information or distort their preferences depending on whether they are the first or second mover or if they move simultaneously. A mediator enlarges the set of incentive-compatible mechanisms, since he or she can collect a full set of information from both parties without revealing private information from one party to the other. A direct revelation mechanism in mediation would allow the mediator to communicate separately and confidentially with each interested individual, gain their truthful private information, and provide recommendations for action on the basis of that information. See also *direct versus indirect revelation mechanism*.

Mergers: see *horizontal integration*.

Minimax regret: public choice theorists have invoked minimax strategies as one of the possible explanation of citizens' (otherwise irrational) participation in political elections. According to the rational abstention theorem, voting is irrational inasmuch as it yields negative expected returns (the cost of voting is higher than its expected benefits). However, prospective voters participate in response to minimax strategies. They participate in voting in order to minimize the maximum possible regret – having abstained when their vote could have been decisive. See also *rational abstention* and *minimax strategy*.

Minimax strategy: a decision that assumes that the most preferable alternative is one in which the worst possible outcome is the least harmful. This assumption is used to sort preferences in game theory, and coincides with the maximin criterion often used in political theory. When an agent faces uncertain prospects for success, a minimax strategy implics that it is better for him or her to choose actions with the lowest risk, even if it means forgoing a chance at the highest payoffs. Suppose that two individuals play chess. If player 1 can win in one move, his or her best move is that winning move. Imagine player 2 has two moves. Move one means player 1 can win in the next move. Move two means player 1 can, at best, tie on the next move. Player 2 should take move two. The minimax strategy allows working back from the end of the game to find the best move at any time. Player 1 will try to maximize his or her own chance of winning on each play, and player 2 will try to minimize player 1's chance of winning. In criminal law contexts, agents who pursue minimax strategies should be very sensitive to increases in punishment. A would-be criminal with a minimax strategy weighs potential losses (prison terms) more heavily than potential gains (big score on a bank robbery). See also *maximin strategy* and *zero-sum game*.

Minimum wages: legal price floors on the price of labor. Minimum wages are generally established by legislation, such that no employer subject to the legislation can legally pay wages lower than this legislated minimum. Economic theory suggests that minimum wage laws prevent employers from reaching the optimizing balance between the marginal value product (i.e., the benefit of an additional worker to the firm) and the worker's wage (i.e., the cost of an additional worker to the firm), hence creating distortions in the production process. For example, minimum wage regulation generally increases unemployment for all workers whose marginal value product falls below the minimum wage (i.e., for low-productivity workers). In order to minimize such shortfalls, the legislated minimum wage should be fixed above the market-clearing wage or should be accompanied by policies aimed at softening the employment reduction by stimulating higher output. See also *marginal value product*.

Minoritarian default rules: default rules are implicit agreements that the law presumes in interpreting contracts but that parties are free to nullify by express agreement. Because forming a "complete" contract expressly anticipating every possible contingency would be impractical, the law introduces default rules as gap fillers so as to reduce the transaction costs for parties negotiating a contract, and also to reduce the court costs associated with resolving contract disputes. The conventional wisdom on default rules is that they should either be majoritarian default rules (i.e., what a majority of similarly situated parties would have chosen) or penalty default rules (i.e., imposing a penalty on parties who fail to specify an essential contract term expressly). Ayres and Gertner (1999) identify four circumstances (for reasons other than penalty) in which minoritarian default rules (i.e., rules that only a minority of contracting parties would have chosen) may be preferred: (a) when the cost of contracting around a majoritarian rule is substantially greater than the cost of contracting around a corresponding minoritarian rule, it may be the case that the selection of a minoritarian rule is efficient, because, even though a greater number of agreements will need to contract expressly around it, the cost of opting out of a minoritarian rule will be lower and a net benefit will result; (b) conversely, when the disparate costs of *failing* to contract around a default rule favor a minoritarian rule over a majoritarian rule (e.g., when the impact of failing to contract around a default rule would be substantially greater for the minority than for the majority), a minoritarian rule may be preferable; (c) when the expected cost of ex ante express contracting are less than the cost of ex post gap filling by courts for a majoritarian rule, the minoritarian rule may be more efficient; (d) when the parties are not similarly informed (e.g., when one type of party tends systematically to lack the legal knowledge to appreciate the significance of the default rule), minoritarian default rules may be preferred (Kim, 1999). See also *majoritarian default rules* and *penalty default rules*.

Mixed strategies: see *pure versus mixed strategies*.

Model calibration: see *calibration*.

Modified selection hypothesis: Fon and Parisi (2003) argue that the avoidance of inefficient rules, a central element advanced by Priest (1977), is only a small factor in the cost–benefit calculations of potential litigants. Fon and Parisi argue instead that, because cases tend overwhelmingly to be brought to court by plaintiffs, plaintiffs will tend to file cases in pro-plaintiff jurisdictions and be more reluctant to settle when their cases appear before pro-plaintiff judges, causing a drift in the evolution of the common law toward pro-plaintiff precedents. The modified selection hypothesis offers an explanation for the expansion of legal rules and remedies over time. The predicted effect of the modified selection hypothesis is orthogonal to arguments for the efficiency of the common law; both may be true. See also *survivor theory of efficiency*, *efficiency of the common law hypothesis*, and *Priest's selection hypothesis*.

Monitoring: see *agency problems*.

Monopolistic competition: an oligopolistic market in which a large number of firms sell differentiated products. The main characteristics of monopolistic competition are the heterogeneity of the goods produced in the market, the presence of a high number of consumers and producers, the absence of entry or exit barriers in the long run, and the perfect information of consumers and producers. Examples of markets fitting the description of monopolistic competition are restaurants and service industries in large cities. The original idea of monopolistic competition is due to Chamberlin (1933) and Robinson (1933). In monopolistic competition, each firm behaves like a monopolist in the short run, generating a positive profit and producing an output level such that the marginal revenue equals the marginal cost. Contrary to a perfectly competitive market, in which each firm faces a perfectly elastic demand curve, in a monopolistic market each firm's demand curve is downward-sloping. In the short run, as in a monopolistic setting, each firm has market power and has excess production capacity, thereby imposing a price higher than marginal cost. In the long run, other firms enter the market, attracted by the positive profits accrued in the short run, and the individual demand of each incumbent firm is reduced. Each firm still produces an output, with the marginal revenue equaling the marginal cost, but at a zero economic profit. The benefits of product differentiation decrease with the increased competition and the market tends toward perfect competition, except for the presence of heterogeneous goods. See also *market structure*.

Monopoly: an important form of market failure. A monopoly is characterized by the presence of a single seller of a unique good with no close substitutes. A monopoly faces the entire market demand for the good it sells and has no competition. A monopolist has the highest degree of market power compared to other market structures. In contrast to a competitive firm, the monopoly charges a price above the marginal cost. Because a monopoly sets its price above the marginal cost, it places a wedge between the consumer's willingness to pay and the producer's cost, causing the quantity sold to fall short of the social optimum, with a resulting social deadweight loss. Monopoly can be sustained only in the presence of barriers to entry. Barriers to entry can arise for a number of reasons, including (a) ownership of a key resource, (b) legal monopolies, whereby governments grant a firm an exclusive right to produce some good, and (c) natural monopolies, when economies of scale make a single large producer more efficient than a large number of small producers. A monopolist, like a competitive firm, maximizes profit by producing quantities that lead marginal cost to equal marginal revenue. Marginal revenue for the monopolist is different from that of a competitive firm. In a competitive market, marginal revenue equals price. A competitive firm can sell as much as it likes at the prevailing price, but, for a monopolist, marginal revenue declines as the quantity of output increases. Each additional unit produced actually reduces the marginal revenue obtained by the producer. Compared to perfect competition, monopoly makes producers better off and generally (but not necessarily) consumers worse off. Legal systems respond to the problem of monopoly in a variety of possible ways, including (a) the adoption of structural remedies to make monopolistic industries more competitive (e.g., the break-up of monopolistic firms, merger guidelines); (b) the adoption of behavioral remedies to regulate the behavior of monopolies (e.g., price regulation, sanctions for the abuse of market power); and (c) the transformation of private monopolies into public enterprises (e.g., the US Postal Service, European rail systems). See also *natural monopoly, market failures, price discrimination, Coase conjecture, Harberger's triangle, barriers to entry, structural versus behavioral remedies, Chadwick–Demsetz scheme, market structure,* and *antitrust paradox.*

Monopsony: a market characterized by the presence of many producers and only one consumer. The term "monopsony," introduced for the first time by Joan Robinson (1933), depicts the mirror image of monopoly on the demand side. The monopsonist – the only buyer of the good on the market – controls its producers in the same manner as a monopolist with its own consumers. At equilibrium, the monopsonist exerts its market power by pushing the price of the good down to the production cost. Examples of monopsony are labor markets dominated by one employer and a universal healthcare system in which the government is the only buyer of healthcare services. See also *market power, monopoly,* and *imperfect competition.*

Monotonicity voting criterion: according to this criterion of voting, the winner of an election should remain the winner in any revote in which all voters change their preference in favor of the winner of the original election. Although the monotonicity may appear unavoidable if we assume rational voting, social choice theory shows that this criterion is not necessarily fulfilled, especially in situations of strategic voting under incomplete information. See also *social choice theory.*

Moral hazard: the undesirable consequence of ex post asymmetric information. Moral hazard is often associated with problems of agency in which the principal is unable either to observe or to verify the agent's behavior. Performance-based contracts, according to which the agent's compensation is linked with observable and verifiable output, represent a solution to moral hazard problems, as they realign the agent's and principal's objectives. Performance-based contracts are second best solutions when the agents are risk-averse, since the agents cannot be fully insured under any contract scheme. Additionally, conveying information through signaling and/or acquiring information through screening can solve moral hazard problems. Unlike adverse selection, which generally materializes before a contract, moral hazard is a form of ex post opportunism. Moral hazard problems arise in a number of situations. In insurance markets, after an individual obtains an insurance policy, he or she faces reduced incentives to take precautions to avoid a loss. After entering into a contract, promisees may invest in excessive reliance when expectation damages would compensate them for their reliance expenditures. Likewise, creditors may not take adequate precautions to mitigate the loss if liability for delayed performance covers the entire creditor's prejudice. In tort law, strict liability rules create a moral hazard problem for potential victims who may not have adequate incentives to take precautions, given the full liability coverage in the event of accidents. See also *asymmetric information, adverse selection, signaling, screening, mechanism design*, and *contract theory*.

Moral pessimism versus moral optimism bias: according to Kant (1781), moral optimism is the view that human beings are morally good, and if they fail to do good it may be because of a lack of knowledge, social conditions, non-culpable negligence, or lack of self-control. On the contrary, moral pessimism is the view that human beings are not morally good and that most individuals fail because of moral deficiency. Behavioral economists and law and economics scholars have identified situations in which individuals make biased assessments about other individuals' moral qualities, and refer to them as moral pessimism (or moral optimism) bias. These biased perceptions may affect the behavior of parties in a relationship. In evolutionary game theory, individual perceptions about other players' moral qualities, regardless of the accuracy of those perceptions, critically affect game outcomes. For example, in a tit for tat game, optimal strategies may be determined by the expectations of other players' moral or cooperative attitudes. A morally optimistic player in certain conditions has a greater probability of successfully triggering long-term cooperation. Conversely, under an identical external environment, a morally pessimistic player would engage in anticipatory defection, forgoing the possibility of future cooperation. In several of these situations, moral optimism and moral pessimism become self-fulfilling prophecies. Policymakers may play an important role in correcting moral pessimism biases to promote self-sustaining cooperation. See also *self-serving bias, social projection bias, Hurwicz optimism–pessimism index*, and *behavioral law and economics*.

Most effective precaution taker: all things being equal, when precautions can be alternatively taken by more than one party (alternative care cases), the law should encourage the individual who can take the most effective precautions (the most effective precaution taker) to do so. An important factor for identifying the party who can most effectively take precautions is given by the impact of the parties' precautions on the probability of the relevant event (e.g., the probability of an accident, the probability of breach, etc.). Consider a probability function $p(x, y)$ in which the probability p is negatively affected by the parties' precautions, x and y. The most effective precaution taker is the party whose precautions have the greatest impact on the probability of the event. Say $\left|\frac{\partial p}{\partial x}\right| > \left|\frac{\partial p}{\partial y}\right|$, then the party who can take precautions x is the most effective precaution taker. When the parties' costs of precaution are different, this criterion should consider the cost-effectiveness of precautions, adjusting for the different precaution costs, $\left|\frac{\partial p}{\partial x}\right|/c_x$ vs. $\left|\frac{\partial p}{\partial y}\right|/c_y$ (the most cost-effective precaution taker). When applying Calabresi's (1970) cheapest cost avoider paradigm, the most effective precaution taker criterion is used in conjunction with other specific elements (including the best risk bearer, the cheapest precaution taker, and the cheapest risk avoider) to determine the optimal allocation of accident costs. These criteria help explain the adoption of different liability regimes and the existence of immunities and exemptions from liability, in tort law and other areas of the law. See also *alternative versus joint care*, *cheapest cost avoider*, *cheapest risk avoider*, *best risk bearer*, and *cheapest precaution taker*.

Multi-peaked preferences: see *single-peaked versus double-peaked preferences*.

Multi-sourcing: see *winner determination*.

Multiple equilibria: the concept of Nash equilibrium does not require uniqueness, and in some games multiple equilibria may arise. The presence of multiple equilibria gives rise to coordination problems, such that players need to coordinate on more than one possible outcome, as in the battle of the sexes game. Game theorists have proposed a number of criteria to select the prevailing Nash equilibrium. These criteria are known as equilibrium selection criteria. Under some of these criteria, outcomes are not necessarily determined by payoffs. See also *equilibrium selection*, *Nash equilibrium*, *coordination games*, *focal point*, *subgame-perfect strategy and equilibrium*, and *Pareto-dominant equilibrium*.

Multiple regression: see *regression analysis*.

Multiple takings problem: if an entitlement is protected by liability-type rules, and damages are set below the subjective valuation of the good for the current owner, a multiple takings problem may arise. A party who values the infringement of the right more than the damages can credibly threaten a non-consensual taking. Under Coasean bargaining, if the current owner values the entitlement more than the infringer, no involuntary transfer should take place. However, the threat of a non-consensual taking could be repeated over time, and the multiple threats of infringement could dissipate the value of the initial Coasean bargaining. A multiple takings problem arises when an entitlement is affected by multiple threats of infringement. Under a liability-type rule, the higher-valuing owner may be forced to give payments to each person threatening to infringe his or her right, far above the value of the good or entitlement. If the owner expects to face a multiple takings problem, he or she may just pay no one in the first place, and this may result in a suboptimal final allocation of the right. See also *normative Coase theorem*, *reciprocal takings problem*, and *property rules versus liability rules*.

Multiplication effect of sticks: legal rules create incentives by threatening sanctions ("sticks") or promising rewards ("carrots"). When the promise of a reward produces its effects, the carrot is given out and consumed. Unlike rewards, threats, when effective, do not need to be carried out. Dari-Mattiacci and De

Geest (2009) have shed light on this feature of legal threats in considering the multiplication effect of sticks. The multiplication effect is due to the fact that, although a punishment can be applied only once, the threat to punish can be made repeatedly, without having to carry out the punishment. Parties' compliance with the law renders punishment unnecessary, allowing the threat to be reused in other situations. The multiplication effect of sticks provides one possible explanation for the fact that legal rules use threats (sticks) more frequently than rewards (carrots) to create incentives. See also *carrots versus sticks*.

Mundus!: in 2004 the Erasmus program in law and economics received recognition by the European Union as an Erasmus Mundus program. This recognition was celebrated with great enthusiasm by the European law and economics community, since the funding allowed the continuation and expansion of the European Master in Law and Economics (EMLE) to an international level. The more substantial funding of EMLE allowed the granting of a substantial number of scholarships (including several full scholarships to non-European students). The announcement was given by the former president of the European Association of Law and Economics, Roger van Den Berg, during the 2004 annual meeting in Zagreb, Croatia, and was communicated to the members of the association during the annual dinner speech by the incoming president, Hans-Bernd Schaefer. The members of the association celebrated this announcement with a toast to "Mundus!" Since then, scholars in the European law and economics community have jokingly been using the word "Mundus!" as a celebratory expression, comparable to the centuries-old Greek term "Eureka!," to cheer an academic accomplishment or a new scientific result. This form of cheering has been continued over time, but the expression is often repeated with no awareness of its origin. See also *Erasmus program in law and economics* and *EALE*.

Myopia: term used by economists to refer to the short-sightedness of agents in a variety of contests. In behavioral economics, the term identifies limitations in cognitive thinking and decision-making. In public choice theory, myopia refers to the short-sightedness of political agents who, moved by political or re-election constraints, give excessive weight to the immediate payoffs relative to the long-term effects of their political decisions. A myopic decision-maker does not give the proper weight to the long-term consequences of his or her actions, and may limit his or her attention to a limited range of values. A myopic decision-maker tends to overestimate present consequences (e.g., the consumption utility or earnings, the effects of policies on short-term unemployment) and may take decisions that are immediately beneficial but suboptimal over the long term. In all its variations, the choices of a myopic agent depart from that of an ideal "rational agent," who employs foresight and is perfectly able to process information on future streams of earnings or utility without exhibiting excessive time preference. See also *time preference*, and *social time preference*, *social discount rate*.

N

Nash bargaining solution: the general consensus, among economists and lawyers alike, is that uncoerced bargaining can allow parties to arrive at the set of alternatives that is best for them, and that is best for society as a whole. Starting with Francis Edgeworth (1881) and John Hicks (1932), economists have tried to understand the process of bargaining. John Nash's (1950b) work on bargaining has provided a valuable paradigm for modeling how human beings make decisions in the process of bargaining. Nash explores the concept of bargaining in a two-person game. In the game, both players have a fixed set of alternatives. If the players choose certain alternatives, they will achieve certain results. If the players fail to agree, they will achieve a certain, less desirable result (called the disagreement point or disagreement payoff). Each player has the power to veto every result aside from the least desirable result. The Nash bargaining solution holds that the two players in this game will, through negotiation, arrive at the set of alternatives that maximizes the product of their utility gains from the bargaining (called the Nash product). On the basis of this result, public choice and social choice scholars (Sen, 1970; Kaneko and Nakamura, 1979; Mueller, 2003) have formulated a Nash social welfare function, in which the welfare of society is maximized through a hypothetical Nash bargaining scheme. See also *axiomatic theory of bargaining* and *Nash criterion of welfare*.

Nash criterion of welfare: John Nash's (1950b) criterion of social welfare departs from the straight utilitarian approach, suggesting that social welfare maximization requires something more than the maximization of the sums of the payoffs for the various members of society. The Nash social welfare function is represented by the grand product of the utility of the members of society. Unlike the typical Kaldor–Hicks utility maximization function $Max \sum_{i=1-n} U_i$, the Nash utility maximization function is represented by the grand product of the utilities of all members in society, $Max \prod_{i=1-n} U_i$. This criterion of welfare builds on Nash's idea that, through bargaining, parties arrive at the set of alternatives that maximizes the product of their utility gains (called the Nash product). On the basis of this result, social choice and public choice scholars (Sen, 1970; Mueller, 2003) have formulated a Nash social welfare function, in which the welfare of society is maximized following a hypothetical bargaining between its members. Kaneko and Nakamura (1979) show that the hypothetical bargaining result is ultimately best for society and derive Nash's scheme "as a unique possible social welfare function in view of the [dominant] social choice theory." A layman's interpretation of this criterion of social welfare is that society is formed by a network of individual relations, and the multiplication captures the important interpersonal effects that are part of societal well-being. Additionally, the Nash criterion captures the welfare implications of distributional inequalities. Like Rawls' (1971) difference principle, the result of the Nash criterion of welfare is relatively straightforward: the well-being of a society is heavily affected by the well-being of its weakest members. The use of the algebraic grand product captures that intuition. Just as the strength of a chain is heavily influenced by the strength of its weakest link, so the chain of products in an algebraic multiplication is heavily affected by the smallest of the multipliers. The policy implications are similar – though not as extreme – as those reached under a Rawlsian maximin criterion of welfare. In the law and economics tradition, these models of social welfare have not enjoyed great popularity. This is not so much for an ideological bias but for a combination of methodological and practical reasons. From a methodological point of view, distributional concerns are generally kept separate from the pursuit of efficiency. Such separation has been rationalized on the basis of the so-called two-step optimization process: the legal system is a costly instrument for distribution and should be used for the creation of incentives; the tax system can be utilized to correct distributive problems and is a cheaper instrument for the wholesale redistribution of wealth (Kaplow and Shavell, 1994). From a practical point of view, the adoption of the Nash criterion would run into the well-known difficulties of normalizing the scale of utility across individuals and estimating diminishing marginal utility effects. See also *Nash bargaining solution*, *aggregation problem*, *Rawlsian maximin*, *Kaldor–Hicks criterion*, *difference principle*, *utility monster*, and *capability approach*.

Nash equilibrium: virtually every legal problem involves interdependent decision-making (e.g., the actions of victims and tortfeasors in the face of accidents, the effort of a promisor and the reliance of a promisee in a contract, the choices of a prospective criminal and the precautions of a prospective victim, etc.). The concept of Nash equilibrium (Nash, 1951) is the most frequently used tool for analyzing interdependent decision problems. The idea of Nash equilibrium is each players in a game will adopt the best strategy for him- or herself, considering the strategy of the other player. At a given point, neither player could do any better, given the strategies adopted by the other player; therefore an equilibrium arises. More formally, then, the equilibrium is defined as the set of strategies and payoffs chosen by *A* and *B* such that *A* cannot improve his or her payoff given *B*'s strategy, and *B* cannot improve his or her payoff given *A*'s strategy. It is worth observing that some games have no equilibria in pure strategies, and also that some games have multiple equilibria. See also *dominant strategy equilibrium*, *pure versus mixed strategies*, and *subgame-perfect strategy and equilibrium*.

Nash product: see *Nash bargaining solution*.

Nash social welfare function: see *Nash criterion of welfare*.

Nash strategy: see *best response*.

Nash, John Forbes (1928–): an American mathematician who made important contributions to the early foundations of game theory, as well as to concepts of differential geometry. He was born on June 13, 1928, in Bluefield, West Virginia. In 1994 Nash was awarded the Nobel Prize in economics, along with fellow game theorists Reinhard Selton and John Harsanyi, for their pioneering analysis of equilibria in the theory of non-cooperative games. While at Princeton University, in 1950, Nash wrote his doctoral dissertation on non-cooperative games that contained the definition and properties of what would later be called the Nash equilibrium. Game theory formalized the process of strategizing on the basis of expected countermoves from the other player(s) in an interaction. This type of exchange characterizes many economic situations, and is thus a critical component of current economic thought. Nash introduced the distinction between cooperative games, in which binding agreements can be made, and non-cooperative games, in which binding agreements are not feasible. He developed an equilibrium concept for non-cooperative games that later came to be called the Nash equilibrium. Among his many important publications, his works on this topic include "Equilibrium points in n-person games" (1950a), "The bargaining problem" (1950b), and "Two-person cooperative games" (1953). See also *game theory* and *Nash equilibrium*.

Natural experiment: an observational study that is not controlled by the experimenter, and in which the assignment of treatments occurs naturally on account of other factors. Like field experiments, natural experiments take place in the real world, as opposed to the laboratory. Unlike field experiments, in a natural experiment the independent variable is naturally occurring (or exogenously determined outside the experiment). Examples of natural experiments in law and economics include the study of the effects of changes in states' minimum wage laws on employment levels, the effects of new criminal-sentencing guidelines on crime rates, the effects of divorce laws on family choices, and the effects of tax rates on tax compliance. Natural experiments are especially useful when they capture an exogenous change in a relevant factor while other factors remain unchanged, so that observed effects can be attributed to the change in that factor. The range of applications of natural experiments nicely complements that of controlled experiments, and their use becomes particularly important in areas in which controlled (field and laboratory) experiments would not be feasible. See also *field experiment*, *laboratory experiment*, and *calibration*.

Natural monopoly: an industry is a natural monopoly when a single firm can supply a good or service to an entire market at a smaller cost than could two or more firms. A natural monopoly arises when there are economies of scale over the relevant range of output. The existence of an incumbent firm in a natural monopoly de facto creates a barrier to entry for other firms. A good example of a natural monopoly is in the power distribution industry. Once an electrical company has developed an infrastructure (e.g., running power lines to a community), it can service every resident there at a low average cost. A new firm would have to face the fixed cost of setting up its own infrastructure before being able to provide a service to its first customer. A significant feature of natural monopoly industries is that promoting competition through market fragmentation in these industries will not necessarily help consumers. When competition is pursued through deconcentration measures (e.g., the break-up and divestiture of a natural monopoly), two countervailing effects are generally produced. First, the entry of one or more additional firms triggers competition and leads to an increase in output and social surplus by decreasing the size of Harberger's triangle (lost surplus due to monopoly underproduction). Second, the presence of multiple firms means that any given quantity of goods is not being produced at the lowest possible average cost. The correction of the monopoly deadweight loss through market deconcentration hence introduces a new inefficiency. This inefficiency is known as Tullock's rectangle (increased production cost due to forgone production economies). A legal reform that forces competition through market deconcentration on a natural monopoly industry will be welfare-enhancing only if the area of Tullock's rectangle (increase in production costs) is smaller than the area of Harberger's triangle (monopoly deadweight loss). Reflecting the peculiar effects of competition in a natural monopoly industry, competition authorities often prefer price regulation to other structural market remedies when dealing with natural monopolies. Competition authorities may therefore allow the natural monopolist to operate as the only firm in an industry (preserving low average costs of production), regulating its price or forcing a higher level of output. However, the price regulation of a natural monopolist is often problematic and fails to approximate marginal-cost pricing, because of the presence of asymmetric information and rent-seeking. See also ***weak monopoly***, ***Ramsey pricing***, ***monopoly***, ***market failures***, ***Harberger's triangle***, ***Tullock's rectangle***, ***marginal-cost pricing***, and ***Chadwick–Demsetz scheme***.

Natural selection theory of legal evolution: see ***survivor theory of efficiency***.

Near-public good: in some economic literature the term "near-public goods" has been used to describe a particular category of goods characterized by non-rivalry in use and the excludability of non-paying individuals. As a result of their feature of excludability, near-public goods could be produced and effectively traded in the market, but their feature of non-rivalry renders public intervention potentially desirable so as to avoid deadweight losses due to excessive levels of exclusion. The concept of anticommons describes a similar category of situations, and has gained much popularity in the recent law and economics literature. See also ***anticommons*** and ***non-rivalry***.

Necessary and sufficient conditions: the concepts of "necessary" and "sufficient" conditions are common to several disciplines, including economics, philosophy, and logic. If A is a necessary condition for B, then B could not have occurred without A. However, B does not necessarily occur as a result of A. Differently, if A is a sufficient condition for B, then A is one of the possible causes of B (i.e., B can occur in the presence of A, but does not necessitate A). Finally, if A is a necessary and sufficient condition for B, then B can occur only, and will occur always, in the presence of A. These concepts play an important role in the law of evidence and are important tools in the assessment of causation. See also *causation*.

Negative expected value suits: see *negative value suits*.

Negative externalities: see *externalities*.

Negative income tax: a concept that constitutes a proposed extension to systems of progressive taxation, whereby taxpayers beneath a certain threshold receive money rather than paying to the government. Historically, laissez-faire economists have been cautiously supportive of negative income tax proposals as an alternative to welfarism. See also *progressive taxation*.

Negative liability: negative and positive externalities are equally harmful to social welfare. In several areas of the law, legal rules provide instruments for internalizing negative externalities. For example, tort liability can be viewed as a way of forcing tortfeasors to internalize the negative external effects of their conduct. Those who cause harm to others without their consent (negative externality) should compensate their victims for their loss (internalization). As pointed out by Dari-Mattiacci (2009), in the presence of positive externalities, negative liability should symmetrically apply: those who create a positive externality should be paid a compensatory award by the gainers. However, legal systems rarely create negative liability and generally adopt other mechanisms and indirect solutions for the internalization of positive externalities. There are several explanations for the asymmetric treatment of negative and positive externalities in the law, among which is the fact that negative liability would pose a number of practical and theoretical problems, relating to intent, incentives, and evidence. See also *externalities*.

Negative reciprocity: see **tit for tat**.

Negative-value suits: there are many instances when parties involved in a dispute do not actually resort to litigation. Law and economics scholars have studied the rules of the litigation process, and the legal and regulatory schemes that apply to specific categories of litigation, to try to understand why potential litigants do or do not file suit. One interesting issue within this line of study is the existence of negative-value suits, or negative-expected-value suits. A negative-value suit is one in which the cost to a plaintiff of litigating the case to the point of achieving a successful judgment outweighs the benefits the plaintiff would receive from the positive judgment. For example, if a person slips and injures him- or herself where a neighbor negligently failed to care for his sidewalk, it might cost the injured person more to litigate the case than what he or she might expect to receive through a judgment against his or her neighbor. The theory is that negative-value suits should not be pursued (there is a negative expected return from litigation) and should not be settled (given the negative expected returns, the threat of litigation is not credible). However, evidence suggests that negative-value claims are occasionally filed, and frequently settled. Scholars have asked why defendants still might settle when faced with a negative-value suit. If the defendant knows that the plaintiff would lose financially from trying to litigate successfully, he or she should dismiss the threat of litigation as non-credible and should not settle. Bebchuk and Klement (2012) summarize a variety of hypotheses as to why defendants might still settle, despite the existence of negative-value suits. These include a lack of information on the part of the defendant, the ability of the plaintiff(s) to divide up the costs of litigation, costs that the defendant might bear upfront that make the defendant less likely to want to allow litigation ever to begin, the possibility of new information coming to light during trial, the reputation of the defendant and other soft factors, and contingency fee arrangements. These explanations show how real-life litigation scenarios are frequently different from a perfect-information scenario, in which a defendant would have little incentive to settle in a negative-value suit.

Neglect probability bias: psychological studies have shown that individuals tend to disregard small levels of uncertainty, acting as if certain events were certain and as if uncertainty surrounding such events did not exist. This phenomenon is known as the neglect probability bias (Redelmeier and Kahneman, 1996). This bias becomes relevant in all situations in which individuals make decisions under uncertainty, and affects the ways in which individuals undertake precautions in tort law (Posner, 2003), inducing individuals to make decisions as if certain facts were certain, and disregarding all other possible outcomes of their choice. See also *optimism bias*, *zero risk bias*, *behavioral law and economics*, and *debiasing*.

Net present value: see *present value*.

Network effects: term generally used to refer to demand-side externalities, when the value of a commodity increases as the number of consumers increases. The literature distinguishes between direct network effects (e.g., the value of owning a telephone increases as more people buy telephones, there potentially being more people who may be called or who may call) and indirect network effects (e.g., the value of owning an electric car increases with the number of electric cars produced and sold, because it will increase the supply of recharging stations in the territory). Less commonly, the term may also refer to decreases in value when the number of consumers increases. See also *spillover* and *economies of scale*.

Network externality: see *network effects*.

Neuroeconomics: field exploring the foundations of economic behavior, bringing together the research tools of psychology, neurology, and economics. Much of the research in neuroeconomics developed as an offspring of experimental economics. A subset of the research in this field, pioneered by Kevin McCabe at the Center for Law and Neuroeconomics at George Mason University, explores the interrelationship between law and human emotions, developing original theory and research with the development of an ambitious research agenda for legal policymakers. See also *happiness research*, *utility maximization*, and *experimental law and economics*.

New institutional economics: it was Oliver Williamson (1975) who first used this term, to describe the then emerging field of the study of the institutions using modern economic tools. Williamson used the term with reference to the work of Ronald Coase and Douglass North. These three scholars were recognized with the Nobel Prize in economics, respectively in 1991, 1993, and 2009. New institutional economics uses economics to analyze the laws, rules, and norms – both formal and informal – that govern modern economies. In contrast to "old institutional economics," which largely criticized neoclassical economics and its focus on the individual and rational behavior, new institutional economics uses traditional economic tools of analysis and continues to focus, in part, on individual behavior. Although in recent years Williamson has pointed out that new institutional economics is still far from a unified theory, the discipline has grown large and developed a clear identity and research agenda. The founding of the International Society of New Institutional Economics (ISNIE) in 1997, and the success and large participation of academics at the annual meetings of the association, are indications of the increased worldwide interest in new institutional economics. See also *transaction-cost economics*, *Coase, Ronald*, *North, Douglas*, *Williamson, Oliver*, and *ISNIE*.

Newcomb's paradox: in 1960, while contemplating the prisoner's dilemma, William Newcomb formulated a hypothetical scenario that illuminates issues of free will and decision-making (Nozick, 1969). Although he did not publish his thoughts on it, it has been termed Newcomb's paradox (also known as Newcomb's problem). It presents a decision-making situation in which two reasonable alternatives exist. The choice between these two alternatives poses a decision paradox, which symbolizes the tension between forward-looking and backward-looking approaches to decision-making. Newcomb's problem considers a person who is presented with two boxes, A and B. Box A always has $1,000 in it and box B will either have $0 or $1,000,000 in it. Newcomb's thought experiment also includes an individual, called the Predictor, who is able to predict the person's decision-making with perfect or near-perfect accuracy. The Predictor decides whether to put $1,000,000 in box B or leave box B empty. The person has the opportunity to take one or two boxes, along with the contents therein. The person must decide, when faced with the two boxes, whether to choose one box or both boxes. If the person chooses one box, he or she will presumably pick box B. If the Predictor predicts that the person will choose boxes A and B, the Predictor will leave nothing in box B. If the Predictor predicts that the person will choose box B alone, the Predictor will put $1,000,000 in box B. The paradox arises because the player should realize that, whatever the Predictor predicted, the choice has already been made. The Predictor might have predicted correctly or incorrectly. No matter what the Predictor predicted, picking both boxes reaps a higher reward by $1,000. However, as the Predictor is almost always correct, it might be wise to play a safe strategy, choosing only one box. The paradox represents the tension between two rational approaches to decision-making. This tension characterizes several conditional cooperation problems, in which individual decisions hinge upon expectations of cooperation and trust by the other player. Albert and Heiner (2003) have shown that, given predictability, evolution favors a backward-looking approach to solving this problem. See also ***backward induction*** and ***prisoner's dilemma***.

No ex post renegotiation assumption: parties can at times renegotiate agreements that were not performed and modify the obligations under a contract. Ex post renegotiation opportunities can affect the parties' ex ante incentives as well as dilute the effectiveness of legal remedies. The law and economics literature often assumes away renegotiation opportunities in order to isolate the effect of legal rules from the effects of ex post renegotiation. Besides this methodological reason, the assumption of no ex post renegotiation applies to the case of material breach when the benefit of the forgone performance is irreversibly lost as a result of non-performance. Examples would include situations in which the time of the performance is of the essence (e.g., catering for a wedding, providing recording equipment for a live performance) or in which the nature of the performance is non-fungible (e.g., breach through the sale to a third party of a piece of art or a unique piece of property). See also ***renegotiation proofness*** and ***no retraction principle***.

No retraction principle: proposed by Ben-Shahar (2004), this principle suggests that the mutual consent requirement for contract formation is too narrow to induce optimal reliance by the parties in the course of their negotiations. The no retraction principle suggests that a party who manifests the intent to enter into a contract under certain terms should not be able to retract from his or her position in the subsequent course of the negotiations. Under a no retraction rule, in a negotiation in which the traditional "meeting of minds" is not reached, the proponent should not be allowed to retract freely from his or her bargaining position. The other party could de facto hold him or her to the terms he or she proposed in the course of negotiations. The no retraction principle rests on the idea that the obligations of the parties should grow stronger as their initial bargaining positions converge toward an agreement. The principle constitutes a departure from the all-or-nothing approach followed by most contract law regimes, and calls for the adoption of an ascending scale of enforceability (similar to that envisioned by Fuller and Perdue, 1936). The no retraction principle leads to the adoption of varying levels of enforceability, similar to those subsequently considered by Bell (2010), as an alternative to the enforceable versus non-enforceable divide, used by modern contract law regimes. Critics of the no retraction principle contend that it imposes liability in conjunction with activities that do not qualify as sources of legal obligations, and that it fails to recognize the reverse effects it might have on parties' willingness to engage in pre-contractual negotiations, given the difficulties of exiting them (Markovits, 2004). See also *graduated consent theory*, *reliance*, *no ex post renegotiation assumption*, and *renegotiation proofness*.

Non-cooperative games: a game is defined as non-cooperative when each player is required to choose his or her strategy independently and cannot sign an enforceable agreement that obliges him or her to play a pre-specified strategy. Cooperation may arise as a solution of a non-cooperative game. However, in the absence of an enforceable agreement, this occurs only in those situations when cooperation is self-enforcing (i.e., the cooperative behavior is the best response for all players because it maximizes their individual payoff function despite the fact that it is a non-cooperative game). A game is defined as cooperative when players form subgroups, called coalitions, that may enforce cooperative behavior through a third party. The game is played by the coalitions, rather than by individual players. Non-legal enforcement mechanisms such as those considered by Kronman (1985) – hostages, collateral, hands tying, and union – as well as legal enforcement mechanisms, such as contract law, can transform non-cooperative games into cooperative ones. See also *self-enforcing contracts*, *hostages*, *collateral*, *hands tying*, *union*, *relational contracts*, and *cooperative games*.

Non-excludability: the property of a good whereby a person cannot be prevented from using it. Non-excludability is one of the two fundamental characteristics of public goods (the other being non-rivalry). Open-access goods and commons are also non-excludable, but, unlike public goods, their use is rivalrous. The combined presence of non-excludability and rivalry in use leads to the possible overuse and exploitation of open-access and common resources – a problem known as the tragedy of the commons. See also *public good*, *non-rivalry*, *open-access resources*, and *commons*.

Non-legal enforcement mechanisms: enforcement gives credibility to contractual promises. Absent enforcement, contracting parties would be faced with a prisoner's dilemma, in which both parties would have dominant defection strategies (trying to capture the other party's performance, without fulfilling their own contractual promise). The opportunity of an exchange could be mutually beneficial, but, if there is no enforcement mechanism that guarantees mutual performance, no beneficial exchange will take place. Legal systems provide enforcement of contracts (with remedies such as specific performance and damages) to help parties overcome this dilemma and to facilitate contracting. In addition to legal enforcement, parties can utilize non-legal enforcement mechanisms. Kronman (1985) examines the role of non-legal enforcement mechanisms in an article on contracts in the state of nature. He considers four types of non-legal enforcement mechanisms, including hostages, collateral, hands tying, and union. Building on the findings of evolutionary game theory, the subsequent literature has added relational contracts to the list of situations in which cooperative exchanges can be sustained in the absence of legal enforcement. See also *self-enforcing contracts*, *hostages*, *collateral*, *hands tying*, *union*, *relational contracts*, *cooperative games*, and *non-cooperative games*.

Non-observable precautions: when ascertaining negligence, courts and juries perform a negligence test by confronting the level of precaution taken by the tortfeasor with the due level of care. While some forms of precaution are easy to ascertain ex post, others are difficult or even impossible to assess. Dari-Mattiacci and Parisi (2005b) observe that, in the presence of non-observable precautions, individuals would rationally limit their investment in non-observable precautions, since investing in non-observable precautions would not reduce the likelihood of being found negligent. In the law and economics literature, the case of non-observable precautions is generally treated under the discussion of care levels versus activity levels. Like activity level incentives, the incentives to invest in non-observable precautions are present only for the party who bears the accident loss in equilibrium. See also *activity level versus care level* and *decoupling*.

Non-rivalry: the property of a good whereby one person's use or consumption does not diminish other people's opportunity to use or consume. Non-rivalry is one of the two fundamental characteristics of public goods (the other being non-excludability). In economic terms, non-rivalrous goods are goods for which an additional user creates no additional cost (i.e., the marginal cost for an additional user is zero). See also *public good*, *near-public good*, and *non-excludability*.

Non-salability: an item, entitlement, or parcel of land is non-salable when it cannot be sold for either legal or quality reasons. Law and economics scholars have explored the role of inalienability rules in the context of the economics of remedies. See also *inalienability rules*.

Non-satiation: individuals are generally assumed to prefer more to less (i.e., to place positive value on greater consumption of desirable goods). This assumption of non-satiation is used for modeling purposes as an axiom of preference. Although it may be a correct characterization of consumer preferences in most real-life situations, it ignores the fact that there are limits to the amount of goods that any one individual can enjoy or consume. In the absence of a resale market, too much of a good can actually become a bad. See also *axioms of preference*, *bliss point*, and *diminishing marginal utility*.

Non-systematic risk: see *systematic versus unsystematic risk*.

Non-tariff barriers: countries use many methods to restrict imports. The most common way to discourage imports is to impose a tariff, or import tax, on imported goods so that they will be more expensive to domestic consumers. Any trade barrier that is not a tariff or import quota is a non-tariff barrier. For example, a country may subject goods to rigorous specification requirements and lengthy inspections. Under ideal conditions, these barriers are disfavored by economists because they distort the relative price of goods facing consumers, which prevents the price system from allocating resources efficiently. The relative price of the imports is artificially high, and too few domestic resources will be spent on them. However, these barriers are used for reasons other than promoting efficiency. Trade barriers are sometimes justified as protecting domestic industries, preventing invasive pests and species from entering a country, or attempting to discourage environmentally insensitive business practices overseas, among other reasons.

Non-zero-sum games: see *variable-sum games*.

Norm entrepreneur: Sunstein (1996) observes that there will often exist a disjunction between private beliefs and public norms. Indeed, for any given member of a community, there will almost certainly be at least one public norm with which that community member privately disagrees. Norm entrepreneurs are political actors who make use of the lacuna between public norms and private beliefs to effect social change. Norm entrepreneurs can be a powerful mechanism for social, cultural, and political change – when the private beliefs of a large number of people quietly begin to diverge from a publicly endorsed norm. The norm entrepreneur sees the opportunity to make expression and endorsement of the dissenting beliefs acceptable, potentially undermining the existing norm and establishing a contrary (or modified) norm. See also *descriptive versus prescriptive norms* and *expressive law*.

Normal distribution: found, intuitively, where a set of data tends to conform to a bell curve. Not all random distributions of data conform to a normal distribution, but, absent special assumptions, most naturally occurring phenomena will. The central limit theorem states that, under many common conditions, random phenomena will tend to conform to a normal distribution. Consequently, the assumption of normal distribution may be a useful "first pass" when encountering new data. Moreover, normal distributions are mathematically convenient, lending themselves to a robust set of analytical tools and corollaries. See also *Pareto distribution*.

Normal good: in economic terminology, this term refers to a good that reacts positively to changes in consumers' income. An increase in income leads to an increase in the consumption of normal goods. A decrease in income leads to a reduction in the consumption of normal goods. For normal goods, the income elasticity of demand is positive. See also *inferior good* and *Giffen good*.

Normal-form versus extensive-form games: the terms "normal-form game" and "extensive-form game" are used in game theory to refer to two representational forms of strategic interactions. Normal-form games are represented by a matrix (box) with two (or more) rows and two (or more) columns. Each side of the box represents a player; the rows and columns represent the players' strategies. The "top" player chooses between the column strategies (hence he or she is called the "column-player"). The "side" player chooses between the row strategies (hence he or she is called the "row-player"). Each possible outcome corresponds to the little box resultant from the chosen strategies. The payoffs are indicated inside each box (the first number generally refers to the payoff of the row-player, the second number to the column-player). The representation of a game in extensive form is significantly different. An extensive-form game has the structure of a decision tree with multiple branches and sub-branches. Players are represented by the nodes in the decision tree. The branches starting at each node represent the strategies available to that player. Payoffs are indicated at the end of each sub-branch by numbers, with the first number being the payoff of the first mover and the second number refers to the payoff of the second mover. The choice of a normal-form as opposed to extensive-form representation of a game does not affect the outcomes. However, the extensive-form representation of a game allows specification of the strategies of the players as well as the sequence of their decisions. The information regarding the sequence of players' moves is not available when the game is represented in normal form. See also *subgame*, *subgame-perfect strategies and equilibrium*, and *Markovian strategies*.

Normative analysis: see *positive versus normative law and economics*.

Normative Coase theorem: according to the positive Coase theorem (Coase, 1960), absent transaction costs, the final allocation of legal entitlements will be efficient, regardless of the initial assignment of rights and choice of remedial protection. In the absence of transaction costs, the law does not matter. When transaction costs are present and exceed the benefits of a transaction, Coasean bargaining will not be carried out, and both the initial assignment of rights and the choice of remedies will affect final allocations. In the presence of positive transaction costs, the law matters, and the efficiency of the final allocation is not independent of the choice of the legal rules and remedies. The so-called normative Coase theorems are corollaries to the positive Coase theorem, explaining how the law matters when transaction costs are present. The plural is used because, even though there is only one positive Coase theorem, there are several normative versions of the theorem formulated by various scholars. A first simple normative corollary to the Coase theorem is that legal systems should lubricate exchange mechanisms and reduce impediments to voluntary bargaining. Legal rules should therefore be designed to lower transaction costs and minimize other costs associated with the transfer. This is, for example, the idea behind the concept of majoritarian default rules. In addition to this simple normative corollary, more complex normative corollaries to the Coase theorem attempt to identify the preferable assignment of rights and choice of remedies to minimize the effects of positive transaction costs. The optimal choice should generate outcomes that mimic those that would have been chosen by the parties in the absence of transaction costs. Demsetz (1972) was among the first scholars to discuss systematically the problems resulting from lifting the assumption of zero transaction costs in the Coase theorem. Demsetz observes that the choice of remedy in the presence of significant transaction costs affects resource allocation. One remedy may be superior to another, because the difficulty of avoiding costly interactions is usually different for the interacting parties. Accordingly, the legal rule should be chosen taking into consideration which party can avoid the costly interaction at the lowest cost. The most notable (and cited) normative restatement of the Coase theorem comes from Calabresi and Melamed (1972), who show that, in the presence of positive transaction costs, liability-type remedies (which they call liability rules) are preferable to property-type remedies (which they call property rules). In their view, liability-type rules are preferable because they allow an entitlement to be appropriated by another party without the consent of the other. As long as the infringer is willing to compensate the original owner for the objectively determined value of the right, the entitlement will change hands, positive transaction costs notwithstanding. Liability-type rules allow the entitlement to be reallocated bypassing the need for a voluntary transaction and the obstacles created by transaction costs. According to Calabresi and Melamed, in these situations liability-type rules can achieve a combination of efficiency and distributive results that would be difficult to achieve under property-type rules. In partial tension with Calabresi and Melamed, Epstein's (1993) restatement is worthy of consideration for being closer in spirit to Ronald Coase's original theorem and resisting some of the bolder implications of the Calabresi and Melamed argument. Epstein stresses the importance of the "single owner test": when resources are under the command of two or more persons, the legal arrangement should attempt to induce all the parties to behave in the same way that a single owner would. When the single owner test yields a unique result, that result should be adopted as the legal rule. However, when the single owner test does not yield clear results, no normative corollary principle should be formulated on the basis of the Coase theorem. Further exploring the choice between property-type and liability-type remedies, Kaplow and Shavell (1996) address several factors casting doubt on the equivalence of these alternatives in low-transaction-cost environments. Their analysis considers several objections to Coasean costless bargaining, including the inability of a party to ascertain what the other is willing to pay or accept, the victims' ability to mitigate harm, the problem posed by one party being judgment-proof, and administrative costs. Kaplow and Shavell find a presumption in favor of liability-type rules over property-type rules in the context of harmful externalities, but that this presumption may be overcome as a result of one or more of the factors they describe. After considering some of the conventional arguments for the use of property-type protection, the authors find a strong theoretical case for the protection of these interests using property-type rules. Their version of the normative Coase theorem thus underlies the choice of the optimal system to ensure the protection of various types of property rights. Also bridging the gap between Coase, for whom liability-type rules and property-type rules are equally efficient, and Calabresi and Melamed, for whom high transaction costs lead to a preference for liability-type remedies, is the work by Ayres and Talley (1995) on private information as a transaction cost. The inefficiency occurs when parties misrepresent their own valuations in order to gain strategic advantage in the bargaining process. When two parties have private information about how much they value an entitlement, endowing each party with a partial claim to the entitlement can reduce the incentive to behave strategically during bargaining by inducing greater disclosure. A bargainer has two Coasean alternatives: buy the other party's claim or sell his or her own claim. The normative formulation of Ayres and Talley is that a liability-type remedy is preferable, because it allows a party's decision to pursue one of these alternative transactions to function as a credible signal of a low or high valuation, thereby encouraging more efficient trade. See also ***Coase theorem***, ***asymmetric Coase theorem***, ***Hobbes theorem***, ***multiple takings problem***, ***reciprocal takings problem***, ***property rules versus liability rules***, ***cathedral***, ***Coase, Ronald***, ***Stigler, George***, ***Demsetz, Harold***, and ***Calabresi, Guido***.

Normative decision theory: see *decision theory*.

Normative overdeterrence: Depoorter, Van Hiel, and Vanneste (2011) discuss the idea of normative overdeterrence resulting from excessive legal sanctions and extreme measures of deterrence. Overdeterrence may be at one and the same time inefficient and counterproductive to the enforcement effort. Overdeterrence can result from excessive penalties and/or excessive enforcement levels and can be counterproductive in terms of compliance, because of the fact that they may trigger principled disobedience, increase the satisfaction involved with rule breaking, and undermine political support for enforcement. See also *countervailing norms*.

Norms: see *descriptive versus prescriptive norms*.

North, Douglass Cecil (1920–): a prominent economic historian who has had an important influence on law and economics, thanks to his contributions to understanding how economic and political institutions change over time. He pioneered the use of econometrics to analyze economic and political history. Douglass North received the Nobel Prize in economics (with Robert Fogel) in 1993 for his research on the economic history of the United States and Europe. North was born on November 5, 1920, in Cambridge, Massachusetts. He received his undergraduate degree from the University of California, Berkeley, in 1942, and after an interruption in his studies to serve in the Merchant Marine during World War II received his Ph.D. in economics from the same university in 1952. During his graduate studies at Berkeley he became interested in economic history, and over the course of his career he has pioneered the application of complex statistical analysis tools to research the formation of political and economic institutions and the consequences of these institutions on the performance of economies over time. He published the bulk of his research on this topic in his most influential work, *Institutions, Institutional Change and Economic Performance* (1990). North has advanced the theory that institutional structures, particularly as they relate to property rights, are the basis for a society's economic well-being. In addition to his investigations into institutional structures he has carried out research in the area of how cognitive and behavioral science affect economic change over time. See also *new institutional economics*.

Null versus alternative hypothesis: statistical analysis involves formulating and testing hypotheses on the observed data set. The concept of the null hypothesis, introduced by Fisher (1949), corresponds to a default position. Typically, the null hypothesis assumes that there is no relationship between two measured phenomena. For example, the frequency at which capital punishment is applied is not related to the average educational level of the jury. The null hypothesis is typically formulated in opposition to the alternative hypothesis, which claims the presence of a relationship between the two observed phenomena (e.g., the frequency at which capital punishment is applied decreases as the percentage of jurors with a college education increases). The concept of the alternative hypothesis was first formulated by Neyman and Pearson (1928). The alternative hypothesis does not necessarily need to be defined as the logical negation of the null hypothesis, and can either be "one-tailed," when the relationship is assumed only in one direction, or "two-tailed," when both directions are admitted. See also *level of significance*, *type I and type II errors*, and *falsifiability*.

Nussbaum's capabilities approach: see *capability approach*.

Oates' decentralization theorem: see *decentralization theorem*.

Observation learning: see *informational cascades*.

Observational studies: see *controlled experiment*.

Ockham's razor: a heuristic for evaluating theories, stating that, when presented with two competing theories, *A* and *B*, that explain phenomenon *X* with equivalent explanatory strength, the "simpler" theory should be preferred. This principle is occasionally used in the law and economics literature to encourage scholars to refrain from unnecessary complexity in their analysis and in the formulation of hypotheses. As a general statement, Ockham's razor raises a number of philosophical problems. First, what is a "theory"? Second, what is "explanatory strength"? Third, what is "simple"? There are no quick answers to these vexing and profound philosophical questions. For practical purposes, it suffices (a) that scientific theories (inclusive of economic theories) are abstract models linked to the real world by sentences expressing hypotheses; (b) that the explanatory strength involves some correlation between predictive success and comprehensiveness; and (c) that simplicity correlates with fewer assumptions. In scientific practice (and in the study of law and economics), Ockham's razor is rarely useful in comparing two fully worked-out theories. Rather, it is most useful at the theory-*building* stage, as a practical principle guiding the construction of models. The designation derives from the medieval philosopher William of Ockham (*c.* 1285–*c.* 1348), though the attribution is dubious; no express declaration of the principle exists in Ockham's work (Brampton, 1964). While Ockham's preoccupation with ontological parsimony was acutely consonant with the gist of the heuristic that bears his name, it is doubtful that *any* philosopher or scientist would prefer multiplying entities beyond necessity. Its normative force is therefore questionable, since everyone seems inclined to parsimony anyway. Finally, it bears keeping in mind that, in philosophy, Ockham's razor is often taken to have particular significance in metaphysics, in which it may (albeit controversially) carry descriptive weight. However, in the sciences, Ockham's razor is merely a practical, normative principle about how one ought to build a model, ceteris paribus. See also *assumptions*, *robustness*, and *falsifiability*.

Oligopoly: a market structure dominated by the presence of a few firms handling most of the market supply for many buyers. The presence of a small number of sellers in oligopolistic industries is generally a consequence of the presence of high barriers to entry, restricted access to innovative or complex production technology, or economies of scale in production. Oligopolistic firms have market power and behave as price setters, as opposed to perfectly competitive firms, which act as price takers and have zero market power. The distinctive feature of oligopolistic markets is represented by the mutual interdependence of strategic decisions among the sellers. The presence of few sellers induces each oligopolistic firm to be aware of the actions undertaken by the other competitors operating in the market. Each firm's choice influences and is influenced by the other firms' choices. When making decisions regarding output and other market strategies, firms in an oligopoly industry must take into account how competitors will likely react. For example, suppose an oligopoly firm can raise its advertising budget and increase revenues by capturing some of its competitors' customers. This strategy will be less attractive if the competitor is likely to increase advertising in response. Oligopoly theorists use game-theoretical analysis to model the interdependence of firms' strategic choices. The most widely known oligopoly models are the Cournot model, according to which firms compete in output quantity, and the Bertrand model, in which firms compete in price. The market outcomes of oligopolistic competition may vary substantially. Oligopolistic firms may collude tacitly or through the formation of cartels and act as monopolists, thereby restricting output quantity and raising prices in the market. In other contexts, the competition may be substantial, and the prices observed on the market may approach the outcome of perfect competition. The welfare analysis of oligopolistic markets is therefore sensitive to the parameters defining market structure. See also ***duopoly***, ***oligopsony***, ***Bertrand competition***, ***Cournot competition***, ***cartels and tacit collusion***, ***market power***, and ***market structure***.

Oligopsony: an industry in which there are only a few buyers for a particular good, but many sellers. Like oligopoly, the interaction of a reduced number of buyers results in mutual interdependence; unlike oligopoly, the mutual interdependence applies to the relationship between buyers, not sellers. Oligopsonists have power in the buyers' market and adopt strategies considering how the other competing buyers would react to their decisions. Typically, oligopsony arises when a few firms are competing for factors of production that are not widely used outside that industry, such as the case of the US auto industry in the 1960s, when a large number of firms competed to supply the three major auto makers with components and raw material. Oligopsony firms have a strong incentive to avoid engaging in price competition for inputs because it would only lower profits for the entire industry. As a result, oligopsony firms also employ various mechanisms of collusive behavior, such as price leaders and cartels, to coordinate the prices they pay for inputs. See also ***duopsony***, ***oligopoly***, and ***market structure***.

Opaque preferences: see ***translucent preferences***.

Open-access resources: scholars generally use this term to describe common-pool resources over which no party can – legally or practically – claim property rights. In some environmental law literature, open-access resources are distinguished from common-pool resources and considered extreme versions of common-pool resources, over which the government or other entities can exert almost no control. Wayburn and Chiono (2010) use the atmosphere as an example of an open-access resource. See also ***common-pool resources***, ***public good***, and ***commons***.

Opportunity cost: the opportunity cost of a decision is the value of the second best (unchosen) alternative. For example, if Smith chooses to spend his evening engaged in activity *A*, but would have otherwise chosen activity *B*, then a consequence of choosing *A* is that Smith loses the opportunity to do *B*. The opportunity cost of *A* is the forgone value of *B*. See also ***Bastiat's unseen costs*** and ***accounting profits versus economic profits***.

Optimal allocation of risk: see ***best risk bearer***.

Optimal scope of negligence: when determining negligence, courts need to determine not only the level of a party's care but also whether a specific precautionary measure should be included in the inquiry about negligence or not. This choice determines the scope of the negligence inquiry. The optimal scope of negligence balances the gains derived from improved accident prevention with the administrative costs of the system. The scope of negligence is important, because it determines whether a certain precautionary measure should be modeled as care (if included in the determination of negligence) or as activity level (if excluded), and hence it affects the optimal choice between strict liability and negligence (Dari-Mattiacci, 2005). See also ***Learned Hand formula***.

Optimal specificity of law: see ***rules versus standards***.

Optimal versus efficient mechanism design: in the terminology of mechanism design and contract theory, scholars draw a distinction between optimal and efficient mechanism design. An optimal mechanism design maximizes the expected payoff of one particular agent. An efficient mechanism design maximizes the total payoff across all agents. In applications of mechanism design to auctions, the agent that receives this special consideration is typically the seller, though this need not be the case. See also ***mechanism design***, ***contract theory***, and ***agency problems***.

Optimism bias: a distortion of perception, also referred to as unrealistic optimism, resulting in an inflated estimation of one's future success. Optimism bias is commonly regarded as a psychologically generated bias in human judgment. An optimism bias may undermine the accurate and calculated estimation of risks. Behavioral scholars classify optimism bias under the "positive illusions" (i.e., unrealistically favorable perceptions about oneself) identified by Taylor and Brown (1988). Optimism bias leads individuals to overestimate the probability of achieving a desirable outcome (e.g., the successful performance of a contract) or to underestimate the probability of undesirable outcomes (e.g., the probability of an accident). To study the effect of the optimism bias in a law and economics model, the bias can be modeled as a false perception about the probability of certain events. Consider the probability p of an accident (or of a breach of contract) and x as the precautions taken by the tortfeasor (or promisor). Optimism bias can be denoted as an underestimated probability of accident or breach, $p(x) < p(x)^*$. Behavioral law and economics scholars have addressed the problem of optimism bias, considering the possible role of law in restraining or correcting this judgment error. Debiasing unrealistic optimism through law is not an easy task. For example, an optimism bias may lead to the assumption of an excessive risk, undermining the deterrent effect of liability rules. Even if the potential tortfeasor knows that the actions driven by his or her optimism may be construed as negligence, the imposition of such liability would not as such correct the bias, and will be unlikely to encourage the adoption of optimal ex ante precautions. See also *illusion of control bias*, *above-average effect*, *Hurwicz optimism–pessimism index*, *self-serving bias*, *false uniqueness bias*, *false consensus bias*, *zero risk bias*, *neglect probability bias*, *blind spot bias*, *behavioral law and economics*, and *debiasing*.

Optimism index: see *Hurwicz optimism–pessimism index*.

Optimization: see *constrained optimization*.

Option to buy: see *call option*.

Option to sell: see *put option*.

Option value: term, originating with the finance literature, that refers to the advantage that the option holder derives when choosing not to exercise an option. The option value increases with the volatility of the underlying market and the time expiration of the option. Option value theory has drastically changed the way of thinking about investment decisions. Traditionally, investment theory suggested that an investment should be undertaken whenever it generated a positive net present value. McDonald and Siegel (1986), Pindyck (1991), and Dixit and Pindyck (1994) have shown that the traditional net present value rule does not yield the optimal result when the investment is irreversible. When decisions entail irreversible investments, the value of the option not to invest should be taken into account. As Polinsky and Shavell (2007) observe, this concept is useful in the field of environmental economics. In assessing the value of environmental quality, it may be necessary to assess the option value of future alternatives. For example, a group of individuals may seek to change local policies so as to protect a small lake, because they want to preserve the option of using it in the future. This concept helps to capture the passive value that individuals sometimes place on the possibility of using or consuming something in the future. The concept has found applications in the law and economics literature, ranging from sequential litigation decisions (Bebchuk, 1996) to the optimal timing of legal intervention (Parisi, Fon, and Ghei, 2004). See also *quasi-option value*.

Ordinal preferences: the idea that alternatives are comparable only on a relative basis, by a ranking (first, second, third, etc.), and are not measurable in objective cardinal values with a numerical scale (one, two, three, etc.). Doctrines of ordinalism view utility as a strictly subjective and non-measurable reaction to external alternatives that may allow for intrapersonal rankings but not for interpersonal quantifications or comparisons according to an objective scale. With ordinal preferences it is possible only to express whether one good is preferred to another (ranking of preferences), without specifying how much more or less one good is preferred (intensity of preferences). See also *cardinal preferences*, *ordinalism*, *preferences*, and *interpersonal utility comparisons*.

Ordinal utility: see *ordinal preferences*.

Ordinalism: the doctrine according to which utility can be expressed only through ordinal preferences, implying that it is possible to express only the ranking between alternatives, not to express the intensity of preferences by means of cardinal numbers. Ordinalism poses a substantial challenge to the utilitarian approaches to policymaking often utilized in law and economics, inasmuch as most mechanisms to aggregate preferences across a large number of subjects assume the measurability and interpersonal comparability of utility. Alternative paradigms of welfare, such as Posner's wealth maximization, overcome the objections of ordinalism, albeit giving rise to different methodological concerns. See also *ordinal preferences*, *cardinalism*, *interpersonal utility comparisons*, and *wealth maximization*.

Ordoliberalism: a term for a German economic and political school of thought that advocates capitalism in conjunction with a strong state to ensure that the free market operates efficiently. It is noted for its view that the proper role of government is to promote a strong legal system and protect individual rights and free market competition in order to prevent economic power from amassing in the hands of a few, thereby stifling competition. This school of thought arose in West Germany after World War II, when the role of capitalism was uncertain there, as many were calling for an economic system characterized by widespread nationalization and central planning as a way to deal with the devastation of the German economy. Ordoliberalism was originally referred to as neoliberalism, but, with its emphasis on the role of the state in promoting capitalism and free markets, it is distinct from modern neoliberalism. It began being referred to as Ordoliberalism in 1950, as a result of its association with the academic journal *ORDO*. Because the school centered on Walter Eucken and Franz Böhm, both of whom taught at the University of Freiburg in southwest Germany, the Ordoliberals have also been referred to as the Freiburg school. The West German adoption of Ordoliberal principles, led in part by the controversial removal of price control measures, allocation decrees, and rationing directives by Ludwig Erhard in 1948, led to a flourishing of the postwar West German economy known as the *Wirtschaftswunder.* This school of thought is still influential on German political and economic leaders today, including Erich Hoppmann, Friedrich Hayek's successor at the Freiburg school, who has attempted to integrate Hayekian principles into a new Ordoliberal framework. See also *Freiburg school of law and economics*.

Organic rationality: see *ecological rationality*.

Original position: see *veil of ignorance*.

Origins of property: the origins of property have been extensively studied by economic theorists. Adam Smith (1776) argued that scarcity is what explains the establishment and enforcement of property rights. This would explain the limited domain of property in early societies and the changing contours of property protection as a result of changes in the economic structure of society. However, as pointed out by Harold Demsetz (1967), scarcity is a necessary but not sufficient condition for the emergence of property. Property rights develop to internalize externalities in the use of scarce resources. There are costs associated with the establishment of property. While scarcity may be necessary for giving objects value and prompting the desire to have property rights, the establishment of such rights also requires that the protection of the rights be economically justified, in the sense that the benefit of private property (internalization of the externalities from common use) should outweigh the cost of establishing and protecting property rights. Property rights emerge only when the gains of internalization become larger than the cost of internalization. The study of the historical evolution of property confirms these economic propositions and reveals that changes in the economy often trigger changes in the social and legal conception of property. Property rights emerge and grow in societies in relation to the cost–benefit calculus regarding the establishment and protection of such rights. Economic change creates new cost–benefit relationships, giving rise to modifications in property regimes (Rose, 1985; Posner, 2010; Parisi, 2007). This gives rise to a grounds-up conception of property, in which the legal notion of property reflects the localized and evolving function performed by property in society. The natural propensity of humans to possess productive and scarce resources and the social acceptance of this human attitude gives rise to the institution of property and its regulation. See also *functional property*, *commons*, and *bundle of sticks*.

Ostrom, Elinor (1933–2012): until her recent death the Arthur F. Bentley Professor of Political Science at Indiana University Bloomington. In 2009 she became the first woman to be awarded the Nobel Prize in economics. She was best known for her innovative analysis of the tragedy of the commons, which she argued was manageable by consumers of common goods without the constraints of government regulation or a collapse into private property. More generally, she was credited with renewing scholarly interest in political economy. She received her B.A. (honors), majoring in political science, in 1954 and her Ph.D. in political science in 1965 – both at the University of California, Los Angeles. Ostrom was the senior research director of the Vincent and Elinor Ostrom Workshop in Political Theory and Policy Analysis at Indiana University Bloomington. She was also the founding director of the Center for the Study of Institutional Diversity at Arizona State University, Tempe. See also ***common-pool resources***.

Other-regarding preferences: social scientists use this term to describe situations in which one individual's preferences are subordinated to the preferences of others (Scott, 1972; Pollak, 1976; Sen, 1977; Elster, 1983). Examples of other-regarding preferences include altruism, envy, and status seeking. McAdams (1992) provides a useful taxonomy of other-regarding preferences, distinguishing between (a) positive and negative other-regarding preferences and (b) relative and absolute other-regarding preferences. A *positive* other-regarding preference is one in which an actor's well-being increases as another actor's well-being increases (e.g., family relationships). A *negative* other-regarding preference is one in which an actor's well-being decreases as another actor's well-being increases (e.g., a bitter enemy). An *absolute* other-regarding preference is one in which the functional relationship is simply correlative with the well-being of the other actor (e.g., both family relationships and bitter enemies). It may be easier to understand absolute other-regarding preferences by contrasting them with *relative* other-regarding preferences, in which an actor's well-being is a ratio of his or her own well-being and that of another (e.g., an egalitarian is not principally concerned with the welfare of others in a vacuum but, rather, the welfare of others in relation to each other; likewise, a competitive socialite may not care about the fame of others per se, but may care about the fame of others relative to him- or herself). Law and economics scholars model other-regarding preferences generally as interdependent utility functions. See also ***relative preferences*** and ***interdependent utility functions***.

Outlier: econometricians collect large amounts of data on which to perform statistical analyses. Most data points will cluster within a certain range of the mean. An outlier is a data point that is far from the mean. These outliers are examined closely to see if they represent the true variability of the data or if the observation shows a data entry error or some spurious departure from the ordinary course of things. Discarding outliers that belong in the data set will result in an underestimation of the variability in the data. Suppose there is a study to compare the length of prison sentences with recidivism rates for violent criminals across states. Most of the observations are clustered around an average sentence length of ten years and a repeat rate of 20 percent in the first year after release. However, one state reports an average sentence length of one year and a repeat rate of only 1 percent. This last observation is an outlier. Perhaps this piece of data was mistakenly reported or recorded or is simply a fluke, and it should be ignored. However, before it is discarded, it must be examined closely to see if there is an explanation. See also *econometric models*.

Overconfidence: see *optimism bias*.

Overcorrection: a form of bias that results when actors are forced to revise their judgments after the discovery of an error in their initial judgments. Empirical studies have shown that test subjects tend to compensate more than necessary in correcting for the initial distortion, leading to distortion in the opposite direction. For example, in a trial in which faulty evidence is presented and subsequently shown to be incorrect, jurors may not simply discount the flawed evidence but take it as affirmative support in favor of the party against whom it was presented. Guttel (2004) suggests that mechanisms exist in the law to mitigate the effect of overcorrection bias. See also *behavioral law and economics*, *anchoring bias*, *bounded rationality*, and *ecological rationality*.

Overlapping generations: see *intergenerational equity*.

P

Pairwise competition voting: with this, candidates (or alternatives) are selected through a sequential one-on-one contest with all other candidates. In a direct pairwise selection, two candidates are matched against each other, the winner competes against a third contender, and so on. The candidate who prevails in the last one-on-one contest is declared the winner. As shown by Condorcet's voting paradox, this form of direct pairwise selection can generate intransitive collective outcomes and is thus vulnerable to agenda manipulation. In order to avoid such a voting problem, a pairwise voting competition should be carried out as a tournament, allowing each candidate to compete one on one against everyone else. Each candidate would gain two points for each one-on-one contest that he or she wins and one point for each contest that results in a tied vote. The candidate with the highest total score is the winner. In such a pairwise voting competition, Condorcet's voting paradox would be prevented. The candidate who wins the higher number of pairwise contests will do so regardless of the sequence of voting, thus avoiding both the intransitivity and the agenda-setting problems. See also *Condorcet voting paradox* and *agenda setting*.

Papers on Non-Market Decision Making: the original title of the journal *Public Choice*. Gordon Tullock founded the journal in 1966. See also **Public Choice** and *Tullock, Gordon*.

Paretian liberal: Paretian liberalism is a dual commitment to (a) some form of liberalism and (b) Pareto optimality. Sen (1970b) has shown that, even when the constraints of liberalism are starkly minimal, the possibility exists that some set of preference orderings will fail to satisfy either the condition of liberalism or Pareto optimality. Hence the title of his paper, "The impossibility of a Paretian liberal." This antinomy is often referred to as "Sen's liberal paradox." See also *Sen's liberal paradox*, *social choice theory*, *interdependent utility functions*, and *meddlesome preferences*.

Pareto distribution: Vilfredo Pareto (1897) observed that the income distribution in a population could be represented with a parametric density function now known as a "Pareto distribution." The distribution envisioned by Pareto is a parametric density function with upper tails that decrease at a polynomial rate (e.g., incomes above a certain threshold, x_0, decrease at a rate $Cx_0^{-\theta}$ for some real C and positive θ). Evidence has confirmed that distributions of income and of several other socio-economic realities follow Pareto's functional form, to the point that Pareto's distributions are often referred to as "Pareto's law." Pareto distributions and their generalizations are frequently used to describe both natural and socio-economic phenomena that are characterized by "fat-tailed" distributions. See also *normal distribution* and *Pareto index*.

Pareto efficiency: according to the criterion of Pareto efficiency (or Pareto opti-mality), an optimal allocation is one that maximizes the well-being of one individual with the well-being of other individuals remaining constant. This cri-terion is named after the welfare criterion formulated by Italian economist and sociologist Vilfredo Pareto (1848–1923). Unlike the Kaldor–Hicks efficiency criterion, the Pareto criterion limits the inquiry to ordinal preferences of the relevant individuals. Given a set of alternative allocations, a Pareto improve-ment (or Pareto optimization) can be achieved by pursuing reallocations that make at least one individual better off without making anyone else worse off. An allocation of resources is Pareto-efficient (or Pareto-optimal) when no fur-ther Pareto improvements can be made. The Pareto criterion has been criticized for two main reasons: (a) it is dependent on the status quo, in that different results are achieved depending on the choice of the initial allocation; and (b) it allows only the ordinal evaluation of preferences, since it does not contain any mechanism to induce parties or decision-makers to reveal or evaluate cardinal preferences (i.e., the intensity of preferences). As a result of these shortcomings, scholars (such as Calabresi, 1991) have questioned the usefulness of the Pareto criterion in its applications to law and economics. See also *Pareto non-compa-rability*, *Pareto-optimal redistribution*, *Kaldor–Hicks criterion*, *utilitarianism*, and *aggregation problem*.

Pareto improvement: see *Pareto efficiency*.

Pareto index: used to characterize the distribution of income (or other resources) across the population. The Pareto index provides information regarding the concentration of wealth in a percentage of the population (e.g., 70 percent of the world's wealth is held by 30 percent of the population). A lower Pareto index denotes a higher concentration of wealth among the few. A higher index denotes a more even distribution of wealth. Formally, the Pareto index is the coefficient used in a Pareto distribution. See also *Pareto distribution*.

Pareto non-comparability: a Pareto-efficient allocation of resources is one that leaves no opportunity for reallocating resources to make at least one party better off without making anyone else worse off (i.e., no further Pareto improvements are possible). In normal situations, there are several possible solutions that could qualify as Pareto-optimal, and the Pareto criterion does not allow any welfare comparison between them; in other words, there is Pareto non-comparability. For example, if the social problem is that of distributing a benefit between two parties, any hypothetical distribution would be Pareto-optimal, since there is no possible alternative redistribution that would make one party better off without harming another party. In these cases, the Pareto criterion is agnostic on which, among these alternative distributions, should be chosen. See also ***Pareto efficiency***, ***Kaldor–Hicks criterion***, ***utilitarianism***, and ***aggregation problem***.

Pareto-dominant equilibrium: one with payoffs that are Pareto-efficient, in the sense that no Pareto improvements are possible. In other words, players cannot make any change such as to create an advantage for at least one player without prejudice to the others. Pareto optimality is used as a refinement of the Nash equilibrium concept in the presence of multiple equilibria. See also ***multiple equilibria***.

Pareto-optimal redistribution: redistribution is generally considered a violation of the Pareto principle, inasmuch as it involves one individual or group gaining at the expense of another. However, redistribution can lead to a Pareto improvement, if the giver draws some satisfaction from his or her giving (e.g., altruistic donation). A Pareto-optimal redistribution can, therefore, exist, to the extent that the individuals who give can experience some benefit from their giving.

Pareto's law: see ***Pareto distribution***.

Participation constraint: when formalizing decision-making processes, this concept is used to capture the idea that a party will choose not to participate in a given activity if the expected payoff of that decision is lower than a given reservation value (generally, the status quo payoff). For example, when deciding whether to enter into a contract, the participation constraint requires that each party is at least as well off in the contract as he or she would have been without signing the contract. More generally, the participation constraint requires that the agent is not worse off by undertaking a given course of action. The concept of participation constraint is of critical importance in mechanism design and in solving agency problems. Any solution to an agency problem should satisfy simultaneously the incentive compatibility constraint and the participation constraint. In the presence of risk aversion, participation constraints often limit the extent to which optimal incentives can be created. For example, optimal incentives often require that risk be borne by the party that can best control it. Hence, for instance, to create optimal incentives the risk of business failure should be borne by managers rather than shareholders. Desirable as it may be from the point of view of incentives (i.e., reallocation of the risk satisfies the incentive compatibility constraint), the reallocation of business risk to individual managers may be unacceptable for most risk-averse individuals (i.e., reallocation of the risk would not satisfy the participation constraint of the prospective manager). See also ***mechanism design***, ***agency problem***, ***incentive compatibility***, and ***strategy proofness***.

Path dependence: in economic analysis, path dependence indicates that "history matters," in the sense that past decisions affect current economic choices. In the presence of path dependence, the economy does not necessarily converge toward a unique equilibrium; multiple equilibria may exist. The prevailing equilibrium will be partly affected by the pattern of past choices made by economic agents in the process of convergence. The concept of path dependence was originally introduced to explain the patterns and processes of technology adoption. For example, the adoption of a technology standard can exhibit path dependence, and inferior standards can survive. Bandwagon and network effects may produce path dependence in industries that converge toward a product design or standard. The concept of path dependence was subsequently utilized in a wide range of applications in evolutionary economics. See also ***herding behavior***.

Penalty default rules: according to the traditional criterion, default rules should aim at minimizing transaction costs by mimicking the content of the rules that the majority of the contracting parties would have contracted for. In a well-known article, Ayres and Gertner (1989) provide a different concept of default rules. In contrast to traditional (majoritarian) default rules, penalty default rules (or penalty defaults) are purposefully chosen to differ from what the parties would have chosen, and are designed to give at least one party an incentive to contract around the penalty default. By doing so, penalty defaults encourage one or both parties to reveal information to the other party and to the courts by affirmatively choosing the contract provision they prefer. An essential premise of the notion of penalty defaults is the idea that contracting costs are not the only reason for contractual incompleteness. In many settings, contractual incompleteness is the result of strategic behavior on the part of contracting parties (e.g., parties who are trying to gain an advantage over the other party by withholding private information). Penalty defaults give parties incentives to negotiate ex ante by penalizing them for leaving inefficient gaps in their contracts. The traditional contracting-cost-minimizing function of default rules is often in conflict with the strategic-cost-minimizing function of penalty default rules. According to Ayres and Gertner, the balance should be struck by giving preference to penalty defaults over majoritarian defaults when it is cheaper for the parties to negotiate a term ex ante than for the courts to estimate ex post what the parties would have wanted. The concept of penalty defaults is very similar to the concept of information-forcing default rules, which had previously been formulated by Goetz and Scott (1980), who suggest that the exclusion of liability for unforeseeable harm or consequential damage in contracts (e.g., the rule set in 1854 by the well-known English case *Hadley* v. *Baxendale* 156 ER 145 [1854]) is a good illustration of a default rule that forces the revelation of private information between the parties. The result of that case was that one party did not receive full expectation damages, despite such damages being the majoritarian default rule, because that party did not reveal enough information when negotiating the contract. The court applied a penalty default rule that would encourage parties to negotiate explicitly in the future. Parties who face a risk of harm that is unforeseeable to the other party will have incentives to reveal such private information to render the risk known (and thus foreseeable) to the other party. In this way, information-forcing default rules and penalty default rules allocate the risk on the party who is in the best position to disclose information relevant to the transaction. Eric Posner, in his analysis of penalty default rules, argues that penalty default rules do not actually exist in real contracts, regardless of whether they encourage more efficient and explicit contracting during negotiations (Posner, 2006). See also *default rules, majoritarian default rules, minoritarian default rules, information harnessing, asymmetric information, altering rules,* and *sticky default rules.*

Penalty defaults: see *penalty default rules.*

Perfect compensation: see *indifference criterion of perfect compensation.*

Perfect competition: description of a market in which consumers and producers act as price takers and have zero market power in setting the price of a homogeneous good. In a perfectly competitive market, each firm is small relative to the size of the whole market (atomistic market), and therefore cannot affect market equilibrium prices (price taker). The conditions characterizing a perfectly competitive market are an infinite number of buyers and sellers, the absence of entry and exit barriers, the homogeneity of the good traded in the market, and perfect information on the part of consumers and producers. In real-world situations, the restrictive conditions for perfect competition are rarely met, and there are few, if any, perfectly competitive markets consistent with this economic definition. Perfect competition constitutes a fundamental benchmark in economic theory for the evaluation of efficiency. Each firm acts as a profit maximizer, choosing its output to maximize profit. In the short term, perfectly competitive firms choose the output level at which price equals marginal cost (allocative efficiency). In the short run, the firm can earn either positive or negative profits. Consider the case when firms earn positive profits in the short run. In the absence of entry barriers, new firms will be attracted and will enter the market, driving profits to zero. A similar reasoning applies in the case of negative profits in the short run. In the long run, perfectly competitive firms produce an output level at which market price equals marginal cost (allocative efficiency) and average cost (productive efficiency). This implies that, in the long run, the firm produces at the minimal production scale (i.e., at the minimum average cost). In a perfectly competitive market, the aggregate surplus and the consumer surplus are maximal. See also *imperfect competition, Bertrand competition, Cournot competition, Stackelberg competition,* and *market structure.*

Perfect equilibria: Nobel laureate Reinhard Selten refined the concept of Nash equilibrium for analyzing dynamic strategic interaction. When applying the concept, we often identify several equilibria in non-cooperative games. Through Selten's refinements, some of the equilibria can be excluded as improbable or unreasonable. Consider, for example, the case of equilibria that could be induced by threats or promises that are not credible. By eliminating outcomes induced by non-credible threats and promises, unique equilibria can often be singled out, allowing for stronger predictions about outcomes in dynamic strategic interactions in the form of so-called perfect equilibria. See also *Nash equilibrium.*

Perfect expectation damages: a refinement of simple expectation damages in contract law, by which damages are liquidated on the basis of the promisee's forgone contractual benefit, evaluated at the "socially optimal" level of reliance. Perfect expectation damages create optimal incentives for the promisor's performance and for the promisee's reliance levels. In view of the difficulty of establishing what constitutes optimal reliance in particular real-world cases, the law and economics literature has shown that coupling an expectation damages rule with a zero marginal damage rule can also create optimal bilateral incentives. See also *zero marginal damages* and *expectation damages*.

Perfect information: see *complete versus perfect information*.

Permanent income hypothesis: see *wealth effect versus income effect*.

Perpetuity: the payment of a fixed sum, P, over an infinite number of periods. The present value of the perpetuity is P/r, where r represents the discount rate. If the payments are made over a finite period of time the payment is called an annuity. See also annuity, *present value*.

Pessimism bias: see **moral pessimism bias**.

Pessimism index: see *Hurwicz optimism–pessimism index*.

Piercing the corporate veil: this expression refers to the courts' ability to impose personal liability on the shareholders, officers, and corporate directors for the wrongful acts of a corporation. This highly litigated doctrine pierces the shield of limited liability granted to corporate entities. Factors such as undercapitalization of the corporation, improper accounting practices and record-keeping, and single-handed management of the corporation by the dominant stockholder, as well as other fundamental principles of justice, are taken into account when courts decide on the application of this doctrine. See, for example, *DeWitt Truck Brokers* v. *W. Ray Flemming Fruit Co.,* 540 F.2d 681, 687 (Fourth Cir. 1976). Critics of this doctrine point out that courts are quite unpredictable in the application of this doctrine, and that lifting the shield of limited liability undermines the ability to attract capital to the corporate business sector (Easterbrook and Fischel, 1985). Supporters of the doctrine, instead, argue that limited liability serves only to shift the cost of wrongful corporate behavior from shareholders to innocent creditors of the corporation, making it harder for the corporation to enter into the credit market (Hansmann and Kraakman, 1991). Given that shareholders, officers, and directors are in a better position (than corporate creditors) to monitor the acts of a corporation, they are the best cost bearers of the losses caused by the wrongful acts of the corporation.

Pigouvian tax: Arthur C. Pigou (1877–1959) was a pioneer in the study of economic externalities. Externalities are a form of market failure that create a discrepancy between the private cost and the social cost of an activity. Pigou

(1920) suggests that these failures can be corrected by imposing a tax on the externality-creating activities. This tax is called a Pigouvian tax. In the case of negative externalities the social cost exceeds the private; in the case of positive externalities, social costs are lower. In order to make actors internalize the externalities they generate, the Pigouvian tax should equal the difference between the social and private costs. Creators of negative externalities should therefore face a positive tax, while the creators of positive externalities should instead pay a negative tax (i.e., receive a Pigouvian subsidy). Consider the textbook case of a polluting factory. Pigou suggests that the problem with pollution is that the firm is using a productive resource (clean air) for which it is not required to pay. When a firm does not have to pay for a productive input, its marginal cost of production is artificially low and its profit-maximizing output is too high, from a social efficiency perspective. The theory is that, if the government could impose a Pigouvian tax equal to the marginal damage from pollution, the firm would be acting as if it took into consideration the costs of its pollution. The marginal costs of production after tax would truly reflect the value of the resources going into production, and production would be reduced to the socially optimal amount. See also ***externalities***, ***internalization***, ***Coase theorem***, and ***polluter pays principle***.

Pliability rules: remedies that combine the features of property-type and liability-type remedies, either sequentially or simultaneously. The term, recently introduced into the literature by Bell and Parchomovsky (2002), obviously refers – by blending the two terms – to the distinction between property rules and liability rules rendered popular by Calabresi and Melamed's (1972) seminal paper. Pliability rules cope with the inherent limitations of property and liability rules, combining the advantages of these remedial solutions. Such mixed remedial protection may be desirable when the legal relationship or entitlement is likely to be affected by changed circumstances or supervening policy goals. See also ***property rules versus liability rules***.

Pluralistic ignorance: term used to describe situations of aggregate misperception by society about an objective fact. Expressive laws may be useful to dispel shared misperceptions and to correct problems of pluralistic ignorance. See also ***expressive law***.

Pluralistic ignorance bias: see ***social projection bias***.

Plurality voting method: there are two main forms of plurality voting methods: simple plurality voting and plurality voting with elimination. In simple plurality voting, the selection of a winner among several candidates (or alternatives) takes place by giving sole attention to the number of voters who gave the candidate their first-choice vote. The candidate who receives the largest number of first-place votes wins the election. When there are more than two candidates, the simple plurality method does not guarantee that the winner will receive a majority of the first-place votes. The method of plurality voting with elimination is a variation of simple plurality voting. In a plurality vote with elimination, the voting contest is carried out in rounds. After each round the candidate who received the fewest first-choice votes is eliminated, until a sole winner is left. The plurality voting method with elimination is vulnerable to potential strategic voting and is not very practical, given the need to hold N–1 successive rounds for a race involving N candidates. See also *Borda count method*.

Point voting: a simple preference voting scheme in which voters assign points to reflect their ordinal preferences – assigning more points to the candidates (or policies) they favor more. More precisely, voters give one point to their least favorite option, two points to their next least favorite, until they have assigned points to all the available options. The candidate (or policies) with most total points is (are) the winner. See also *Borda count method* and *preferential voting*.

Policy stream: see *policy window*.

Policy window: Kingdon (1995) distinguishes three "streams" that are relevant to policymaking: the problem stream, the policy stream, and the politics stream. The problem stream refers to the process by which problems arise and capture the attention of policymakers. This stream includes both the method of identification (i.e., how policymakers and the public become aware of the problem) and the method of defining or assessing the problem. The policy stream refers to the intellectual process of developing alternative policy proposals from which policymakers can choose to attempt to tackle a specific policy problem. Finally, the politics stream refers to the political environment that affects the choices and behavior of policymakers (e.g., the mood of constituencies, the national political climate, a change in the majority party in charge of the legislature, the influence of interest groups, etc.). A policy window arises when these streams converge, allowing policymakers actually to choose a policy to address a problem. See also *agenda setting*.

Polinsky, A. Mitchell (1948–): an American economist and legal scholar who has pioneered the application of economic theory to the study of law. Born on February 6, 1948, Polinsky received his undergraduate degree from Harvard University in 1970. He went on to receive his Ph.D. in economics from the Massachusetts Institute of Technology in 1973, and his Master of Studies in Law from Yale University in 1976. He has published numerous academic articles, applying economic analysis to the areas of tort, contract, property and criminal law. In one of his best-known articles, "Decoupling liability: optimal incentives for care and litigation" (Polinsky and Che, 1991), it is proposed that a "decoupled" liability system – one in which the award to the plaintiff differs from the payment by the defendant – is optimal, because it reduces the plaintiff's incentive to sue, hence lowering litigation costs without sacrificing the defendant's incentive to exercise care. He has also written one of the leading textbooks on law and economics, *An Introduction to Law and Economics* (1989). Polinsky is currently a professor in both the Law School and Department of Economics at Stanford University. See also *decoupling*.

Political Coase theorem: Cooter first utilized the term "political Coase theorem" in his book *The Strategic Constitution* (2000a), to refer to the application of the Coase theorem to political markets. Parisi (2003) has developed the concept more formally, to consider the effect of a market for votes on democratic outcomes. The political Coase theorem shows that, if all voters are allowed to enter into Coasean bargaining over the policy outcome to be adopted by the majority coalition (i.e., if political bargains are possible and are enforceable), uniqueness and stability are obtained. Analysis of the Nash bargaining equilibrium in a political market yields an interesting geometric intuition. If voters have similar utility functions centered around different ideal policy points, the Coasean bargaining will be conducive to the "center of mass" of the policy space, which weighs the agents' preferences as revealed in the bargaining process. The equilibrium obtainable in such a world of frictionless politics satisfies most criteria of social welfare. Parisi's formulation of the political Coase theorem contains two additional propositions. According to the first, if the conditions for the Coase theorem are present for all voters, different initial majority coalitions will lead to the same final policy outcome. This proposition is the political analogue of a core result of the traditional Coase theorem, according to which the efficient final allocation of resources is achieved independently of the initial assignment of rights. The second proposition shows that, in a world of zero transaction costs, the choice of alternative decision rules has no effect on the policy outcome. The absence of transaction costs guarantees that the final policy outcome will not depend upon the choice of a particular voting rule. As easily recognizable, this proposition is the political analogue of another important result of the traditional Coase theorem, according to which, in a world of zero transaction costs, the choice of remedies is irrelevant for the efficient final allocation of resources. These results rest on the insightful assertion of the efficiency of vote trading, expressed by Buchanan and Tullock in a well-known passage of their *Calculus of Consent*: "Permitting those citizens who feel strongly about an issue to compensate in some way those whose opinion is only feebly held can result in a great increase in the well-being of both groups, and the prohibition of such transactions will serve to prevent movement toward the conceptual social optimality surface, under almost any definition of this term" (Buchanan and Tullock, 1962: 133). In the real world of politics, collective action and agency problems affect political bargaining. The normative implications of the political Coase theorem in real-world political markets remain for the most part unexplored in the literature. See also *logrolling*, *Benholz theorem*, *Coase theorem*, and *political markets*.

Political markets: metaphors of politics-like markets form an established foundation of much of the work in public choice and political economy. Stigler (1971), Becker (1983), and Peltzman (1990), among others, have provided seminal formulations of the efficiency hypothesis of political markets. The thrust of this foundational hypothesis is that political markets are generally clearing, at least in the sense that, in equilibrium, no individual can improve his or her wealth (or utility) without reducing the wealth (or utility) of at least one other individual. However, in real politics, legislative and political bodies seldom work like markets. Cooter (2000) points out four main challenges to the politics-like market analogy. The first is that political agents are limited to the extent to which they can enter into binding political contracts. The second reason why political markets do not function like ordinary markets is that the value of a legislator's vote often depends upon how other legislators vote. There are pervasive externalities and resulting free-riding incentives in political action. The third reason is that real-life politics has too many political actors for each one to bargain with everyone else. Unlike the atomistic marketplace of traditional economics, bilateral negotiations would be prohibitively expensive in real-life politics. Fourth, ordinary citizens are rationally ignorant about legislative bargains, and pervasive agency and accountability problems are present in real-life political markets. See also *logrolling*, *economic theory of politics*, and *political Coase theorem*.

Politics stream: see *policy window*.

Politics-like market metaphors: see *political markets*.

Polluter pays principle: an important principle of international and national environmental law. The principle states that those who cause environmental damage and degradation should pay for it. In economic terms, the principle requires the internalization of the externalities imposed on the environment. In many cases, the principle would support the imposition of a Pigouvian tax. The principle has old roots, and enjoys different interpretations in national legal systems. Already, in a celebrated passage by Plato, we find a statement of the principle, according to which "[i]f anyone intentionally spoils the water of another ... let him not only pay damages, but purify the stream or cistern which contains the water" (Plato, 1953 [355 BC]: book 8, sect. 485[e]). See also *Pigouvian tax*.

Pooling equilibrium: see *pooling versus separating equilibria*.

Pooling versus separating equilibria: a pooling equilibrium is an equilibrium in which players of different types all choose the same equilibrium strategy (for example, sellers with goods of different qualities all offering the same return policies so as to attract customers). A separating equilibrium, in contrast, is an equilibrium in which different types of players select a different equilibrium strategy depending on their characteristics (for example, buyers with different valuations of the same good may have different degrees of willingness to stand in line to purchase it). The concept of separating equilibrium has important applications in contract theory and mechanism design. For example, in order to convey credible information, signaling techniques should be able to create a separating equilibrium. A full product warranty offered at low cost by a reputable seller may be conveying credible information about the quality of the good, since only sellers of high-quality goods could afford to offer a full warranty at a low price. See also *signaling*, *mechanism design*, and *multiple equilibria*.

Popitz's law: according to Johannes Popitz (1927: 348–9), "In a realistic consideration of politics, the power of attraction of the central government becomes inevitable. There is no effective panacea against it." This hypothesis was pronounced so emphatically by Popitz as to become known as "Popitz's law." See also *decentralization theorem*, and *subsidiarity*.

Pork barrel legislation: the promotion of projects that serve the interest of a small minority of the population, diverting taxpayers' money into local districts or concentrated interest groups. In order to obtain legislative support that could not otherwise be achieved, pork barrel legislation is often carried out through logrolling. A small group of legislators, who are willing to trade away their votes on other issues in exchange for support for their special interest bills, can skillfully promote proposals that benefit their local constituents at the expense of the larger population. Game-theoretic representations of pork barrel legislation show that, in the absence of other accountability constraints, dominant strategies will lead to equilibria with too much local interest legislation and too little general interest legislation. See also *logrolling* and *political markets*.

Portfolio theory: Markowitz (1952) first proposed the modern idea of portfolio diversification in investment theory. Portfolio theory dramatically changed the way individuals and firms invest. Prior to portfolio theory, investors would often construct an investment portfolio by analyzing the risks associated with individual investments. For example, an investor might recommend investing largely in one type of stock or bond, because of its relative security and consistent return on investment. This strategy led to homogeneous investment portfolios with little diversity. Markowitz instead showed how diversification could provide greater overall security, without the need to identify inversely correlated risks and rewards with an investment-by-investment evaluation. The concept of diversification has been applied broadly in the law and economics literature to study the optimal allocation of legal risk. All things being equal, the law should allocate risks and liabilities on the individuals who can best bear them (best risk bearers). The possibility of diversifying multiple legal risks is one of the factors taken into account by policymakers in choosing the optimal allocation of risks. See also *diversification*, *systematic versus unsystematic risk*, *hedging*, *best risk bearer*, and *residual bearer*.

Positive analysis: see *positive versus normative law and economics*.

Positive externalities: see *externalities*.

Positive law and economics: see *positive versus normative law and economics*.

Positive versus normative law and economics: scholars in the law and economics field use economic tools to analyze the incentive effects of various laws and regulations on the behavior of actors in society and to gauge the extent to which existing laws and regulations incentivize socially optimal behavior. While law and economics scholars largely use the same analytical tools to evaluate the law, different schools of thought have developed about the ultimate aim of the legal system and the proper role of law and economic scholars within that system. Various scholars studying the history of the law and economics field have identified different methodological approaches in law and economics, and have drawn a distinction between positive and normative approaches. The so-called positive approach to law and economics (which is often associated with the Chicago school) encompasses the use of economics as analytical and descriptive instruments. Positive law and economics mostly uses economics to predict the effects of various legal rules. Economics is used to describe the effects of law and to formulate testable predictions on the effects of law on behavior. The efficiency of the common law hypothesis is also associated with the positive approach in law and economics. The hypothesis suggests that the development of judge-made rules can be explained in terms of their economic efficiency. The normative approach to law and economics (often associated with the Yale school) uses economic analysis as a prescriptive tool: economics is used to prescribe what law should be. When used normatively, economic analysis becomes an instrument of policy and institutional design to gauge legal intervention and to make policy recommendations on the basis of the economic consequences of alternative legal rules. See also *functional law and economics*, *Chicago school*, *Yale school*, and *Virginia school*.

Posner, Richard Allen (1939–): considered one of the founders of the field of law and economics. He was born on January 11, 1939, in New York. Posner received his undergraduate degree from Yale University in 1959, and his law degree from Harvard Law School, where he graduated first in his class and served as president of Harvard Law Review. He joined the faculty of the University of Chicago Law School in 1969, where he became a major proponent and later patriarch of the law and economics movement. He was the founding editor of *The Journal of Legal Studies* in 1972 and served as co-editor (with Orley Ashenfelter) of the *American Law and Economics Review*, from its creation in 1999 until 2008. His early academic work addressed the law and economics approach to a variety of legal subjects, including torts, contracts, procedure, antitrust, public utility, and common carrier regulation. In these articles, he called for major antitrust reforms, proposed and explored an economic efficiency theory for the judicial decisions of common law, and urged wealth maximization as an important goal of social and legal policy. Judge Posner has also written about the economics of legislation and regulation and has extended the scope of law and economics analysis to encompass such areas as family law, primitive law, racial discrimination, jurisprudence, and privacy. Judge Posner's more recent academic work includes law and economics studies of criminal, labor, and intellectual property law, law and literature, the interpretation of constitutional and statutory texts, sexuality, and old age. His current academic research concerns the subjects of judicial administration, evidence, intellectual property, health economics and policy, citations analysis, antitrust, and jurisprudence and moral theory. Posner has written thirty books and more than 300 articles and book reviews. His numerous books include *Economic Analysis of Law* (8th edn., 2010), *Preventing Surprise Attacks* (2005), *Catastrophe: Risk and Response* (2004), *Law, Pragmatism, and Democracy* (2003), *Antitrust Law* (2nd edn., 2001), *The Problematics of Moral and Legal Theory* (1999), *Law and Literature* (2nd edn., 1998), *The Federal Courts: Challenge and Reform* (rev. edn., 1996b), *Law and Legal Theory in England and America* (1996a), *Overcoming Law* (1995), *The Essential Holmes* (1992b), *Sex and Reason* (1992a), *The Problems of Jurisprudence* (1990b), *Cardozo: A Study in Reputation* (1990a), and *The Economics of Justice* (1981). Posner currently serves as a judge on the United States Court of Appeals for the Seventh Circuit. He is the recipient of the 2010 Ronald H. Coase medal for his lifetime work in law and economics. His son, Eric Posner, is also an influential and prolific scholar in law and economics at the University of Chicago Law School. See also *Chicago school*, *Ronald H. Coase medal*, **Journal of Legal Studies**, and *American Law and Economics Review*.

Post-experience goods: see *experience goods versus search goods*.

Potential compensation: the Kaldor–Hicks criterion of potential compensation requires that the increase in value (gain) for those who are advantaged by a change be sufficiently large to compensate the losers. In the Kaldor–Hicks system the compensation is hypothetical. For this reason, this criterion is some- times called "potential Pareto superiority." See also *Kaldor–Hicks criterion* and *Bentham's imperative*.

Potential Pareto superiority: see *potential compensation*.

Power index: see *Shapley–Shubik power index*.

Precaution externalities: in a tort situation, both tortfeasors and victims can typically take precautions. When parties choose their care level, they may affect the cost or benefits of precautionary care for other parties. For example, in some situations one party's precautions can affect the effectiveness of the precautions for the other party (e.g., the use of a reflective vest by pedestrians increases the effectiveness of headlights used by drivers). These effects can be viewed as (positive or negative) externalities of precaution. When choosing their course of action, parties do not always take into account such externalities. See also *alternative versus joint care*, *activity level externalities*, *double-edged torts*, and *hybrid precautions*.

Precaution technologies: see *durable versus non-durable precautions*.

Precautionary principle: a decision-making paradigm that gives extra weight to unknown but potentially irreversible harms, rather than discounting them. The principle suggests that society should avoid courses of action that pose an unknown risk of large or irreversible negative impacts. The precautionary principle is often used in the context of human interaction with the natural environment. For example, a statement such as "We should avoid using up fossil fuels because we do not know the full range of bad outcomes associated with global warming" illustrates the precautionary principle. Advocates of the precautionary principle suggest that it is rational to be cautious in the face of unknown harms. Opponents argue that the principle is irrational, because it ignores the opportunity cost of precautions and the potential positive effects of a future course of action, which are also unknown. Opponents of the precautionary principle prefer more inclusive techniques of policy choice such as risk assessment, which accounts for potential gains and losses of alternative actions. The prescriptions of the precautionary principle are often shown to be at odds with conventional cost–benefit analysis, calling for precautionary choices even when such choices have a negative expected present value. These two competing frameworks often lead to different conclusions regarding the extent and optimal timing of precautionary choices. In law, the precautionary principle has been used to argue against the legalization of same-sex marriage in the United States. Under this principle, uncertainty surrounding the (potentially irreversible) effects of same-sex marriage on social institutions that are supported by marriage indicates that same-sex marriage should be disfavored. A cost–benefit analysis would require considering the – equally irreversible – costs of delaying such a change as well. See also *cost–benefit analysis*.

Precommitment strategies: actions adopted by an individual or a firm that increase the credibility of its own promises or threats by reducing the set of options available in the future. The concept of precommitment strategies was introduced by Schelling (1966), who considers the use of precommitment strategies to increase the deterrence power of threat strategies. One example would be a monopolist who chooses to build additional capacity to discourage potential entrants from entering the monopolistic market. This action makes more credible the monopolist's threat to "play tough," expanding production above the oligopolistic equilibrium level, and imposes a loss on those who decide to enter the market. A famous historical example of precommitment strategies was the choice of Hernán Cortés to destroy his ships upon arrival to Mexico, to discourage his crew from betraying him and fleeing the country. A similar concept is used by Kronman (1985) to describe situations in which a party adopts actions that increase the credibility of one's own promise by imposing a conditional cost in case of breach. Kronman refers to these strategies as hands-tying strategies. See also *hands tying*, *cooperative games*, and *non-cooperative games*.

Predatory pricing: firms with market power are often accused of employing anti-competitive tactics to drive new competitors out of their markets. One of these tactics is predatory pricing. Predatory pricing occurs when a larger, incumbent firm charges a very low price in order to force a smaller, new firm out of the market (through bankruptcy or voluntary shutdown). The new firm is forced to match the incumbent's low price or lose market share. The implicit premise of this argument is that an incumbent firm can absorb short-run losses better than a new firm. This practice is most often observed in oligopoly industries. Predatory pricing has been outlawed by antitrust laws. Courts recognize two degrees of predatory pricing. When the incumbent charges a price below average variable cost, the price is necessarily below the short-run shutdown price. In theory, there is no viable economic reason for a firm to charge a price this low, and companies that are caught doing so are punished by the courts. When the incumbent firm charges a price above average variable cost but below average total cost, it is difficult to prove that the incumbent has bad motives for charging the low price. It may be rational for firms to operate with a short-run loss as long as the price is above the shutdown price. Predatory pricing of this latter type is probably quite common, but often goes unpunished because it is difficult to prove.

Preference revelation: see *revealed preferences*.

Preference shaping: see *endogenous versus exogenous preferences*.

Preferences: economists generally use an individual's rankings of goods to explain and forecast his or her economic decisions. The concept of preference is of central importance to any such ranking. Preferences are the individual likes and dislikes that inform an individual's ranking of goods over one another. Today most economists measure preference through an agent's actual choice behavior, described as revealed preference, as opposed to relying on first personal descriptions of preferences, which yields less precise or inconsistent data. In direct relation to the importance of preferences, economists disagree about how it should be measured. Some economists argue that preferences should be attributed and described with the use of cardinal values, and should be measured with respect to a scale of absolute intensity. Cardinal preferences are useful for solving problems requiring interpersonal comparisons of utility. However, most economists hold that preferences can be attributed only ordinal values, and are useful only to express an intra-personal ranking of alternatives. Economists generally require preferences to be rational with respect to one another, meaning that preferences must be reflexive, transitive, and complete within any given ranking. When an individual has no preference between options, then he or she is said to be indifferent. See also *cardinal preferences* and *ordinal preferences*.

Preferential voting: a general term used to describe a class of democratic voting arrangements (e.g., instant runoff, Borda count, Condorcet method) in which voters rank their preferences ordinally. Preferential voting may be contrasted with single-winner voting, in which voters express only their first choice; and cardinal voting, in which voters express both the ordinal ranks of their preferences *and* the magnitude of those preferences. See also ***Borda count method*** and ***point voting***.

Prescriptive norms: see ***descriptive versus prescriptive norms***.

Present value: also called discounted present value; measures the discounted value of a stream of future payments, evaluated at a given date. Present value calculation usually employs a risk-free interest rate. Suppose that a person receives $110 in one year, which is subject to a risk-free interest rate of 10 percent. The person will be indifferent between the option to receive the $110 in a year and the option to receive the payout's present value today, or $100. If there are risks involved, present value calculations typically add a risk premium to the interest rate, which reflects the degree of uncertainty involved. The present value of a stream of future cash flows is equal to the sum of the present value of each single cash flow. Present value calculations commonly apply a model of compound interest to estimate the current value of future cash flows. See also *discounting*.

Price discrimination: a producer engages in price discrimination when it sells the same good at different prices to different customers, even though production costs do not change. Economists distinguish different types of price discrimination. First-degree or perfect price discrimination refers to the situation when the producer knows exactly each customer's willingness to pay and is able to charges each customer a different price for the first and each subsequent unit of the good consumed. With first-degree price discrimination, the producer effectively charges the highest possible price for each unit. Moving along each buyer's demand curve, the seller charges sequential prices that leave buyers with no consumer surplus. Second-degree price discrimination refers to the case when a producer charges different prices for different quantities of a good. Second-degree price discrimination is possible when different types of buyers with different demand elasticity are likely to buy different quantities. This form of price discrimination is somewhat legitimized because the price is based on the quantity sold. However, when quantities are used as a proxy for the characteristics of the buyer, price differences reflect different demand elasticity, rather than production costs. Finally, third-degree price discrimination is the most common form of price discrimination. With third-degree price discrimination, a seller is able to separate buyers on the basis of observable characteristics, such as age, location, gender, and ethnic group. Price discrimination of any degree is possible only in the presence of market power. In an atomistic market, the opportunity to increase profits through price discrimination would be competed away, forcing all firms to sell at the same market price. Given its non-sustainability in competitive market conditions, price discrimination is often used by antitrust authorities as an indicium of market power. Additional conditions for the sustainability of price discrimination include the ability of the seller to identify two or more groups that are willing to pay different prices, maintain segmented markets, and avoid the rise of secondary markets in which buyers in one group resell the good to another group. Price discrimination has three important effects: (a) increasing the producer's profit, (b) reducing or eliminating the consumer's surplus, and (c) reducing the overall deadweight loss, allowing producers to increase output without undermining their profit. The United States prohibits discrimination "in price between different purchasers of commodities of like grade and quality" with some exceptions (see 15 US Code section 1930 [1914]). Many pricing and discount strategies can be viewed as forms of price discrimination in disguise. Examples include quantity discounts, targeted discount (discount coupons, senior citizen discounts), financial aid (adjusted according to ability/willingness to pay), airline prices (discounts for Saturday night stays, higher fares for direct flights), and higher gasoline prices on highways. See also *market power*.

Priest–Klein selection hypothesis: this hypothesis (sometimes simply "the selection hypothesis") states that, when parties have symmetrical stakes, the disputes that actually go to trial, rather than being settled, will tend to be those with at least a 50 percent plaintiff success rate (Priest and Klein, 1984; Priest, 1985). The intuition is that, the further away from 50 percent the anticipated rate of success, the more likely parties are to settle. A corollary point is that, when stakes are not symmetrical, cases may be litigated even where the anticipated success rate is above or below 50 percent. Subsequent empirical research results have been mixed, but tend to confirm the selection hypothesis (Coursey and Stanley, 1988; Stanley and Coursey, 1990). The dominance of pro-plaintiff legal precedents and the gradual expansion of the domain of legal protection have been explained on the basis of the selection hypothesis (Fon, Parisi, and Depoorter, 2005) See also *survivor theory of efficiency*, *efficiency of the common law hypothesis*, and *modified selection hypothesis*.

Priest, George L. (1947–): currently the Edward J. Phelps Professor of Law and Economics and Kauffman Distinguished Research Scholar in law, economics, and entrepreneurship at Yale Law School. He was formerly the John M. Olin Professor of Law and Economics at Yale Law School from 1986 to 2009. Priest was a major influence in the early development of the economic analysis of law and continues to be one of the most influential and frequently cited legal scholars. He has written on a wide range of subjects, and he is known particularly for his expertise in the area of antitrust law and insurance law. He has also been a key figure in the development of the efficiency of the common law hypothesis. Priest earned his B.A. from Yale University in 1969 and his J.D. from the University of Chicago Law School in 1973. He has been director of the John M. Olin Center for Studies in Law, Economics and Public Policy at Yale since 1983. He is chairman of the Council of Academic Advisers of the American Enterprise Institute. Prior to settling at Yale, he taught at the University of Puget Sound from 1973 to 1975; the University of Chicago Law School from 1975 to 1977; the State University of New York, Buffalo, from 1977 to 1980; and the University of California, Los Angeles, from 1979 to 1981. See also *Priest's selection hypothesis* and *survivor theory of efficiency*.

Primacy effect: see *serial position effect*.

Principal–agent problem: see *agency problems*.

Principle of self-preference: Jeremy Bentham's (1823) principle of self-preference states that "man, from the very constitution of his nature, prefers his own happiness to that of all other sensitive beings put together." This skeptical view of human nature stands in contrast with Bentham's imperative: men do not spontaneously desire the greatest happiness for the greatest number. See also *Bentham's imperative* and *Bentham, Jeremy*.

Priority pricing: Harris and Raviv (1981) refer to priority pricing as a pricing scheme in which various prices are charged and buyers paying higher prices have priority over others in the event of excess demand. Examples of priority pricing include natural gas and electric power for industrial consumers in which users that pay lower rates are cut off before those paying higher prices in the event of a shortage. See also *auction theory*.

Prisoner's dilemma: one of the most famous problems studied in game theory. It shows that cooperation may not arise even if it would be mutually beneficial for the players in the game. Analytically, the prisoner's dilemma is a two-player non-zero sum non-cooperative game, originally presented by Flood and Dresher in 1950 for a conference at the RAND Corporation and formalized by Tucker (1950). The story associated with the prisoner's dilemma is that two suspects are arrested and brought to two different rooms. The police have insufficient evidence for a conviction and offer to each suspect the following deal: if one prisoner confesses and the other does not, the confessor is free while the reticent prisoner receives a ten-year sentence. If both remain silent, they are both prosecuted for a minor charge and are sentenced to a six-month period in prison. If both confess, each prisoner receives a five-year sentence. Each prisoner chooses either to confess or stay silent. The police guarantee to each prisoner that the other would not be informed about the confession before the end of the investigation. Under the standard assumption that each player is interested in maximizing his or her own payoff (i.e. minimize the time in jail), the unique equilibrium of the game occurs when both prisoners confess. This equilibrium is Pareto-suboptimal, since each prisoner cannot realize the higher gain associated with cooperation when using individual rationality. The description of the game fits every situation in which individuals can either cooperate or defect, but individual rationality is not consistent with aggregate rationality and cooperation does not emerge as a self-enforcing solution of the game. Consider the following matrix illustrating the prisoner's dilemma game in the general case, where $C > A > D > B$ and $c > a > d > b$.

	Cooperate	Defect
Cooperate	A,a	B,c
Defect	C,b	D,d

In the absence of any enforceable agreement among the players, the prisoner's dilemma presents a unique Nash equilibrium in pure strategies, (D,d), in which both players defect and no cooperation arises in equilibrium. In the classic form of this game, cooperating is strictly dominated by defecting. There is currently a debate in the literature as to the extent to which the result of the prisoner's dilemma changes in the event of repeated interactions (iterated prisoner's dilemma). There are a wide array of applications of the prisoner's dilemma to law. The first set of applications considers the role of law and legal institution in helping individuals overcome a prisoner's dilemma problem. For example, contract enforcement can be viewed as an instrument that fosters the formation and fulfillment of contractual obligations: absent contract enforcement mechanisms, parties would be unable to trust one another when making reciprocal promises in a contract. The second set of applications considers the potential use of the prisoner's dilemma to discourage undesirable activities. For example, the so-called "clean hand rule" denies legal action for the enforcement of illegal contracts. The lack of legal enforcement puts the contracting parties in a prisoner's dilemma. This would in turn discourage parties from entering into illicit agreements. See also *iterated prisoner's dilemma*, *chain-store paradox*, *folk theorem*, and *evolution of cooperation*.

Private enforcement: the recent law and economics literature has emphasized the important role played by extra-legal enforcement mechanisms in promoting compliance with legal rules. According to this literature, compliance with law is driven not only by the legal threat of sanctions or the promise of rewards carried out by the law but also by the individuals' internalization of the values it embodies (Cooter, 1998, 2000b). According to this literature, private enforcement mechanisms include three main interrelated situations, respectively described as first-party, second-party, and third-party enforcement mechanisms. These mechanisms may change observed patterns of behavior by changing individual preferences and tastes and, in some cases, by affecting social norms and values, even in the absence of other external incentives. See also *first-party enforcement*, *second-party enforcement*, *third-party enforcement*, and *expressive law*.

Private good: this term has different meanings in the legal and economic lexicons. Property law distinguishes between public and private goods, looking at the ownership of the good. A private good is a good that is privately owned. In the economic lexicon, a private good is instead defined as a good that is excludable (i.e., non-owners can be prevented from using the good or consuming its benefits) and rivalrous in use (i.e., its use or consumption by one individual prevents that of another). The legal and economic meanings of the term bear some interesting relationships. Demsetz (1967) notes that not all private goods (in an economic sense) are privately owned (in the legal sense). Revisiting Adam Smith's (1776) idea that scarcity is what gives origin to private property, Demsetz shows that property rights develop to internalize externalities in the use of scarce resources. Scarcity is necessary for giving objects value and prompting the creation of private property rights. However, there are costs associated with the creation of property. The costs of establishing, monitoring, and enforcing property rights are not always justified by the benefits arising from the creation of private property (propertization). Demsetz therefore shows that scarcity is a necessary – but not sufficient – condition for the establishment of private property rights. For this reason, not every good that is (a) scarce and rivalrous in use and (b) excludable and reducible to private property will necessarily be privately owned. Property rights emerge only when the gains of propertization are larger than the cost of establishing, monitoring, and enforcing private property rights. See also ***public good***, ***commons***, ***anticommons***, ***commodification***, and ***origins of property***.

Private information: term used in economic analysis to refer to information that is unobservable to other individuals. The presence of private information leads to asymmetric information and to the associated problems of adverse selection and moral hazard. See also ***asymmetric information***, ***adverse selection***, ***moral hazard***, and ***penalty default rules***.

Private-value auctions: in a private-value auction, bidders generally compete for the acquisition of a good that they intend to keep for private consumption rather than treat it as a resale or investment opportunity. The valuation of one bidder is driven by his or her subjective preferences, and the valuation made by one bidder is independent of the valuations made by others. The observation of other bidders' valuations through the bidding process, although revealing information on the market valuation of the good, reveals no additional information concerning the private value of the individual bidder. Unlike common-value auctions, winning a private-value auction by being the highest bidder does not give rise to the winner's curse. See also ***common-value auctions***, ***winner's curse***, ***direct versus indirect revelation mechanism***, and ***auction theory***.

Probability density function: measures the likelihood that a continuous random variable assumes a given value. The probability density function presents the same properties characterizing the probability in probability theory. The probability density function takes non-negative values and its integral is equal to one.

Problem of social cost: see ***Coase theorem***.

Problem stream: see ***policy window***.

Procedural preferences: according to standard economic analysis, individual choices are motivated by self-interest and economic outcomes, such as monetary payoffs or consumption opportunities. However, experimental evidence shows that individuals also have preferences about the procedure or process used to reach a given outcome. So, for example, a reward that was gained fairly may be preferred to a reward that was obtained unfairly. The concept of procedural preferences refers to the preferences that individuals have over alternative outcome-generating procedures. In this context, these procedures include processes governing decision-making, the allocation of resources, and the resolution of conflicts. Procedures are perceived as crucial in many situations. Experimental evidence shows that individuals exhibit a preference for procedural fairness (or procedural justice). In other words, individuals may prefer that the allocation of resources or the resolution of conflicts occur according to a procedure designed to be fair. Note that procedural fairness concerns the design of the process, but provides no assurance about the distributive fairness of the economic outcome (Rabin, 1993). The law and economic literature is slowly incorporating these important findings in the study of legal rules and procedures. Procedural fairness is probably a necessary ingredient for the legitimacy and social acceptance of the legal process. See also *kindness function* and *distributive reciprocity*.

Procedural reciprocity: see *kindness function*.

Procurement auctions: auctions at which an object or service is being purchased rather than sold. The auctioneer is the buyer of the good or service and the bidders are the sellers, competing to secure the procurement contract. A procurement auction can follow any of the specific mechanisms followed in traditional sale auctions, including first- and second-price auctions, English, and Dutch auctions. See also *first-price auctions*, *second-price auctions*, *Dutch auctions*, and *English auctions*.

Prodigal son's effect: term used in the public choice and political science literature to suggest that, in a political exchange, it may be necessary to pay larger amounts of "pork" (or other political currency) to get support from those further away ideologically. See also *pork barrel legislation* and *logrolling*.

Producer profit: generally defined as the difference between total revenue and the total cost of production. The producer profit is generally lower than the producer surplus, since the fixed production costs are subtracted from the producer profit but are not subtracted when computing the producer surplus. See also *producer surplus*.

Producer sovereignty: see *consumer versus producer sovereignty*.

Producer surplus: the benefit accrued by a producer when selling the output at a market price higher than the producer's reservation price (i.e., the minimum price at which the producer would be willing to sell). The size of the producer surplus depends on the market structure and the degree of market power. The concept of producer surplus differs from that of producer profit, which is generally defined as the difference between total revenue and the total cost of production. The producer surplus is generally higher than the producer profit, since the fixed production costs are not subtracted from the producer surplus but are subtracted when computing profits. In a perfectly competitive market, the highest efficiency is attained (first theorem of welfare) and aggregate surplus (measured as the sum of consumer and producer surplus) is maximized. However, under competitive conditions the producer surplus is at its lowest, and it may even be null when all firms face the same constant marginal cost, with zero economic profit for each producer. Market power enables producers to raise prices above marginal cost, thereby increasing the producer surplus. It is maximized when a monopolist practices first-degree price discrimination. From a social perspective, in market structures with positive market power, the increase in the producer surplus comes at the expense of a decrease in the consumer surplus and total surplus, which causes a social deadweight loss (Harberger's triangle). The deadweight loss is often used to justify government intervention and regulation in monopoly industries. See also *producer profit*, *consumer surplus*, *aggregate surplus*, *deadweight loss*, *Harberger's triangle*, and *fundamental theorems of welfare*.

Production cost: the aggregate of expenditures (including raw materials, labor, and interest on loans and taxes paid) required to produce a good. See also *production function*.

Production efficiency: see *X-inefficiency*.

Production function: a mapping between all the possible combinations of inputs and their maximum output. Alternatively stated, the production function can be interpreted as the minimum level of input required to produce a level of output for a given good. By mapping the possible relationship between inputs and outputs for a given technology, the production function sets the production possibility frontier, which represents the set of all technologically feasible combinations of output and inputs. See also *marginal product* and *diminishing marginal product*.

Production possibility frontier: see *production function*.

Profit: see *accounting profits versus economic profits*.

Progressive taxation: under a system of progressive taxation, the marginal rate of taxation increases as income increases. By contrast, under a flat tax system, while wealthier citizens still pay more money than poorer citizens in absolute terms, wealthier and poorer citizens both pay an equal percentage of their income. See also *marginal tax rates*, *flat tax versus lump-sum tax*, and *negative income tax*.

Proper equilibrium: see *trembling hand*.

Propertization: see *commodification*.

Property rules versus liability rules: the law protects individual entitlements and provides remedies against their infringement. Property rules and liability rules are two of the key tools that legal systems use to protect entitlements. When an individual or entity suffers contractual breach, negligent harm, or trespass, for example, the law works to enforce the victim's rights by either mandating damages or granting an injunction that will stop a wrong from happening again. Scholars use the term "liability rule" to refer to remedies granting damages and "property rule" to refer to remedies granting an injunction. The terms originate from the fact that damages are the standard remedy in torts and contracts (liability) and injunctions are the standard remedy for the protection of real rights (property). Calabresi and Melamed (1972) have formulated a simple and powerful economic theory to explain the use of these two, readily distinguishable, forms of protection. Their landmark contribution has given origin to what Ayres and Goldbart (2001) have described as a "scholarly revolution," which makes the property rules versus liability rules distinction a central pillar in the economic analysis of law. Calabresi and Melamed look at the efficiency of the two sets of remedies. Property rule allows the entitlement holder to protect his or her entitlement and sell it only for a price he or she deems sufficient. The liability rule allows a taker to take the holder's entitlement, so long as he or she pays the holder damages. While it may be common practice for courts to use the liability rule in tort and contract cases and the property rule in property cases, Calabresi and Melamed examine the efficiency properties of these rules in relation to transaction costs. When transaction costs are low, property rules have a comparative advantage over liability rules, because they are more efficient and clear and will allow parties to bargain easily. However, when transaction costs are high, parties may be unable to transfer entitlements voluntarily, and liability rules will prove superior. Although the conclusions reached by Calabresi and Melamed (1972) have been challenged, their article remains among the most cited in the legal and economic literature, and continues to provide a solid foundation for the understanding of the advantages and limits of liability-type and property-type remedies. See also ***undefinable kicker***, ***Coase theorem***, ***normative Coase theorem***, ***multiple takings problem***, ***correlated-value claim***, ***reciprocal takings problem***, ***Calabresi, Guido***, ***dual-chooser rules***, and ***defendant choice rules***.

Proportional liability: under tort law, various rules exist that courts apply to compensate a victim for injury caused by a tortfeasor. These rules also deter potential tortfeasors from taking action, or failing to take precaution, in a way that might increase the chance of causing harm to others. Scholars have used economic tools to analyze various tort rules to determine which rules encourage potential tortfeasors and potential victims to take efficient levels of precaution and engage in efficient levels of behavior. A full liability rule would generally require a negligent tortfeasor to compensate a victim for all the harm done in the occurrence of an accident. If A was driving negligently and hit B, A would be responsible for all the harm that occurred, regardless of the extent to which A caused all the harm experienced by B. In contrast, Stremitzer and Tabbach (2009) consider a rule of proportional liability, incorporating the probability that the tortfeasor's negligence caused the harm at issue. Proportional liability would set the measure of the tortfeasor's damages at the cost of harm "multiplied by the probability that it was caused by the [tortfeasor's] negligence" (Stremitzer and Tabbach, 2009). For example, if a tortfeasor's negligence increases the chance of injury or harm from 10 percent to 30 percent, the probability that his or her negligence caused the harm is 40 percent $\left(\text{ie.,} \frac{30\%-10\%}{50\%}\right)$. The tortfeasor would therefore be proportionally liable for 40 percent of the total cost of the harm resulting from the accident. In analyzing the proportional liability rule, Stremitzer and Tabbach find that proportional liability performs at the same level of efficiency as the full liability rule, and outperforms threshold liability and strict liability, if the standard of due care is set at or above the social optimum. Furthermore, if the standard of due care is set above the social optimum, the proportional liability will outperform all the other liability rules listed. This is in large part due to the fact that the proportional liability rule encourages efficient behavior while also mitigating the judgment-proof problem, to some extent. See also ***threshold liability***, ***market share liability***, and ***comparative causation***.

Prospect theory: introduced by Kahneman and Tversky (1979), this is a psychology-based utility theory that characterizes decisions among risky alternatives with known probabilities. Contrary to the expected utility framework, which projects optimal decisions, prospect theory is a descriptive model that attempts to capture real-life choices, starting from empirical psychological evidence on how people make choices under uncertainty. Psychological evidence shows that individuals set reference points and evaluate risky outcomes on the basis of potential losses and gains, which are defined respectively as lower and larger outcomes. Contrary to the expected utility framework, prospect theory measures losses and gains with respect to the reference point, and does not measure the absolute wealth yielded by the risky prospects. Prospect theory applies an "S"-shaped value function that assumes the value of zero at the reference point, and is concave on the space of gains and convex on the space of losses. The "S"-shaped value function used by prospect theory embeds loss aversion, according to which a gain generates a utility increase lower than the disutility caused by the same-sized loss. Empirical evidence shows that individuals tend to underreact to large probabilities events and overreact to small ones. Prospect theory applies a probability weighting function that makes estimations in the same way. According to prospect theory, individuals evaluate potential outcomes (with the "S" value function) and their respective probabilities (with the weighting function) and choose the risky prospect having the highest utility. Prospect theory has been invoked to explain evidence inconsistent with economic rationality, such as the equity premium puzzle, the excess returns puzzle, the status quo bias, and the endowment effect. Prospect theory is not an axiomatic theory; its original formulation violates first-order stochastic dominance. Cumulative prospect theory and rank-dependent expected utility theory offer refinements of prospect theory, but at the cost of introducing violations of the transitivity of preferences. See also ***expected utility***, ***risk preferences***, ***reference points***, *loss aversion*, *settlement versus trial*, *endowment effect*, and *willingness to pay versus willingness to accept*.

Proxy variable: in statistical analysis and empirical research, some variables of interests can be non-measurable. In some cases, researchers can use a proxy variable to substitute a non-measurable variable. A proxy variable should be closely correlated, though not necessarily in a linear or positive way, with the non-measurable variable of interest. For example, the quality of life can be proxied with per capita GDP, and class attendance can be used to proxy student motivation in class. Dummy proxy variables, or indicator variables, are widely used in statistical analysis and take either the value zero or one to indicate the absence or presence of an effect of interest. See also *dummy variable*.

***Public Choice*:** the leading academic journal in the field of public choice theory. The journal was established in 1966 under the editorship of Gordon Tullock, who served as active editor until 1991. The original title of the journal was *Papers on Non-Market Decision Making*. During Tullock's editorship additional scholars served as co-editors, including Peter Ordeshook (1973–6), Kenneth Shepsle (1975–80), and Peter Aranson (1981–9). Charles Rowley and Robert Tollison later took the editorship, serving as editors from 1991 to 2007. William Shughart II has been serving as editor since 2007. *Public Choice* publishes articles in the field of public choice theory, with the inclusion of several areas of scholarship that are relevant to law and economics. See also *law and economics journals*.

Public choice theory: one of the most important interdisciplinary developments in the latter half of the twentieth century was the application of economic analysis to politics and policymaking. Whereas the domain of economics is traditionally regarded to be the marketplace and private actors, upon which the government acts as an exogenous force, public choice theory looks at choices from the perspective of the government and politicians, analyzing the costs and benefits of policy decisions, issue bundling, political bargaining, the preferences of voters, elections, and the structure of governmental institutions. Public choice is generally considered distinct from, though deeply entwined with, the law and economics movement. It is associated with the Virginia school style of economics. Historically, Duncan Black, James Buchanan, and Gordon Tullock are considered the founders of public choice theory. The core literature includes "On the rationale of group decision-making" (Black, 1948), *The Theory of Committees and Elections* (Black, 1958), and *The Calculus of Consent: Logical Foundations of Constitutional Democracy* (Buchanan and Tullock, 1962). Buchanan and Tullock co-founded the journal *Public Choice*, which was instrumental in the development of the discipline. See also *Buchanan, James*, *Tullock, Gordon*, *social choice theory*, and *Virginia school*.

Public good: a form of market failure. A public good is a commodity with two characteristics: (a) non-excludability, and (b) non-rivalry in consumption. The non-rivalry element distinguishes public goods from commons and open-access resources. Non-rivalry in consumption means that the use of a public good by one person does not deprive others of its use (e.g., the use of a lighthouse's signal by one ship does not preclude its use by other ships). Therefore, unlike commons and open-access resources, public goods does not lead to overconsumption but, rather, undersupply. The characteristic of non-excludability implies that it is either impossible or not cost-effective to exclude nonpaying third parties from the enjoyment of a public good. This leads to a free-rider problem. Examples of public goods range from national defense to basic research and crime control. Samuelson (1954, 1955) made the concept of public goods widely recognized, suggesting public provision as the only practical solution to the free-riding problem. Political economists generally point to the need to supply public goods as the main justification (and limit) to the scope of governments. Benevolent governments can improve social welfare by providing public goods when the total benefits exceed the costs, financing the production of the public goods with tax revenue. A practical problem often associated with the governmental supply of public goods is given by the difficult determination of the optimal quantity of such goods to produce. The public good problem arises because there is no easy way to induce parties to reveal their valuation of the public good through the price system. The absence of a price system that could capture the public's valuation of public goods creates difficulties in carrying out reliable cost–benefit analysis. Recent empirical research has studied the extent to which markets actually fail in the supply of public goods, with special emphasis on the private solutions to the public good problem. See also *local public good*, *near-public good*, *free riding*, *non-rivalry*, *market failures*, *commons*, *private goods*, *Tiebout competition*, and *collective action problem*.

Public good game: this requires each subject to choose secretly the amount of money he or she will contribute to a public pot. The payoff for each subject is the amount kept in his or her own pocket (net of the contribution to the public pot) plus an even split of the money placed in the pot. Individual contributions placed in the pot increase in value (i.e., they are multiplied by an amount smaller than the number of players and greater than one). The socially optimal solution is reached when every subject contributes all his or her money into the public pot. However, contributing to the public good is privately "irrational." The Nash equilibrium of the game requires every subject to contribute zero to the public pot. In game theory terminology, those who contribute nothing are called defectors or free riders and those who contribute a positive amount are called cooperators. This game can be used to described situations in which individuals are asked to contribute to the production of a public good. The public good game has been widely studied by experimental economists. The actual levels of contribution in experimental settings may vary substantially on account of individual heterogeneity (ranging from 0 percent to 100 percent of the initial endowment). However, the Nash equilibrium of the game is rarely observed, indicating a systematic departure from pure self-interest. The public good game has been tested in the context of repeated play to investigate the roles of trust and reciprocity. The standard experimental result indicates a declining proportion of public contribution with respect to the average contribution in the one-shot game. The common explanation is that trusting contributors may decide to reduce their individual level of contribution when they observe that the others do not contribute as much as they did in the previous stage of the game. Repeated interactions of players lead to a substantial reduction in the contribution level, which, however, rarely drops to zero, because of the presence of a hard-core group of altruistic individuals. Inequity aversion and reciprocity have often been invoked to explain the experimental evidence of the declining contribution rate. Subjects reduce their contribution level once they perceive the injustice or unfair behavior associated with the fact that the other players receive a bigger share for a smaller contribution. See also ***prisoner's dilemma***, ***inequity aversion***, and ***kindness function***.

Punitive damages: a measure of damages that goes beyond compensatory damages. Unlike compensatory damages, which are quantified on the basis of the plaintiff's loss, punitive damages also seek to penalize the defendant. Although there is little to guide courts when calculating punitive damages, they are often expressed as a multiple of compensatory damages. The law and economics literature identifies the appropriate function of punitive damages in the maintenance of deterrence in the presence of enforcement errors. Enforcement errors occur because some victims do not bring a claim against their tortfeasor. Prospective tortfeasors would anticipate the enforcement errors and could rationally expect lower levels of liability. If properly gauged, punitive damages could help mitigate enforcement error and incentivize efficient levels of care. Punitive damages should be imposed with a multiple (of compensatory damages) equal to the inverse of the enforcement error (e.g., an enforcement error of 0.5 should be offset with a punitive damage multiplier of two). By doing so, punitive damages would maintain the level of expected liability equal to the actual harm, with a full internalization of the harm in expected terms. See also ***compensatory damages*** and ***disgorgement damages***.

Pure versus mixed strategies: two variants of Nash strategies. A pure strategy identifies the move a player will make with a probability equal to one. A mixed strategy identifies the set of moves that a player will make with a probability less than one. A player will play a mixed strategy only if the payoff from either pure strategy is the same. Mixed strategies are generally interpreted as strategies picked through a random process, although they can also be the result of imperfect decision processes that lead to mixed outcomes (e.g., trembling hand strategies). Pure strategies can be viewed as a special case of mixed strategies, in which one particular strategy is selected all the time and all other strategies are never picked. A pure strategy equilibrium exists when each player in the game picks his or her strategy with perfect certainty. A mixed strategy equilibrium occurs when players adopt mixed strategies. The existence of multiple Nash equilibria in a given game makes it harder to predict which strategy a player will pick and presents the possibility that neither player will pick a strategy that is in his or her best interest. This problem may present an instance in which policies or regulations could intervene to help influence the choices of players. See also *dominant strategies*.

Pure conflict games: in the law and economics literature, this term (or strictly competitive games) is used to refer to situations in which parties cannot achieve any gain through their cooperation or coordination. Zero-sum games and constant-sum games fall within the category of pure conflict games, inasmuch as in all such games one player's gain always equals the other player's loss. See also *zero-sum games*, *constant-sum games*, and *inessential games*.

Put option: this (also called an option to sell) confers the right to sell goods or shares at the sole discretion of the potential seller at a future date within a determined time limit. A put option is generally granted through a contract between two parties that gives one party the option to sell a particular quantity of a good or security at a set price (the strike price) before some agreed-upon date (the expiration date). The purchaser of the put option profits when the price drops below the strike price. This can be used as a way to mitigate the risk of owning a commodity that may drop in value or as an instrument of speculative investment. See also *call option*, *chooser's call/put option*, and *option value*.

Qualitative versus quantitative models: the distinction between qualitative and quantitative analysis has different meanings in different disciplines. In the social sciences, quantitative analysis aims at developing mathematical models and investigates empirically social phenomena and their relationships. Quantitative research requires the collection of quantitative data and measurable information, and involves testing theoretical predictions and hypotheses on the available empirical data set. Qualitative analysis, instead, focuses on case studies, and collects qualitative information through participant observations in experiments, interviews, surveys, and case studies. The results obtained by researchers adopting a qualitative approach cannot be generalized, contrary to some of those obtained through quantitative methods. However, qualitative data is rich and better able to describe contextual details. There is considerable debate as to whether quantitative methods are superior to qualitative methods in the social sciences. Researchers in favor of quantitative analysis argue that such methods are the only ones that reflect a truly scientific approach. Researchers in favor of qualitative models argue, on the contrary, that qualitative analysis is better able to capture the complexity of social phenomena, which could be excessively simplified under quantitative analysis. In law and economics modeling, the qualitative versus quantitative distinction acquires a different meaning (both of which would fall under the heading of "quantitative analysis," as used in the social sciences). Qualitative economic models are mathematical models that use generic variables (often represented with letters or symbols, rather than real numbers) that can take on any numerical value, and use implicit functional forms that do not stipulate any specific functional relationship between the variables. The use of qualitative mathematical models to formulate the problem can produce more general results. However, at times the results reached with a qualitative model are indeterminate. The model needs the imposition of some restrictions (e.g., limiting the possible values of the variables or specifying the functional relationships between the variables) to generate determinate results. Restrictions are imposed with the adoption of assumptions, on the basis of which determinate results are derived. The results obtained with qualitative mathematical models can provide the basis for formulating qualitative predictions (e.g., they can tell if, on the basis of given assumptions, an increase in tort liability may lead to a decrease in accident rates), but they cannot, as such, generate quantitative predictions (e.g., by telling us the actual fall in accident rates). When data is available, qualitative models can be calibrated and turned into quantitative models. This would entail giving actual numerical values to parameters and variables and specifying all the functional relationships in explicit form. Quantitative models, when accurately calibrated, can provide a basis for formulating quantitative predictions. See also *calibration*.

Quasi-option value: many decisions made in the present generate costs and/or benefits in the future. Some of these costs and benefits are uncertain. Information can be acquired over time to reduce uncertainty. Delaying the decision until after new information is acquired can be beneficial. The term "quasi-option value" (at times simply referred to as "option value") refers to the benefit of delaying a decision so as to make a more informed decision in the future. In most cases, the opportunity to acquire information may delay the optimal timing of a decision. However, as Arrow and Fisher (1974) and Henry (1974) have pointed out, when there are irreversibilities on the benefits side (e.g., forgone benefits that cannot be recouped in the future), the quasi-option value of waiting may be negative. A negative quasi-option value would entail an additional cost from waiting, and a desirable acceleration of the decision process. See also *option value*.

Quasi-rent: the difference between total revenues and total avoidable costs – the measure of how much a given firm benefits from staying in business. In the long run, when all costs are variable, and non-avoidable costs are zero, quasi-rent coincides with economic profit. See also *rent*.

R

Race over the top: see *race to the top versus race to the bottom*.

Race to the top versus race to the bottom: states share borders with each other, and they often compete to encourage businesses to reside within their borders. States compete for businesses and residents by offering bundles of services and regulations (e.g., Delaware is frequently viewed as a state that uses business-friendly regulation to encourage companies to incorporate within its borders). This form of jurisdictional and regulatory competition is often metaphorically described as leading to a race to the top or a race to the bottom. The conventional theory postulates that the regulatory competition between states will lead to a race to the top (Tiebout, 1956). The alternative view expresses concern that jurisdictional competition can actually create a race to the bottom because of jurisdictional externalities (Parisi, Schulz, and Klick, 2006; Yablon, 2007). The law and economics literature has attempted to identify the conditions under which jurisdictional and regulatory competition is likely to lead to "top" or "bottom" outcomes, but the theoretical literature still lacks a general criterion for distinguishing between these two hypotheses. An interesting possibility emerges in the case of self-regulation, in which firms and organizations subject themselves to self-selected standards (e.g., environmental quality ratings, voluntary compliance audits, work safety certifications) to signal information to customers and business partners. Here a possibility arises that competition and signaling externalities may lead to a race over the top, in which firms may voluntarily adhere to inefficiently strict standards in order to send a stronger signal to customers and business partners. See also *Tiebout competition* and *regulatory competition*.

Ramsey pricing: a method of regulating prices whereby government regulators set a price and quantity for monopolists that maximizes the total surplus, subject to the monopolists' break-even constraint. Ramsey pricing is named after the philosopher, mathematician, and economist Frank P. Ramsey (1903–1930), who first exposited the idea in a paper on taxation (Ramsey, 1927). The pricing scheme requires that regulators find the monopolist's break-even price (i.e., a price equal to average cost) that is closest to the marginal cost and minimizes deadweight loss. A price below the Ramsey price would cause a loss to the monopolist, while a higher price would increase the deadweight loss, increasing the monopolist's profit (and deadweight loss) at the expense of the consumer surplus. Ramsey pricing is a second best pricing scheme. The inefficiency imposed by Ramsey pricing is measured by the deadweight loss. This inefficiency increases with economies of scale and with the elasticity of demand. First best regulation in a natural monopoly would consist of marginal cost pricing, and is achievable only in the case of a weak monopoly. Marginal cost pricing imposes a loss to the monopolist, since the marginal cost falls below the average cost. In the event of a strong monopoly, first best regulation could be sustained only by subsidizing the monopolist for an amount equal to the loss imposed by marginal cost pricing. However, subsidizing the monopolist would be politically problematic, and such policies are rarely adopted. See also ***natural monopoly*** and ***weak monopoly***.

Random walk: introduced by Karl Pearson (1905), this mathematically describes a random process in time (i.e., a process that formalizes a trajectory consisting of taking successive random steps). In economic applications, random walk processes are used to describe the evolution of a fluctuating stock price in the market or a gambler's financial wealth. A number of applications of the random walk analysis are available in computer science, physics, ecology, and psychology.

Ranking of preferences: see ***ordinal preferences***.

Rate of time preference: see ***time preference***.

Rational abstention: social scientists frequently study the decision-making process of voters in public elections. Starting with Downs (1957), public choice scholars have acknowledged the obvious fact that, in large elections, individual voters have a minimal impact on the outcome of the election. A rational choice model of voting would therefore suggest that investing private resources to vote is irrational. This raises a paradox of voting: voters incur costs to participate in elections, even though their vote by itself will almost certainly not impact the outcome of the election. The paradox has been explained in various ways, including minimax regret theory, the consumption value of voting, and expressive voting theory. While explaining the voters' participation paradox, these explanations raise the rational ignorance paradox: when voters participate in elections they should do so without investing private resources in information. See also ***rational ignorance***, ***voting paradoxes***, ***expressive voting***, ***minimax regret***, and ***public choice theory***.

Rational actor model: much of the early work in the economic analysis of law builds upon the rational actor model, explicitly assuming that individuals are strictly rational utility maximizers. The rational actor model enjoys the great advantage of predictability and tractability. Rational actors are generally assumed to possess stable preferences, to make informed choices, to make unbiased judgments when acting under uncertainty, and typically, though not necessarily, to be self-interested (their utility function generally includes only arguments that relate to their own personal well-being). On the basis of the rational actor model, the law and economics literature has generated normative models guiding the design of legal rules and institutions, in several areas of the law. Recent scholarship in both experimental and behavioral law and economics has identified the limitations of these assumptions, developing alternative models of rationality that take into account cognitive imperfections, judgment biases, and other departures from rational choice. See also *decision theory*, *behavioral law and economics*, and *experimental law and economics*.

Rational choice theory: the implicit model undergirding most mainstream microeconomic research today. Rational choice theory posits that self-interested (i.e., "rational") actors behave in such a way as to maximize their self-interests, whatever those interests may be (Elster, 1986). In law and economics, rational choice theory has often been employed to study the behavior of individuals under the law. While rational choice theory furnishes the background assumptions for most mainstream economics, it is not entirely without controversy. The rational, self-interested actor is an abstraction, convenient for modeling behavior with tremendous clarity and precision in an ideal world. However, humans do not always behave "rationally" in the real world; and the use of rational choice principles to model human choice under the law at times undermines the predictive value of economic analyses. New generations of law and economics scholars are beginning to explore the implications of this methodological controversy. Behavioral economics and experimental economics have developed instruments that may prove increasingly useful to develop notions of ecological rationality with the descriptive and predictive power needed for law and economics applications. See also *ecological rationality*, *behavioral law and economics*, and *experimental law and economics*.

Rational expectations: the idea behind rational expectations is that people make efficient use of all the information available to them when forecasting future events. When the assumption of rational expectations is invoked, the model postulates that people learn very quickly from past experience and do not make systematic forecasting errors. With rational expectations, individuals' forecasts are on average correct. The theory suggests that individuals use all the available and relevant information up to the point at which marginal information costs equal the marginal benefits derived from the information. This implies that, when information is complete or costlessly available, individuals have perfect foresight. However, since information is generally incomplete and costly, models of rational expectations allow forecasts to be inaccurate. John Muth (1960, 1961) is credited with introducing the term into economics. However, it is thanks to the models of rational expectations developed in the 1970s by macroeconomic theorists such as 1995 Nobel laureate Robert Lucas that the concept has become influential in economics, and in law and economics. See also *adaptive expectations* and *credibility*.

Rational herding: see *herding behavior*.

Rational ignorance: Anthony Downs (1957) introduced this term into the public choice literature. The term has since then acquired broader significance and application in the law and economics literature. Ignorance is said to be rational when the cost of acquiring the information exceeds the potential benefit that the information could provide. Downs uses this idea in the context of political voting. In political elections, the vote of any one individual is very unlikely to influence the outcome. Two consequences follow from this realization: (a) individuals should rationally abstain from voting (rational abstention); and (b) rational voters should not invest in information to make the right choice (rational ignorance). Given that virtually no voter is likely to be decisive individually, abstention or uninformed participation are rational for most individuals. Rational ignorance has consequences for the quality of the decisions process and for the value of collective decision-making. See also *rational abstention*, *voting paradoxes*, and *public choice theory*.

Rational racism: see *statistical discrimination*.

Rawls, John Bordley (1921–2002): in addition to being one of the most prominent American political philosophers of the twentieth century, John Rawls has also been a very influential figure for the law and economics movement. John Rawls was born on February 21, 1921, in Baltimore, Maryland. He received his undergraduate degree from Princeton University in 1943, and, after an interruption in his studies due to military service, earned his Ph.D. in moral philosophy from Princeton in 1950. In 1952 Rawls received a Fulbright Fellowship to Oxford University. In 1971 he published *A Theory of Justice*, a work that revolutionized the contemporary thinking on justice. Rawls' theory, sometimes called justice as fairness, seeks to identify a concept of justice by examining the principles that people would generally agree upon. Since these values would be influenced by people's socio-economic status, Rawls introduces a condition he dubs a "veil of ignorance." Rawls argues that only when people are ignorant of their socio-economic status are they able to make a truly just decision about the governance of their society. In his theory of justice, Rawls concludes that, through a veil of ignorance, people would agree on the following principles: (a) each person should have equal rights to basic liberties, (b) social and economic benefits should be arranged in such a way that they maximize the situation of the least advantaged person, and (c) the privilege of office and position should be formulated in such a way as to ensure the maximum amount of fair opportunity (the difference principle). The conception of justice developed by Rawls has inspired welfare economists, in their attempt to formulate an economic welfare function capable of capturing the tradeoffs between aggregate wealth and fairness in distribution. In addition to his contributions to the theory of justice, Rawls also had an important impact on the debates regarding the obligation to obey the law, the role of religion in the public arena, and international human rights. In addition to

A Theory of Justice, Rawls' major works include *Political Liberalism* (1993), *Justice as Fairness: A Restatement* (2001), and *The Law of Peoples* (1999). See also *veil of ignorance* and *difference principle*.

Rawlsian justice: law and economics scholars often use this term as synonymous with a system of justice that is both efficient and fair. The reference is to John Rawls' (1971) *A Theory of Justice*. Rawls argues that a just arrangement of society is that which individuals would choose under a "veil of ignorance" (a veil that prevents them from knowing their position in the world and that removes them from their own worldly vested interests). Given their risk aversion in the face of uncertainty, individuals would choose allocations of rights and entitlements that are at the same efficient and distributively fair. Inequalities would be acceptable only to the extent that they are necessary to create efficient incentives for overall social welfare. Law and economics models that are inspired by an objective of Rawlsian justice, capturing the difficult tradeoff between efficiency and fairness in distribution, are usually modeled with a Nash social welfare function. See also *veil of ignorance*, *difference principle*, and *impartial observer theorem*.

Rawlsian maximin: the maximin principle is a guiding principle in Rawls' *A Theory of Justice* (1971), and is often used to refer to what Rawls calls the difference principle. According to this, social policy should pursue the maximization of the minimum gain to be achieved, so that social and economic inequalities can be "of the greatest benefit to the least-advantaged members of society." Rawls argues that the legitimacy of his difference principle is validated by maximin strategies being the most rational strategies for actors choosing under conditions he describes as the veil of ignorance. See also *utility monster*, *difference principle*, *veil of ignorance*, *Nash criterion of welfare*, and *capability approach*.

Ray economies: ray economies of scale extend the concept of economies of scale to multiproduct settings. Ray economies occur when the average cost of production increases as the scale of production increases for a given bundle (mix) of products. See also *economies of scale* and *economies of scope*.

Reaction function: the reaction function of a player identifies the best response when the strategic variable that the player chooses is a continuous variable. The reaction function specifies the optimal choice of a strategic variable by one player as a function of the choice of another agent. The most familiar example of reaction function is in the Cournot function in an oligopoly, which specifies the output level that maximizes firm's individual profits, for any output level chosen by other firms active in the market. See also *Nash equilibrium* and *Cournot competition*.

Recency effect: see *serial position effect*.

Reciprocal takings problem: if an entitlement is protected by liability-type rules, and damages are set below the subjective valuation of the good for two parties, a reciprocal takings problem may arise. Parties will continually take the good from each other knowing that they will have to pay only an amount lower than their valuation of the good. When the court does not know each party's subjective valuations of a good and damages are set too low, what will occur is a form of auction. Observing the reciprocal takings, the court will set higher damages each time the good is taken by the other party. Each litigant will continue to take the good from the other until damages are set above their valuation of the good and the taking will no longer be efficient. See also *dispositive takings principle*, *normative Coase theorem*, *multiple takings problem*, and *property rules versus liability rules*.

Reciprocity: in the existing law and economics literature, this term refers to a fairly broad range of concepts. Consider the following colloquialisms: "Do unto others as you would have done unto you," "If you scratch my back, I'll scratch yours," and "Tit for tat." These pieces of collective wisdom come to mind for many people when they think of reciprocity. Besides these common intuitions, it is possible to distinguish different concepts of reciprocity, according to their structure and mode of operation. In spite of great variation of ethical values from one culture to another, norms of reciprocity and retaliation stand as universal principles in virtually every human society. Historically, reciprocity norms first materialize in their negative form (e.g., the talionic principle of "an eye for an eye, a tooth for a tooth") and subsequently take up a positive connotation (e.g., the command to "love thy neighbor as thyself"). Economists and behavioral scientists have devoted considerable attention to both positive and negative connotations of reciprocity. Several studies provide an evolutionary explanation of reciprocity. The common ground of understanding is that, as a result of evolution, be it genetic or cultural, humans have developed an innate sense of fairness. This sense of fairness is the foundation for both positive and negative reciprocity attitudes (Fon and Parisi, 2003). Experimental and behavioral evidence confirms the claim that people exhibit a strong tendency toward both reciprocation and retaliation. The law and economics literature identifies reciprocity as an important condition for fostering the emergence and sustainability of spontaneous order, whenever the strategic conditions of the social interaction are such that socially optimal outcomes are not achievable through Nash strategies. See also *tit for tat strategies*.

Reciprocity-induced cooperation: Fon and Parisi (2003) have studied the effects of externally imposed reciprocity constraints on players' cooperative strategies. They label this type of cooperation "reciprocity-induced cooperation." Fon and Parisi examine the effects of external reciprocity constraints on the parties' strategies and label these "reciprocity-induced strategies." A key benefit of reciprocity is that it encourages parties to reveal their preferences truthfully. In the reciprocity context, "neither party would have an incentive to withhold cooperation below the privately optimal level of reciprocal cooperation" (Fon and Parisi, 2003). The reciprocity-induced equilibrium (i.e., the pattern of cooperation that parties reach when faced with exogenous reciprocity constraints) is often closer to the social optimum than the unconstrained Nash equilibrium. Reciprocity constraints are much more effective in inducing an optimal level of cooperation when parties are symmetrical. When parties are asymmetrical, reciprocity may still lead to an improvement over the unconstrained Nash equilibrium, but fail to induce socially optimal levels of cooperation. These concepts relate to the work of Hirschleifer (1983) and Cornes and Sandler (1996), all of whom have studied the effects of weak-link constraints on players' voluntary cooperation strategies. See also *fairness equilibrium*, *kindness function*, and *procedural preferences*.

Recontracting robustness: see *renegotiation proofness*.

Redistribution through law: see *two-step optimization*.

Reference point dependence: see *prospect theory*.

Reference points: psychological evidence shows that individuals set reference points in order to evaluate the outcomes of available alternatives. When evaluating the possibility of participating in a lottery, for example, individuals may set their reference point equal to their current wealth level and evaluate each outcome as a gain when it is larger than the reference point and a loss in the opposite case. Reference points may cause the so-called endowment effect, according to which individuals evaluate more highly the goods or services they already possess and belong to their reference points. Hart and Moore (2008) have suggested a promising application of reference points to behavioral law and economics, modeling contracts as reference points. An understanding of individuals' use of reference points in decision-making helps to explain long-term contracts and features of the employment relationship. Another study, performed by Fehr, Hart, and Zehnder (2011), examines the tradeoff between rigidity and flexibility in the presence of incomplete contracts and uncertainty. Through an experimental analysis, the authors show that rigid contracts may be preferred to flexible contracts by parties who engage in ex ante competition on the contract terms, accepting the contract as a reference point. See also *prospect theory*, *endowment effect*, and *behavioral law and economics*.

Reflexive preferences: see *axioms of preference*.

Regional impact multiplier system: see *input/output analysis*.

Regression analysis: a set of techniques used to discover statistical correlations. Given a set of data S, consisting of two (or more) elements $< x_0, x_1, \ldots >$, regression analysis "explains" the statistical relationship between x_0 and x_1 (or x_n, holding all other $x_{i \neq n}$ constant) with a formula of the form $x_0 = a + bx_1 + n$, where the value of x_0 is dependent on the value of x_1, a denotes a baseline value of x_0, and n denotes "noise." Intuitively, imagine the data set represented in a scatter plot. Regression analysis may be thought of as an attempt to draw a line through the cluster of points, minimizing the aggregate space between all of the points and the line – that is, trying to "fit" a line that most closely matches the scatter of points. In practice, a useful regression analysis tends to deal with multiple independent variables. Regression analysis today is a routinely used analytical tool and has proved invaluable to empirical research. It is worth observing that methodological issues are raised when causation is inferred from statistical correlation, and therefore care is required when interpreting the results of a regression analysis. See also *type I and type II errors*, *level of significance*, and *multiple regression*.

Regulatory capture: see *capture theory*.

Regulatory competition: governments at various levels, through legislatures and administrative bodies, create laws and rules that govern behavior. Tiebout (1956) first developed an economic model of jurisdictional and regulatory competition by arguing that states and municipalities will compete by generating policies that reflect the preferences of the local population. Individual states can serve as laboratories to generate effective policies, and, when faced with regulatory competition from other states, each state is more likely to work diligently to explore new and better policy schemes. This competition can ultimately generate better laws and regulations. There are various other ways in which the concept of regulatory competition has been used in the law and economics literature. Parisi, Schulz, and Klick (2006) use the concept of regulatory competition to describe the ways in which regulatory competences can be allocated within a unified state, among multiple legislative or administrative bodies. They observe that, when regulatory authority is shared among multiple bodies, there are two important dimensions that characterize the relationship between their actions. The first dimension concerns the effects of the action: positive effects (e.g., granting rights or privileges) and negative effects (e.g., restricting the rights and privileges already vested). The second dimension concerns the relationship between the actions of different regulatory bodies: joint competence (e.g., situations in which the joint action of the various bodies is needed) and alternative competence (e.g., situations in which the action of one or another body is sufficient). In economic terms, with joint competence the actions of the relevant bodies can be viewed as complements, with alternative competence the actions can be viewed as substitutes. Parisi, Schulz, and Klick (2006) show that the interaction between these two dimensions of regulatory action can affect regulatory outcomes. See also *Tiebout competition* and *race to the top versus race to the bottom*.

Regulatory impact analysis: governments at various levels, through legislatures and administrative bodies, create laws and rules that govern behavior. Over time, countries have developed different types of assessment procedures to evaluate (prospectively or retrospectively) the impact of their laws and regulations. These assessment procedures are generally called regulatory impact analysis, or just impact analysis. Generally, a regulatory impact analysis attempts to assess the

impact a specific regulation will have (or has had) on the regulated environment. The purpose of such analysis is to evaluate the cost-effectiveness and
welfare effects of laws and regulations. The field of law and economics provides
valuable methodological foundations for regulatory impact analysis. Different
techniques are used to carry out ex ante versus ex post impact analysis. Ex ante
assessments are often carried out on the basis of qualitative models, simulations,
and experimental studies, while ex post assessments are carried out with quantitative and empirical models, considering the actual impact of regulation on the
affected industry or region.

Relational contracts: informal agreements governed by unwritten codes of conduct and sustained by reputational concerns. Law and economics scholars and
new institutional economists have extensively studied relational contracts. Relational contracts become a desirable alternative to formal contracting when the
nature of the relationship is such that it would be prohibitively costly to specify
ex ante all possible future contingencies, and parties need to reach accommo-
dations to deal with unforeseen or uncontracted-for events. Relational contracts
are also particularly desirable when the implementation of the contract relies
on the parties' specialized knowledge, such as to render the enforcement and
adjudication of the contract by a third party extremely problematic and unpredictable. Game theory models have been used to identify the conditions under
which informal contracts can be sustained. Each party's reputation must be
sufficiently valuable to mutual performance obtainable through Nash strategies
even in the absence of legal enforcement. Put differently, relational contracts
must be self-enforcing. See also *self-enforcing contracts*.

Relative preferences: a form of other-regarding preferences, in which the well-
being of one individual involves a comparison with others. Examples of relative
preferences are those reflecting egalitarianism, and a desire for social status,
hierarchical positions, and fame. Early economists such as Adam Smith (1759,
1776) and John Rae (1834) recognized the relativity of wants and needs, but
much of the economic theory that followed focused on absolute preferences and
self-interest as the driving forces of human actions. Relative preferences can be
distinguished between positive and negative. With positive relative preferences,
one person's well-being increases as other people's well-being increases relative
to his or hers. This may be the case of an affluent individual who has a preference for equality or, more generally, for an individual who has a preference for
modesty. With negative relative preferences, one person's satisfaction, instead,
decreases as other people do better relative to him or her. This might be the
case for individuals driven by a desire to be ahead of others, or individuals who
care about social ranking or seek higher status, prominence, or fame relative
to others. Recent empirical and experimental work has brought new interest on
the question of relative preferences. McAdams (1992) has brought the concept
of relative preferences into the mainstream legal literature, and several other
law and economics scholars have considered the issue from the perspective of

policy design (such as Weisbach, 2008; Posner and Sunstein, 2010). Although negative relative preferences may foster competition, behavior driven by relative preferences may lead to an excessive dissipation of resources and a destruction of value. Relative preferences can be modeled with the use of some modified specification of interdependent utility functions. See also ***other-regarding preferences*** and ***interdependent utility functions***.

Relative price: the relative price of a good or service is its value compared with another good or service. Formally, it is the ratio of the prices of two goods or services. Economically, the relative price represents a measure of an opportunity cost. The opposite of relative price is nominal or absolute price, which is merely the cost of a good or service measured in money currency (e.g., dollars). In economics, agents react to changes in relative prices and not to changes in absolute prices. In consumer theory, the agent chooses the optimal consumption bundle by equating the marginal rate of substitution (i.e., the ratio between the marginal utility of two goods) to the relative price of the goods. The legal system, by imposing penalties (or rewards), changes the relative price of certain activities, discouraging (or encouraging) their undertaking. For example, the price of a criminal activity is the expected punishment threatened by the law. A thief will consider the relative price of petty theft and grand larceny when deciding how much to steal. If the sentence for petty theft is a month in jail and the sentence for grand larceny is five years in jail, the relative price of a grand larceny conviction is sixty petty theft convictions. See also ***marginal rate of substitution***.

Reliance: in the law and economics literature, contract reliance is defined as an investment undertaken by the promisee in light of a promisor's performance. Reliance investments increase the value of performance (if performance is received) but at the same time increase the value of the loss if the contract is breached. An important objective of contract law is to induce optimal levels of reliance. The problem of optimal reliance arises because, in many situations, reliance investments are contract-specific investments. The cost of such investments is sunk if the contract is irreversibly breached. See also ***incentives***, ***reliance damages***, ***expectation damages***, ***perfect expectation damages***, ***sunk costs***, ***asset specificity***, and ***zero marginal damages***.

Reliance damages: contract law penalizes parties who breach their contractual obligations. Contract law often forces a breaching party to pay some amount of damages to the non-breaching party. One way to calculate damages is to pay the non-breaching party an amount equal to the amount spent in reliance on the contract. Scholars and courts refer to this type of damages as reliance damages. Unlike expectation damages, which give the non-breaching party the benefit of the bargain, reliance damages leave the non-breaching party in the position he or she would have been in had he or she never agreed to the contract in the first place. Put differently, reliance damages are the amount of damages necessary to make the non-breaching party indifferent between breach and no contract. In economic terms, reliance damages bring the promisee on the same indifference curve he or she was on prior to entering into the contract. The law and economics literature has shown that, because of the lack of full internalization of externality, reliance damages provide insufficient incentives for performance, encouraging a promisor to breach a contract too soon (Cooter and Ulen, 2008). The reason is that reliance damages do not induce a full internalization of the externality caused by the breach. The expected benefit to the promisee of the contract is frequently greater than the amount the promisee expended in reliance on the contract. Reliance damages also create excessive incentives for reliance, inasmuch as all reliance investments are compensated through damages in the event of breach. See also *incentives*, *reliance*, *expectation damages*, and *efficient breach*.

Renegotiation: see *no ex post renegotiation assumption*.

Renegotiation proofness: one of the main concerns of mechanism design theory relates to the incentives of players to change the rules of the game they are playing. Renegotiation proofness (also known as recontracting robustness) requires that the mechanism design chosen by the player is invariant to renegotiation. Renegotiation may take the form of changes in the game rules that are mutually beneficial for the players and may occur at different stages of the contractual process. We can distinguish between interim renegotiation, which occurs before the mechanism is played and determines a mechanism and an equilibrium change, and ex post renegotiation, occurring after the mechanism is played and involving a change of the outcome proposed by the mechanism. The idea of renegotiation proofness is that the mechanism designer can anticipate exactly how any mechanism will be renegotiated and incorporate the changes in the original mechanism. In mechanism design theory, a renegotiation-proof mechanism is robust to both interim and ex post renegotiation. See also *mechanism design*, *contract theory*, *no ex post renegotiation assumption*, and *no retraction principle*.

Rent: economic rent is the remuneration of a production factor above the normal level required to employ the factor in the production process (i.e., above the factor owner's opportunity cost). Economic rent closely relates to producer surplus, but it is measured in input units rather than output units. See also *quasi-rent*.

Rent dissipation: see *rent seeking*.

Rent extraction: see *rent seeking*.

Rent seeking: competition is a fundamental ingredient of efficient markets. However, not every form of competition is productive and socially desirable. Gordon Tullock's (1967) seminal article lays the foundations for the understanding of unproductive and destructive competition. Tullock's pioneering contribution into the nature of unproductive competition by individuals and groups through the political process was followed by the work of Anne Krueger, who coined the term "rent seeking," which has now become a fundamental concept of economic theory, with applications spanning from civil litigation to international trade, to government regulation and political lobbying, and, more generally to situations in which agents engage in the costly pursuit of economic rents. Tullock's and Krueger's insight into how self-interested parties incur costs in the pursuit of rents has provided a valuable key for the understanding of economic behavior of actors outside the traditional profit-maximizing framework. Unlike conventional situations of productive competition, rent-seeking expenditures are unproductive. Rent-seeking models consider players who engage in a contest in which each player expends costly efforts to increase the probability (probabilistic models) or the share (deterministic models) of a given prize. Much of the theoretical literature that followed Tullock's and Krueger's lead focused on how much effort each player expends, and how the degree of rent dissipation varies with the value of the prize, the number of contestants, and the allocation rules (Posner 1975; Demsetz, 1976; Bhagwati, 1982; Tollison, 1982; and many others). This important strand in the literature has turned most of conventional welfare economics on its head. In a long-run equilibrium, investments in a competitive market yield the normal market rate of return. Shaking this conventional wisdom, the rent-seeking literature unveiled the different nature of unproductive competition, identifying conditions under which competitive rent seeking could lead to under- or over-dissipation. Rent-seeking models are frequently used in law and economics to study litigation and adjudication processes. The rent-seeking literature is also of great practical and theoretical significance for the understanding of unproductive contests such as redistributive political competition and special interest group lobbying. See also *rent extraction*, *Tullock's paradox*, *lost treasure effect*, *Tullock*, *Gordon*, and *public choice theory*.

Representativeness bias: a cognitive bias that causes people to evaluate the probability of an event/hypothesis by assessing how closely the event/hypothesis relates to available data. According to the representativeness bias, people do not estimate the likelihood of an event according to Bayes' theorem. The representativeness bias was identified by Tversky and Kahneman (1974), who also identified the availability bias and the anchoring bias. One of the implications of the representativeness bias is the so-called law of small numbers (identified by Rabin, 2002), according to which people tend to extract too much inference from small samples (or personal experience), thereby neglecting the relevance of base rates in assessing event probability. See also *law of small numbers*, *hindsight bias*, *anchoring bias*, *availability bias*, and *serial position effect*.

Representativeness heuristics: see *representativeness bias*.

Reputation tax: individual deviations from prescriptive norms (i.e., norms that reflect an "ought to" sense of obligation) usually carry consequences in terms of social sanctions and social stigma. Scholars analogize the cost that individuals face due to such sanctions and stigma to a tax on their reputation (Tirole and Benabou, 2006). See also *descriptive versus descriptive norms* and *reputational incentives*.

Reputational cascades: see *informational cascades*.

Reputational incentives: the effects of present actions on future opportunities and payoffs affect incentives. Signals previously sent by an individual affect how other parties predict the future behavior of that individual. Therefore, signals and choices made by a party can lead to future costs and benefits unrelated to the present situation. In response to reputational incentives, parties consider the long-term consequences of their actions (e.g., how present choices will influence their future ability to reach agreements). Take, for example, a producer committed to making high-quality shoes. Consumers trust the producer to make high-quality products, and for each breach of that trust (part of the mixed strategy of the producer) the producer gets a present benefit (selling a low-quality shoe for a high-quality price). If the producer exploits that benefit too frequently, it gains a reputation as a low-quality producer and can no longer sell shoes for a high-quality price. See also *reputation tax* and *crowding out versus crowding in effects*.

Reservation price: the maximum price a given consumer would be willing to pay for a particular good or service. The reservation price reflects the subjective value that an individual attaches to a good. The reservation price is the benchmark against which the consumer surplus is measured (the total savings with respect to the willingness to pay and the price actually paid by each consumer). See also *consumer surplus*.

Residual bearer: term used in tort law and economics to identify the party who bears the accident loss in equilibrium (i.e., the party who bears the loss when both parties adopt the due level of care and an accident occurs). The concept of the residual bearer is particularly important to understand the parties' incentives. The idea is that there are several factors that influence the likelihood of an accident, but courts and juries take only some of these factors into consideration when assessing negligence. For example, the number of miles that a person drives, or the number of times that a person crosses the street, affect the likelihood of an accident, but are not taken into consideration to establish negligence. When establishing negligence, courts and juries generally do not look at the "quantity" (activity level) of the parties' behavior, but only at their "quality" (care level). A reduction in activity level does not reduce the likelihood of being found negligent, and only the party who expects to bear the accident loss in equilibrium will have incentives to reduce his or her activity level (Shavell, 1980b). Dari-Mattiacci and Parisi (2005b) point out that, for a similar logic, the incentives to invest in non-observable precautions also follow the residual bearer. See also *activity level versus care level*, *non-observable precautions*, *best risk bearer*, *cheapest risk avoider*, and *cheapest cost avoider*.

Residual decoupling: the law and economics literature has introduced the idea of decoupling liability from compensation as an instrument to promote an optimal balance of costly litigation and valuable deterrence. Residual decoupling reduces victims' recovery while keeping tortfeasors fully liable when both parties are diligent. Unlike standard decoupling, residual decoupling can maintain a credible threat of liability without drastically changing the normal workings of the liability system. Residual decoupling affects only the allocation of the residual loss, and can therefore be used in combination with negligence and strict liability regimes to encourage a socially desirable reduction of tort activity levels. See also *decoupling, activity level versus care level, non-observable precautions, comparative causation, Shavell's activity level theorem*.

Residual loss: see *residual bearer*.

Retaliation: see *reciprocity* and *tit for tat strategies*.

Returns to scale: the relationship between changes in production input and the resultant changes in output. There are three general categories of returns to scale: (a) constant returns to scale, (b) decreasing returns to scale, and (c) increasing returns to scale. When each increase in input is matched by an equal increase in output, then the returns to scale are constant. When each increase in input causes a greater increase in output, the returns to scale are increasing; and when each increase in input causes proportionally less increase in output, then the returns to scale are decreasing. See also *economies of scale*.

Revealed preferences: the theory of revealed preferences, introduced by Paul Samuelson (1938), elicits consumers' preferences on the basis of observed consumer behavior. Contrary to standard consumer theory, the revealed preference theory identifies consumer preferences and constructs indifference curves starting from the observation of consumers' purchasing habits, thereby overcoming the measurability problem of utility functions. Samuelson (1950) demonstrates the equivalence of consumer theory and revealed preference theory. The functional school of law and economics builds on the idea that individuals can reveal their preference over alternative legal rules through contracting and choice of law. Whenever possible, legal systems should adopt rules and mechanisms that foster the revelation of preferences by the subjects of the law, avoiding otherwise complex revelation and measurement problems. See also *revelation principle, demand-revealing processes*, and *strategy proofness*.

Revelation principle: This principle (Gibbard, 1973) states that for any equilibrium of any general Bayesian game (one characterized by incomplete information regarding payoffs), there is an incentive-compatible direct revelation mechanism that provides equivalent payoffs or outcomes. When a central mediator has collected all the relevant true information known by all individuals participating in a game, he or she can simulate outcomes on the basis of that information. Therefore, a mediator can also predict how the players would behave under different mechanisms. In mechanism design, the revelation principle allows a designer first to consider whether any mechanisms exist that would induce parties to reveal private information to the designer. If that mechanism cannot be found, no mechanism can be designed to achieve the outcome desired by the designer. See also *revealed preferences* and *mechanism design*.

Revenue equivalence theorem: this theorem (Vickrey, 1961) states that the most popular auction formats (e.g., English auctions, Dutch auctions, first-price sealed bid auctions and second-price sealed bid auctions) on average yield the same price in a single item allocation problem with symmetric agents. This result follows from the fact that all these auctions can be shown to be efficient in a simple private-value setting. See also *auction theory*, *first-price auctions*, *second-price auctions*, *Dutch auctions*, *English auctions*, and *common-value auctions*.

Reverse adverse selection: term used in the law and economics literature to describe the possible strategy of insurers cherry-picking low-risk categories of customers. Siegelman (2004) points out that reverse adverse selection may take place when insurers are better able to recognize the risk faced by insureds. Insurers may take advantage of this asymmetric information to carry out cream-skimming or cherry-picking of desirable insureds (e.g., by reaching out or selectively advertising to the healthiest or lowest-risk groups). See also *adverse selection* and *inverse adverse selection*.

Reverse auctions: see *double auctions*.

Reverse causation: see *instrumental variable approach*.

Reverse damages: damages one might have to pay under a reverse liability rule. When a party creates a positive externality that benefits another party, the receiving party may be reverse-liable to the party producing the benefit. In order to correct the externality, the benefitting party might have to compensate the party producing the benefit for the value of the positive externality that he or she produced (reverse damages). Although legal systems generally impose liability for the internalization of negative externalities, positive externalities are often left without compensation. Dari-Mattiacci (2009) provides several examples of reverse damage rules for the compensation of uncontracted-for benefits and positive externalities, such as unjust enrichment and *negotiorum gestio* rules. One of the main reasons for the different legal treatment of negative versus positive externalities lies in the fact that those who create a positive externality have control over it, while victims of a negative externality do not have control over the choice of the other party. See also *reverse liability rule* and *positive externalities*.

Reverse liability rule: liability can be viewed as a form of internalization of negative externalities. Reverse liability may be considered the inverse of standard liability for the internalization of positive externalities. Dari-Mattiacci (2009) has studied the use of reverse liability rules, considering the case in which liability is imposed on a person who has received a gain (the gainer) toward the person who contributed to produce it (the benefactor). See also *reverse damages* and *positive externalities*.

Review of Law and Economics: established in 2005 as the official journal of the European Association of Law and Economics (EALE) in collaboration with the Berkeley Electronic Press. It publishes theoretical and empirical interdisciplinary research in law and economics-related subjects. Unlike other journals in law and economics, the *Review of Law and Economics* is published over the internet, avoiding the delays of print publication. The electronic content in the journal appears continuously, as articles are accepted for publication. The journal also publishes two special issues at the end of every year on special topics. Robert Cooter, Ben Depoorter, Gerrit De Geest, Nuno Garoupa, Lewis Kornhauser, and Francesco Parisi served as the founding editors of this review until 2009, and were subsequently joined by editors serving on a three-year rotating basis and elected by EALE: Stefan Voigt (2009–12), Giuseppe Dari-Mattiacci (2010–13), Fernando Gomez (2011–14), Tonja Jacobi (2012–15), Thomas Ulen (2013–16), and Dominique Demougin (2014–17). See also *law and economics journals* and *EALE*.

Right of first purchase: see *call option*.

Risk aversion: see *risk preferences*.

Risk-loving: see *risk preferences*.

Risk management: the four main strategies of risk management are avoidance, diversification, hedging, and insurance. Avoidance is a preventive strategy, which involves ex ante precaution investments. Diversification and hedging are strategies aimed at minimizing the impact of risk. Specifically, diversification mitigates the effects of unsystematic risk through a portfolio, while hedging is a form of management of systematic or market risk through financial and derivative market instruments. Insurance is a strategy of ex post transfer and spreading of risk. See also insurance, *futures*, *diversification*, *hedging*, and *systematic versus unsystematic risk*.

Risk preferences: individuals can exhibit different attitudes toward risk: risk aversion, risk neutrality, and risk-loving. To understand the distinction, consider a gamble with $\frac{1}{x}$ odds of success and $y : 1$ payout. When $x = y$, a gambler repeatedly making the bet will tend to break even. However, risk-averse people will refuse to gamble even when $x < y$, while risk-loving people will gamble even when $x > y$. Risk aversion is usually shown as the natural consequence of the diminishing marginal utility of wealth. As pointed out by Adam Smith (1776), people are generally unwilling to enter into an actuarially fair gamble, when they might face a fifty-fifty chance of doubling their wealth or losing it all. This is because the utility gain (joy) of doubling one's assets is lower than the utility loss (pain) of losing one's entire wealth. Under these assumptions, rationality entails risk aversion rather than risk neutrality. In the presence of risk aversion, uncertainty and the risk of a loss may create welfare losses that exceed the actual expected or materialized loss, if the risk cannot be insured or diversified. Risk-averse individuals are thus willing to pay an insurance premium (an insurance price that exceeds the expected loss) to avoid the risk. A risk-neutral individual is, instead, an individual who is indifferent to uncertainty and who is unwilling to pay a positive premium to insure against a risk. Finally, a person is said to be risk-loving if he or she exhibits a preference for uncertainty, such as to be willing to pay in order to face uncertainty (e.g., a gambler who is willing to buy a lottery ticket at a price higher than the expected win). The assumptions concerning the risk preferences of individuals are often of critical importance in legal policymaking. In several situations, legal remedies are chosen taking instrumental account of the risk propensities of the relevant subjects. For example, Becker's (1968) analysis of optimal criminal penalties accounts for the risk aversion of prospective criminals in identifying the optimal combination of probability and severity in terms of the imposed sanction. In several situations, legal rules often create incentives by reallocating risk or liability. The reallocation of risk is a double-edged sword, since it may create welfare gains through the incentive system but, at the same time, create welfare losses due to the risk aversion of the affected individuals. This implies that, if alternative efficient legal solutions are available, preference should be given to those solutions that "spread" the risk rather than concentrate it on one or the other party. When risk spreading is unfeasible or excessively costly, legal policymakers should, ideally, proceed to design law that balances the gains obtained by creating optimal incentives with the possible welfare losses occasioned by reallocations of risk. When risk neutrality can be assumed, or when there are cost-effective opportunities for risk diversification or insurance, legal rules and remedies can be designed to optimize primary and residual incentives, setting aside concerns for risk allocation problems. See also *prospect theory*, *diminishing marginal utility*, *loss aversion*, and *Hurwicz optimism–pessimism index*.

Risk premium: risk-averse individuals generally prefer to receive a sum with certainty than to face a bet with an equal expected value paid with uncertainty. A risk premium is the difference in amount that would leave an individual indifferent between the certain and the expected values. Put differently, a risk premium is the price that a risk-averse individual would pay to avoid risk. A risk premium is equal to zero in the case of risk neutrality and actually becomes negative when risk-loving individuals are concerned (i.e., a risk lover would be willing to pay to participate in a fair gamble). Besides its obvious applications to risk, insurance, and gambling, the concept of the risk premium is relevant and frequently used in law and economics. Legal rules create incentives by allocating risk and liability (e.g., tort rules reallocate the risk of a loss from victims to tortfeasors, contract rules reallocate the risk of non-performance from promisees to promisors, and legal warranties reallocate the risk of failure of a product from buyers to sellers). In the absence of a market for insurance, individuals face a utility loss when legal rules shift a risk on them. In designing legal rules, policymakers should attempt to maximize social welfare taking these two interrelated dimensions – optimal incentives and optimal risk allocation – into account. The concept of risk premium is used in these contexts as a monetary proxy for the utility loss occasioned by legal rules through the reallocation of risk and liability. See also *risk preferences*, *certainty equivalence*, and *disruption costs*.

Rivalrous in use: see *non-rivalry*.

Rivalry: see *non-rivalry*.

Robustness: economic modeling often necessitates the use of simplifying assumptions. The term "robustness" refers to the validity of the results of an economic model when the underlying assumptions or specifications of a model are relaxed. For example, in many tort and contract law problems, the model assumes the risk neutrality of the parties. The robustness of the analysis depends on whether the qualitative results hold when the initial assumptions are relaxed and risk aversion is introduced. In a different setting, robustness refers to the sensitivity of the policy results to the specification of the social welfare function. For example, a given allocation of rights or liabilities may be efficient under a Kaldor–Hicks social welfare function but not equally efficient if a different social welfare function is utilized. The term here could refer to the validity of the policy results when there are changes in the initial specification of the social welfare function. Robust results are generally preferable, providing a more solid foundation for normative interventions. See also *assumptions*, *Ockham's razor*, *falsifiability*, and *trembling hand*.

Romano, Roberta (1952–): the Sterling Professor of Law at Yale Law School. Romano is a prolific scholar, having authored three books and hundreds of articles. Her work centers primarily on corporate law and financial regulation. Romano received her A.B. (highest honors) from the University of Rochester in 1973, majoring in history and English; her M.A. in history from the University of Chicago in 1975; and her J.D. from Yale in 1980. Romano clerked for Hon. Jon O. Newman on the Second Circuit from 1980 to 1981. Prior to moving to Yale, where she was Allen Duffy/Class of 1960 Professor of Law from 1991 to 2005, and Oscar M. Ruebhausen Professor of Law from 2005 to 2011, she taught at Stanford Law School from 1981 to 1985. She was president of the American Law and Economics Association from 1998 to 1999. In 1995 she was inducted as a Fellow of the American Academy of Arts and Sciences. She is director of the Yale Law School Center for the Study of Corporate Law.

Ronald H. Coase medal: in 2008 the board of the American Law and Economics Association decided to establish the Ronald H. Coase medal. The medal is awarded biennially in recognition of lifetime contributions to the field of law and economics. The first medal recipients were Richard Posner in 2010 and Guido Calabresi in 2012. See also *Coase, Ronald*, *Posner, Richard*, and *Calabresi, Guido*.

Rotten kid theorem: this theorem holds that the members of a household, acting in their own self-interests, will attempt to maximize household income, even when such activities negatively affect their individual private income (Becker, 1974). Subsequent research on the topic has revealed that the rotten kid theorem relies upon several assumptions that were not obvious in Becker's paper, which therefore weakens its general applicability (Lindbeck and Weibull, 1988; Bergstrom, 1989; Lundberg and Polak, 2003). See also *Becker, Gary*, and *transferable utility*.

Rubin, Paul H. (1942–): the Samuel Candler Dobbs Professor of Economics and Law at Emory University. He is a central figure in the history of law and economics, having written on a large range of legal topics. He is known particularly for his work on regulation and evolutionary processes in the law, and for his seminal work on the efficiency of the common law hypothesis. He received his B.A. from the University of Cincinnati in 1963 and his Ph.D. from Purdue University in 1970. Rubin is currently editor-in-chief of *Managerial and Decision Economics. See* also *efficiency of the common law hypothesis*.

Rubinfeld, Daniel L. (1945–): the Robert L. Bridges Professor of Law and a professor of economics at the University of California, Berkeley. Rubinfeld is a prolific author, having published over 100 articles and two textbooks in the areas of law and economics, microeconomics, and econometrics. His areas of expertise include applied econometrics, antitrust law, and public finance. Rubinfeld majored in mathematics, graduating from Princeton University with a B.A. (magna cum laude) in 1967; he received his Ph.D. in economics from the Massachusetts Institute of Technology in 1972. He taught at the University of Michigan from 1972 to 1983, prior to moving to Berkeley. He served on the staff of the President's Council of Economic Advisers in 1969, and as deputy assistant attorney general in the antitrust division of the US Department of Justice from 1997 to 1998. Rubinfeld was an editor of the *International Review of Law and Economics* from 1988 to 2002. He served as president of the American Law and Economics Association from 2005 to 2006.

Rules versus standards: laws govern a complex and interconnected world and cannot be specified with reference to every possible fact pattern. The law and economics literature refers to the choice of the specificity of legal regulations as a choice between rules (laws with high levels of specificity) and "standards" (laws with low levels of specificity). When legislators choose between rules and standards, they must consider whether the law should be given content ex ante or ex post, and calculate the costs associated with each option (Kaplow, 1992). Standards give a greater degree of flexibility to judges and allow them to consider the specific circumstances of the case (e.g., driving at a reasonable speed). Rules, conversely, contain a higher degree of specificity and often provide unambiguous criteria for the resolution of a legal issue (e.g., driving at 55 miles per hour). Rules are very clear but often are unhelpful as new fact patterns arise. Standards are ambiguous but they can apply more broadly. With greater specificity comes less flexibility, often at the expense of an optimal fit between the objective of the rule and the regulated conduct. Rules with a higher degree of specificity require greater ex ante investments compared to the cost of developing a less specific standard. However, standards are more difficult to interpret, since they require determinations of the law's content to be made ex post by courts and juries. Parisi and Fon (2009) analogize the lawmaking process to a production process, in which the lawmaker incurs both fixed and variable costs. The creation of the law requires the lawmaker to invest in the fixed cost required for the production of a legal rule. Increasing the fixed investment (i.e., the degree of specificity) lowers the variable costs of adjudication. A standard requires a smaller initial investment, but requires larger outlays in its implementation and interpretation by courts and juries. Furthermore, with changes in the regulated environment, detailed rules are subject to a higher rate of obsolescence compared to general standards. See also ***acoustic separation***.

S

Safety in numbers versus danger in numbers: the idea of safety in numbers developed from empirical evidence showing that, for any given individual in a group, the probability of being the victim of a bad event decreases with group size. The concept was first introduced into the statistical literature by Reuben Smeed (1949), who found an exponential relationship (known as Smeed's law) between per capita accident rates and the number of drivers. There are several explanations of the safety in numbers rule, ranging from biological explanations of group behavior to the idea that mass behavior is more predictable and easier to control, to the idea that greater precaution investments are taken by prospective tortfeasors when risks are multiple. The expressions "danger in numbers" and "safety in prominence" have been used to describe the opposite hypothesis, that per capita risk may actually increase with group size. Rather than describing some empirical regularities, these concepts find applications in a limited set of situations, mostly characterized by intentional mass harm. For example, the use of a popular software platform may increase the per capita risk of being the victim of a cyber-attack. In the case of terrorist attacks, the probability of being a victim of a suicide bomber may increase when traveling on a crowded bus or being in a busy restaurant. Being alone or in prominence pose lower risks of an attack. See also *Smeed's law*.

Safety in prominence: see *safety in numbers versus danger in numbers*.

Salience: the perceived importance or quality of an element relative to neighboring and competing elements. Behavioral law and economics scholars use salience to describe a mechanism that attracts the attention of individuals with limited cognitive resources. Focusing on the more salient elements facilitates learning and the decision-making process. However, behavioral law and economics point to the possible biasing effects of salience in decision-making. See also *salience and dominance in experiments*, *cognitive bias*, *behavioral law and economics*, and *debiasing*.

Salience and dominance in experiments: in experimental economics, salience and dominance are essential requirements for the validity of an experiment. The concept of salience refers to the requirement that individuals' payoffs should be affected by their choices and actions in the experiment. The concept of salience distinguishes economic experiments from other forms of experiments used in the social sciences, such as some psychological experiments, surveys containing self-reported behavior, or questionnaires on hypothetical choice scenarios. Economic incentives should be dominant, in the sense that participants' choices should be predominantly driven by the reward structure. The requirements of salience and dominance generally hinge upon the additional assumption that the utility of the participants increases monotonically with an increase in the payoff or reward. Assuming non-satiation in the relevant range of the experiment's payoffs generally satisfies monotonicity. See also *laboratory experiment* and *experimental law and economics*.

Sanctions as prices: a fundamental insight of the economic analysis of law is the notion that legal sanctions are "prices" set for given categories of legally relevant behavior. This idea develops around the positive conception of law as a command backed by an enforceable sanction. The law and economics discipline uses the well-developed tool of price theory to predict the effect of changes in sanctions on individual behavior. Although the legal system sometimes borrows a price from the actual market (e.g., when the sanction is linked to the compensatory function of the rule of law), there are a wide range of situations in which legislative and judicial bodies set prices in the absence of a proper market mechanism (Parisi, 2001). This poses an essential question as to how the legal system can set efficient prices if there is no market process that generates them. See also *carrots versus sticks* and *incentives*.

Satisficing: a decision-maker who chooses the best available alternative according to some objective function is said to optimize. However, there are computational and decision costs involved in such optimal decision-making. When decisions are too complex or when the decision costs are too high, a decision-maker may look for a satisfactory solution, rather than an optimal first best solution. In this case the decision-maker is said to satisfice, rather than optimize. The term "satisfice" was coined by Herbert Simon (1956) in "Rational choice and the structure of the environment," and subsequently it has become a term of art in the bounded rationality literature. See also *rational choice theory* and *bounded rationality*.

Scale economies: see *economies of scale*.

Schelling point: see *focal point*.

Schumpeter's creative destruction: Marx (1993 [1857]) used the term "creative destruction" to describe the tension between the creative and destructive effects of production in capitalism. In the current literature, the idea of creative destruction is generally discussed in connection with Joseph Schumpeter's (1942) book *Capitalism, Socialism and Democracy* (1994). Schumpeter uses the term to describe the destructive effects of innovation. New products destroy the value of older products, destabilize industries, and dissipate the value of the human capital associated with their production. Law and economics scholars have considered the issue when examining the effect of intellectual property protection on optimal rates of innovation. See also *Coase conjecture*.

Scope economies: see *economies of scope*.

Screening: in the context of asymmetric information, screening represents a strategy adopted by the uninformed party to extract information from the informed party. Like the effect of signaling, screening can correct the problem of asymmetric information and prevent the undesirable effects of asymmetric information (adverse selection and moral hazard). Screening can take place by having the uninformed party offer a menu of choices to the informed party. The selection made by the informed party may reveal the content of the private information and could be used by the uninformed agent to optimize. Although screening and signaling are both strategies for correcting asymmetric information and for minimizing the problems of adverse selection and moral hazard, the two mechanisms operate differently. A distinguishing feature of screening is that, unlike signaling, it requires the uninformed agent to move first. Nobel laureate A. Michael Spence (1973) introduced the concept of screening in the economics literature, considering an application of the screening strategy in employee selection. An employer who is uninformed about the applicant's quality can offer a menu of choices, such as an employment contract formed by pairs of pay rates and working hours, to the candidate. The selection of a certain combination of pay rate and working hours provides information about the candidate. Screening is also used by banks to select potential borrowers on the basis of their financial history or job security. See also *asymmetric information*, *adverse selection*, *signaling*, and *moral hazard*.

Search costs: see *information costs*.

Search goods: see *experience goods versus search goods*.

Second theorem of welfare: see *fundamental theorems of welfare*.

Second best: see *first best versus second best*.

Second-degree price discrimination: see *price discrimination*.

Second-mover advantage: see *last-mover advantage*.

Second-order rules: Ayres (2005) refers to second-order rules as rules (either bargained for or established by law) that allow a party to purchase additional entitlements after a first-order entitlement has been violated. Contract law provides a useful example of a potential second-order rule. During contract formation, parties might stipulate a clause that states: "If either party must breach, the non-breaching party may bargain with the breaching party for specific performance." The first-order rules still apply – the party may seek expectation or reliance damages for breach – but the additional second-order rule allows for specific performance even when the court would not choose that option. See also *Coase theorem* and *single-price allocation*.

Second-party enforcement: the law may serve as a focal point delineating legal entitlements and empowering right holders to exert second-party enforcement against their own violators. The concept of second-party enforcement is based on the idea that laws may affect behavior not only through external incentives such as sanctions or rewards but also by triggering responses in other subjects and changes in social norms. Second-party enforcement can be carried out through the withdrawal of future cooperation and reputational and social sanctions and also through self-help and reprisal. The common ground for the explanation of second-party enforcement is that, as a result of evolution, be it genetic or cultural, humans have developed an innate sense of fairness (Marongiu and Newman, 1987). Research in behavioral and experimental economics provides support for the stylized fact that humans are predisposed toward second-party enforcement. Human actors are particularly skilled at detecting cooperators and cheaters in social interactions. People are in many ways better at solving problems that require cheater detection (deciding whether a social contract has been violated) than those that involve detecting cooperators (Cosmides and Tooby, 2003). This suggests that human psychology developed in such a way as to facilitate, and at the same time place great reliance on, second-party enforcement. Experimental and behavioral evidence have attempted to "measure" individuals' "taste" for justice through their willingness to engage in costly second-party enforcement. The results consistently show that, in the absence of legal enforcement, people will engage in second-party enforcement against their violators, even when it is not cost-effective to do so. People demonstrate distaste for wrongful behavior and a willingness to punish violators of shared norms, even when punishment is materially costly and there are no plausible future benefits from so behaving (Gintis, 2000). Although payoff consequences are important, other motives not captured by the objective payoffs of the game provide the motivation for second-party enforcement, through retaliatory behavior. These retaliatory attitudes are triggered when humans interact with other humans, but are not present when the game is played against impersonal entities or when the violation was involuntary or unavoidable under the circumstances (Fon and Parisi, 2005). Second-party enforcement is carried out even in one-shot interactions in which reputational and cooperative motives are not at work. See also *first-party enforcement*, and *third-party enforcement*, *private enforcement*, and *expressive law*.

Second-price auctions: in these the highest bidder wins the auction and is awarded the object at a price equal to the second highest bid. These auctions are also called Vickrey auctions, after the Nobel laureate William Vickrey, who studied and classified them. For a single item auction, Vickrey describes these auctions as a variant of Dutch auctions. Quoting Vickrey (1961): "On the other hand, the Dutch auction scheme is capable of being modified with advantage to a second-bid price basis, making it logically equivalent to the second-price sealed-bid procedure . . . " Second-price auctions can be used in procurement auctions. In this case, the lowest bidder wins the procurement and is paid an amount equal to the second lowest bid. One would naturally wonder why any seller would choose second-price auctions to sell his or her goods: a seller could collect higher bid payments using a first-price auction. In fact, as pointed out by Vickrey, the idea that sellers should prefer first-price auctions to second-price auctions has been shown to be untrue. Second-price auctions have the nice property of creating incentives for bidders to reveal their true value through the bidding process: in sale (procurement) auctions, bidding one's full private valuation (cost) becomes a dominant strategy for all bidders. See also *first-price auctions*, *Dutch auctions*, *English auctions*, *common-value auctions*, and *auction theory*.

Selection of cases for trial: see *settlement versus trial*.

Self-defeating subsidiarity: according to the subsidiarity principle, the optimal allocation of competences between local and central levels of government can be thought of in terms of cost advantages arising from economies of scale and economies of scope. When transferring competences from one level of government to another, economies of scope signify that, if one or more competences are shifted to the central level, the cost of carrying out the remaining activities at the local level will be greater. This implies that, once the process of centralization has begun, further progressive centralization is facilitated and often unavoidable. Carbonara, Luppi and Parisi (2009) refer to this process as "self-defeating subsidiarity" and use it to explain the paradox pointed out by Alesina, Angeloni, and Schuknecht (2005), according to which the subsidiarity test, introduced in the European Union to limit excessive centralization, has instead led to a wave of intense centralization. See also *subsidiarity* and *subsidiarity test*.

Self-enforcing contracts: contracts in which mutual performance can be achieved through Nash strategies in the absence of legal enforcement. Game theory and relational contract theory have identified the conditions under which contracts can be self-enforcing. In most legally relevant relationships, parties face unilateral defection strategies, and reputation becomes a critical ingredient to sustain cooperation. Evolutionary game theory also provides instruments to identify the environments and strategies that can foster spontaneous cooperation between parties engaged in repeat-game interactions. See also *relational contracts*.

Self-serving bias: an individual's tendency to attribute his or her successes to internal and personal factors while ascribing his or her failures to factors outside personal control. For example, a student who receives a good grade for an exam might attribute his or her performance to the quality of his or her study, level of commitment, and intelligence; however, if he or she performs poorly, he or she might attribute his or her failure to the teacher's unfair grading or other exogenous factors. Individuals who exhibit a self-serving bias tend to extract patterns of biased causal inference from the observed reality, perceiving ambiguous information as material that supports their preferred outcome or vision of reality. Self-serving bias may occur in conjunction with unrealistic optimism and false uniqueness bias, according to which an individual believes that he or she can perform better than the average person in areas linked to the individual's self-esteem. Researchers have observed this phenomenon when individuals are asked to evaluate their own driving skills, communication effectiveness, or leadership ability. The self-serving bias may surface in an individual because of his or her need to protect his or her self-esteem; in order to convey a more favorable social self-representation; or simply because individuals tend to recall internal reasons for success better than the external ones. When the self-serving bias occurs at the group level, it is labeled "group-serving bias." Self-serving bias is especially relevant in out-of-court settlement opportunities. Experiments investigate subjects playing the role of either the plaintiff or defendant in a hypothetical tort law case. Studies show that the self-serving bias affects the bargaining process when parties interpret the facts of the dispute in their own favor. This effect leads litigants to overestimate their assessment of damages or success probabilities, and may lead to higher litigation rates and forgone settlement opportunities. See also *false consensus bias, optimism bias, false uniqueness bias, blind spot bias, moral pessimism versus moral optimism bias, Hurwicz optimism–pessimism index*.

Sen, Amartya (1933–): best known for his pioneering contributions to the field of social choice theory. Sen received the Nobel Prize in economics in 1998, for his work in welfare economics, specifically for his work addressing poverty and famine. Sen was born on November 3, 1933, in Santiniketan, Bengal, in India. He received a Bachelor of Arts degree from Presidency College in Calcutta with a major in economics. He then went on to receive another Bachelor of Arts from Trinity College in Cambridge in 1956, as well as a Ph.D. in economics in 1959. He completed his thesis there on "the choice of techniques." Sen is perhaps best known for the eponymous Sen's liberal paradox, put forth in his article "The impossibility of a Paretian liberal" (1970b), which demonstrates the incompatibility of classical liberalism and Pareto optimality in even very simple preference scenarios. His book *Collective Choice and Social Welfare* (1970a) proved a groundbreaking work in the field of welfare economics, attempting to navigate a middle ground between those who advocates absolute adherence to the free market, and statists who advocate complete government control over markets. Sen argues that perfection in social decision-making is not necessary, and that majority decisions should be followed, as long as the interests of minority groups are not overlooked. He is also known for his contributions to the fields of welfare economics, and work to fight poverty and famine in developing countries. See also *Sen's liberal paradox, Paretian liberal,* and *capability approach*.

Sen's capabilities approach: see *capability approach*.

Sen's liberal paradox: formulated by Amartya Sen in his article "The impossibility of a Paretian liberal" (1970b). The paradox is presented in the form of an impossibility theorem. Sen states that collective decision-making, through the social choice function, cannot simultaneously satisfy the conditions of Pareto optimality and minimal liberalism. Far from suggesting a general inconsistency between Pareto efficiency and liberalism, the theorem suggests that there is no assurance that the two principles can be reconciled (the problem does not necessarily arise, as when the preferences of the single individual and those of society do not collide). Society can overcome the drawback implied by Sen's paradox in several ways. One possibility proposed by Sen consists of giving individuals the ability to constrain their own choice, and to accept that other persons in the society also have freedom of choice. An alternative solution proposes allowing individuals in the society to sign a contract wherein each individual trades away his or her right to act in his or her own self-interest and in return gains control over the right of others to act selfishly. These solutions could allow society to move toward Pareto-efficient solutions, while respecting liberal choice principles. See also *Paretian liberal* and *meddlesome preferences*.

Separating equilibrium: see *pooling versus separating equilibria*.

Serial position effect: psychologists and behavioral economists have observed that, when subjects are presented with items of information serially, they are able to remember the earlier items (primacy effect) and later items (recency effect) better than information in the "middle" of the list (Murdock, 1962). For example, when given a list of words to memorize, test subjects tend to have good recall of words at the end of the list, somewhat worse recall of words at the beginning, and worst recall for words in the middle of the list. Interestingly, the primacy and recency effects have also been observed in animals (Castro and Larsen, 1992). The two biases are acutely relevant in jury trials, when evidence is often presented serially, and when primacy and recency may distort the persuasive weight that jurors assign to it (Kassin and Wrightsman, 1979; Furnham, 1986). See also *behavioral law and economics*, *anchoring bias*, *availability bias*, and *representativeness bias*.

Settlement versus trial: parties to litigation face decisions about whether to settle or proceed to trial. Law and economics scholars have explored how individuals make decisions about whether to settle or proceed to trial. Kahneman and Tversky (1979) have found that human beings are averse to loss and that this will impact how they make decisions in litigation and other contexts. Cooter and Ulen (2008) use a helpful hypothetical: if a person must choose between a sure gain of $50 and a 50 percent chance at $100 or nothing, the person will choose the sure gain of $50. However, if a person must choose between a sure loss of $50 or a 50 percent chance at a loss of $100 or a loss of nothing, he or she will choose the gamble. In other words, the person is averse to loss and will therefore be more willing to face litigation than to settle for a certain loss of $50. Kahneman and Tversky's insight is helpful in understanding how individuals behave in litigation, and the critical role played by settlement offers in setting a reference point for the parties' litigation decisions. See also *prospect theory*.

Shadow price: in many situations, decisions are taken when there is no market price, or the price is not known, or does not reflect the real opportunity cost. The expression "shadow price" refers to the implicit cost of a change in the objective function in all such situations. The technical significance of the term changes according to the specific uses. In constrained optimization in economics, the shadow price reflects the value change of the objective function at the optimal solution obtained by relaxing the constraint by one unit. In mathematical language, the shadow price measures the value of the Lagrange multiplier at the optimal solution. In consumer theory, the shadow price measures the marginal utility of adding one unit of income in the budget constraint. In production theory, the shadow price measures the marginal production cost of adding one unit of output in the output constraint. In public policy applications, the shadow price refers to the social opportunity cost of a hypothetical public policy or project. In law and economics, the idea of shadow price provides a powerful metaphor to refer to the implicit costs of legal policy choices – a metaphor that is particularly convenient when policy choices affect situations that are not characterized by explicit markets and lack a price system. See also ***constrained optimization***.

Shapley–Shubik power index: developed by Shapley and Shubik (1954), it measures voting power. Consider the simplest case of a committee with three members, each casting one vote. In this case, the three members have equal power. If one of the three members casts three votes and the other two members cast only one vote between them, the first member would instead have all the voting power. The Shapley–Shubik index provides a formula to measure voting power as a function of the distribution of the votes, and the resulting opportunity for voters to form a majority coalition. When some coalitions are harder to form than others (e.g., ideological differences), the index needs to be adjusted in consideration of the actual opportunities to form a coalition. Applications of this index range widely, from an analysis of weighted voting in European Union contexts to United Nations deliberations, to predictions of US Supreme Court case outcomes.

Shavell, Steven M. (1946–): the Samuel R. Rosenthal Professor of Law and Economics at Harvard Law School. He was born in Washington, DC, on May 29, 1946. He received his B.A. from the University of Michigan in 1968 and a Ph.D. in economics from the Massachusetts Institute of Technology in 1973, and graduated as a Harvard Law School Liberal Arts Fellow in 1977. Shavell has written a number of influential articles and books, several of which have provided major theoretical contributions to the field of law and economics. Shavell's major contribution to the field of law and economics is in the development of the economic modeling of legal problems. Examples include "Strict liability versus negligence" (1980b), "Damage measures for breach of contract" (1980a), and "Economic analysis of accident law" (2003). Shavell has also contributed valuable insights in less conventional areas of law and economics, with seminal articles such as "Fairness versus welfare" with Louis Kaplow (2001) and his work on the role of law in shaping morality. His book *Foundations of Economic Analysis of Law* (2004) provides an analysis and synthesis of the economic approach to various topics within the legal system, namely property law, tort law, contract law, criminal law, the litigation process, and welfare economics. See also *Shavell's activity level theorem*.

Shavell's activity level theorem: an ideal remedy in tort law incentivizes optimal precautionary care levels and optimal activity levels for both potential tortfeasors and potential victims. Shavell (1980b) shows that this ideal is not achievable under negligence-based regimes, because, while negligence-based regimes may incentivize optimal care levels (i.e., observable precautions), only the bearer of residual liability will be incentivized to adjust his or her activity level (i.e., unobservable precautions). This is because the non-bearer of residual liability wants only to avoid liability (for which he or she need only demonstrate due care), whereas the bearer of residual liability wants to avoid harm. Therefore, only the bearer of residual liability will be incentivized to exercise the optimal unobservable care/activity level. Consequently, Shavell's theorem states that no negligence-based regime can incentivize optimal activity levels for both parties. See also *care level versus activity level*, *decoupling*, and *residual decoupling*.

Signaling: in the context of asymmetric information, screening represents a strategy adopted by the informed party to reveal private information to the uninformed party. Like the effect of screening, signaling can correct the problem of asymmetric information and prevent the undesirable effects of asymmetric information (adverse selection and moral hazard). The uninformed party adjusts his or her expectations on the basis of the received signal and optimizes on the basis of the adjusted expectations. Screening and signaling strategies are both adopted to correct asymmetric information. Unlike screening, signaling requires the informed agent to move first. A. Michael Spence (1973) originally introduced the concept of signaling by examining the process of applications in the job market. Potential employees send a signal about their ability to the employer by investing in education. Better candidates face a lower opportunity cost to acquire the signal (i.e., it is easier for better candidates to be enrolled in more prestigious schools, or to have better grades). Although the score obtained in a given college class may have little relevance for the applied position, the education record of a candidate can credibly signal information about his or her work ethic and may serve as a good indicator of the employee's ability and productivity. For a signal to be a valuable source of information (rather than cheap talk), a separating equilibrium is necessary. Different types of individuals should face different costs of sending a given signal, such that only a subset of them will be able or willing to send the signal in equilibrium. Upon receiving a credible signal, the uninformed party adjusts his or her expectations and optimizes accordingly (e.g., the employer attempts to recruit or offers higher wages to more qualified prospective employees). See also *asymmetric information*, *adverse selection*, *screening*, *moral hazard*, *cheap talk*, and *pooling versus separating equilibrium*.

Significance test: see *level of significance*.

Simons, Henry Calvert (1899–1946): an economist who taught at the University of Chicago Law School. His main substantive work was in developing monetarism and promoting laissez-faire policies. However, perhaps more than his substantive contributions, he is remembered for his stylistic influence on the Chicago school of economics and the University of Chicago Law School. He was in many ways a pioneer in the interdisciplinary use of economic analysis in studying the law. See also *Chicago school*.

Simulations: since the early years of computing, economists and social scientists have taken advantage of computer technology to study market and social phenomena. The term "simulations" includes a variety of techniques that can shed light on problems that cannot be solved with other mathematical techniques. After its initial advent, the use of simulations in economics has undergone a period of decline, followed by a period of resurgence. In law and economics, simulations played a marginal role during the early decades of the discipline. Law and economics required simple models, and the mathematical formalizations could generally yield determinate results without having to resort to computer simulations. This has relegated simulation to a secondary role (mainly to produce visual illustrations or to generate numerical examples), rather than to derive actual results. Starting in the 1990s the problems tackled by law and economics scholars grew in complexity, and the field has witnessed an increasing use of simulations to understand more complex social dynamics. In future years the use of simulations in law and economics will likely grow larger, expanding the domain of traditional law and economics. In the foreseeable future, problems in law and economics will remain mathematically simple. Therefore, the use of simulations will not be that of providing solutions to complex mathematical problems that cannot be solved through qualitative mathematical models. Rather, simulations will be increasingly useful for addressing dynamic problems, and for the study of phenomena such as the propagation of norms, the evolution of preferences under the law, and modeling law as a complex adaptive system. See also *comparative statics* and *calibration*.

Sin taxes: see *meddlesome preferences*.

Single-monopoly profit theorem: antitrust scholars traditionally held the view that a firm with the potential for monopoly in both markets could leverage its monopoly position in one market to create a monopoly in the second market, thereby creating double monopoly profits. Posner (1976), and others in the Chicago school, have argued against this view. Chicago school scholars argue that the combination of multiple markets ends up creating one product or service and, therefore, one monopoly. Firms with powerful positions in both markets will not use leverage to create monopolies in both markets because it will ultimately mean an increase in prices for the combined product in question and a decrease in revenue for the double-monopoly firm. This theorem, called the single-monopoly profit theorem, critiques the traditional assumption that two monopolies are worse than one. In its application to tying, the theorem implies that tying may produce benefits, such as increased convenience for consumers and lower transaction costs, with no deadweight loss, and it should therefore be treated as per se legal. Carlton and Waldman (2002) have partially criticized the single-monopoly profit theorem, showing that tying may be undertaken for anticompetitive reasons, not so much to increase monopoly profits but to deter entry in the monopoly tying market. These post-Chicago considerations have been used to argue for a rule of reason approach in the antitrust treatment of tying cases (Ahlborn, Evans, and Padilla, 2004). See also ***tie-ins*** and ***bundling***.

Single-chooser rules: those that give either the plaintiff or the defendant control over the ultimate allocation of an entitlement. Choosers can engage in bargaining with the other party over the final allocation of that entitlement, but have the ultimate say as to how the entitlement will be allocated if bargaining fails. When a court has complete or near-complete valuation information for one of the parties in dispute, the court can allocate the entitlement through single-chooser rules to the rival. The party with less hidden information has less of an opportunity to withhold information strategically from the other party, and an equitable result is more likely to occur. This differs from dual-chooser rules, whereby the plaintiff and the defendant both have some measure of control over the allocation of an entitlement, bargaining to determine who values it more. See also ***dual-chooser rules***, ***chooser's call/put option***, ***first-order rules***, ***single price allocation***, ***property rules versus liability rules***, and ***Coasean bargaining***.

Single-peaked versus double-peaked preferences: the concept of "single-peaked preferences" was first formulated by Duncan Black (1948), and it has proved extremely useful in the study of collective decision-making. A decision-maker's preferences are single-peaked if his or her alternative preferences are positioned on either side of his or her preferred preference. If one imagines a line graph that connects a decision-maker's preferences, which are plotted according to how much he or she prefers them, single-peaked preferences would create the image of a hill with a single peak at the decision-maker's top preference. As an example, imagine a voter who is considering various candidates for public office. There are six candidates, and their views are all different. They are all roughly positioned along a line between left- and right-wing ideological extremes. Imagine the voter is a moderate. His or her favorite candidate resides in the middle of the ideological spectrum. His or her second- and third-choice candidates reside on either side of his first preferences. He or she is less favorable toward the three remaining candidates, who inhabit the extremes of the ideological spectrum. Because the voter's alternative preferences hover right near his or her top preference, his or her preferences are single-peaked. Preferences are double-peaked or multi-peaked when the individual's top alternatives are separated by less preferred options (e.g., a voter may put high levels of expenditures for public education as his or her first choice, but may put very low expenditures as his or her second choice, with intermediate expenditures as the third choice). See also *median voter theorem* and *Arrow's impossibility theorem*.

Single price allocation: when a court recognizes or enforces a property entitlement, it may set a single price for damages in the event of a taking or breach of an injunction. That single price, when interpreted by the relevant parties, provides them with a commonly recognized starting point in the Coasean bargaining that may lead to the reallocation of the entitlement (Ayres, 2005). See also *Coasean bargaining* and *second-order rules*.

Single-sourcing: see *winner determination*.

Smeed's law: using empirical evidence from sixty-two countries, Smeed (1949) shows that it is safer to drive in countries with more driving. The relationship that Smeed finds is that of an exponential curve, and it has become known as Smeed's law. This relationship has been confirmed by empirical studies in a variety of other contexts, and it is generally referred to with the expression "safety in numbers." See also *safety in numbers versus danger in numbers*.

Smith, Vernon Lomax (1927–): an American economist known for his work in the fields of experimental economics, industrial organization, property rights economics, and neuroeconomics. In 2002 Smith received the Nobel Prize in economics, along with Daniel Kahneman, for his seminal contributions to the field of experimental economics. He was born on January 1, 1927, in Wichita, Kansas. He received his undergraduate degree from the California Institute of Technology in 1949, a Master's degree in economics from the University of Kansas in 1952, and his Ph.D. from Harvard University in 1955. Among his many contributions to the field, he has developed an array of methods and standards for laboratory experiments in economics. He has also developed laboratory trials of new, alternative market designs. During his years at George Mason University, where he held a joint appointment with the law school and the economics department, he became actively involved with the law and economics research and with the study of the law and economics of irrational behavior. See also *experimental law and economics* and *Kahneman, Daniel*.

Social benefit: the sum of private benefits and the spillover benefits to society. While private benefits are accrued to the individual consumers and producers, spillover benefits arise from positive externalities that benefit the overall society. The external benefits are not captured by the price system. Positive spillovers or externalities create a discrepancy between the private and social benefits of an activity. The estimation of the spillover or externality benefit requires the estimation of the monetary value of external benefit of the activity to third parties and society as a whole. Like the estimation of social costs, this quantification is at times difficult, since it can involve monetary quantifications, in the absence of explicit market prices. See also *externalities* and *social cost*.

Social choice theory: one of the main offshoots of economics, which shares many commonalities with law and economics, and public choice theory. The term has both a broad and narrow sense: in its more inclusive sense, social choice is the study of the relationship between individuals and societies in terms of preferences and collective action; on a narrower conception, social choice theory is concerned with a set of particular technical problems and their policy implications. Central to the study of social choice theory are the voting paradoxes of Condorcet and Arrow (1951). Two prominent social choice theorists have been awarded the Nobel Prize in economics: Kenneth Arrow in 1972 and Amartya Sen in 1998. See also *Arrow, Kenneth*, *Sen, Amartya*, *public choice theory*, and *voting paradoxes*.

Social contract: see *contractarianism*.

Social cost: the sum of private costs and the spillover or externality costs to society. While private costs are borne by individual consumers and producers, spillover costs (or benefits) arise from negative (or positive) externalities to society, which are not captured by the price system. Both negative and positive externalities create a divergence between private and social costs. For example, when a firm's activity causes an externality, the social cost of the activity will be the sum of the private cost of the firm (e.g., the production costs required to manufacture the goods) and the cost of the externality (e.g., air pollution borne by the entire society). Absent an internalization of the externality (e.g., liability for pollution costs), the price system will transmit only the private cost of the activity, but will not reflect the full social cost. The estimation of social cost requires the estimation of the monetary value of externalities. These costs are at times difficult to quantify, since they will require estimation on the basis of the preferences of the population, in the absence of explicit market prices. See also *externalities*, *Pigouvian tax*, and *Coase theorem*.

Social discount rate: the rate at which society trades off present consumption for future consumption. In assessing the proper social discount rate, two factors should be taken into account: (a) humans tend to undervalue the future consequences of their actions; and (b) the costs and consequences of current choices may be borne by future generations. The choice of social discount rates poses a substantial challenge to policymakers and economists alike, given the lack of consensus on the criteria that should guide intergenerational economic policy. In day-to-day practice, the social discount rate is occasionally proxied by the opportunity cost of capital (e.g., twenty-year Treasury bonds for comparable-term policies) or the productivity growth rate (to estimate the incremental social benefit generated by public policies). Although there are good reasons to say that the social discount rate should be proxied by these market-based rates, when evaluating alternatives, policymakers often base their cost–benefit analysis on other considerations (such as the equitable distribution of consumption over time) and prefer to use overlapping generation models to estimate the impact of proposed policies on social welfare. See also *intergenerational equity*, *myopia*, *social time preference*, and *present value*.

Social norms: see *descriptive versus prescriptive norms*.

Social projection bias: human beings consider what other human beings do when making decisions or when formulating moral or ethical judgments. Sometimes the perception of what other human beings do can influence their behavior or judgment. Cooter, Feldman, and Feldman (2006) point out that, in this process, a social projection bias becomes possible. With a social projection bias an individual selectively finds in the outside world support and confirmation for his or her chosen path of action. For example, when individuals are prone to engaging in negative behavior, they may fall prey to a social projection bias and overestimate the number of other individuals who are engaging in negative behavior (Cooter, Feldman, and Feldman, 2006). This will lead the individual to engage in more negative behavior him- or herself. Sometimes an individual's perceptions of other human beings do not actually impact his or her propensity to take a certain action. An individual may already be inclined to engage (or not to engage) in certain activities, and the social projection bias leads him or her only to overestimate the extent to which other individuals do the same (e.g., an individual who is already inclined to steal will overestimate how many other individuals in the world steal). Like a Freudian projection bias, a social projection bias works only at a psychological level, to assuage guilt and provide self-assurance, but it does not actually affect the number of people who engage in good (or bad) actions or activities. See also *uniqueness bias*, *moral pessimism versus moral optimism bias*, and *behavioral law and economics*.

Social response theories: see *countervailing norms*.

Social sanctions: scholars and legal policymakers have long realized that legal rules and sanctions are not the only factors that impact behavior; social norms and social sanctions also play an important role in influencing behavior. Social sanctions are external, non-legal pressures to engage in certain behavior. Social pressures can come from oneself, friends, neighbors or co-workers, or the community as a whole. The literature distinguishes three forms of social sanctions (first-party, second-party, and third-party sanctions), based on who enforces the sanction. A fundamental question addressed by the recent law and norms literature considers the critical interaction between legal and social sanctions in promoting socially desirable behavior. Anecdotal and empirical evidence has shown that, when the legal system regulates a situation already governed by informal social norms, several possible dynamics may be triggered. In some cases, the creation of a legal sanction may trigger or reinforce preexisting social sanctions (Rasmusen, 1996; Kahan and Posner, 1999; Cooter, 2000b); in other cases, it may corrode existing social sanctions and even trigger backlash effects

(Kahan, 2000; Stuntz, 2000; Parisi and von Wangenheim, 2006). An interesting study by Gneezy and Rustichini (2000) provides experimental evidence of the non-linear relationship between legal and social sanctions. The field experiment tested the effects of the introduction of a fine for latecomers on parents' behavior in several day care centers. Gneezy and Rustichini find that the introduction of the fine produced an increase in the number of children picked up late by parents. One of the explanations for this paradox is that the introduction of a fine corroded other informal enforcement mechanisms, such as guilt, shame, and community reprobation. Legal policymakers should be conscious of these effects, in order to avoid unintended results from legal intervention. See also *private enforcement, first-party enforcement, second-party enforcement, third-party-enforcement,* and *expressive law.*

Social time preference: the discount rate used by policymakers when weighing costs or benefits that materialize at different times. See also *social discount rate* and *myopia.*

Social welfare: in standard economic applications, social welfare represents the sum of the consumer surplus and the producer surplus. However, in law and economics applications, social welfare becomes a more complex concept requiring the evaluation of the effects of the introduction of legal rules. There are two interrelated dimensions in which social welfare analysis plays out in law and economics models. The first involves the choice of the maximand (what should be maximized), the second involves the techniques of aggregation (how we should maximize). Scholars in law and economics are often in disagreement as to the appropriate definition of social welfare for legal policy. In the law and economics literature, an important debate involves the appropriate choice of the maximand for legal policy. The two competing criteria – utility maximization and wealth maximization – each offer advantages and disadvantages in actual applications. Although the majority of theoretical economists believe that utility is the appropriate maximand for welfare analysis, in practical applications the difficulties involved in measuring utility and undertaking interpersonal utility comparisons render utility maximization unfit for policy analysis. Several law and economics scholars have come to utilize wealth-based methods for evaluating social welfare. However, many scholars criticize the paradigm of wealth maximization for its indifference to distributive concerns, arguing that distributive justice should be included as a fundamental ingredient of social welfare. A related debate concerns whether the components of social welfare should be aggregated in an additive form (according to the Kaldor–Hicks criterion) or in a multiplicative or non-linear form (as in the Nash or maximin criteria of welfare). See also *maximand, utility maximization, wealth maximization, utility monster, Kaldor–Hicks criterion, Nash criterion of welfare, Rawlsian maximin, Pareto efficiency, capability approach, welfare analysis,* and *interpersonal utility comparisons.*

Spatial competition: see *Hotelling competition*.

Spatial property: see *functional property*.

Spatial voting: spatial voting models are used in public choice and social choice theory. In spatial voting models, policy alternatives are represented as points in a multidimensional policy space and voters' preferences are represented with Euclidean indifference curves, usually shaped as concentric circles. Indifference curves that are closer to a voter's ideal point represent policy alternatives that are preferred to those lying on more peripheral indifference curves. Spatial voting models use these tools to model the effect of alternative voting rules, agenda setting, and the forming of alternative coalitions on policy outcomes. See also *Euclidean preferences*, *median voter theorem*, and *Hotelling competition*.

Specific assets: see *asset specificity*.

Specific risk: see *systematic versus unsystematic risk*.

Spillover: an externality effect (either a benefit or a cost) caused by an economic activity that affects individuals or firms that are not directly involved in the activity that creates the spillover. Spillover effects, just like externalities, are not captured by the price system. An important case of spillovers is that of knowledge spillovers stemming from scientific research and discovery. The dissemination and exploitation of the discovery or information create benefits for individuals not associated with its original production. Given the non-excludable nature of most knowledge spillovers, intellectual property law is often unable to regulate situations of knowledge spillovers, and different instruments of industrial and fiscal policy are utilized to align private and social incentives for scientific research and discovery. See also *network effects* and *externalities*.

Spot contracts versus forward contracts: spot contracts are standard sales contracts involving one person agreeing to buy a present good from another person or entity for a certain price, referred to as the spot price. In forward contracts, two parties agree to buy or sell something at a future date for a price that is set at the time of the contract, referred to as the forward price. Forward contracts allow contracting parties to reallocate the risk of future price or commodity fluctuations (hedging). The difference between the spot price and the forward price is called the forward premium, and it is analogous to the insurance premium that the seller pays to the buyer for taking the risk of a future price change.

Spot price: see *spot contracts versus forward contracts*.

Spur Industries* v. *Del E. Webb Development Co.*:** law and economics scholars often cite the 1972 case *Spur Industries* v. *Del E. Webb Development Co.*, 494 P. 2d 700 (1972), as an example of a court decision based on efficiency considerations. This famous case deals with the laws of nuisance. Spur Industries owned a livestock feedlot that produced a powerful stench of manure. Webb Development was in the process of constructing a retirement community, which would later become Sun City, Arizona. Initially there was no interference between the two activities. As both activities began to expand, the stench from the feedlot upset residents too close to the lot. The court, instead of simply granting an injunction to Webb Development, decided that, although the feedlot was creating a negative externality (the stench) on the residents of Sun City, the development was also creating a negative externality on the feedlot as it expanded, forcing its eventual shutdown. Therefore, the court ordered the feedlot to be relocated, but decided that Webb had to pay for the relocation. Although the court reached this decision by applying a variation of the coming to the nuisance principle, law and economics scholars often view this solution as inspired by hypothetical Coasean bargaining. See also ***coming to the nuisance.

St. Petersburg paradox: in this paradox, individuals are faced with a proposed gamble that gives them the opportunity to win an infinite amount of money with a very small probability (e.g., a coin is tossed repeatedly and the participant wins an amount of 2^n, where n is the number of consecutive tails observed in the game). Although the expected value of this gamble is infinite, most individuals would not be willing to pay a large fee to participate in the game. The St. Petersburg paradox is generally used to illustrate the difference between expected value and expected utility theory. Individuals' choices are driven by their perception of expected utility and not by expected values. Expected utility theory plays an important role in guiding the choice of legal instruments, such as in the choice of the optimal probability/severity of penalties and in the optimal design of rewards and incentives under uncertainty. See also ***expected utility***.

Stackelberg competition: the Stackelberg leadership model (1934) describes the competition between firms that choose their quantity of production sequentially. The model is often used to characterize the optimal strategy of an incumbent monopolist in the industry (the so-called Stackelberg leader) and a potential entrant (the so-called Stackelberg follower). In this competition model, the Stackelberg leader has a commitment power: it can credibly commit itself to undertake a specific action. This idea is translated into game-theoretical language by allowing the leader to move first in a sequential game. The Stackelberg leadership model is therefore defined as a sequential game in which firms compete on quantity. The firm that moves first is labeled the leader of the game and the firm that moves in the second stage of the game is labeled the follower. Players have perfect information: the follower can observe the leader's move, and the leader knows ex ante that the follower observes his or her action. The Stackelberg model is solved by backward induction and has a subgame-perfect Nash equilibrium. In equilibrium, the follower chooses its quantity on its reaction function, given the leader's quantity observed at the first stage of the game. The leader chooses its output to maximize its profits, anticipating that the follower will react rationally based on its reaction function. In the Stackelberg game, the aggregate output produced is higher and the price is lower than in the Cournot game. Additionally, the leader (follower) produces a higher (lower) quantity with respect to the Cournot solution. The intuition behind this first-mover advantage is that the leader can credibly commit itself to the production of a given output level. Hence, the leader can expand its output level beyond the Cournot equilibrium level, thereby forcing the follower to optimize on the residual demand in the market. In some situations, the Stackelberg leader can credibly deter a competitor's entry by holding excess capacity, which can be interpreted as the monopolist's precommitment to an aggressive competitive strategy. Any non-credible threat on the part of the follower is ruled out in the solution of the game, given its sequential nature. The assumption of perfect information plays a key role in the Stackelberg game. In the event of imperfect information, the follower cannot observe the quantity chosen by the leader, and the game reduces to a Cournot setting, in which firms compete on quantity simultaneously. See also *Cournot competition*, *oligopoly*, and *first-mover advantage*.

Stackelberg's duopoly model: see *Stackelberg competition*.

Stag hunt game: also known as the assurance game, this is a two-player game with a mix of cooperation and trust issues, characterized by multiple equilibria. The story associated with the game was originally suggested by the French philosopher Jean-Jacques Rousseau. Two hunters can choose to hunt either a stag or a rabbit. Hunting stags is a difficult task, with a minimal probability of success if either hunter acts alone. Hunting stags is more beneficial for society but requires trust and cooperation between the hunters. In contrast, hunting rabbits is an easier task, which can be accomplished by hunters acting alone. The stag hunt game has two pure strategy equilibria: one equilibrium is Pareto-optimal (payoff-dominant), while the other is risk-dominant. The risk-dominant equilibrium is Pareto-suboptimal, but involves less riskiness since the payoff variance over the other player's strategies is lower. The following matrix illustrates the stag hunt game in the general case, where $a > b > d > c$ and $A > B > D > C$. The two Nash equilibria are (A,a), the Pareto-optimal equilibrium, in which both parties hunt a stag, and (D,d), the risk-dominant equilibrium, in which both parties hunt a rabbit. The stag hunt game is often cited in the law and economics literature as an illustration of the relevance of trust for sustainable cooperation. The choice between playing it safe or taking a risk with the prospect of a higher reward hinges upon the players' level of trust. See also *coordination games*, *multiple equilibria*, *Nash equilibrium*, *prisoner's dilemma*, and *chicken game*.

		Hunter 1	
		Stag	Rabbit
Hunter 2	Stag	A,a	C,b
	Rabbit	B,c	D,d

Standards: see *rules versus standards*.

Stationary state: dynamic models start by describing an equilibrium state. This equilibrium, called a steady state equilibrium, is characterized by stock variables with constant proportional growth rates. If the steady state growth rates are zero, the model is said to be in a stationary state. Stationary state models can be analyzed using comparative statics. See also *steady state*, *comparative dynamics*, *comparative statics*, and *dynamic models*.

Statistical causation: the criterion of statistical causation is used in tort law when liability is imposed on a group of defendants on the basis of the statistical probability that their activity caused the plaintiff's loss. The criterion is used when it cannot be shown which specific defendant caused the loss to the plaintiff, but it is known that they all carried out an activity similar to the one that caused the harm to the plaintiff. The criterion was adopted in the 1980 case *Sindell* v. *Abbott Laboratories,* 26 Cal. 3d 588 (1980), in the context of product liability, to impose liability on multiple defendants on the basis of the market share they had in the production of a harmful drug. In this case, multiple defendants had produced a drug that had injured the plaintiffs, and the plaintiffs were unable to show which defendant had produced the specific drug that harmed them. Traditional criteria of causation would have required the case to be dismissed, but the court decided to impose the liability on all producers of the harmful drug, in proportion to their market share at the time of the injury. Calabresi and Cooper (1996) discuss the scope of application of this criterion in recent tort law. When applying statistical causation, courts have limited the imposition of liability to the percentage market share (i.e., several liability). In the event of insolvent or disappearing defendants, the remaining loss was left without compensation (i.e., no joint liability). The adoption of statistical causation and market share liability creates liability externalities. These externalities can be particularly problematic when different production techniques and precaution levels are adopted in manufacturing the good. See also *market share liability*, *proportional liability*, and *comparative causation*.

Statistical discrimination: discrimination against subsets within a population may occur, even in the absence of irrational personal prejudices, as when employers use racial or gender stereotypes formed on the basis of statistical information about a demographic (Arrow, 1973). The resort to using statistical demographic data in lieu of particularized information about a potential employee can be explained as a consequence of information costs and uncertainty. Legally, statistical discrimination tends to be permissible (e.g., discriminating in favor of more educated or more experienced potential employees) except when applied against constitutionally protected groups (e.g., on the basis of race). See also *taste for discrimination*.

Status quo bias: see *endowment effect*.

Steady state: in economic applications, the steady state identifies the long-term equilibrium of an economy. If the economic system deviates from its steady state, the economy will be in a transient state, and gradually move back toward the steady state. See also *dynamic models* and *stationary state*.

Sticks versus carrots: see *carrots versus sticks*.

Sticky default rules: McDonnell (2007) and Ayres (2012) use this term to refer to situations in which the law increases the parties' costs for opting out of a default rule. Default rules may be made sticky in order to reduce parties' errors, or for a variety of other paternalistic reasons. See also *altering rules, penalty default rules*, and *default rules*.

Sticky defaults: see *sticky default rules*.

Sticky norms: social norms govern the behavior of individual communities, and community members often take them as seriously as they do the law. Social norms sometimes reflect troublesome values or views that governments intend to change, by enacting statutes. Kahan (2000) introduced the term "sticky norms" into the law and economics literature. The problem of sticky social norms considered by Kahan is that sometimes social norms are so entrenched in a society that it becomes difficult, if not impossible, to change them. Sticky social norms often reflect outdated viewpoints on race, gender, age, or behavior in general. As Kahan points out, examples of these types of troublesome sticky norms include the view that a woman who says "No" to sexual advances might actually mean "Yes" or that drinking and driving do not constitute a serious offense. In response, governments often enact strict statutes that attempt to change sticky norms. However, governments frequently fail to change social norms, and prohibited behavior continues despite new statutes. Police officers might fail to enforce new statutes or juries might fail to recognize or acknowledge the requirements of the new statutes that run contrary to existing social norms (Kahan, 2000). This attitude undermines legislative efforts to reform troublesome sticky norms and presents a challenge for policymakers. See also *hard shoves versus gentle nudges, countervailing norms*, and *backlash effect*.

Stigler, George Joseph (1911–1991): an American economist who won the 1982 Nobel Prize in economics for his seminal work on industrial structures, the functioning of markets, and the causes and effects of public regulation. Stigler received his Ph.D. from the University of Chicago in 1938. He joined the faculty of the Graduate School of Business and the department of economics at the University of Chicago in 1958. He was the Charles R. Walgreen Distinguished Service Professor of American Institutions at the University of Chicago. Stigler is considered one of the pioneers of law and economics and is well known for his analysis of government regulation and the public sector. In particular, he developed the capture theory of regulation, an important component of public choice economics. This microeconomic theory set out to discover the ways in which the legislative process is an endogenous rather than an exogenous part of the economy. More specifically, Stigler's notion of regulatory capture

hypothesizes that corporate actors and interest groups may hijack the government's regulatory power to further their own interests. Stigler is also recognized
as a leader in the field of industrial organization, the study of markets and
industrial structure. Additionally, he is a founder of the field of the economics
of information, which applies economic tools and methodology to study the
acquisition of information. His publications include *Memoirs of an Unregulated
Economist* (1988), *The Essence of Stigler* (1986), *The Citizen and the State:
Essays on Regulation* (1975), *The Organization of Industry* (1969), *The Theory
of Price* (3rd edn., 1966), *Essays in the History of Economics* (1965), and *Five
Lectures on Economic Problems* (1950).

Strategic behavior: concept at the core of game theory and defined as interdependent decision-making. Contrary to negative connotations of the term "strategic,"
most rational human behavior is strategic under this definition: actions taken by
one individual matter for the decision of other individuals. Most situations relevant to law involve strategic decision-making. The decisions of a creditor and a
debtor, of a tortfeasor and a prospective victim, of a promisor and a promisee, are
all examples of interdependent decision-making. What is best for one individual
hinges upon the choice of his or her counterpart. The strategic nature of most
legally relevant behavior renders the tools of game theory particularly useful in
law and economics. See also *game theory*.

Strategic complements versus strategic substitutes: in legal and economic contexts, the actions of certain players frequently impact the behavior or standing
of other players. In the game theory context, this means that the actions of
the players are interdependent. The concepts of strategic complementarity and
strategic substitutability specify the type of interdependence between the players' strategies. The players' decisions are called strategic complements when
they reinforce one another, and they are strategic substitutes if they mitigate
one another. Several results in strategic decision-making depend on whether
the players' actions are strategic complements or substitutes. The distinction
between the two hinges upon the finding of whether an action by one player
increases or decreases the effectiveness of a counteraction by the other player.
For example, strategies are strategic complements when aggressive behavior by
one player increases the marginal benefit of aggressive behavior for the second player. Strategies are strategic substitutes when aggressive behavior by the
first player decreases the marginal benefit of aggressive behavior by the second
player. Industrial organization scholars have applied these concepts to study
the impact of a firm's actions in one market on the strategies of competitors
in a different market (see, for example, Bulow, Geanakoplos, and Klemperer,
1985). Often the assessment of whether strategies are strategic complements
or strategic substitutes requires a close empirical analysis of the relevant markets. In mathematical terms, a positive sign for the cross-partial derivative of
a payoff function denotes strategic complements, while a negative sign for the
cross-partial derivative denotes strategic substitutes.

Strategic complexity: term used in contract theory and game theory to describe the complexity of the game-theoretic problem facing an agent. Players are assumed to act rationally and compute and play equilibrium strategies given information about the preferences, rationality, and beliefs of other agents. In order to play equilibrium strategies, agents must be able to compute them. If strategies are excessively complex, it would be unrealistic to expect agents to undertake them in equilibrium. Although there is no general consensus on how to measure the complexity of a strategic problem, experimental economics has been used to verify the computational abilities of agents faced with different strategic problems. Recent theoretical models attempt to incorporate strategic complexity to verify the robustness of results when agents have limited cognitive or computational abilities. See also *Nash equilibrium*, *evolutionary game theory*, *experimental law and economics*, and *contract theory*.

Strategic constitution: drawing upon contractarian ideas, economic analysis, and social choice theory, Robert Cooter's book *The Strategic Constitution* (2000a) compares and contrasts varying constitutional approaches, introducing the concept of the strategic constitution – a constitution that aims at satisfying the preferences of its citizens by designing institutions and procedures that create the best set of incentives for its citizens, lawmakers, and officials to satisfy those preferences. See also *constitutional political economy* and *Cooter, Robert*.

Strategic entry deterrence: firms that already exist in a market have expended resources establishing themselves and developed a reputation. This initial position of dominance gives the early entrant to a market a significant advantage over other potential entrants. As Salop (1979) points out, this scenario creates an asymmetry advantage for the earlier entrant, giving the early entrant a first-mover advantage. In this position, the incumbent firm may engage in strategic entry deterrence. In other words, the early entrant may take strategic steps to make it more difficult for other firms to enter the market. Entry deterrence strategies may include binding commitments with customers, overcapacity investments, and other precommitment strategies. These commitments are made known to potential entrants, deterring the prospective entrants from attempting to enter. See also *barriers to entry*.

Strategic substitutes: see *strategic complements versus strategic substitutes*.

Strategic voting: voting mechanisms do not always elicit the expression of true preferences. With strategic voting, voters do not vote according to their true preferences but falsify them in order to manipulate the voting outcome. Strategic voting is particularly effective in sequential voting decisions (e.g., primaries and general elections). Strategic voting may lead to inefficient collective outcomes. Public choice theorists have studied the robustness of alternative voting mechanisms to strategic voting.

Strategy proofness: mechanisms can be tested by their strategy proofness; when a mechanism is strategy-proof, the strategic choices of the players are trivial and truthfully reflect the players' preferences. Players will always reveal their true preferences while adhering to their dominant strategies. See also *revealed preferences, incentive compatibility constraint*, and *strategy-proof allocation mechanism*.

Strategy-proof allocation mechanism: bargaining mechanism that prevents parties from acting strategically by withholding information. These mechanisms reduce the failures associated with asymmetric information and can lead parties away from the Nash equilibrium to a cooperation equilibrium and enhanced profits. See also *strategy proofness*.

Strictly competitive games: see *pure conflict games*.

Structural adjudication of norms: in complex societies, standards of behavior arise in multiple ways. While policymakers obviously enact laws that govern behavior, social norms arise outside the legislative process. These norms, whether simple or complicated, govern the behavior of persons and entities. Cooter (1994) calls this development of norms outside the standard lawmaking process the "new law merchant." However, in complex societies, in which courts face challenges to their ability to obtain needed information, courts must determine the extent to which they should enforce these norms. For instance, if in one region small companies have developed a norm regarding the proper procedure one should follow to cancel a contract, a court might ask to what extent it should enforce this norm. Courts will want to enforce some of these norms, because informal enforcement fails to achieve optimal levels of cooperation. In order for courts to determine which of these norms they should enforce, Cooter (1994) proposes a structural approach to the adjudication of norms. The structural adjudication of social norms involves three steps. First, courts would "identify the actual norms that have arisen" in a certain area, such as a business community. Courts could look here to whether persons have internalized the norm and are enforcing it among the relevant group. Second, courts would need to analyze the incentive structure underlying the norm. Cooter states that this analysis would require a testing of the norm in a model that "characterizes the norm as an equilibrium in a game." Finally, through this analysis, the court would determine whether the underlying incentive structure is efficient (i.e., resulting in repeated transactions). Courts could then enforce a norm that is supported by an efficient incentive structure. See also *descriptive versus prescriptive norms* and *customary law*.

Structural equation models: see *instrumental variable approach*.

Structural versus behavioral remedies: antitrust law uses both structural remedies and behavioral remedies. Structural remedies concentrate on the creation or conservation of a competitive market structure. Examples include the divestment and break-up of monopolistic firms, the prevention of mergers, etc. Behavioral remedies allow imperfectly competitive market structures to exist and focus on the prevention of the undesirable side effects of imperfect competition. Examples include the prevention of anti-competitive activities, sanctions for the abuse of a dominant position, etc. From a welfare point of view, behavioral approaches should be preferred to their structural alternatives when natural monopolies with substantial economies of scale are involved. Historically, structural remedies have been typically adopted by US antitrust law, while behavioral remedies have been preferred by European antitrust law (e.g., articles 85 and 86 of the 1957 Treaty of Rome), although important steps have recently been taken in the European Union, toward an increasingly structural approach in antitrust policy.

Structure-induced equilibrium: public choice scholars have analyzed the decision-making processes of collective decision-making bodies, such as legislatures. Scholars have struggled to explain adequately the decision-making behaviors of groups of decision-makers, in part because of the complex nature of such decisions. In his work on collective decision-making, Shepsle (1979) focuses on the "institutional properties" that govern the decision-making activities of a collective body. Specifically, Shepsle identifies three types of institutional properties that tend to affect decision-making in an organization, namely committee systems, jurisdictional arrangements, and control systems. Shepsle analyzes these various structural elements and finds that these structures affect the ways in which individual preferences are aggregated toward an equilibrium outcome. Shepsle (1979) calls this structure-induced equilibrium. A structure-induced equilibrium is contingent upon the chosen institutional arrangement and is often not robust to institutional changes. However, in the absence of a Condorcet winner, structural arrangements can, at least, offer the "prospect of equilibrium." Organization leaders can shape institutional structures and indirectly influence the resulting equilibria generated by those institutions (Shepsle, 1979). See also ***Condorcet winner***.

Subgame: the extensive-form game models the actions of players and the sequence within which they take those actions. A subgame is a subset of actions or interactions, within the broader extensive-form game, that can be viewed and studied separately from the rest of game interaction. An extensive-form game can be made up of multiple subgames. In a subgame the players play only a smaller part of the larger game. Formally, a subgame begins at a decision node of the game and includes only the decision node that begins the subgame and the nodes that follow, but none of the previous nodes of the original game. Baird, Gertner, and Picker (1994) illustrate the concept using the example of a debtor and a lender. The lender must first make the decision about whether to lend money to the debtor or not. The debtor must then determine whether to repay the lender. If the debtor does not repay, the lender must decide whether or not to sue the debtor. These stages represent subgames of the entire extensive-form game. See also *subgame-perfect strategy and equilibrium* and *normal-form versus extensive-form games*.

Subgame-perfect strategy and equilibrium: any subset of actions or interactions within a bigger extensive-form game that can be viewed and studied separately from the rest of the game interaction is a subgame. A strategy is called subgame-perfect if it represents a Nash strategy for every subgame of the original game. Put differently, the strategies are subgame-perfect when the players' strategies at each subgame are the best responses, given the choices of the other player(s), and the players would choose that strategy for any smaller subgame of the original larger game. A subgame-perfect equilibrium is one that is reached when parties play subgame-perfect strategies. See also *subgame* and *normal-form versus extensive-form games*.

Subjective value: subjective value (the value that an individual attaches to an object) is generally different from the market value (or price) of an object. The reason why individuals are willing to buy a good at price X is because they attach a higher subjective value Y to the good, such that Y > X. Likewise, individuals are willing to sell a good at price X because they attach a lower subjective value Z to the good, such that Z < X. Thus, sellers are getting a "bargain" by selling at X what they value at Z. Market values are determined by the subjective valuations of buyers and sellers; the market value only accurately reflects the valuations of the marginal buyers and sellers. A challenge from the point of view of the law is trying to determine how best to award damages when one person or entity suffers a loss. One problem in accurately calculating damages is the assessment of the subjective value (Cooter and Ulen, 2008). Sometimes a party attaches a subjective value to an item of property or a promised level of performance that far exceeds its market value. Courts must then decide how to incorporate this subjective value, if at all, into the overall damages calculation. Muris (1983) identifies the subjective value problem, observing that if an individual owns an object he or she must value it above the market price (otherwise he or she would have sold it, or not purchased it). Based on this observation, Muris has argued that compensation based on market value may lead to a systematic under-compensation. The existence of subjective value adds to the complexity of calculating damages in the law, ranging from takings compensation to tort damages and breach of contract. See also *consumer surplus*.

Subsidiarity: the subsidiarity principle is a principle of governance designed to guide the allocation of power and responsibility between the central government and state governments in a federal system (Inman and Rubinfeld, 1997). The subsidiarity principle was formally adopted in 1992 by the European Union (in the Maastricht Treaty) to limit the excessive centralization of competences. According to the so-called subsidiarity test, a given policy responsibility should be allocated at the lowest possible level of government, unless there is evidence that the central government has a comparative advantage in fulfilling the task under consideration. The subsidiarity principle is currently included in article 5 of the consolidated version of the Treaty Establishing the European Community (and is included in the proposed European constitution, under article 9), and reads as follows: "The Community shall act within the limits of the powers conferred upon it by this Treaty and of the objectives assigned to it therein. In areas which do not fall within its exclusive competence, the Community shall take action, in accordance with the principle of subsidiarity, only if and in so far as the objectives of the proposed action cannot be sufficiently achieved by the Member States and can therefore, by reason of the scale or effects of the proposed action, be better achieved by the Community. Any action by the Community shall not go beyond what is necessary to achieve the objectives of this Treaty." There is a flourishing economic and legal literature examining the concept of subsidiarity as an instrument for achieving an optimal level for the centralization of policy responsibilities. This literature focuses on the optimal allocation of policy functions in multi-level governments, discussing the interplay between economies of scale, economies of scope, and the heterogeneity of preferences. It has been noted in the empirical literature that, contrary to its stated goal, the adoption of the subsidiarity principle has been followed by a wave of intense centralization (Alesina, Angeloni, and Schuknecht, 2005). Carbonara, Luppi, and Parisi (2009) use the term "self-defeating subsidiarity" to refer to the paradox of progressive centralization triggered by the subsidiarity principle. See also *subsidiarity test*, *self-defeating subsidiarity*, *decentralization theorem*, *Popitz's law*, and *Tiebout competition*.

Subsidiarity test: according to this, the centralization of governmental functions should be permitted only if the reallocation of functions brings added value over and above what local governments could achieve locally. This test has been used in the European Union since its formal adoption in 1992 by the Maastricht Treaty to evaluate the proposed centralization of competences. The test can be carried out in three different forms: (a) a centralized subsidiarity test; (b) a decentralized subsidiarity test; and (c) a democratic subsidiarity test. See also *subsidiarity*, *self-defeating subsidiarity*, *centralized subsidiarity*, *decentralized subsidiarity*, and *democratic subsidiarity*.

Substitutes: goods that tend to be consumed alternatively (one or the other) are called substitutes (e.g., white sugar and cane sugar, or butter and margarine). If there is a shift in demand for a good, demand for its substitutes will shift in the opposite direction. Likewise, if the price of a good increases, demand for its substitutes increases. In economic terms, this effect is described as a positive cross-price effect: $\partial j/\partial P_i > 0$, where j represents the quantity demanded of good j and P_i represents the price of its substitute good i. The economic concept of substitutes is of particular importance in legal applications. When studying the effect of legal intervention on a given industry and in order to separate the effect of the enacted policy from the effect of other environmental parameters, it is useful to look at the movement of the stock prices of producers of substitute goods and compare them against the stock prices of the regulated industries. In other contexts, legal rules may create incentives for a primary activity by taxing (or subsidizing) activities that are substitutes to it. For example, in order to deter some hard-to-monitor activities, the legal system may choose to criminalize or to tax substitute goods or activities. Tort law distinguishes between cases of alternative care (i.e., situations in which the parties' precautions are substitutes and it is enough that only one party takes precautions) and joint care (i.e., situations in which the parties' precautions are complements and both parties need to take precautions to avoid an accident). See also ***complements***, ***cross-price effect***, and ***alternative versus joint care***.

Substitution effect: this measures consumers' reaction (in terms of a change in consumption levels) to a change in the relative price of the consumption goods, in the absence of wealth effects. A change in relative price leads consumers to substitute away from the more expensive good, increasing their consumption of the cheaper good, in order to reach the highest available indifference curve. To calculate the substitution effect, the consumer needs to be compensated for the wealth effects of a price change. On the basis of the substitution effect, the goods are classified as net substitutes if the consumption of the relatively cheap good increases at the expense of the relatively expensive one, or net complements in the opposite case. The legal system, with the use of sanctions and rewards, affects the relative price of alternative human activities, creating incentives for individuals to substitute away from socially undesirable or illegal behavior toward socially desirable and legal behavior. See also ***normal good***, ***inferior good***, ***Giffen good***, ***wealth effect versus income effect***, ***Coase theorem***, and ***relative price***.

Sufficient conditions: see ***necessary and sufficient conditions***.

Sunk costs: non-recoverable costs incurred in the past. According to economic theory, sunk costs are irrelevant for future choices. Suppose a firm buys a call option for $500,000 providing the right to buy a plant at $3.5 million in three months. Suppose the firm finds an opportunity to buy a plant with similar characteristics at $3.25 million. Economic rationality requires the firm to disregard the sunk cost of $500,000 associated with the call option. The firm should buy the plant at the lowest cost and let the call option expire without exercising it. See also ***asset specificity*** and ***sunk cost fallacy***.

Sunk cost fallacy: experimental economics shows that, contrary to the prediction of economic theory, sunk costs affect economic decisions, often because of an aversion to loss. The agent considers the price paid as a benchmark for the value of the good and is unwilling to sell for a price lower than the price paid. This is called the sunk cost fallacy, which has important effects on financial and economic decisions. See also ***sunk costs***.

Supply side economics: see ***demand-side versus supply-side economics***.

Supreme Court Economic Review: established in 1982 as the first law and economics journal focused on the work of the Supreme Court: its decision-making, its functioning as an organization, and the economic reasoning and the social welfare analysis that the court employs in reaching its decisions. The editors of the *Supreme Court Economic Review* have been Peter Aranson (1982–3); Harold Demsetz (1993–7); Ernest Gellhorn (1993–9); Nelson Lund (1995–8, 2001); Larry Ribstein (1999–2001); Todd Zywicki (2002, 2009–present); Francesco Parisi (2003–8); Daniel Polsby (2003–8); Lloyd Cohen (2006–8); Ilya Somin (2009–12); and Joshua Wright (2012–present). The *Supreme Court Economic Review* is one of the three journals in the field of law and economics published by the University of Chicago Press (together with *The Journal of Law and Economics* and *The Journal of Legal Studies*). See also *law and economics journals.*

Survivor theory of efficiency: the efficiency of the common law hypothesis is one of the most important and controversial positive claims in law and economics. The understanding of the mechanisms that weed out inefficient laws has required considerable elaboration. A well-known theoretical explanation of the efficiency of the common law hypothesis is Priest's (1977) survivor theory of efficiency, which proceeds from the premise that inefficient laws impose larger stakes on parties than efficient laws. The consequence of higher stakes is that disputes arising from inefficient laws will be litigated more frequently. The more often a law runs the metaphorical "gauntlet" of trial and appellate review, the more chances it has of being overturned. The result is that efficient laws will have an easier time "surviving" than inefficient laws over time, and the body of common law precedents will trend toward efficient rather than inefficient laws, due to a cumulative "weeding out" process. It is notably *not* a premise of the survivor theory that judges ever *intend* to create efficient laws, or that efficient judicial decisions tend to be efficient at all. Rather, the survivor theory is a "demand-side" theory, explaining the development of precedent in terms of the probability that *litigants* bring certain cases (i.e., the ones arising from inefficient laws) to court. See also *efficiency of the common law hypothesis*, *Priest's selection hypothesis*, and *modified selection hypothesis*.

Systematic versus unsystematic risk: systematic risk (also known as undiversifiable risk or market risk) is the risk inherent in the entire market or market segment. Systematic risk reflects the social costs borne by the entire economy associated with the occurrence of a negative event. For example, the global default risk stemming from banking activity in the economy represents a systematic risk. Banks bear only the private cost associated with the default risk of their own portfolios. Although systematic risk can be hedged with the use of financial instruments, including forward contracts, swaps, options, and futures, the presence of high levels of systematic risk may justify regulation in order to realign private and social costs. Systematic risk cannot be mitigated through portfolio diversification, since all investments in the portfolio are equally affected by market risk (e.g., a market collapse affects all companies in the portfolio). Unsystematic risk (also known as diversifiable risk, idiosyncratic risk, or specific risk) is the risk inherent in a specific company or industry investment. Unlike systematic risk, the magnitude of unsystematic risk can be mitigated through appropriate diversification. For example, as the number of diverse stocks in a portfolio increases, the unsystematic risk of the portfolio decreases. See also *risk management*, *diversification*, *hedging*, and *portfolio theory*.

Systemic risk: see *systematic versus unsystematic risk*.

T

Tacit collusion: see *cartels and tacit collusion*.

Take-it-or-leave-it offer: term (also shortened as tioli offer) used in a variety of contexts in the law and economics literature. The most common use of this term is descriptive of actual contractual practices. In a take-it-or-leave-it contract, one party is dictating all the terms of the contract and the other party has the choice of either accepting the terms of the offer or refusing to contract. This descriptive use of the term refers to all situations in which the offeree has no power to alter the terms of the contract. Standard-form contracts and adhesion contracts can therefore be described as take-it-or-leave-it contracts to emphasize the fact that, in such contracts, one party has greater bargaining power than the other (Kessler, 1943). Cooter and Ulen (2008), in an analysis of Kessler's work and of tioli contracts, point out that criticisms of take-it-or-leave-it offers are justified when one side has monopolistic bargaining power and is using its power to reduce competition. However, they also note that take-it-or-leave-it offers (in the form of standard-form contracts) can at times increase the efficiency of exchange by reducing product differentiation and reducing transaction costs. The second usage of the term is normative, as it identifies take-it-or-leave-it offers as optimal bargaining strategies that should be adopted to maximize payoffs under certain conditions. Game theory helps identify the strengths and weaknesses of these strategies, highlighting the difficulty of pre-committing oneself to a no-renegotiation strategy that could give credibility to the "or-leave-it" threat. Finally, the term "take-it-or-leave-it offer" can be found in formal law and economics papers as a modeling short cut to avoid having to employ a formal bargaining game to derive a price, the value of which may be immaterial for the actual analysis. When found in those contexts, a price generated through a take-it-or-leave-it offer is equivalent to an arbitrary price, chosen by the modeler to study the problem at hand.

Taste for discrimination: Becker (1971) gives a systematic treatment of discrimination, whereby an individual's preference to be associated with some persons rather than others (i.e., their taste for discrimination) is assigned a money value – that is, what the person would pay for the privilege of living out their discriminatory preference. Becker models this cost as a coefficient in the cost–benefit function of economic actors. Discrimination may not necessarily express negative biases (i.e., preferring *not* to be associated with a certain group). Nepotism, for example, is the result of a positive bias toward favoring a friend or family member, but one that imposes similar costs. A taste for discrimination in this model leads to effects that are similar to transaction costs, and the long-term consequence of tastes for discrimination will tend to be a reduction in efficiency. See also *statistical discrimination*.

Taste for fairness: social scientists have advanced the idea that individuals may have internalize certain other-regarding norms, developing a "taste for fairness." Experimental economists have tested this idea, and have found confirmation that humans exhibit distaste for outcomes that they perceive as unfair. Fehr and Schmidt's (1999) theory of inequity aversion develops a functional form of a utility function that incorporates a taste for fairness. In experimental games, players have revealed their willingness to sacrifice part of their personal payoffs in the interest of fairer outcomes. These experiments show that the intensity of this "taste" is not insignificant. An interesting application of this concept in the law and economics literature is found in Kaplow and Shavell's (2002) *Fairness versus Welfare*. Kaplow and Shavell consider whether fairness or welfare should be the goal of policies and laws. They note that a focus on fairness could result in perverse effects on welfare and argue that laws and policies should be considered solely based on their impact "on the well-beings of individuals." While the authors argue against using fairness (i.e., a sense of justice or equity) to judge laws and policies, they do define welfare broadly enough to include what they term a "taste for the notion of fairness" (Kaplow and Shavell, 2002: 982). A taste for fairness is the pleasure an individual derives from fairness. For example, a person may derive pleasure or happiness from knowing that a victim has received just compensation. This taste for fairness is incorporated into Kaplow and Shavell's definition of welfare. A policy that maximizes individual well-being can do so in part by maximizing the feeling of fairness an individual might derive from certain actions or activities. However, the taste for fairness is tied to the well-being of and pleasure experienced by an individual, and so is different from a general conception of fairness. See also *fairness equilibrium*, *inequity aversion*, *kindness function*, *ultimatum game*, *dictator game*, and *experimental law and economics*.

Theory of clubs: see *club goods*.

Theory of the firm: in his classic work on the economic theory of the firm, Coase (1937) argues that firms will emerge and that transactions will take place within the firm when the costs of using the market mechanism (i.e., transaction costs) exceed the cost of organizing and managing the same resources within the firm: "The main reason why it is profitable to establish a firm would seem to be that there is a cost of using the price mechanism" (Coase, 1937: 336). Without a firm, all the factors of production that are organized within the firm would be managed and allocated through market transactions requiring potentially costly contractual arrangements. Williamson has provided extensive contributions to the economic theory of the firm, sometimes labeled transaction-cost economics or new institutional economics. These contributions show that firm structure and industries evolve naturally to economize on transactions costs. See also *transaction costs*, *Coase, Ronald*, and *holdup problem*.

Third-degree price discrimination: see *price discrimination*.

Third-party enforcement: one of three forms of extralegal enforcement mechanisms. Third-party enforcement refers to situations in which punishment is carried out in a decentralized fashion by third-party members of society. In this context, third-party members include all members of a community other than the rule violator (the first party), its victim (the second party), and those formally entrusted with law enforcement (central law enforcers). Recent empirical and anecdotal evidence shows that the enactment of a new law may serve as a focal point delineating legal entitlements and facilitating private enforcement (McAdams, 2000). The law acts as a signal for others witnessing violations, empowering members of a community to exert third-party enforcement against violators under the form of social sanctions and reprobation. See also *first-party enforcement*, *second-party-enforcement*, *private enforcement*, and *expressive law*.

Threat point: see *disagreement point*.

Threshold liability: law and economics scholars have used economic tools to analyze various tort rules to determine which rules encourage potential tortfeasors and potential victims to take efficient levels of precaution and engage in efficient levels of activity. Under tort law, a negligent tortfeasor is generally required to compensate a victim for all the harm done in the occurrence of an accident. Stremitzer and Tabbach (2009) have used the term "threshold liability" to describe a causation-incorporating criterion of compensation, in which a tortfeasor should be "liable for damages if he acted negligently *and* if his negligence caused the accident." Threshold liability, with its focus on causation, is the prevalent approach to tort law in the United States. Stremitzer and Tabbach compare threshold liability to a different criterion of compensation, which they call "proportional liability," and conclude that threshold liability, by generating higher damage awards, exacerbates the judgment-proof problem, without providing any true gain in efficiency terms. See also *proportional liability*.

Tie-ins: tying links the sale of one good to the sale of another. Tying can be secured either technologically or contractually. Examples of technological tying include proprietary lens attachments for cameras or ink cartridges for printers. While a different producer could supply these components, tying limits the compatibility of the additional component to those produced by the producer of the original device. Producers can legally protect technological tying by patenting the specific additional components. Contractual tying relies on exclusivity contractual clauses, which require retailers of the primary good to sell only add-on components supplied by the primary producer. For example, car dealers may be required to sell only optional accessories supplied by the automaker. A restaurant that wishes to offer coke as a beverage might be able to sell only other drinks manufactured by Coca-Cola. Both forms of tying extend the market power of the primary good to the market for accessories or complementary products. For this reason, antitrust authorities closely scrutinize tying practices, as they could signal the presence of market power and could become instruments of price discrimination. In a tying arrangement, the proportions of the quantities of the tied goods are left to the choice of the consumer. When consumers purchase a camera body, they also decide how many additional lenses they would like. On the contrary, bundling arrangements fix the proportion of bundled goods. See also ***bundling*** and ***single monopoly profit theorem***.

Tiebout competition: Charles Tiebout's (1956) model of jurisdictional competition postulates that local governments compete in the provision of local public goods. Local governments offer different bundles of public services, taxes, and regulations, and individuals and firms can indicate their preferences over alternative bundles by moving between one locality and another. The analysis requires that local governments actively compete in the provision of public goods and that individuals have an opportunity to relocate at relatively low cost. Tiebout's model is often invoked in support of arguments against centralization and standardization, inasmuch as they would curtail the healthy effects of jurisdictional competition. See also ***regulatory competition***, ***voting with your feet***, ***subsidiarity***, ***race to the top versus race to the bottom***, and *fiscal federalism*.

Time inconsistency: see ***dynamic inconsistency***.

Time preference: individuals generally exhibit positive time preference, since they prefer to obtain something nearer in time rather than at a later time in the future. Consumers with a positive time preference are willing to pay a premium to obtain something earlier in time. The time discount rate represents the rate at which an individual is willing to trade present for future consumption. An individual with a high time preference (a high time discount rate) is likely to want to spend or consume now, rather than save for the future. Time preference provides an explanation for market interest rates. There are various explanations for the human tendency to exhibit positive time preference, including shortsightedness and a tendency to underestimate future needs, the value of goods as factors of production, optimism about future income potential, limited life expectancy, and the uncertain protection of property rights. See also ***present value***, ***social discount rate***, and ***myopia***.

Time series: a set of data obtained over regular time intervals, such as census data and annual GDP figures. The crucial feature that distinguishes time series from common data sets is the temporal ordering of the data. Time series analysis comprises techniques to identify patterns in time series data, and modeling techniques to represent time series data and extract predictions. In the economic analysis of law, time series data is particularly valuable for studying the impact of new laws on observed behavior. For example, by studying the time series data regarding auto accidents in a certain locality, it is possible to measure the impact of a given change in speed limits or other traffic law. When such inferences are drawn, it is important to control for other changes that may have taken place during the same period. See also *regression analysis*.

Time discount rate: see *time preference*.

Tioli offer: see *take-it-or-leave-it offer*.

Tit for tat strategies: the tit for tat strategy for repeated prisoner's dilemma games was formulated in a four-line computer program by game theorist Anatol Rapoport, who successfully entered a contest run by Robert Axelrod (Axelrod and Hamilton, 1981; Axelrod, 1984). Rapoport's tit for tat strategy starts with cooperation, and thereafter matches the other player's last action, defecting in response to a defection, and returning to cooperation if the other player resumes cooperation. Critics note that, while successful in Axelrod's experiment, tit for tat is an evolutionarily unstable strategy: if there are enough defectors in the population, the tit for tat strategy could be outperformed by pure defection. Likewise, in a tit for tat strategy, multiple parties could get trapped in a cycle of mutual defection and retaliatory punishment. Tit for tat strategies are much more forgiving than grim strategies, because in tit for tat strategies retaliation follows for only one period, while in grim strategies retaliation is triggered for an indefinite period, basically putting an end to cooperation after a single defection. See also *grim strategies*, *evolution of cooperation*, *reciprocity*, and *prisoner's dilemma*.

Tragedy of the anticommons: see *anticommons*.

Tragedy of the commons: see *commons*.

Transaction costs: all costs associated with transactions among individuals and firms. The notion of transaction costs has acquired particular importance in law and economics, as the absence of transaction costs represents a fundamental condition for the applicability of the positive Coase theorem. The category of transaction costs includes both ex ante bargaining costs associated with the negotiation and conclusion of the contract and the ex post costs of monitoring and enforcing the contracts. Legal systems can affect the magnitude of transaction costs, and one of the policy objectives in the design of law is indeed the reduction of transaction costs. For this reason, transaction cost considerations are fundamental to any analysis of legal regimes and the design of contracting processes, governance mechanisms, and institutions. See also *Coase theorem*, *theory of the firm*, *default rules*, *majoritarian default rules*, and *boilerplate*.

Transaction-cost economics: this dominant methodological approach within the larger field of new institutional economics views the firm and the market as alternative means of contracting. Building upon Coase's (1937) seminal work and Williamson's (1985) extensive systematization, transaction-cost economists identify the limitations of the neoclassical analysis of models of perfect competition. Transaction-cost economics, along with new institutional economics, reaches beyond the assumptions of the neoclassical analysis to consider the roles played by other crucial variables. Specifically, transaction-cost economics explains the emergence and functioning of economic and legal institutions, not only as a production function but as an intricate mode of contracting, and as a governance framework alternative to the market. The allocation of economic activity between firms and markets is taken as exogenous under the neoclassical approach; firms are characterized as production functions; markets serve as signaling devices; contracting is accomplished through an auctioneer; and disputes are disregarded because of the presumed efficacy of court adjudication. Williamson and other new institutional economists criticize the neoclassical economic approach to the market and the firm for relying on such simplistic assumptions, which too often limit the explanatory power of their models. In the classical model of economics, the market is a frictionless institution characterized by perfect competition, ease of entry and exit, product homogeneity, unbounded rationality, and perfect information. Self-interest and opportunism are not ignored in the classical model, but are accounted for only in the bargaining stage of contract, not in the execution stage. The pragmatic methodology of transaction-cost economics is very attentive in formulating plausible assumptions and in keeping models in close contact with phenomena. In doing so, transaction-cost economists generally make three additional assumptions regarding contracts: (a) contracting is characterized by actors with bounded rationality; (b) those contracting act opportunistically in the execution stage; and (c) the dimension of asset specificity must be added to the model assumptions. When these elements are present, the contracting outcome calls for a governance solution. Transaction-cost economics attempts to explain how institutions with a governance structure emerge as transaction-cost-minimizing devices. More specifically, transaction-cost economics criticizes the alternative perspectives for their unconditional reliance on unrealistic assumptions: planning assumes perfect cognitive competence; contract as promise assumes the absence of ex post opportunism in the execution stage of the contract; and the perfect competition model ignores the crucial role played by asset specificity in the execution stage of the contract. Within this literature, concepts of contract as governance and contract as framework are valuable paradigms for explaining the governance structures and the non-standard forms of contracting that emerge in response to these shortcomings. See also *new institutional economics, theory of the firm, transaction costs, contracts as governance, Williamson, Oliver,* and *Coase, Ronald.*

Transferable utility: an informal conceptual device employed to simplify situations in which members of a group tend to (or are assumed to) coordinate their action and behave as a single decision-maker. The underlying idea is that, if the gainers in a group could costlessly transfer utility to losers within the same group, the members of the group would collectively act to maximize the aggregate utility of the group, acting as a single agent. However, unlike wealth, which can be transferred (or "trickle down") from one individual to another, utility often cannot. The aggregation properties of transferable utility models make it appealing to modeling, but the implications of the transferable utility assumption are often more restrictive than recognized. See also ***Kaldor–Hicks criterion*** and ***rotten kid theorem***.

Transient state: see *steady state*.

Transitive choices: see *transitivity of preferences*.

Transitivity of preferences: one of the fundamental axioms of rational choice. Transitive preferences imply that, if an individual prefers *x* to *y* and *y* to *z*, then he or she must also prefer *x* to *z*. The axiom of preference transitivity is fundamental in consumer theory, according to which consumers choose between alternative consumption bundles, and transitivity is interpreted as a rationality requirement for the consistency of consumer choice. As shown by Condorcet's voting paradox and Arrow's impossibility theorem, most collective decision-making processes do not guarantee that transitive preferences held by individual voters will translate into transitive collective outcomes. See also ***rational choice theory***, ***axioms of preference***, ***Condorcet voting paradox***, and ***Arrow's impossibility theorem***.

Translucent preferences: human preferences are said to be translucent, in the sense that people can observe other people's preferences, albeit not perfectly. The term "preferences" in this context includes attributes such as the character, moral values, and willingness to cooperate of the individual. In statistical terms, translucence means that external observers can infer true preferences with higher accuracy than mere chance. Cooter and Eisenberg (2000) point out that, if people could not distinguish a cooperator from a defector at a rate higher than chance, then rational people would never try to recognize character. If no one ever attempted to make character assessments, then no one could deceive anyone about character. The theory of translucent preferences thus suggests that the very possibility of deceit implies that (a) some people internalize norms and values into their preferences (i.e., there are "good" citizens and "bad" citizens), and (b) external observers can recognize those that internalized such values with less error than chance would produce. The concept of translucent preferences is used in the law and norms literature inasmuch as the ability to observe true character and to distinguish cooperators from defectors is one of the key factors for the emergence and sustainability of conditional cooperation. Translucent preferences are generally advantageous to parties involved in cooperative games but are undesirable in pure conflict games. Since translucence is a human trait that requires long-term internalization, one should expect to see greater transparency in societies in which cooperation-type interactions are somewhat more frequent than conflict-type interactions. See also *revealed preferences*.

Treatment conditions: scientists, economists, attorneys, policymakers, and the public in general all use different types of experiments to discover truths about the world. Through an experiment, one can test and prove hypotheses. Most experimenters try to reach conclusions by observing how actors behave under various pressures and circumstances. In a controlled experiment, the designer of the experiment will designate some actors to experience certain pressures and circumstances. These pressures or circumstances are called treatment conditions. The designer will designate other actors to be part of a control group. This control group will often experience no unusual pressures or circumstances – showing the designer what happens under normal conditions. For example, imagine that one wants to test the impact of frequent exposure to safety information and warnings on actual behavior. One group would be the experimental group, and that group would receive the treatment condition, by being exposed to safety information and warnings frequently. The act of being exposed to safety information and warnings would be the treatment condition, so the experimental group would be exposed to such information on a frequent basis. The control group, on the other hand, would be the same as the experimental group in all ways except that the control group would not be subjected to abnormal exposure to safety information and warnings. The treatment condition is what the experiment is set up to test. See also *controlled experiment* and *control group*.

Treatment group: see *control group*.

Trebilcock, Michael J. (1941–): the chair in law and economics at the University of Toronto Faculty of Law, where he has taught since 1972. Trebilcock has played a key role in the development of law and economics, having founded the Canadian Law and Economics Association (CLEA) and serving as president of the American Law and Economics Association in 2002. His work has focused on contracts, trade, and regulation. Trebilcock earned his LL.B. from the University of Canterbury in New Zealand in 1962 and an LL.M. from the University of Adelaide in 1965. Prior to settling at the University of Toronto Faculty of Law, he taught at the University of Adelaide from 1965 to 1969, and McGill Law School from 1969 to 1972. He was elected a Fellow of the Royal Society of Canada in 1987. See also *CLEA*.

Trembling hand: most legal problems that involve interdependent decision-making are analyzed with the game-theoretic concepts of Nash strategies and Nash equilibrium. In a Nash equilibrium, players will adopt the best strategy for them, considering the strategy of the other player; neither player could do any better, and hence we have an equilibrium. The rigor of game theory, useful as it may be for theoretical analysis, does not always reflect the imperfect nature of human choice. The concept of the trembling hand was first introduced by

Selten (1975) as a refinement of the Nash equilibrium concept, and has been adopted and extensively used in law and economics to capture the possibility of human error in strategic decision-making. A tremble occurs when one player makes a mistake (e.g., picks the wrong strategy), which moves the players out of equilibrium. As Baird, Gertner, and Picker (1994) point out, this term conjures up the image of a player whose hand is trembling while he or she makes a play during the game and therefore makes a mistake. Because the player merely makes a mistake, it is possible to consider the options that remain after the mistake, without considering how the players reached this position. If a player deliberately took an erroneous move, this would be considered in analyzing the game ahead of time. However, players can make erroneous moves that they did not plan to make, and the other players may in turn account for such possibility. A simple tort problem will provide a compelling illustration. According to a Nash equilibrium model of negligence liability, rational tortfeasors should always avoid liability by taking due care. In turn, if tortfeasors never choose to be negligent, prospective victims should not expect to receive any compensation in the event of an accident. Victims would therefore have incentives to take precautions to reduce their expected accident loss. On the basis of this Nash logic, law and economics scholars have shown that a rule of simple negligence creates optimal care incentives on both parties. However, in real life, tortfeasors are often found to be negligent. People make mistakes, and due to their "trembling hand" even perfectly rational tortfeasors may be found negligent. In turn, prospective victims may account for this possibility when choosing their level of care, and a different, less desirable, equilibrium may emerge. Trembling hand problems may be very common in certain domains of human action. The law and economics literature has derived most of its standard results on the basis of Nash assumptions, and should over time consider the robustness of these results in light of trembling hand problems. A variation of the trembling hand equilibrium, called proper equilibrium, has been formulated by Myerson (1978), by assuming that players try to avoid more costly mistakes, such that they can be expected to happen with lower probability. See also ***Nash equilibrium*** and ***robustness***.

Triangulation: public choice scholars have applied a vast array of economic tools to analyze the world of political decision-making. Downs' (1957) median voter theorem shows how the desires of political candidates affect the policy positions they take as candidates. In a two-party system, in which one candidate wins who takes the majority of the votes and voters are fully informed about the policy platforms of the candidates, candidates will take on the policy preferences of the median voter. The support of the median voter will bring with it the support of the largest possible number of voters, making victory more likely for the candidate adopting the median voter's position. In real-world political markets, the term "triangulation" (Broder, 1997) has been used to describe the result of efforts to legislate in the middle ground between ideological extremes, in which vote-trading transaction costs are high (Luppi and Parisi, 2012a). Candidates "legislate to the middle ground," trying to maneuver between two ideological extremes on either side. When viewed in a two-dimensional policy space, policy proposals can be seen as forming a policy triangle. Broder labeled the strategy of President Clinton's 1996 re-election campaign as triangulation, in which Clinton legislated and campaigned toward the middle of the ideological spectrum, leaving elected officials on either side of the ideological spectrum seeming extreme. Triangulation describes an effective strategy to seek out the median voter and secure electoral victory. See also ***logrolling*** and ***political Coase theorem***.

Tullock, Gordon (1922–): considered one of the founders of public choice theory and one of the leading exponents of the Virginia school of law and economics. He was born in Rockford, Illinois, on February 13, 1922. He attended the University of Chicago, and after an interruption due to military service received his law degree in 1947. Tullock never received an undergraduate degree, though he was awarded an honorary Ph.D. by the University of Chicago in 1994. His 1962 book *The Calculus of Consent,* co-authored with Nobel laureate James Buchanan, is considered to have founded the field of public choice theory. This book provided a clear link between empirical decision-making and normative principles. He also identified the concept of unproductive competition (a concept that later became known as rent seeking), the extraction of value from others without any reciprocal contribution, in his 1967 paper "The welfare costs of tariffs, monopolies, and theft," and later expanded his work on that subject into a 1993 book, *Rent Seeking.* His 1971 book *The Logic of the Law* and his 1980 book *Trials on Trial* have been at the same time influential and controversial, even within the law and economics community. Going against the conventional wisdom in law and economics, Gordon Tullock's work is critical of the common law process and sheds a positive light on the legal systems based on legislation. In addition to his work in public choice theory and law and economics, he has contributed important research to other fields of economics, as well as law and sociobiology, the study of social behavior within the context of evolution. See also ***Tullock's rectangle***, ***Tullock's paradox***, ***public choice theory***, ***rent seeking***, ***constitutional political economy***, ***Virginia school***, ***Buchanan, James***, **Papers on Non-Market Decision Making**, and **Public Choice**.

Tullock's paradox: Gordon Tullock (1967) has originated a variety of rent-seeking models for an understanding of the economic behavior of players who engage in a contest in which each player expends efforts to increase his or her probability (probabilistic models) or his or her share (deterministic models) of a given prize. Much of the early literature focused on how much effort each player expends, and how the degree of rent dissipation varies with the contestants' returns to effort, the value of the prize, and the number of contestants. The early wisdom in the literature analogized rents to profits, maintaining that both were likely to be competed away in the long-run equilibrium, with rent-seeking activities yielding the normal market rate of return. Tullock (1980) identified the conditions under which competitive rent-seeking could lead to under- or over-dissipation. Tullock's paradox arises in situations of increasing returns to rent-seeking expenditures. Here, the aggregate rent-seeking expenditures could exceed the value of the prize, with negative expected returns for the participants. Rational players should realize that participation in the rent-seeking contest would give negative expected returns, and should consequently choose to exit the contest. Tullock's paradox arises because, if all players exit, any one of them could win the prize with a minimal effort by re-entering the contest. This would destabilize the no-participation equilibrium. Tullock's paradox thus suggests that, even in negative expected return situations, we should not safely assume lack of participation. The subsequent literature considered participation with mixed strategies (Hillman and Samet, 1987) and mixed-participation strategies (Dari-Mattiacci and Parisi, 2005a) as a solution to Tullock's paradox. See also *lost treasure effect*, *rent seeking*, and *Tullock, Gordon*.

Tullock's rectangle: in a natural monopoly, production can be most cheaply carried out by a single firm. Forcing competition in a natural monopoly would increase consumer welfare and reduce the monopoly deadweight loss (Harberger's triangle), but would increase production costs. The area corresponding to the increase in production costs is known as Tullock's rectangle. The welfare effects of the divestment and break-up of a natural monopoly can be evaluated by comparing the areas of Harberger's triangle and Tullock's rectangle. If the area of Tullock's rectangle is larger than the area of Harberger's triangle, a break-up of a natural monopoly would be undesirable from a welfare point of view. Price regulation or nationalization of the industry are two traditional solutions considered in such cases of natural monopoly. The so-called Chadwick–Demsetz scheme provides an alternative to the traditional solutions, allowing the economies of scale of the natural monopoly to be preserved, while avoiding the pitfalls of the traditional regulatory and nationalization solutions. See also *Harberger's triangle*, *efficiency defense*, *Chadwick–Demsetz scheme*, *natural monopoly*, and *Tullock, Gordon*.

Two-part tariffs: pricing schemes used by monopolists or firms with substantial market power to discriminate between consumers when they cannot identify consumer types. A two-part tariff requires consumers to pay a fixed fee or lump-sum payment for the service regardless of the quantity purchased and a variable charge for each unit actually purchased. With homogeneous consumers, two-part tariffs allow monopolists to extract the entire consumer surplus by charging a price equal to the marginal cost and a fixed fee equal to the consumer's surplus at the marginal price. In the presence of two or more types of consumers with different demand schedules, the optimal two-part tariff occurs when monopolists charge a variable price above the marginal cost and a fixed fee equal to the consumer's surplus. Two-part tariffs are price schemes often implemented for utilities (e.g., gas, energy), amusement parks (e.g., Disneyland), athletic clubs, etc. Two-part tariffs were first studied by Oi (1971) in his well-known paper "A Disney dilemma: two-part tariffs for a Mickey Mouse monopoly." See also *monopoly*, *price discrimination*, and *marginal-cost pricing*.

Two-sided markets: the concept of a two-sided market describes a situation in which one platform exists that must attract economic players to both sides of the platform. The platform provides some intermediate service or plays some role that is useful only if both of the relevant parties on either side of the platform come to the table. There are many examples of two-sided markets in complex modern economies, ranging from the organization of trade shows and fairs to cellphone service providers. A trade show organizer needs to attract exhibitors and at the same time bring visitors to the show; likewise, a cellphone service provider needs to attract both cellphone users and cellphone producers. Rochet and Tirole (2004) point out that the price structure of a two-sided market must always be one that attracts customers on both sides of the platform. A two-sided market firm can increase prices on one side while decreasing prices on the other side (e.g., decrease ticket price to the show and increase expositors' fees) so as to keep both sides coming to the platform.

Two-stage least squares: see *instrumental variable approach*.

Two-step optimization: legal systems pursue several policy goals, among which efficiency and distributive justice stand as important objectives. The prevailing wisdom in the literature is that substantive legal rules in areas such as contracts or torts are very costly instruments for redistribution. The tax system has an intrinsic advantage over other areas of substantive law for carrying out reallocation of wealth. On the basis of these considerations, scholars have argued in favor of a two-step optimization of efficiency and distributive justice, whereby substantive law is designed to maximize aggregate wealth, and the tax system can be used to correct the distributive inequalities created by substantive law (Kaplow and Shavell, 1994). See also *welfare analysis*.

Tying: see *tie-ins*.

Type I and type II errors: two categories of errors that may occur when testing hypotheses. A type I error happens when the researcher rejects as false a hypothesis that is actually true. A type II error happens when the researcher does not reject a hypothesis that is actually false. These terms are used most often in statistics or econometrics tests, but sometimes they are used more loosely to describe errors. For example, a researcher considering the criminal justice system may start with the null hypothesis that every defendant is innocent. A type I error occurs when the null hypothesis is erroneously rejected – that is, when an innocent defendant is found guilty (a false positive). A type II error consistent with this null hypothesis, then, is when a guilty defendant is set free (a false negative). Using this null hypothesis, the US criminal justice system has many additional protections, such as the right to due process, that guard against type I errors. See also ***Blackstonian error ratio***, ***level of significance***, ***null versus alternative hypothesis***, and ***carrots versus sticks***.

Ugly princess: the protection of the weaker contractual party against the opportunistic behavior of his or her stronger counterpart may require contractual safeguards. Law and economics and new institutional economics scholars have explored the role of alternative contractual solutions that extend beyond the standard contractual agreement to correct for problems of opportunistic behavior (Williamson, 1983; Baumol, 1986). The idea of a "hostage" has been used in this literature to refer to an atypical bonding mechanism (Kronman, 1985; Williamson, 1985; Baumol, 1986). A hostage is a bonding instrument characterized by the fact that it is of value to the promisor (the hostage giver), but of little or no value to the promisee (the hostage taker) or to society in general. This characteristic distinguishes hostages from collateral (which is, generally, equally valued by the two parties). Williamson (1983) explains this essential feature of a hostage with the "ugly princess" analogy. When a king is under siege and needs to give a hostage, he gives away the uglier of his two daughters. This action makes the hostage takers less apt simply to run away with the hostage. In a contractual context, when a promisee offers a hostage-type bonding mechanism, it is similarly important that he provides an unattractive hostage, to avoid opportunism by his promisee. For example, individuals who invest in firm-specific specialized human capital often will require some bonding (e.g., golden parachutes) in order to guard against the risk of exploitation by their employers (Baumol, 1986). However, the employer should be careful not to offer anything too attractive in the way of bonding to his or her worker, or else the worker may find a way to trigger the termination condition and run away with it. One of the difficulties in applying the ugly princess concept in the design of hostages is that, in some cases, hostages do not have an objective market value, and it may be difficult for the promisee to ascertain the actual value of the hostage to the promisor. See also ***hostages***.

Ultimatum game: a two-player game in which the proponent offers an allocation of a monetary endowment S to the responder, according to which the proponent gets x and the responder $S - x$. The responder can either accept or refuse the proposal. If he or she accepts, the division of the sum S is implemented and the proponent gets x and the responder $S - x$. If the responder refuses, the sum S is lost and both players get zero. The Nash equilibrium of the ultimatum game is one in which the proponent offers the smallest possible positive amount (for example, one cent or one dollar), and the responder accepts the proposal. Contrary to Nash equilibrium predictions, experimental evidence has shown that people behave in a systematically different way in ultimatum game settings. Proponents tend to offer a share of *S* between 40 percent and 50 percent, and rarely offer less than 20 percent or more than 50 percent. Responders tend to accept offers close to 50 percent, but systematically refuse offers lower than 20 percent. These results are interpreted as evidence of motivations, such as altruism, inequity aversion, a taste for fairness and similar other-regarding motivations, in explaining economic behavior. See also *dictator game*, *experimental law and economics*, *inequity aversion*, *taste for fairness*, and *kindness function*.

Undefinable kicker: when the sanction for a violation of property rights is equal to the value of the property, then the distinction between property rules and liability rules evaporates. Consequently, in order to prevent property rules from collapsing into liability rules, property remedies should impose an additional cost to the violator, raising deterrence above mere restitution. Calabresi and Melamed (1972) refer to this additional sanction as the undefinable kicker. The result is that actors may knowingly incur liability when it is efficient, while being strongly deterred from violating the property interests, even when such a violation may result in an efficient exchange. The reasons for preserving the division between liability and property rules are manifold. First, because a violation of property rules does not involve bargaining, and because a property owner's private valuation of his or her property is not disclosed, it is impossible to determine whether any given violation is in fact efficient. Indeed, there is no reason to suppose it would be efficient generally, even if particular violations might be. Second, allowing the efficient trampling of property rights imposes an externality on the legal system as a whole. Third, imperfect detection creates a situation in which, for example, an attempted theft becomes a win-or-break-even situation for potential thieves. The undefinable kicker may be small or large; what matters is simply that it raise the sanction for property violations above that of restitution, effectively discouraging involuntary transfers outside the marketplace. This often takes the form of criminal penalties. See also *zero-order liability rule* and *property rules versus liability rules*.

Undiversifiable risk: see *systematic versus unsystematic risk*.

Unilateral accidents: accidents whose occurrence is sensitive only to the injurer's behavior, and cannot thus be reduced by altering the behavior of the victim. In such unilateral situations, precautions taken by the victim are unnecessary and socially undesirable. Unilateral accidents are distinguished from bilateral accidents, whose occurrence depends upon the behavior of both parties. See also *bilateral accidents* and *alternative versus joint care*.

Unilateral precautions: see *unilateral accidents*.

Unintended consequences: see *Bastiat's unseen costs*.

Union: term used in the law and economics literature to refer to one of the four non-legal enforcement mechanisms (the others being hostages, collateral, and hands tying) considered by Kronman (1985). Union refers to situations in which the promisor and promisee merge into one entity. This may include situations of two firms merging into one, or situations of vertical integration, when an upstream (downstream) company acquires its downstream (upstream) counterpart, business partnerships, and family unions. In all these situations, the independent interests of the parties are united into one. This leads to a full (or partial) internalization of the costs and benefits of cooperation for both parties, facilitating the sustainability of cooperative equilibria. In the context of contract performance, after a union, parties internalize the costs and benefits of breach and will engage in optimal performance and reliance of contractual promises. See also *self-enforcing contracts*, *hostages*, *collateral*, *hands tying*, *relational contracts*, *cooperative games*, and *non-cooperative games*.

Uniqueness bias: see *false uniqueness bias*.

***United States* v. *Carroll Towing*:** see *Learned Hand formula*.

Unproductive competition: see *rent seeking*.

Unraveling: see *backward induction*.

Unrealistic optimism. see *optimism bias*.

Unsystematic risk: see *systematic versus unsystematic risk*.

Utilitarianism: in the nineteenth century and early twentieth century economists and philosophers developed welfare paradigms according to which the degree of all affected individuals had to be taken into account in any comparative evaluation of different states of the world. This methodological trend, related to utilitarian philosophy, is best represented by philosophers and jurists such as Bentham (1789) and later economists such as Kaldor (1939) and Hicks (1939), who in different ways formulated criteria of social welfare that accounted for the *cardinal* preferences of individuals. In his *Principles of Morals and Legislation*, Bentham (1789) presents his theory of value and motivation. He suggests that mankind is governed by two masters: "pain" and "pleasure." The two provide the fundamental motivation for human action. Bentham notes that not all individuals derive pleasure from the same objects or activities, and not all human sensibilities are the same. Bentham's moral imperative, which has greatly influenced the methodological debate in law and economics, is that policymakers have an obligation to select rules that give "the greatest happiness to the greatest number." This formulation of Bentham's imperative is quite problematic, since it identifies two maximands (i.e., degree of pleasure and number of individuals) without specifying the tradeoff between one and the other. Later economists, including Kaldor (1939), Hicks (1939), and Scitovsky (1941), have formulated welfare paradigms that avoid these ambiguities. However, these formulations present a different set of difficulties in their implementation. Mathematically, both the Bentham and the Kaldor–Hicks versions of efficiency are carried out by comparing the aggregate payoffs of the various alternatives and selecting the option that maximizes such summation (Klick and Parisi, 2005). See also ***wealth maximization, utility maximization, utility monster, Bentham, Jeremy***, and ***Beccaria, Cesare***.

Utility maximization: the field of law and economics studies the effect of regulation on social welfare. A notable debate in the literature involves the question of the appropriate maximand for legal policy. The maximand is the object of maximization by the policymaker (i.e., what the policymaker intends to maximize). In the choice of the maximand, law and economics scholars are divided between two main alternative approaches: utility maximization and wealth maximization. Although the majority of conventional economists believe that utility is the appropriate maximand for welfare analysis, several law and economics scholars believe that the utility maximization approach falters because of the fact that utility cannot be measured objectively making interpersonal comparisons of utility almost impossible, and rendering any balancing across groups or individuals largely arbitrary. This limitation makes utility maximization unviable for practical policy purposes and has led practitioners in the field of law and economics increasingly to use the alternative paradigm of wealth maximization. See also ***wealth maximization, utility monster, Kaldor–Hicks criterion, Nash criterion of welfare, Rawlsian maximin, Pareto efficiency, capability approach, welfare analysis, interpersonal utility comparisons, happiness research***, and ***neuroeconomics***.

Utility monster: in utilitarianism, if one must choose between two possible actions, one should choose the action that results in the greater overall happiness. The most common version of utilitarianism adopts a social welfare function in which the utility of the members of society is summed up with a Kaldor–Hicks welfare function (the sum of the utility of all members of society). If one action produces aggregate utility that is higher than another action, the former action should be preferred. In the law and economics context, these forms of aggregation are very frequently utilized when evaluating the efficiency properties of alternative legal rules. Nozick (1974) has criticized the concept of utilitarianism, in part by a theoretical discussion of the so-called "utility monster." A utility monster is a person who receives increasing amounts of happiness with each additional unit of consumption. Unlike normal consumers, who eventually experience diminishing returns on their increased consumption, the utility monster becomes increasingly happy as he or she continues to consume. In deciding between various policies, Kaldor–Hicks utilitarianism would likely favor policies that continue to provide increasing levels of resources to the utility monster, because his or her level of enjoyment continues to increase at an increasing rate. The supply of resources to the utility monster might be at the expense of the provision of resources to other people who are needy but do not experience the same levels of increasing marginal utility. Nozick uses this paradox to criticize utilitarianism by pointing to the absurd consequences of utilitarian welfare policies, whereby the utility monster would continues to receive preference over other more needy people. An interesting variation of the utility monster occurs when utility maximization is combined with different aggregation techniques, such as the Nash criterion of welfare (the maximization of the product of the utilities) or the Rawlsian maximin (the maximization of the utility of the least well off). Under these criteria, the opposite paradox of a "disutility monster" may take place. Since these criteria of welfare are heavily influenced by the well-being of individuals with the lowest levels of utility, members of a group who are "hard to please" would receive disproportionate reallocations of wealth. See also *marginal utility*, *Kaldor–Hicks criterion*, *Nash criterion of welfare*, *Rawlsian maximin*, *utilitarianism*, and *aggregation problem*.

Value: see *subjective value*.

Vanderbilt Ph.D. in law and economics: program launched at Vanderbilt University in 2006 by W. Kip Viscusi and Joni Hersch, both formerly of Harvard University. The program constitutes the first example of a Ph.D. program issued by a law school faculty in the United States. The Vanderbilt program is designed to allow students to pursue a joint J.D./Ph.D. with a focus on law and economics. The program addresses the growing interest in exploring the intersection of law and applied economics, and is a result of the growing importance and influence of the field of law and economics itself. The courses are taught by a combination of law, economics, and business professors and are open to students in the law, economics, and business programs. Students complete coursework in microeconomic theory, econometrics, and law and economics theory. As is often the case, the principal fields for upper-level concentrations are dictated by the research specialties of the teaching faculty, and currently include behavioral law and economics, labor and human resources, and risk and environmental regulation. See also *EDLE*, *EMLE*, and *Erasmus program in law and economics*.

Variable-sum games: unlike zero-sum and constant-sum games, variable-sum games are characterized by a variable aggregate payoff, either positive (positive-sum games) or negative (negative-sum games). Many economic and legally relevant situations can be described as variable-sum games, in which the interaction among parties can create a gain or avoid a loss through the players' coordination or cooperation. For policymakers seeking to maximize aggregate social welfare, variable-sum games will be the only relevant form of interaction since the aggregate welfare in a constant-sum game will be constant and "maximization" will be trivially satisfied regardless of the choice of policy – or, indeed, the players' moves. Examples range from contract rules used to foster efficient bargains (positive-sum game) or procedural rules used to discourage inefficient litigation (negative-sum game). See also *constant-sum games*, *zero-sum games*, and *inessential games*.

Veil of ignorance: in *A Theory of Justice* (1971), John Rawls gives a philosophical analysis of justice (distributive justice especially) as fairness. Fairness is the product of objective and impartial decision-making. Recognizing that fairness is a notion susceptible to relativism and subjectivity, Rawls unpacks the concept using a thought experiment he terms the veil of ignorance. In determining what is "fair," Rawls asks people to suspend knowledge of their particular identities – their social class, their race, their personal preferences and tastes. They then make choices in a rational, self-interested manner, ignorant of how those choices might impact them particularly. The power and persuasiveness of the veil of ignorance is that it provides an armchair mechanism for testing the fairness of proposals, relying not on altruism or virtuousness but, rather, the assumption of rationality that undergirds so much of economics. This construct closely resembles Harsanyi's (1953) veil of uncertainty, as expressed in his impartial observer theorem. See also ***impartial observer theorem***, ***veil of uncertainty***, ***Rawls, John***, and ***difference principle***.

Veil of uncertainty: John Harsanyi (1975) developed the veil of uncertainty construct in conjunction with impartial observer theorem, which had been independently introduced by Vickrey (1945) and Harsanyi (1953). The idea is, when a policymaker chooses between alternative policies (e.g., alternative income distributions, etc.), the merits of the policies should be evaluated from the viewpoint of an impartial observer – that is to say, from the point of view of an individual who does not know which position he or she would occupy, and gives an equal chance to receiving each possible allocation. A very similar concept (the veil of ignorance) was used by John Rawls (1971) in his well-known book *A Theory of Justice*. Rawls formulates his problem by implicitly assuming risk aversion. Harsanyi (1975) critiques Rawls' version of the veil of ignorance, offering a defense of the utilitarian model as one that most ably allows society to consider the circumstances of individuals equally. Harsanyi specifically critiques Rawls' theory that the maximin principle can serve as a basis for morality. However, Harsanyi acknowledges the power of the veil of ignorance concept, but he prefers to distinguish it from his original impartial observer scenario, recasting it in the terminology of modern decision-making theory: the veil of uncertainty. The decision-makers, when under the veil in what Rawls calls the "original position," operate in a position of uncertainty "because, by assumption, the participants would be uncertain about what their personal circumstances would be under any particular institutional framework to be agreed upon" (Harsanyi, 1975). In the more general usage of these concepts, Harsanyi's veil of uncertainty and Rawls' veil of ignorance are often invoked interchangeably. These frameworks have generated much debate and analysis since they were first proposed, providing an important foundation for modern theories of justice. See also ***veil of ignorance*** and ***impartial observer theorem***.

Vertical integration: in a complex global economy, firms often consolidate to create economies of scale and control more and more of their production processes. Firms engage in vertical integration when they consolidate up and down the line of production. While vertical integration can create economies of scale that make it cheaper for a firm to operate, it can also lead to higher costs for consumers. Instead of there being market competition at different levels of the production chain, the firm now controls the entire process and sells directly to consumers, giving it greater control over the prices consumers pay. Williamson

(1985) points out that vertical integration is, in part, a firm's response to market failures and the ineffectiveness of market governance mechanisms. There is probably some amount of optimal vertical integration for a firm, which allows the firm to gain efficiency through both economies of scale and a correction in the failure of market governance. The idea is an extension of Coase's (1937) theory of the firm, inasmuch as, when transaction costs become high, spot contracts between vertically related firms may break down, and vertical integration of the firms gives them an opportunity to internalize the costs and benefits of their activities and avoid the losses caused by strategic and opportunistic behavior. See also *backward integration*, *forward integration*, *double marginalization*, and *union*.

Vickrey auctions: see *second-price auctions*.

Vickrey impartial observer theorem: see *impartial observer theorem*.

Virginia school: often associated with the functional approach to law and economics, the Virginia school builds on the methodological foundations of constitutional political economy, public choice theory, and Austrian economics, and has gradually developed a critical view of both the positive and normative approaches to law and economics, often espoused by the Chicago and Yale schools. Scholars such as Gordon Tullock, James Buchanan, Charles Rowley, Todd Zywicki and several others associated with George Mason University have, through their own work, developed a distinctive methodological approach to law and economics. The Virginia school is wary of generalized efficiency hypotheses, especially when applied to sources of law outside the common law. The Virginia school is also skeptical of the normative and prescriptive uses of economic analysis to design laws and legal remedies. The Virginia school builds on the methodological premises of normative individualism and believes that the dominant methodology of law and economics overlooks the unintended consequences of legal intervention, advocating a greater emphasis on the decision-making power of individuals. See also *functional law and economics*, *positive versus normative law and economics*, *public choice theory*, *Chicago school*, and *Yale school*.

Vote trading: see *logrolling*.

Voting paradoxes: situations in which the preferences of voters contradict certain desirable or common-sense assumptions. For example, in one of the earliest examples, Condorcet's voting paradox, it follows from a particular assignment of preferences in a three-voter model that a majority will prefer option *A* over *B*, *B* over *C*, and *C* over *A*, contradicting the assumption of transitivity. Contemporary interest in voting paradoxes originates with Arrow (1951), and much subsequent research has been an extension of Arrow's work. See also *Condorcet voting paradox*, *Arrow's impossibility theorem*, *Sen's liberal paradox*, *rational abstention*, and *rational ignorance*.

Voting with your feet: individuals live in different states, and are subject to different laws, institutions, and social norms. The expression "voting with your feet" refers to the fact that, if a citizen of a certain state does not like the laws and policies of his or her state, he or she can either attempt to change those policies from within, through the democratic process, or vote with his (or her) feet, relocating to a different state where he or she finds the policies, protections, and norms of the state's government and people more agreeable. The expression is generally associated with Tiebout's (1956) model of public expenditures, and is used in support of individuals, freedom of movement and choice of law. Although this concept could apply to any person who chooses to move from one democracy to another, in lieu of using his or her vote to generate change in his or her first location, Laycock (2009) points out that federalist scholars argue that voting with one's feet is a benefit of the federalism inherent in federal structures, such as that of the United States. In its practical application, the voting metaphor is in many respects incomplete. The cost of relocating is high relative to the cost of voting; local governments can therefore extract some rent from individuals in their jurisdiction before triggering relocation. Further, the relocation choices of individuals may be affected by adverse selection and moral hazard (e.g., localities with better health care may attract a higher percentage of individuals with health problems or may reduce incentives to invest in preventive health). The institutional design of a federal system should therefore anticipate such problems and correct possible jurisdictional externalities. In discussing the conceptual framework of voting with your feet, Laycock (2009) points out that the opportunity to vote with one's feet should not be seen as an excuse for government to fail to enforce constitutional protections rigorously. See also *Tiebout competition* and *exit/voice model*.

Warranties: the law and economics literature considers a warranty as a promise of the seller to assume specific responsibilities in case the quality or the performance of the purchased item does not conform to the specifications and the legitimate contractual expectations of the buyer. Warranties can be conventional (i.e., chosen and made into a contract by the contracting parties) and legal (i.e., created by operation of law). From an economic point of view, three main functions are played by legal and conventional warranties: (a) the information-revealing function; (b) the incentive function; and (c) the insurance function. As has been shown in the literature, the pursuit of these three functions is not always possible with the choice of a single warranty instrument. With respect to the information-revealing function, the main idea is that most consumer transactions are chronically affected by asymmetric information, whereby sellers are assumed to have a natural advantage in gathering information concerning the true quality of the sold item. In the presence of asymmetric information, the seller's willingness to offer a warranty is a credible signal of the information available to the seller. Through the mechanism of contractual warranties, sellers of products of different quality will be able to offer easily observable and credible information to potential buyers. Buyers may also possess private information that is not available to the seller. The demand for warranties by buyers could also signal the existence of private information on the part of the consumer, namely the expected level of harm that he or she faces in the event of product failure. Highly sensitive consumers will demand more warranties, while low-sensitivity buyers may forgo the warranty in return for a discount. In addition, in this case, the contractual choice of a warranty may serve a socially valuable signaling function. When both asymmetric information problems are present, we should expect a broad variety of warranty coverage to become available. In equilibrium, low-quality sellers will be matched with low-sensitivity buyers (with the choice of limited warranties or the exclusion of warranties) and high-quality sellers will be matched with high-sensitivity buyers (with the choice of full warranties or extended warranties). With respect to the incentive function, the main idea is that the quality and the probability of failure of a good can be influenced by the behavior of the parties. Warranties operate as incentives for the parties to invest in the production and preservation of high quality. As Priest (1981) has pointed out, a warranty is an instrument with which the parties control the efforts of the seller and buyer to provide and to maintain a functioning product. With respect to the insurance function, warranties operate as a way to allocate the risk of a product defect between a buyer and a seller. In addition to the signaling and incentive effects, warranties reallocate the risk and operate as insurance for the buyer, in that the seller is giving assurances as to the quality of the product. In this case, the optimal warranty instrument and resulting allocation of the risk are determined by the relative risk aversion of the parties (Parisi, 2004). See also *adverse selection* and *signaling*.

Weak monopoly: a monopoly that operates in a contestable market. Although the weak monopoly faces no competition in the present, its monopolistic position could be challenged by the entry of a competitor. See also *contestable markets*, *natural monopoly*, and *Ramsey pricing*.

Weak link problem: term used to describe situations in which the value or effectiveness of something is determined by the weakest of its components. Examples range from defense systems to immigration enforcement, network integrity, import duties, professional licensing, and welfare policy. Consider the case of import controls within a union of states with a common market (e.g., the European Union). If member states adopt different levels of import control enforcement, illegal imports would flow into the common market utilizing the "weakest link." The effectiveness of the union's import control is determined by its weakest link. Toughening controls at one port of entry would be ineffective if other ports keep weaker levels of enforcement. Weak link problems often arise in contexts of international cooperation, the voluntary provision of public goods, and multi-level governance (Cornes and Sandler, 1996; Sandler, 2006). In social welfare analysis, the weak link concept has been used to characterize the implications of Rawls' difference principle and of his maximin criterion (the idea that the weakest member within a group determines the strength and welfare of that group). See also *best shot problem*, *maximin strategy*, *Rawlsian maximin*, *difference principle*, and *capability approach*.

Wealth effect versus income effect: individuals react to changes in their financial well-being by changing their patterns of consumption, investment and savings. Economists distinguish between wealth effects (changes in an individual's "stock" of wealth) and income effects (changes in the "flow" of wealth, or income) that may accompany a change in financial well-being. The wealth effect measures the reaction of a consumer to a change in his or her wealth level. The income effect measures the reaction of a consumer to a change in his or her real income. Both effects are measured in terms of a change in the consumption or investment level, in the presence of constant relative prices of the goods in the consumption bundle. Generally, economic agents respond to perceived increases in wealth and income by increasing their spending. In these cases, the income and wealth effects are positive, and they occur for the so-called "normal" goods. Macroeconomists further distinguish between the effects of permanent and transitory changes in income, to study the different patterns of spending that the two changes may produce. The permanent income hypothesis, formulated by Friedman in 1957, is that changes in consumption mostly depend on changes in permanent income (i.e., what people expect to earn over an extended period of time), while transitory changes in income mostly affect investments. Economists have also observed that people experience a positive wealth effect when they are richer (due to an increase in real income) or when they feel richer (due to an increase of purchasing power or a decrease in the price of something they buy). However, these differences may affect the amounts and composition of the goods and services consumed by the agent. On rare occasions, an increase in wealth may have a negative impact on consumption (for the so-called "inferior" goods). One important application of the wealth effect occurs in conjunction with the Coase theorem. This states that, if property rights are fully assigned, liability rules have no effect on resource allocations as long as there are no transaction costs and no wealth effects from the initial assignment. The presence of a wealth effect may undermine the equivalence proposition of the Coase theorem. Finally, behavioral and experimental economists have observed that the magnitude of the wealth effect depends on the reference point: people feel differently about gaining wealth from how they do about losing it. Hence, changes in wealth of equal magnitude provoke wealth effects of different magnitude according to whether they involve gains or losses of wealth. This may explain the poor results achieved when promoting economic stimulus through redistributive fiscal policy. See also ***normal good***, ***inferior good***, ***Giffen good***, ***substitution effect***, ***Coase theorem***, and *fiscal delusion*.

Wealth maximization: under wealth maximization principles, a transaction is desirable if it increases the sum of wealth for the relevant parties (where "wealth" includes all tangible and intangible goods and services). Several practitioners of the economic analysis of law have adopted paradigms of wealth maximization in their work, departing from the nineteenth-century utilitarian ideal of utility maximization. Richard Posner is probably the most notable exponent of the wealth maximization paradigm. In several of his writings, Posner defends the criterion of wealth maximization, advancing reasons for regarding it as a worthy standard for evaluating legal rules. Posner (1979) formulates an intuitive justification of wealth maximization. According to this view, wealth maximization can be regarded as a superior ethical principle because it is consistent with ethical intuitions, provides for a more sound theory of justice, and yields more definite results than the alternative economic views on justice. By promoting the efficient use of resources, wealth maximization encourages traditional capacities, such as intelligence, and traditional virtues, such as honesty. In later years Posner (1985) explicitly advocates wealth maximization as a criterion that should guide judicial rule making. In order to make the case for wealth maximization, he defines it and compares it with the alternative theories of utilitarianism and libertarianism. Wealth maximization occurs when a transaction increases the total amount of goods and services, weighted by offer prices and demand prices. Because of the market's ability to capture subjective values and preferences, wealth maximization is a comprehensive measure of social welfare. Besides Posner's defense of wealth maximization as a superior ethical criterion, other scholars defend the wealth maximization criterion on pragmatic grounds. Unlike utility, wealth can more easily be measured. Furthermore, interpersonal comparisons of utility are impossible, rendering any attempt to balance or aggregate utility across groups or individuals largely arbitrary. However, the use of wealth maximization in policy analysis attracts many criticisms, both from within and without the law and economics community. Bentham (1789) challenged the use of objective factors, such as wealth or physical resources, as a proxy for human happiness. Despite the difficulties in quantifying values such as utility or happiness, the pursuit of pleasure and happiness and the avoidance of pain are the motivating forces of human behavior, and wealth is a mere instrument to achieve such human goals. According to Coleman (1982), wealth maximization is a form of Kaldor–Hicks maximization in disguise. The practical advantages of wealth maximization over utility maximization relate to the fact that it is easier to ascertain actual changes in wealth as opposed to utility. In spite of such practical superiority, according to Coleman, Posner's defense of wealth maximization as a normative criterion remains subject to several of the shortcomings of the Kaldor–Hicks criterion, including its difficult moral defensibility. Posner's defense of wealth maximization has been further criticized for building upon notions of implied, rather than actual, consent. Coleman (1982) recognizes the usefulness of tests of hypothetical consent à la Rawls, but questions the uniqueness of wealth maximization as a dominant criterion of justice from the perspective of ex ante social choice. The indeterminacy of such hypothetical social choice poses a challenge to the consent-based moral justification of wealth maximization. Legal scholars (such as Malloy, 1988) have often argued that wealth maximization and other efficiency-based theories of justice promote "disrespect for individual liberty," are "indeterminative and elitist," and "can hardly be viewed as anything other than amoral, if not immoral." Posner (1988) suggests that these critiques miss the mark, in that they treat the methodology of law and economics as a political theory. Affirming that wealth maximization is the best normative and positive theory of common law rights and remedies does not imply that the wealth maximization criterion should override moral concerns. Several other prominent scholars and political theorists have also openly criticized the wealth maximization paradigm, arguing that an increase in wealth cannot constitute a social improvement unless it furthers some other social goal, such as utility, equality, and freedom to fulfill human capabilities (Calabresi, 1980; Sen, 1985, 1993; Nussbaum, 2000). Future scholarship in law and economics should attempt to systematize the terms of this debate, showing the conditions under which the methodological choice of a specific maximand will lead to relevant differences in normative policy analysis (Klick and Parisi, 2005). See also *utility maximization*, *Kaldor–Hicks criterion*, *Nash criterion of welfare*, *Rawlsian maximin*, *Pareto efficiency*, *welfare analysis*, *utilitarianism*, and *capability approach*.

Welfare analysis: much research in law and economics is concerned either with determining whether a law (or set of laws) is efficient or, alternatively, with designing laws that effect efficient results. In such cases, "efficiency" denotes maximal social welfare. However, there are several competing analyses of what maximal social welfare means. The choice of analysis has two dimensions: (a) what is being "maximized," and (b) how it is being "maximized." Along the first dimension, there are two candidates for maximization: (i) wealth, and (ii) utility. When wealth is the maximand (the object being maximized), the "efficient" allocation is the one that maximizes the total wealth in a society. It is the same for utility. The choice of maximand depends on a number of practical and technical considerations. Certainly, the ultimate aim of any policy is to maximize utility; however, supernumerary practical problems (not the least of which is the difficulty in measuring utility) often make wealth a more useful yardstick. The second dimension concerns how the maximand is aggregated. In the theoretical framework of welfare analysis, social welfare is an aggregation of the private welfare of the members of society. There are at least four commonly used ways of aggregating the maximand to determine what distribution is maximal: (a) Pareto, (b) Kaldor–Hicks, (c) Nash, and (d) Rawls. Using Pareto efficiency, a distribution is maximal when it cannot be changed without making at least one party worse off. Using the Kaldor–Hicks criterion (Kaldor, 1939; Hicks, 1939), a distribution is maximal when the summation of all the private values of the parties is maximal. Using the Nash criterion (Nash, 1950b), a distribution is maximal when the product of all the private values of the parties is maximal. Finally, using Rawls' difference principle (Rawls, 1971), a distribution is maximal when the least well-off party is maximal. While there has historically been discussion about the merits of one maximand or aggregation technique over others, in practice the choice of maximand or aggregation technique will largely depend on the subject of the analysis, as well as practical and technical considerations. See also *efficiency*, *wealth maximization*, *utility maximization*, *Kaldor–Hicks criterion*, *Nash criterion of welfare*, *difference principle*, *Pareto efficiency*, *capability approach*, *two-step optimization*, *constrained optimization*, and *robustness*.

Williamson, Oliver Eaton (1932–): a prominent American economist, whose work has been highly influential in the field of law and economics. He was awarded the Nobel Prize in economics (with Elinor Ostrom) in 2009. Williamson's areas of interest include new institutional economics, transaction-cost economics with applications to organization theory, corporate structure, and public policy (antitrust and regulation). He was born on September 27, 1932, in Superior, Wisconsin. Williamson received his undergraduate degree from the Sloan School of Management in 1955, his M.B.A. from Stanford University in 1960, and his Ph.D. from Carnegie Mellon University in 1963. He taught at the University of Pennsylvania and Yale University, and has been a professor of business administration, economics, and law at the University of California, Berkeley, since

1988. He currently serves as a professor at the graduate faculty, and the Edgar F. Kaiser Professor Emeritus of Business, Economics, and Law. Some of his major publications include "The economics of governance" (2005), "The theory of the firm as governance structure" (2002), *The Mechanisms of Governance* (1996), *The Economic Institutions of Capitalism: Firms, Markets, Relational Contracting* (1985), *Markets and Hierarchies: Analysis and Antitrust Implications* (1975), *Corporate Control and Business Behavior: An Inquiry into the Effects of Organization Form on Enterprise Behavior* (1970), and *The Economics of Discretionary Behavior: Managerial Objectives in a Theory of the Firm* (1964). See also **Ostrom, Elinor**, **transaction-cost economics**, and **new institutional economics**.

Willingness to pay versus willingness to accept: these terms, abbreviated as WTP and WTA, constitute alternative subjective measures of commodity values. WTA is the maximum amount of money at which a person is willing to sell a good or service that he or she has access to. WTP, on the other hand, is the minimum amount a person is willing to pay for a commodity. Sellers consider WTA when deciding how much to supply at various prices, while consumers use WTP when deciding how much to pay for goods and services. Neither WTA nor WTP requires an actual exchange. WTP is limited by an agent's wealth, while WTA is theoretically boundless. There is room for trade wherever WTP exceeds WTA. The difference between WTP and WTA constitutes the gains from trade. WTA and WTP are important concepts in cost-benefit analysis, in which economists are asked to estimate individuals' valuations of items that are not traded in the marketplace. For example, a researcher can estimate the value of an enforceable contract by discerning how much a promisor would have to be compensated in order to forgo the contract; alternatively, one might estimate what the promisor is willing to pay for the chance to enter the contract. In market transactions, involving standard commodities, in which the object of the exchange has little subjective or sentimental value, WTA is likely to equal WTP. In the presence of budget constraints, the values of WTA and WTP are less often equivalent. For example, a crime victim may be willing to pay only $10,000 to avoid the crime if that is all the money he or she has. While his or her WTP may be $10,000, his or her WTA value might be much higher. Experimental evidence suggests that the magnitude of the gap between WTA and WTP is larger when a subject already possesses the item being evaluated (endowment effect). See also **endowment effect**, **endowment effect theory**, **loss aversion**, and **contingent valuation**.

Winner determination: a fundamental function of auctions and exchanges is clearing markets by an appropriate matching of supply to demand. In auction theory, the choice of matching mechanism is referred to as winner determination. There are two forms of winner determination: (a) single sourcing, and (b) multi-sourcing. Single sourcing maps buyers to sellers one to one, while multi-sourcing allows multiple sellers to be mapped to a single buyer or, alternatively, multiple buyers to a single seller. The choice of winner determination mechanism affects the complexity of auction mechanisms as well as the allocative efficiency of the outcomes. See also *auction theory*.

Winner's curse: in a common-value auction, in which bidders bid for the purchase of a good to be resold on the market, there is often uncertainty as to the value of the item. In the face of uncertainty, the bid represents the bidder's guess as to the worth (or potential resale value) of the good. There will be a distribution of guesses and corresponding bids. The winner is the bidder who made the highest guess, but the correct value is likely to be close to the average guess. The winner's curse (or buyer's remorse) comes from the realization that in a common-value auction, in which bidders have reasonable information about the worth of the item, the winner is the bidder who made the largest positive valuation error. See also *common-value auctions*.

World systems theory: see *dependency theory*.

Worst risk bearer: see *best risk bearer*.

WTP versus WTA gap: see *willingness to pay versus willingness to accept*.

X-inefficiencies: the concept of X-inefficiency was introduced by Harvey Leiben-stein (1978) as a measure of the distance between a firm's actual production behavior and a perfectly competitive firm's technically efficient choice. X-inefficiencies are sustainable only in imperfectly competitive markets, in which there is a lack of competitive pressure. In perfect competition, X-inefficiency may arise in the short run, but it will disappear in the long run under the effect of competition. Potential market entrants are willing to employ the most efficient production technology to realize a profit, and thereby increase competition, driving all firms to produce efficiently. However, under imperfect competition, X-inefficiency may persist, leading firms to adopt inefficient production techniques and realize positive profits. A monopolist producing below the efficient scale of production distorts production below the perfectly competitive level of output, and enables X-inefficiency to surface. Since it is limited to the estimation of production inefficiencies, the concept of X-inefficiency does not capture other factors that may lead to economic inefficiency, such as market failures. See also *imperfect competition*.

Yale school: Yale Law School has played – and continues to play – an important role in the establishment of law and economics. Starting in the 1960s with the work of then professor Guido Calabresi, and through the work of scholars such as George Priest, Susan Rose-Ackerman, Alan Schwartz, Roberta Romano, Jerry Mashaw, and Anthony Kronman, Yale Law School has secured its position as a leading intellectual center for the study of law and economics. Over the years Yale Law School has attracted leading scholars in the field of law and economics, and related disciplines, including Bruce Ackerman, Ian Ayres, Richard Brooks, Robert Ellickson, Henry Hansmann, Christine Jolls, Jonathan Macey, and Daniel Markovits. The Yale school is often compared and contrasted to its historic rival, the Chicago school, for its method and focus in law and economics. In the context of this comparison, the Yale school is often described as being somewhat more inclined to use normative economic analysis, and to believe that there is a larger need for legal intervention to correct market failures, and for correcting distributive problems. A notable element of some of the seminal contributions that originated from the Yale school is the attention paid to the competing goals of fairness and efficiency in the legal system, and the resulting formulation of normative propositions as to what the law ought to be like in light of those goals. Unlike the Chicago school, Yale scholars have been relatively eclectic in their views and methodology – sufficiently so as to render any generalization about Yale-style methodology difficult and possibly sterile. See also *functional law and economics*, *positive versus normative law and economics*, and *Chicago school*.

Z

Zermelo's algorithm: see *backward induction*.

Zero marginal damages: rule identified in the law and economics literature as one of the conditions of optimality for contract damages. The damages that the breaching promisor is required to pay in the event of a breach of contract affects the promisee's level of reliance. Expectation damages (i.e., damages that make the promisee indifferent between breach and actual performance) may lead to excessive reliance investments. The promisee is induced to invest in reliance, knowing that, in the event of a breach, greater reliance expenditures will be recovered through a larger damage award. To avoid the overreliance problem, the zero marginal damage rule indicates that the liquidation of contract damages should be invariant to the promisee's level of reliance (formally, the derivative of damages with respect to reliance should be equal to zero). This will encourage promisees to internalize both the cost and the benefit of their reliance choices, limiting their investment to an efficient level of reliance. The practical problem of implementing a zero marginal damage rule in contracts is that, under this rule, the liquidation of damages might occasionally lead either to under-compensation (some reliance expenditures will remain uncompensated) or to over-compensation (damages are paid for reliance expenditures that were not actually made). The law and economics literature has suggested that perfect expectation damages (i.e., damages based on the promisee's forgone benefit, evaluated at the "socially optimal" level of reliance) could be viewed as an implementation of the zero marginal damage rule. See also *perfect expectation damages*.

Zero risk bias: psychological studies have shown that individuals tend to disregard risks that are perceived to be very small, treating them as if the probability of their occurrence was zero. This phenomenon is called zero risk bias (Baron, Gowda, and Kunreuther, 1993). Posner (2003) analyzes the implications of the zero risk bias in tort law, examining the effectiveness of alternative liability regimes in response to this decision-making bias. See also *optimism bias*, *neglect probability bias*, *behavioral law and economics*, and *debiasing*.

Zero-order liability rule: liability-type rules, unlike property-type rules, allow non-consensual takings. A zero-order liability rule is a liability rule that ensures that there will be no non-consensual takings. This is done by setting the liability for the non-consensual takings so high that it effectively discourages any involuntary transfer. The concept of the zero-order liability rule, as used by Ayres (2005), can be viewed as complementary to the concept of the undefinable kicker, introduced by Calabresi and Melamed (1972). A property-type rule can add a kicker for its violation to avoid the possibility of collapse into a mere liability rule. A zero-order liability rule, instead, can set the price for a non-consensual taking so high as to induce every rational person not to infringe the right without the prior consent of the current owner. See also ***undefinable kicker*** and ***property rules versus liability rules***.

Zero-sum games: a category of games, also called pure conflict games or strictly competitive games, in which each player's gain (or loss) is exactly counterbalanced by the loss (or gain) of the other player(s). Analytically, in a zero-sum game the players' payoffs always add up to zero. In a two-player game, let π_1 and π_2 be the payoffs of players 1 and 2; the condition $\pi_1 + \pi_2 = 0$ holds for any possible outcome of the game. The matrix illustrates a zero-sum game in the general case.

		Player 1	
		Strategy X	Strategy Y
Player 2	Strategy X	a,–a	–b,b
	Strategy Y	c,–c	–d,d

For two-player finite zero-sum games, the minimax and maximin strategies yield the same mixed-strategy Nash equilibrium. Analytically equivalent results obtain in constant-sum games, in which the players' payoffs always add up to the same constant sum. Unlike zero-sum and constant-sum games, variable-sum games are characterized by variable aggregate payoff, either positive (positive-sum games) or negative (negative-sum games). In the law and economics literature zero-sum games are the standard illustration for the so-called "pure conflict situations." This is rather intuitive: one player's gain is the other player's loss. In a zero-sum game there is no surplus that parties can pursue through cooperation or coordination. Litigation over a fixed-value claim can be seen as a zero-sum game. However, once litigation costs are taken into consideration, litigation becomes a variable-sum game: the parties can in fact avoid litigation costs by settling their case out of court. See also ***constant-sum games***, ***variable-sum games***, ***inessential games***, ***minimax strategies***, and ***maximin strategies***.

REFERENCES

Ahlborn, Christian, David S. Evans, and A. Jorge Padilla. 2004. "The antitrust economics of tying: a farewell to per se illegality," 49 *Antitrust Bulletin* 287–341.

Ainslie, George W. 1992. *Picoeconomics: The Strategic Interaction of Successive Motivational States within the Person*. Cambridge University Press.

Akerlof, George A. 1970. "The market for 'lemons': quality uncertainty and the market mechanism," 84 *Quarterly Journal of Economics* 488–500.

Akerlof, George A., and Paul M. Romer. 1993. "Looting: the economic underworld of bankruptcy for profit," 1993 *Brookings Papers on Economic Activity* 1–73.

Akerlof, George A., and Janet L. Yellen. 1986. *Efficiency Wage Models of the Labor Market*. Cambridge University Press.

Albert, Max, and Ronald A. Heiner. 2003. "An indirect-evolution approach to Newcomb's problem," 20 *Homo Oeconomicus* 161–94.

Alchian, Armen A., and Harold Demsetz. 1972. "Production, information costs, and economic organization," 62 *American Economic Review* 777–95.

Alesina, Alberto. 1987. "Macroeconomic policy in a two-party system as a repeated game," 102 *Quarterly Journal of Economics* 651–78.

Alesina, Alberto, Ignazio Angeloni, and Ludger Schuknecht. 2005. "What does the European Union do?," 123 *Public Choice* 275–319.

Arlen, Jennifer, and Eric Talley (eds.). 2008. *Experimental Law and Economics*. Cheltenham: Edward Elgar.

Arnold, Craig Anthony. 2002. "The reconstitution of property: property as a web of interests," 26 *Harvard Environmental Law Review* 281–364.

Arrow, Kenneth J. 1951. *Social Choice and Individual Values*. New York: John Wiley.
  1971. "A utilitarian approach to the concept of equality in public expenditure," 85 *Quarterly Journal of Economics* 409–15.
  1973. "The theory of discrimination," in Orley Ashenfelter and Albert Rees (eds.), *Discrimination in Labor Markets*, 3–33. Princeton University Press.

Arrow, Kenneth J., and Anthony C. Fisher. 1974. "Environmental preservation, uncertainty, and irreversibility," 88 *Quarterly Journal of Economics* 312–19.

Arrow, Kenneth J., and Leonid Hurwicz (eds.). 1977. *Studies in Resource Allocation Processes*. Cambridge University Press.

Axelrod, Robert M. 1984. *The Evolution of Cooperation*. New York: Basic Books.

Axelrod, Robert M., and William D. Hamilton. 1981. "The evolution of cooperation," 211 *Science* 1390–6.

Ayres, Ian. 2005. *Optional Law: The Structure of Legal Entitlements*. University of Chicago Press.
  2012. "Regulating opt-out: an economic theory of altering rules," 121 *Yale Law Journal* 2032–117.

Ayres, Ian, and Robert H. Gertner. 1989. "Filling gaps in incomplete contracts: an economic theory of default rules," 99 *Yale Law Journal* 87–130.

1999. "Majoritarian vs. minoritarian defaults," 51 *Stanford Law Review* 1591–613.

Ayres, Ian, and Paul Goldbart. 2001. "Optimal delegation and decoupling in the design of liability rules," 100 *Michigan Law Review* 1–79.

2003. "Correlated values in the theory of property and liability rules," 32 *Journal of Legal Studies* 121–51.

Ayres, Ian, and Eric Talley. 1995. "Solomonic bargaining: dividing a legal entitlement to facilitate Coasean trade," 104 *Yale Law Journal* 1027–117.

Babcock, Linda, George Loewenstein and Samuel Issacharoff. 1997. "Creating convergence: debiasing biased litigants," 22 *Law and Social Inquiry* 401–13.

Babcock, Linda, George Loewenstein, Samuel Issacharoff, and Colin Camerer. 1995. "Biased judgments of fairness in bargaining," 85 *American Economic Review* 1337–43.

Baird, Douglas G., Robert H. Gertner, and Randal C. Picker. 1994. *Game Theory and the Law*. Cambridge, MA: Harvard University Press.

Banerjee, Abhijit V. 1992. "A simple model of herd behavior," 107 *Quarterly Journal of Economics* 797–817.

Baron, Jonathan, Rajeev Gowda, and Howard Kunreuther. 1993. "Attitudes toward managing hazardous waste: what should be cleaned up and who should pay for it," 13 *Risk Analysis* 183–92.

Barton, John H. 1972. "The economic basis of damages for breach of contract," 1 *Journal of Legal Studies* 277–304.

Bastiat, Frédéric. 1850. *Ce qu'on voit et ce qu'on ne voit pas, ou l'économie politique en une leçon* [*That Which Is Seen and That Which Is Unseen, or Political Economy in One Lesson*]. Paris: Guillaumin.

Baumol, William J. 1882. "Contestable markets: an uprising in the theory of industry structure," 72 *American Economic Review* 1–15.

1986. "Williamson's *The Economic Institutions of Capitalism*," 17 *Rand Journal of Economics* 279–92.

Baumol, William J., and Alan S. Blinder. 2011. *Economics: Principles and Policy*, 12th edn. Cincinnati: South-Western College Publishing.

Baumol, William J., John C. Panzar, and Robert D. Willig. 1983. "Contestable markets: an uprising in the theory of industry structure: reply," 73 *American Economic Review* 491–6.

Bebchuk, Lucian A. 1996. "A new theory concerning the credibility and success of threats to sue," 25 *Journal of Legal Studies* 1–25.

Bebchuk, Lucian A., and Alon Klement. 2012. "Negative-expected-value suits," in Chris W. Sanchirico (ed.), *Procedural Law and Economics*, 2nd edn., 341–9. Cheltenham: Edward Elgar.

Beccaria, Cesare. 1764. Dei delitti e delle pene [*On Crimes and Punishments*]. Livorno: Coltellini.

Becker, Gary S. 1968. "Crime and punishment: an economic approach," 78 *Journal of Political Economy* 169–217.

1971. *The Economics of Discrimination*. University of Chicago Press.

1974. "A theory of social interactions," 82 *Journal of Political Economy* 1063–93.

1983. "A theory of competition among pressure groups for political influence," 98 *Quarterly Journal of Economics* 371–400.

Bell, Abraham, and Gideon Parchomovsky. 2002. "Pliability rules," 101 *Michigan Law Review* 1–79.

2003. "Of property and anti-property," 102 *Michigan Law Review* 1–70.

Bell, Tom W. 2010. "Graduated consent in contract and tort law: toward a theory of justification," 61 *Case Western Law Review* 1–68.

Bender, Keith A., and Peter J. Sloane. 1998. "Job satisfaction, trade unions and exit-voice revisited," 51 *Industrial and Labor Relations Review* 222–40.

Bennett, Christopher. 2011. "Expressive punishment and political authority," 8 *Ohio State Journal of Criminal Law* 285–301.

Ben-Shahar, Omri. 2004. "Contracts without consent: exploring a new basis for contractual liability," 152 *University of Pennsylvania Law Review* 1829–72.

Bentham, Jeremy. 1789. *An Introduction to the Principles of Morals and Legislation.* London: T. Payne.

1823. *Leading Principles of a Constitutional Code for Any State.* London: A. Valpy.

1830. *Official Aptitude Maximized, Expense Minimized.* London: R. Heward.

Bergstrom, Ted. 1989. "A fresh look at the rotten kid theorem," 97 *Journal of Political Economy* 1138–59.

Berla, Edward P., Michael L. Brookshire, and Stan V. Smith. 1990. "Hedonic damages and personal injury: a conceptual approach," 3 *Journal of Forensic Economics* 1–8.

Bernholz, Peter. 1982. "Externalities as a necessary condition for cyclical social preferences," 47 *Quarterly Journal of Economics* 699–705.

Bernoulli, Daniel. 1954 [1738]. "Exposition of a new theory on the measurement of risk [trans. Lousie Sommer]," 22 *Econometrica* 22–36.

Bertrand, Joseph. 1883. "Theorie mathematique de la richesse sociale," 67 *Journal des Savants* 499–508.

Bhagwati, Jagdish N. 1982. "Directly unproductive, profit-seeking (DUP) activities," 90 *Journal of Political Economy* 988–1002.

Bikhchandani, Sushil, David Hirshleifer, and Ivo Welch. 1992. "A Theory of fads, fashion, custom, and cultural change as informational cascades," 100 *Journal of Political Economy* 992–1026.

Black, Duncan. 1948. "On the rationale of group decision-making," 56 *Journal of Political Economy* 23–34.

1958. *The Theory of Committees and Elections.* Cambridge University Press.

Blackstone, William. 1766. *Commentaries on the Laws of England.* Oxford: Clarendon Press.

Blair, Roger D., David L. Kaserman, and Richard E. Romano. 1989. "A pedagogical treatment of bilateral monopoly," 55 *Southern Economic Journal* 831–41.

Bork, Robert H. 1978. *The Antitrust Paradox: A Policy at War with Itself.* New York: Basic Books.

Brampton, C. Kenneth. 1964. "Nominalism and the law of parsimony," 41 *The Modern Schoolman* 273–81.

Brennan, Geoffrey, and James M. Buchanan. 1980. *The Power to Tax: Analytical Foundations of a Fiscal Constitution.* Cambridge University Press.

1985. *The Reason of Rules: Constitutional Political Economy.* Cambridge University Press.

Brennan, Geoffrey, Hartmut Kliemt, and Robert D. Tollison (eds.). 2002. *Method and Morals in Constitutional Economics: Essays in Honor of James M. Buchanan.* Berlin: Springer.

Brennan, Geoffrey, and Loren Lomasky. 1993. *Democracy and Decision: The Pure Theory of Electoral Preference*. Cambridge University Press.

Broder, David. 1997. "Age of catatonic politics," *Washington Post*, A19.

Buchanan, James M. 1954. "Individual choice in voting and the market," 62 *Journal of Political Economy* 334–43.

1974. "Good economics – bad law," 60 *Virginia Law Review* 483–92.

1988. "Politics and meddlesome preferences," in Robert D. Tollison (ed.), *Clearing the Air: Perspectives on Environmental Tobacco Smoke*, 107–15. Lanham, MD: Lexington Books.

Buchanan, James M., and Gordon Tullock. 1962. *The Calculus of Consent: Logical Foundations of Constitutional Democracy*. Ann Arbor: University of Michigan Press.

1990. "The domain of constitutional economics," 1 *Constitutional Political Economy* 1–18.

Buchanan, James M., and Yong J. Yoon. 2000. "Symmetric tragedies; commons and anti-commons," 43 *Journal of Law and Economics* 1–14.

Bulow, Jeremy, John Geanakoplos, and Paul Klemperer. 1985. "Multimarket oligopoly: strategic substitutes and strategic complements," 93 *Journal of Political Economy* 488–511.

Calabresi, Guido. 1961. "Some thoughts on risk distributions and the law of torts," 70 *Yale Law Journal* 499–553.

1968. "Transaction costs, resource allocation and liability rules: a comment," 11 *Journal of Law and Economics* 67–73.

1970. *The Costs of Accidents: A Legal and Economic Analysis*. New Haven, CT: Yale University Press.

1980. "An exchange about law and economics: a letter to Ronald Dworkin," 8 *Hofstra Law Review* 553–62.

1991. "The pointlessness of Pareto: carrying Coase further," 100 *Yale Law Journal* 1211–37.

1996. "Address," 6th annual meeting of the American Law and Economics Association, Chicago, May 10.

Calabresi, Guido, and Jeffrey Cooper. 1996. "New directions in tort law," 30 *Valparaiso University Law Review* 859–84.

Calabresi, Guido, and Douglas A. Melamed. 1972. "Property rules, liability rules, and inalienability: one view of the cathedral," 85 *Harvard Law Review* 1089–128.

Carbonara, Emanuela, Barbara Luppi, and Francesco Parisi. 2009. "Self-defeating subsidiarity," 5 *Review of Law and Economics* 741–83.

Carlton, Dennis W., and Michael Waldman. 2002. "The strategic use of tying to preserve and create market power in evolving industries," 33 *Rand Journal of Economics* 194–220.

Castro, Carl A., and Thomas Larsen. 1992. "Primacy and recency effects in nonhuman primates," 18 *Journal of Experimental Psychology: Animal Behavior Processes* 335–40.

Chamberlin, Edward H. 1933. *The Theory of Monopolistic Competition: A Reorientation of the Theory of Value*. Cambridge, MA: Harvard University Press.

Chung, Shin-Ho, and Richard J. Herrnstein. 1961. "Relative and absolute strengths of response as a function of frequency of reinforcement," 4 *Journal of the Experimental Analysis of Animal Behavior* 267–72.

Coase, Ronald H. 1937. "The nature of the firm," 4 *Economica* 386–405.

1959. "The Federal Communications Commission," 2 *Journal of Law and Economics* 1–40.

1960. "The problem of social cost," 3 *Journal of Law and Economics* 1–44.

1988. *The Firm, the Market, and the Law*. University of Chicago Press.

Cohen, Wesley M., and Daniel A. Levinthal. 1990. "Absorptive capacity: a new perspective on learning and innovation," 35 *Administrative Science Quarterly* 128–52.

Coleman, Jules L. 1982. "The economic analysis of law," in J. Roland Pennock and John W. Chapman (eds.), *Nomos XXIV: Ethics, Economics and the Law of Property*, 83–103. New York University Press.

Cooter, Robert D. 1982. "The cost of Coase," 11 *Journal of Legal Studies* 1–33.

1994. "Structural adjudication and the new law merchant: a model of decentralized law," 14 *International Review of Law and Economics* 215–31.

1997. "Punitive damages, social norms, and economic analysis," 60 *Law and Contemporary Problems* 73–91.

1998. "Expressive law and economics," 27 *Journal of Legal Studies* 585–608.

2000a. *The Strategic Constitution*. Princeton University Press.

2000b. "Do good laws make good citizens? An economic analysis of internalized norms," 86 *Virginia Law Review* 1577–601.

Cooter, Robert D., and Melvin Eisenberg. 2000. "Fairness, character, and efficiency in firms," 149 *University of Pennsylvania Law Review* 1717–33.

Cooter, Robert D., Michal Feldman, and Yural Feldman. 2006. "The misperception of norms: the psychology of bias and the economics of equilibrium," unpublished manuscript; available at www.escholarship.org/vc/item/0t6420jb.

Cooter, Robert D., Stephen Marks, and Robert H. Mnookin. 1982. "Bargaining in the shadow of the law: a testable model of strategic behavior," 11 *Economic Analysis* 225–51.

Cooter, Robert D., and Ariel Porat. 2000. "Does harm to self increase the care owed to others? Law and economics in conflict," 29 *Journal of Legal Studies* 19–34.

2002. "Anti-insurance," 31 *Journal of Legal Studies* 203–32.

Cooter, Robert D. and Hans-Bend Schäfer. 2011. *Solomon's Knot: How Law Can End the Poverty of Nations*. Princeton University Press.

Cooter, Robert D., and Thomas Ulen. 1997. *Law and Economics*. 2nd edn. Boston: Addison-Wesley.

2008. *Law and Economics*, 5th edn. Boston: Addison-Wesley.

Cornes, Richard, and Todd Sandler. 1996. *The Theory of Externalities, Public Goods, and Club Goods*, 2nd edn. Cambridge University Press.

Cosmides, Leda, and John Tooby. 2003. "Evolutionary psychology: theoretical foundations," in Lynn Nadel (ed.), *Encyclopedia of Cognitive Science* vol. I, 54–64. London: Macmillan.

Cournot, Antoine-Augustin. 1838. Recherches sur les principes mathématiques de la théorie des richesses [*Researches on the Mathematical Principles of the Theory of Wealth*] Paris: Hachette.

Coursey, Don L., and Linda R. Stanley. 1988. "Pretrial bargaining behavior within the shadow of the law: theory and experimental evidence," 8 *International Review of Law and Economics* 161–79.

Dan-Cohen, Meir. 1984. "Decision rules and conduct rules: on acoustic separation in criminal law," 97 *Harvard Law Review* 625–77.

Dari-Mattiacci, Giuseppe. 2005. "On the optimal Scope of negligence," 1 *Review of Law and Economics* 331–64.

2009. "Negative liability," 38 *Journal of Legal Studies* 21–60.

Dari-Mattiacci, Giuseppe, and Francesco Parisi. 2005a. "Rents, dissipation, and lost treasures: rethinking Tullock's paradox," 124 *Public Choice* 411–22.

2005b. "The economics of tort law: a precis," in Jürgen Backhaus (ed.), *The Elgar Companion to Law and Economics*, 2nd edn., 87–102. Cheltenham: Edward Elgar.

Dari-Mattiacci, Giuseppe, and Gerrit De Geest. 2005. "The filtering effect of sharing rules," 34 *Journal of Legal Studies* 207–37.

2010. "Carrots, sticks, and the multiplication effect," 26 *Journal of Law, Economics, and Organization* 365–84.

Dari-Mattiacci, Giuseppe, Sander Onderstal, and Francesco Parisi. 2011. "Inverse adverse selection: the market for gems," Legal Studies Research Paper no. 10–47, Law School, University of Minnesota.

Davis, Michael. 1991. "Criminal desert, harm, and fairness," 25 *Israel Law Review* 524–48.

De Caritat, Marie-Jean-Antoine-Nicolas. 1785. *Essai sur l'application de l'analyse à la probabilité des décisions rendues à la pluralité des voix [Essay on the Application of Analysis to the Probability of Majority Decisions]* Paris: Imprimerie Royale.

Dekay, Michael L. 1996. "The difference between Blackstone-like error ratios and probabilistic standards of proof," 21 *Law and Social Inquiry* 95–132.

Demsetz, Harold M. 1967. "Toward a theory of property rights," 57 *American Economic Review* 347–59.

1968. "Why regulate utilities?," 11 *Journal of Law and Economics* 55–65.

1972. "When does the rule of liability matter?" 1 *Journal of Legal Studies* 13–28.

1976. "Economics as a guide to antitrust legislation," 19 *Journal of Law and Economics* 371–84.

Depoorter, Ben. 2010. "Law in the shadow of bargaining: the feedback effect of civil settlements," 95 *Cornell Law Review* 957–87.

Depoorter, Ben, Francesco Parisi, and Sven Vanneste. 2005. "Problems with the enforcement of copyright law: is there a social norm backlash?" 12 *International Journal of the Economics of Business* 361–9.

Depoorter, Ben, Alain Van Hiel, and Sven Vanneste. 2011. "Copyright backlash," 84 *Southern California Law Review* 1051–292.

Dixit, Avinash, and Mancur Olson. 2000. "Does voluntary participation undermine the Coase theorem?," 76 *Journal of Public Economics* 309–55.

Dixit, Avinash, and Robert S. Pindyck. 1994. *Investment under Uncertainty*. Princeton University Press.

Dnes, Antony W. 1995. "Franchising and privatization," Note no. 40, World Bank, Public Policy for the Private Sector, Washington, DC.

Dodgson, Charles L. 1876. *A Method for Taking Votes on More than Two Issues*. Oxford: Clarendon Press.

Douglas, Paul H., and Aaron, Director. 1931a. *Unemployment*. London: Macmillan.

1931b. *The Problem of Unemployment*. London: Macmillan.

Downs, Anthony. 1957. *An Economic Theory of Democracy*. Cambridge University Press.

Duff, R. Anthony, and Stuart P. Green. 2011. "Introduction: searching for foundations," in R. Anthony Duff and Stuart P. Green (eds.) *Philosophical Foundations of Criminal Law*, 1–19. Oxford University Press.

Dworkin, Ronald. 1977. *Taking Rights Seriously.* Cambridge, MA: Harvard University Press.

Easterbrook, Frank H., and Daniel R. Fischel. 1985. "Limited liability and the corporation," 52 *University of Chicago Law Review* 89–117.

Edgeworth, Francis Y. 1881. *Mathematical Physics: An Essay on the Application of Mathematics to the Moral Sciences.* London: Kegan.

Edlin, Aaron S. 2007. "A Christmas warning," 4 *Economists' Voice,* http://works.bepress.com/aaron_edlin/47.

Ehrlich, Isaac, and Richard A. Posner. 1974. "An economic analysis of legal rulemaking," 3 *Journal of Legal Studies* 257–86.

Ellickson, Robert C. 1991. *Order without Law: How Neighbors Settle Disputes.* Cambridge, MA: Harvard University Press.

  2001. "The market for social norms," 3 *American Law and Economic Review* 1–49.

Elster, Jon. 1983. "The crisis in economic theory," 5 *London Review of Books* 5–7.

  1986. *Rational Choice.* Oxford: Basil Blackwell.

Emons, Winand, and Nuno Garoupa. 2004. "The economics of US-style contingent fees and UK-style conditional fees," Discussion Paper no. 0407, Department of Political Economy, University of Bern.

Epstein, Richard A. 1985. *Takings: Private Property and the Power of Eminent Domain.* Cambridge, MA: Harvard University Press.

  1993. "Holdouts, externalities, and the single owner: one more salute to Ronald Coase," 36 *Journal of Law and Economics* 553–86.

  1995a. *Simple Rules for a Complex World.* Cambridge, MA: Harvard University Press.

  1995b. "The harm principle – and how it grew," 45 *University of Toronto Law Journal* 369–417.

Etner, Johanna, Meglena Jeleva, and Jean-Marc Tallon. 2009. "Decision theory under uncertainty," Working Paper no. 09064, Centre d'Economie, Université Panthéon-Sorbonne, Paris.

Fama, Eugene F. 1965. "The behavior of stock-market prices," 38 *Journal of Business* 34–105.

Faure, Michael (ed.). 2009. *Tort Law and Economics.* Cheltenham: Edward Elgar.

Feeley, Andrew, and David Schap. 2006. "(Much) more on the collateral source rule," paper presented at the Eastern Economic Association meeting, Philadelphia, February 25.

Fehr, Ernst, Oliver Hart, and Christian Zehnder. 2011. "Contracts as reference points: experimental evidence," 101 *American Economic Review* 493–525.

Fehr, Ernst, and Klaus M. Schmidt. 1999. "A theory of fairness, competition, and cooperation," 114 *Quarterly Journal of Economics* 817–68.

Fisher, Ronald A. 1949. *The Design of Experiments,* 5th edn. London: Oliver & Boyd.

Fon, Vincy, and Francesco Parisi. 2003. "Reciprocity-induced cooperation," 159 *Journal of Institutional and Theoretical Economics* 76–92.

  2005. 'The behavioral foundations of retaliatory justice," 7 *Journal of Bioeconomics* 45–72.

Fon, Vincy, Francesco Parisi, and Ben Depoorter. 2005. "Litigation, judicial path dependence, and legal change," 20 *European Journal of Law and Economics* 43–56.

Forsythe, Robert, Joel L. Horowitz, N. E. Savin, and Martin Sefton. 1994. "Fairness in simple bargaining experiments," 6 *Games and Economic Behavior* 347–69.

Frederick, Shane, George Loewenstein and Ted O'Donoghue. 2002. "Time discounting and time preference: a critical review," 40 *Journal of Economic Literature* 351–401.

Frey, Bruno S., and Alois Stutzer, 2008. "The thirst for happiness," 1 *Journal of International Business Ethics* 7–17.

Fried, Charles. 1981. *Contract as Promise: A Theory of Contractual Obligation.* Cambridge, MA: Harvard University Press.

Friedman, David D. 2000. *Law's Order: What Economics Has to Do with Law and Why It Matters.* Princeton University Press.

Friedman, Milton. 1953. *Essays in Positive Economics.* University of Chicago Press.

   1957. *A Theory of the Consumption Function.* Princeton University Press.

   1958. "The permanent income hypothesis: comment," 48 *American Economic Review* 990–1.

   1962. *Capitalism and Freedom.* University of Chicago Press.

   1976. *Price Theory.* Piscataway, NJ: Transaction.

Friedman, Milton, and Anna Jacobson Schwartz. 1963. *A Monetary History of the United States, 1867–1960.* Princeton University Press.

   1981. *Monetary Trends in the United States and the United Kingdom: Their Relation to Income, Prices, and Interest Rates, 1867–1975.* University of Chicago Press.

Fuller, Lon, and William R. Perdue. 1936. "The reliance interest in contract damages," 46 *Yale Law Journal* 52–96.

Furnham, Adrian. 1986. "The robustness of the recency effect: studies using legal evidence," 133 *Journal of General Psychology* 351–7.

Garoupa, Nuno, and Matteo Rizzolli. 2008. "Why pro-defendant criminal procedure might hurt the innocent," Working Paper no. 137, Department of Economics, University of Milano – Bicocca.

Geanakoplos, John, David W. Pearce, and Ennio Stacchetti. 1989. "Psychological games and sequential rationality," 1 *Games and Economic Behavior* 60–80.

Gibbard, Allan. 1973. "Manipulation of voting schemes: a general result," 41 *Econometrica* 665–81.

Gintis, Herbert. 2000. "Strong reciprocity and human sociality," 206 *Journal of Theoretical Biology* 169–79.

Glaeser, Edward, and Andrei Shleifer. 2002. "Legal origins," 117 *Quarterly Journal of Economics* 1193–229.

Gneezy, Uri, and Aldo Rustichini. 2000. "A fine is a price," 29 *Journal of Legal Studies* 1–17.

Goetz, Charles J., and Robert E. Scott. 1977. "Liquidated damages, penalties and the just compensation principle: some notes of an enforcement model and a theory of efficient breach," 77 *Columbia Law Review* 554–94.

   1980. "Enforcing promises: an examination of the basis of contract," 89 *Yale Law Journal* 1261–300.

Gordon, H. Scott. 1954. "The economic theory of common-property resource: the fishery," 62 *Journal of Political Economy* 124–42.

Grady, Mark F. 1983. "A new positive theory of negligence," 92 *Yale Law Journal* 799–829.

   1988. "Why are people negligent? Technology, nondurable precautions, and the medical malpractice explosion," 82 *Northwestern University Law Review* 293–334.

Granger, Clive W. J. 1969. "Investigating causal relations by econometric models and cross-spectral methods," 37 *Econometrica* 424–38.

Granovetter, Mark. 1985. "Economic action and social structure: the problem of embeddedness," 91 *American Journal of Sociology* 481–510.

Grey, Thomas C. 1980. "The disintegration of property," in Roland Pennock and John W. Chapman (eds.) *Property*, 69–85. New York University Press.

Grossman, Sanford J., and Joseph Stiglitz. 1976. "Information and competitive price systems," 66 *American Economic Review* 246–53.

Grotius, Hugo. 1625. *De Jure Belli ac Pacis [Law of War and Peace]*, Paris: Buon.

Grundmann, Stefan, Wolfgang Kerber, and Stephen Weatherill. 2001. *Party Autonomy and the Role of Information in the Internal Market*. Berlin: Walter de Gruyter.

Guttel, Ehud. 2004. "Overcorrection," 93 *Georgetown Law Journal* 241–83.

Hansmann, Henry, and Reiner Kraakman. 1991. "Toward unlimited shareholder liability for corporate torts," 100 *Yale Law Journal* 1879–934.

Hardin, Garrett. 1968. "The tragedy of the commons," 162 *Science* 1243–8.

Harris, Milton, and Artur Raviv. 1981. "Allocation mechanisms and the design of auctions," 49 *Econometrica* 1477–500.

Harsanyi, John C. 1953. "Cardinal utility in welfare economics and in the theory of risk-taking," 61 *Journal of Political Economy* 434–5.

  1955. "Cardinal welfare, individualistic ethics, and interpersonal comparisons of utility," 63 *Journal of Political Economy* 309–21.

  1975. "Can the maximin principle serve as a basis for morality? A critique of John Rawls's theory," 69 *American Political Science Review* 594–606.

Hart, Oliver. 2009. "Hold-up, asset ownership, and reference points," 124 *Quarterly Journal of Economics* 267–300.

  2011. "Noncontractible investments and reference points," Working Paper no. 16929, National Bureau of Economic Research, Cambridge, MA.

Hart, Oliver, and John Moore. 1988a. "Incomplete contracts and renegotiation," 56 *Econometrica* 755–85.

  1988b. "Incomplete contracts and the theory of the firm," 4 *Journal of Law, Economics, and Organization* 119–39.

  1990. "Property rights and the nature of the firm," 98 *Journal of Political Economy* 1119–58.

  2008. "Contracts as reference points," 123 *The Quarterly Journal of Economics* 1–48.

Hayek, Friedrich. 1944. *The Road to Serfdom*. University of Chicago Press.

Heller, Michael A. 1998. "The tragedy of the anticommons: property in the transition from Marx to markets," 111 *Harvard Law Review* 621–88.

  1999. "The boundaries of private property," 108 *Yale Law Journal* 1163–223.

Henry, Claude. 1974. "Investment decisions under uncertainty: the irreversibility effect," 64 *American Economic Review* 1006–12.

Hicks, John R. 1932. *The Theory of Wages*. London: Macmillan.

  1939. "The foundations of welfare economics," 49 *Economic Journal* 696–712.

Hillman, Arye L., and Dov Samet. 1987. "Dissipation of contestable rents by small numbers of contenders," 54 *Public Choice* 63–82.

Hirshleifer, Jack. 1983. "From weakest-link to best-shot: the voluntary provision of public goods," 41 *Public Choice* 371–86.

  1985. "From Weakest-Link to Best-Shot: Correction," 46 *Public Choice* 221–23.

Hirschman, Albert O. 1970. *Exit, Voice, and Loyalty: Responses to Decline in Firms, Organizations, and States*. Cambridge, MA: Harvard University Press.

Hobbes, Thomas. 1651. *Leviathan, or The Matter, Forme and Power of a Common Wealth Ecclesiasticall and Civil*. London: Andrew Cooke.

Hodgson, David H. 1967. *Consequences of Utilitarianism*. Oxford University Press.

Hotelling, Harold. 1929. "Stability in competition," 39 *Economic Journal* 41–57.

1931. "The generalization of student's ratio," 2 *Annals of Mathematical Statistics* 360–78.

Hurwicz, Leonid. 1972. "On informationally decentralized systems," in C. B. McGuire and Roy Radner, eds. *Decision and Organization: A Volume in Honor of Jacob Marschak*, 2nd edn., 297–336. Minneapolis: University of Minnesota Press.

Inman, Robert P., and Daniel L. Rubinfeld. 1997. "Rethinking federalism," 11 *Journal of Economic Perspectives* 43–64.

1998. "Subsidiarity and the European Union," Working Paper no. 6556, National Bureau of Economic Research, Cambridge, MA.

Jolls, Christine, and Cass R. Sunstein. 2006a. "Debiasing through law," 35 *Journal of Legal Studies* 199–241.

2006b. "The law of implicit bias," 94 *California Law Review* 969–96.

Jolls, Christine, Cass R. Sunstein, and Richard Thaler. 1998. "A behavioral approach to law and economics," 50 *Stanford Law Review* 1471–550.

Kahan, Dan M. 1998. "Social meaning and the economic analysis of crime," 27 *Journal of Legal Studies* 609–22.

2000. "Gentle nudges vs. hard shoves: solving the sticky norms problem," 67 *University of Chicago Law Review* 607–45.

Kahan, Dan M., and Eric A. Posner. 1999. "Slamming white-collar criminals: a proposal for reform of the federal sentencing guidelines," 42 *Journal of Law and Economics* 365–92.

Kahan, Marcel. 1989. "Causation and incentives to take care under the negligence rule," 18 *Journal of Legal Studies* 427–47.

Kahneman, Daniel. 2002. "Maps of bounded rationality: a perspective on intuitive judgment and choice," Nobel lecture, December 8, Stockholm.

Kahneman, Daniel, and Amos Tversky. 1973. "On the psychology of prediction," 80 *Psychological Review* 237–51.

1979. "Prospect theory: an analysis of decision under risk," 47 *Econometrica* 313–27.

Kalai, Ehud. 1977. "Proportional solutions to bargaining situations: interpersonal utility comparisons," 45 *Econometrica* 1623–30.

Kaldor, Nicholas. 1939. "Welfare propositions in economics and interpersonal comparisons of utility," 49 *Economic Journal* 549–52.

Kaneko, Mamoru, and Kenjiro Nakamura. 1979. "The Nash social welfare function," 47 *Econometrica* 423–35.

Kant, Immanuel. 1781. *Critik der reinen Vernunft* [*The Critique of Pure Reason*] Riga: Hartknoch.

Kaplow, Louis. 1992. "The optimal probability and magnitude of fines for acts that definitely are undesirable," 12 *International Review of Law and Economics* 3–11.

Kaplow, Louis, and Steven M. Shavell. 1994. "Why the legal system is less efficient than the income tax in redistributing income," 23 *Journal of Legal Studies* 667–81.

1996. "Property rules versus liability rules: an economic analysis," 109 *Harvard Law Review* 713–90.

2001. "Fairness versus welfare," 114 *Harvard Law Review* 961–1388.

2002. *Fairness versus Welfare*. Cambridge, MA: Harvard University Press.

Kassin, Saul M., and Lawrence S. Wrightsman. 1979. "On the requirements of proof: the timing of judicial instruction and mock juror verdicts," 37 *Journal of Personality and Social Psychology*, 1877–87.

Katz, Avery W., and Chris William Sanchirico. 2010. "Fee shifting in litigation: survey and assessment", Research Paper no. 10–30, Institute for Law and Economics, University of Pennsylvania.

Kaye, David H., David A. Freedman, David L. Faigman, Michael J. Saks, Joseph Sanders, and Edward K. Cheng. 2010. *Modern Scientific Evidence: The Law and Science of Expert Testimony*. St. Paul, MN: West Publishing.

Kerin, Roger A., R. Rajan Varadarajan, and Robert A. Peterson. 1992. "First-mover advantage: a synthesis, conceptual framework, and research propositions," 56 *Journal of Marketing* 33–52.

Kessler, Friedrich. 1943. "Contracts of adhesion: some thoughts about freedom of contracts," 43 *Columbia Law Review* 629–42.

Kim, Pauline. 1999. "Norms, learning, and law: exploring the influences on workers' legal knowledge," 1999 *University of Illinois Law Review* 447–515.

Kingdon, John W. 1995. *Agendas, Alternatives, and Public Policy*, 2nd edn. New York: HarperCollins College Publishers.

Llick, Jonathan, and Francesco, Parisi. 2005. "Wealth, utility and the human dimension," 1 *New York University Journal of Law and Liberty* 590–608.

Kronman, Anthony T. 1985. "Contract law and the state of nature," 1 *Journal of Law, Economics, and Organization* 5–32.

Kuhn, Thomas. 1962. *The Structure of Scientific Revolutions*. University of Chicago Press.

Laffer, Arthur. 2004. "The Laffer curve: past, present, and future," Heritage Foundation; available at www.heritage.org/research/reports/2004/06/the-laffer-curve-past-present-and-future.

Laibson, David. 1997. "Golden eggs and hyperbolic discounting," 112 *Quarterly Journal of Economics* 443–77.

Landes, William, H. and Richard A. Posner 1987. *The Economic Structure of Tort Law*. Cambridge, MA: Harvard University Press.

Laycock, Douglas. 2009. "Voting with your feet is no substitute for constitutional rights," 32 *Harvard Journal of Law and Public Policy* 29–44.

Leibenstein, Harvey. 1978. *General X-Efficiency Theory and Economic Development*. New York: Oxford University Press.

Lindbeck, Assar, and Jörgen W. Weibull. 1988. "Altruism and efficiency: the economics of fait accompli," 96 *Journal of Political Economy*, 1165–82.

Lloyd, William Forster. 1833. *Two Lectures on the Checks to Population*. Oxford University Press.

Loewenstein, George, and Drazen Prelec. 1992. *Choices over Time*. New York: Russell Sage Foundation.

Lundberg, Shelly, and Robert A. Pollak 2003. "Efficiency in marriage," 1 *Review of the Economics of the Household* 153–67.

Luce, R. Duncan, and Howard Raiffa. 1957. *Games and Decisions: Introduction and Critical Survey*. New York: John Wiley.

Luppi, Barbara, and Francesco Parisi. 2011. "Toward an asymmetric Coase theorem," 31 *European Journal of Law and Economics* 111–22.

2012a. "Politics with(out) Coase," 59 *International Review of Economics* 175–87.

2012b. "Jury size and the hung-jury paradox," Legal Studies Research Paper no. 12–01, Law School, University of Minnesota.

Luppi, Barbara, Francesco Parisi, and Daniel Pi. 2012. "Double-edged torts," Legal Studies Research Paper no. 12–57, Law School, University of Minnesota.

Malloy, Robin Paul. 1988. "Invisible hand or sleight of hand? Adam Smith, Richard Posner and the philosophy of law and economics," 36 *University of Kansas Law Review* 209–59.

Mandeville, Bernard. 1714. *The Fable of the Bees: or, Private Vices, Publick Benefits.* London: Edmund Parker.

Manne, Henry G. 1965. "Mergers and the market for corporate control," 73 *Journal of Political Economy* 110–20.

1966. *Insider Trading and the Stock Market.* New York: Free Press.

Markovits, Daniel. 2004. "The no-retraction principle and the morality of negotiations," 152 *University of Pennsylvania Law Review* 1903–21.

Markovits, Richard S. 2008. *Truth or Economics: On the Definition, Prediction, and Relevance of Economic Efficiency.* New Haven, CT: Yale University Press.

Markowitz, Harry M. 1952. "Portfolio selection," 7 *Journal of Finance* 77–91.

Marongiu, Pietro, and Graeme Newman. 1987. *Vengeance: The Fight Against Injustice.* Totowa, NJ: Rowman & Littlefield.

Marshall, Alfred. 1890. *Principles of Economics.* London: Macmillan.

Marshall, Kevin, and Patrick Fitzgerald. 2005. "The collateral source rule and its abolition: an economic perspective," 15 *Kansas Journal of Law and Public Policy* 56–84.

Marx, Karl. 1993 [1857]. *Grundrisse* (trans. Martin Nicolaus). London: Penguin Books.

Maynard Smith, John, and George Price. 1973. "The logic of animal conflict," 245 *Nature* 15–18.

McAdams, Richard H. 1992. "Relative preferences," 102 *Yale Law Journal* 1–104.

2000. "A focal point theory of expressive law," 86 *Virginia Law Review* 1649–729.

McDonald, Robert and Daniel R. Siegel. 1986. "The value of waiting to invest," 101 *Quarterly Journal of Economics* 707–27.

McDonnell, Brett. 2007. "Sticky defaults and altering rules in corporate law," 60 *Southern Methodist University Law Review* 383–440.

Merges, Robert P. 2005. "A transactional view of property rights," 20 *Berkeley Technology Law Journal* 1477–520.

Michelman, Frank I. 1982. *Ethics, Economics, and the Law of Property.* New York University Press.

Mises, Ludwig von. 1966. *Human Action: A Treatise on Economics,* 3rd edn. Chicago: Henry Regnery.

Mnookin, Robert H., and Lewis Kornhauses. 1979. "Bargaining in the shadow of the law: the case of divorce," 88 *Yale Law Journal* 950–97.

Mueller, Dennis C. 2003. *Public Choice III.* Cambridge University Press.

Mukhopadhaya, Kaushik. 2003. "Jury size and the free rider problem," 19 *Journal of Law, Economics, and Organization* 24–44.

Murdock, Jr., Bennet B. 1962. "The serial position effect of free recall," 64 *Journal of Experimental Psychology* 482–8.

Muris, Timothy J. 1983. "Cost of completion or diminution in market value: the relevance of subjective value," 12 *Journal of Legal Studies* 379–400.

Muth, John F. 1960. "Optimal properties of exponentially weighted forecasts," 55 *Journal of the American Statistical Association* 299–306.

1961. "Rational expectations and the theory of price movements," 29 *Econometrica* 315–35.

Myerson, Roger B. 1978. "Refinements of the Nash equilibrium concept," 7 *International Journal of Game Theory* 73–80.

Nash, John F. 1950a. "Equilibrium points in n-person games," 36 *Proceedings of the National Academy of Sciences* 48–9.

1950b. "The bargaining problem," 18 *Econometrica* 155–62.

1951. "Non-cooperative games," 54 *Annals of Mathematics* 286–95.

1953. "Two-person cooperative games," 21 *Econometrica* 128–40.

Nelson, Phillip. 1970. "Information and consumer behavior," 78 *Journal of Political Economy* 311–29.

Neyman, Jerzy, and Egon S. Pearson. 1928. "On the use and interpretation of certain test criteria for purposes of statistical inference," 20 *Biometrika* 175–240.

North, Douglass C. 1990. *Institutions, Institutional Change and Economic Performance.* Cambridge University Press.

Nozick, Robert. 1969. "Newcomb's problem and two principles of choice," in Nicholas Rescher (ed.), *Essays in Honour of Carl G. Hempel*, 107–33. Dordrecht: Reidel.

1974. *Anarchy, State, and Utopia.* New York: Basic Books.

Nussbaum, Martha C. 2000. *Women and Human Development: The Capabilities Approach.* Cambridge University Press.

Nussbaum, Martha C., and Amartya Sen (eds.). 1993. *The Quality of Life.* Oxford University Press.

Oates, Wallace E. 1972. *Fiscal Federalism.* New York: Harcourt Brace Jovanovich.

1985. "Searching for Leviathan: an empirical study," 75 *American Economic Review* 748–57.

Oi, Walter Y. 1971. "A Disneyland dilemma: two-part tariffs for a Mickey Mouse monopoly," 85 *Quarterly Journal of Economics* 77–96.

Olson, Mancur. 1965. *The Logic of Collective Action: Public Goods and the Theory of Groups.* Boston: Harvard University Press.

1982. *The Rise and Decline of Nations: Economic Growth, Stagflation, and Social Rigidities.* New Haven, CT: Yale University Press.

Ostrom, Elinor. 1990. *Governing the Commons: The Evolution of Institutions for Collective Action.* New York: Cambridge University Press.

Ostrom, Elinor, Roy Gardner, and James Walker. 1994. *Rules, Games and Common-Pool Resources.* Ann Arbor: University of Michigan Press.

Panzar, John C., and Robert D. Willig. 1977. "Economies of scale in multi-output production," 91 *Quarterly Journal of Economics* 481–93.

Parchomovsky, Gideon, and Alex Stein. 2010. "The distortionary effect of evidence on primary behavior," 124 *Harvard Law Review* 518–48.

Pareto, Vilfredo. 1897. "The new theories of economics," 5 *Journal of Political Economy* 488–502.

Parisi, Francesco. 2000. "Spontaneous emergence of law: customary law," in Boudewijn Bouckaert and Gerrit De Geest (eds.). *Encyclopedia of Law and Economics,* vol. V, *The Economics of Crime and Litigation*, 603–30. Cheltenham: Edward Elgar.

2001. "The genesis of liability in ancient law," 3 *American Law and Economics Review* 82–124.

2002. "Entropy in property," 50 *American Journal of Comparative Law* 595–622.

2003. "Political Coase theorem," 115 *Public Choice* 1–36.

2004. "The harmonization of legal warranties in European sales law: an economic analysis," 52 *American Journal of Comparative Law* 403–31.

2007. "The fall and rise of functional property," in Donatella Porrini and Giovanni Ramello (eds.), *Property Rights Dynamics: A Law and Economics Perspective*, 19–39. Abingdon: Routledge.

Parisi, Francesco, and Vincy Fon. 2004. "Comparative causation," 6 *American Law and Economics Review*, 345–68.

2009. *The Economics of Lawmaking*. Oxford University Press.

Parisi, Francesco, Vincy Fon, and Nita Ghei. 2004. "The value of waiting in lawmaking," 18 *European Journal of Law and Economics* 131–48.

Parisi, Francesco, Barbara Luppi, and Vincy Fon. 2011. "Optimal remedies for bilateral contracts," 40 *Journal of Legal Studies* 245–71.

Parisi, Francesco, Norbert Schulz, and Ben Depoorter. 2005. "Duality in property: commons and anticommons," 25 *International Review of Law and Economics* 578–91.

Parisi, Francesco, Norbert Schulz, and Jonathan Klick. 2006. "Two dimensions of regulatory competition," 26 *International Review of Law and Economics* 56–66.

Parisi, Francesco, and Ram Singh. 2010. "The efficiency of comparative causation," 6 *Review of Law and Economics*; available at ideas.repec.org/a/bpj/rlecon/v6y2010i2n5.html.

Parisi, Francesco, and Georg von Wangenheim. 2006. "Legislation and countervailing effects from social norms," in Christian Schubert and Georg von Wangenheim (eds.), *Evolution and Design of Institutions*, 25–55. Abingdon: Routledge.

Pearson, Karl. 1905. *On the General Theory of Skew Correlation and Non-Linear Regression*. London: Dulau.

Peltzman, Sam. 1990. "How efficient is the voting market?," 33 *Journal of Law and Economics* 27–63.

Pigou, Arthur C. 1920. *The Economics of Welfare*. London: Macmillan.

Pindyck, Robert S. 1991. "Irreversibility, uncertainty and investment," 29 *Journal of Economic Literature* 1110–48.

Plato. 1953 [355BC]. *The Dialogues of Plato*, vol. IV, *The Laws* (trans. Benjamin Jowett), 4th edn. Oxford: Clarendon Press.

Plott, Charles R., and Kathryn Zeiler. 2007. "Exchange asymmetries incorrectly interpreted as evidence of endowment effect theory and prospect theory?," 97 *American Economic Review* 1449–66.

Polinsky, A. Mitchell. 1980. "Strict liability vs. negligence in a market setting," 70 *American Economic Review* 363–70.

1989. *An Introduction to Law and Economics*, 2nd edn. Boston: Little, Brown.

Polinsky, A. Mitchell and Yeon-Koo Che. 1991. "Decoupling liability: optimal incentives for care and litigation," 22 *RAND Journal of Economics* 562–70.

Polinsky, A. Mitchell, and Steven Shavell. 2007. "The theory of public enforcement of law," in A. Mitchell Polinsky and Steven Shavell (eds.), *Handbook of Law and Economics*, vol. I, 403–54. Amsterdam: North-Holland.

Pollak, Robert A. 1976. "Interdependent preferences," 66 *American Economic Review* 309–20.

Popitz, Johannes. 1927. "Der Finanzausgleich," in *Handbuch der Finanzwissenschaft*, vol. II, 338–75. Tübingen: T. C. B. Mohr.

Popper, Karl. 1959. *The Logic of Scientific Discovery*. London: Hutchinson.

Porat, Ariel, and Avraham Tabbach. 2011. "Willingness to pay, death, wealth, and damages," 13 *American Law and Economics Review* 45–102.

Posner, Eric A. 2003. "Probability errors: some positive and normative implications for tort and contract law," 11 *Supreme Court Economic Review* 125–41.

  2006. "There are no penalty default rules in contract law," 33 *Florida State University Law Review* 563–87.

Posner, Eric A., and Cass R. Sunstein. 2010. *Law and Happiness*. University of Chicago Press.

Posner, Richard A. 1975. "The social costs of monopoly and regulation," 83 *Journal of Political Economy* 807–27.

  1976. *Antitrust Law: An Economic Perspective*. University of Chicago Press.

  1979. "Utilitarianism, economics, and legal theory," 8 *Journal of Legal Studies* 103–40.

  1981. *The Economics of Justice*. Cambridge, MA: Harvard University Press.

  1981. "The positive economic theory of tort law," 15 *Georgia Law Review* 851–924.

  1985. "Wealth maximization revisited," 2 *Notre Dame Journal of Law, Ethics and Public Policy* 85–105.

  1988. "The ethics of wealth maximization: reply to Malloy," 36 *University of Kansas Law Review* 261–5.

  1990a. *Cardozo: A Study in Reputation*. University of Chicago Press.

  1990b. *The Problems of Jurisprudence*. Cambridge, MA: Harvard University Press.

  1992a. *Sex and Reason*. Cambridge, MA: Harvard University Press.

  1992b. *The Essential Holmes: Selections from the Letters, Speeches, Judicial Opinions, and Other Writings of Oliver Wendell Holmes, Jr.* University of Chicago Press.

  1994. "What do judges and justices maximize? (The same thing everybody else does)," 3 *Supreme Court Economic Review* 1–41.

  1995. *Overcoming Law*. Cambridge, MA: Harvard University Press.

  1996a. *Law and Legal Theory in England and America*. Oxford University Press.

  1996b. *The Federal Courts: Challenge and Reform*, rev. edn. Cambridge, MA: Harvard University Press.

  1998. *Law and Literature*, 2nd edn. Cambridge, MA: Harvard University Press.

  1999. *The Problematics of Moral and Legal Theory*. Cambridge, MA: Belknap Press.

  2001. *Antitrust Law*, 2nd edn. University of Chicago Press.

  2003. *"Law, Pragmatism, and Democracy*. Cambridge, MA: Harvard University Press.

  2004. *Catastrophe: Risk and Response*. New York: Oxford University Press.

  2005. *Preventing Surprise Attacks: Intelligence Reform in the Wake of 9/11*. Lanham, MD: Rowman & Littlefield.

  2010. *Economic Analysis of Law*, 8th edn. New York: Aspen Law & Business.

Postema, Gerald J. 1986. *Bentham and the Common Law Tradition*. New York: Clarendon Press.

Priest, George L. 1977. "The common law process and the selection of efficient rules," 6 *Journal of Legal Studies* 65–82.

  1981. "A theory of the consumer product warranty," 90 *Yale Law Journal* 1297–352.

1985. "Reexamining the selection hypothesis: learning from Wittman's mistakes," 14 *Journal of Legal Studies* 215–43.

2010. "Market share liability in personal injury and public nuisance litigation: an economic analysis," 18 *Supreme Court Economic Review* 109–33.

Priest, George L., and Benjamin Klein. 1984. "The selection of disputes for litigation," 13 *Journal of Legal Studies* 1–55.

Pronin, Emily, and Matthew B. Kugler. 2007. "Valuing thoughts, ignoring behavior: the introspection illusion as a source of the bias blind spot," 43 *Journal of Experimental Social Psychology* 565–78.

Pronin, Emily, Daniel Y. Lin, and Lee Ross. 2002. "The bias blind spot: perceptions of bias in self versus others," 28 *Personality and Social Psychology Bulletin* 369–81.

Rabin, Matthew. 1993. "Incorporating fairness into game theory and economics," 83 *American Economic Review* 1281–302.

2002. "Inference by believers in the law of small numbers," 117 *Quarterly Journal of Economics* 775–816.

Rae, John. 1834. *Statements of Some New Principles on the Subject of Political Economy.* Boston: Hillard, Gray.

Ramsey, Frank P. 1927. "A contribution to the theory of taxation," 37 *Economic Journal* 543–59.

Rasmusen, Eric B. 1996. "Stigma and self-fulfilling expectations of criminality," 39 *Journal of Law and Economics* 519–44.

Rawls, John B. 1971. *A Theory of Justice.* Cambridge, MA: Belknap Press.

1993. *Political Liberalism.* New York: Columbia University Press.

1999. *The Law of Peoples.* Cambridge, MA: Harvard University Press.

2001. *Justice as Fairness: A Restatement.* Cambridge, MA: Harvard University Press.

Redelmeier, Donald A., and Daniel Kahneman. 1996. "Patients' memories of painful medical treatments: real-time and retrospective evaluations of two minimally invasive procedures," 66 *Pain* 3–8.

Regan, Donald H. 1980. *Utilitarianism and Co-operation.* Oxford: Clarendon Press.

Ricardo, David. 1817. *On the Principles of Political Economy and Taxation.* London: John Murray.

Riker, William H. 1986. *The Art of Political Manipulation.* New Haven, CT: Yale University Press.

Rizzo, Mario J., and Frank S. Arnold. 1980. "Causal apportionment in the law of torts: an economic theory," 80 *Columbia Law Review* 1399–429.

Rizzolli, Matteo, and Margherita Saraceno. 2009. "Better that X guilty persons escape than that one innocent suffer," Working Paper no. 168, Department of Economics, University of Milan – Bicocca.

Robbins, Lionel. 1935. *An Essay on the Nature and Significance of Economic Science*, 2nd edn. London: Macmillan.

Robinson, Joan. 1933. *The Economics of Imperfect Competition.* London: Macmillan.

Rochet, Jean-Charles, and Jean Tirole. 2004. "Two-sided markets: An overview," working paper, Institut d'Economie Industrielle, Toulouse.

Rose, Carol M. 1985. "Possession as the origin of property," 52 *University of Chicago Law Review* 73–88.

1994. *Property and Persuasion: Essays on the History, Theory, and Rhetoric of Ownership.* Boulder, CO: Westview.

Rothschild, Michael, and Joseph Stiglitz. 1976. "Equilibrium in competitive insurance markets: an essay on the economics of imperfect information," 90 *Quarterly Journal of Economics* 629–49.

Rowley, Charles K. 1984. "The relevance of the median voter theorem," 140 *Journal of Institutional and Theoretical Economics* 104–26.

1989. "The common law in public perspective: a theoretical and institutional critique," 12 *Hamline Law Review* 355–83.

Rubin, Paul H. 1977. "Why is the common law efficient?," 6 *Journal of Legal Studies* 51–63.

Salop, Steven C. 1979. "Monopolistic competition with outside goods," 10 *Bell Journal of Economics* 141–56.

Samuelson, Paul A. 1938. "A note on the pure theory of consumer's behaviour," 5 *Economica* 61–71.

1950. "The problem of integrability in utility theory," 17 *Economica* 355–85.

1954. "The pure theory of public expenditure," 36 *Review of Economics and Statistics* 387–9.

1955. "Diagrammatic exposition of a theory of public expenditure," 37 *Review of Economics and Statistics* 350–6.

Sanchirico, Chris W. 2000. "Taxes versus legal rules as instruments for equity: a more equitable view," 29 *Journal of Legal Studies* 797–820.

Sandler, Todd. 2001. "On financing global and international public goods," Policy Research Working Paper no. 2638, World Bank, Washington, DC.

2006. "Regional public goods and international organizations," 1 *Review of International Organizations* 5–25.

Schelling, Thomas C. 1960. *The Strategy of Conflict*. Cambridge, MA: Harvard University Press.

1966. *Arms and Influence*. New Haven, CT: Yale University Press.

Schkade, David, Cass R. Sunstein, and Daniel Kahneman. 2000. "Do people want optimal deterrence?," 29 *Journal of Legal Studies* 237–53.

Schulz, Norbert, Francesco Parisi, and Ben Depoorter. 2002. "Fragmentation in property: towards a general model," 158 *Journal of Institutional and Theoretical Economics* 594–613.

Schumpeter, Joseph A. 1994 [1942]. *Capitalism, Socialism and Democracy*. London: Routledge.

Schweizer, Urs. 2006. "Cooperative investments induced by contract law," 37 *RAND Journal of Economics* 134–45.

Scitovsky, Tibor. 1941. "A note on welfare propositions in economics," 9 *Review of Economic Studies* 77–88.

Scott, Robert E., and Jody S. Kraus. 2007. *Contract Law and Theory*, 4th edn. Newark, NJ: Matthew Bender.

Scott, Robert Haney. 1972. "Avarice, altruism, and second party preferences," 86 *Quarterly Journal of Economics* 1–18.

Seidmann, Daniel. 2005. "The effects of the right to silence," 72 *Review of Economic Studies* 593–614.

Seidmann, Daniel, and Alex Stein. 2000. "The right to silence helps the innocent: a game-theoretic analysis of the Fifth Amendment privilege," 114 *Harvard Law Review* 430–510.

Selten, Reinhard. 1975. "Re-examination of the perfectness concept for equilibrium points in extensive games," 4 *International Journal of Game Theory* 25–55.

1978. "The chain store paradox," 9 *Theory and Decision* 127–59.

Sen, Amartya. 1970a. *Collective Choice and Social Welfare*. San Francisco: Holden-Day.

1970b. "The impossibility of a Paretian liberal," 78 *Journal of Political Economy* 152–7.

1977. "Rational fools: a critique of the behavioral foundations of economic theory," 6 *Philosophy and Public Affairs* 317–44.

1985. *Commodities and Capabilities*. Oxford: Elsevier.

1989. "Development as capability expansion," 19 *Journal of Development Planning* 41–58.

1993. "Capability and well-being," in Martha Nussbaum and Amartya Sen (eds.), *The Quality of Life*, 30–53. Oxford University Press.

Shapley, Lloyd S., and Martin Shubik. 1954. "A method for evaluating the distribution of power in a committee system," 48 *American Political Science Review* 787–92.

Shavell, Steven M. 1980a. "Damage measures for breach of contract," 11 *Bell Journal of Economics* 466–90.

1980b. "Strict liability versus negligence," 9 *Journal of Legal Studies* 1–25.

1986. "The judgment proof problem," 6 *International Review of Law and Economics* 45–58.

1987. *Economic Analysis of Accident Law*. Cambridge, MA: Harvard University Press.

2003. "Economic analysis of accident law," Working Paper no. 9694, National Bureau of Economic Research, Cambridge, MA.

2004. *Foundations of Economic Analysis of Law*. Cambridge, MA: Harvard University Press.

Shepsle, Kenneth A. 1979. "Institutional arrangements and equilibrium in multidimensional voting models," 23 *American Journal of Political Science* 23–57.

Siegelman, Peter. 2004. "Adverse selection in insurance markets: an exaggerated threat," 113 *Yale Law Journal* 1223–81.

Simon, Herbert A. 1956. "Rational choice and the structure of the environment," 63 *Psychological Review* 129–38.

Simons, Kenneth W. 1995. "The puzzling doctrine of contributory negligence," 16 *Cardozo Law Review* 1693–748.

Singh, Nirvikar, and Xavier Vives. 1984. "Price and quantity competition in a differentiated duopoly," 15 *RAND Journal of Economics* 546–54.

Smeed, Reuben J. 1949. "Some statistical aspects of road safety research," 112 *Journal of the Royal Statistical Society* 1–34.

Smith, Adam. 1759. *The Theory of Moral Sentiments*. London: A. Millar.

1776. *An Inquiry into the Nature and Causes of the Wealth of Nations*. London: Strahan & Cadell.

Spence, A. Michael. 1973. "Job market signaling," 87 *Quarterly Journal of Economics* 355–74.

Stanley, Linda R., and Don L. Coursey. 1990. "Empirical evidence on the selection hypothesis and the decision to litigate or settle," 19 *Journal of Legal Studies* 145–72.

Stevenson, Betsey, and Justin Wolfers. 2006. "Bargaining in the shadow of the law: divorce laws and family distress," 121 *Quarterly Journal of Economics* 267–88.

Stigler, George J. 1950. *Five Lectures on Economic Problems*. London: Macmillan.

1965. *Essays in the History of Economics*. University of Chicago Press.

1966. *The Theory of Price*, 3rd edn. New York: Macmillan.

1969. *The Organization of Industry*. University of Chicago Press.

Stigler, George. 1970. "The optimum enforcement of law," 78 *Journal of Political Economy* 526–36.

1971. "The theory of economic regulation," 3 *Bell Journal of Economics and Management Science* 3–18.

1975. *The Citizen and the State: Essays on Regulation*. University of Chicago Press.

1986. *The Essence of Stigler* (eds. Kurt R. Leube and Thomas G. Hoore). Stanford CA: Hoover Institution Press.

1988. *Memoirs of an Unregulated Economist*. New York: Basic Books.

Stiglitz, Joseph E. 1974. "Alternative theories of wage determination and unemployment in LDCs: the labor turnover model," 88 *Quarterly Journal of Economics* 194–227.

1976. "The efficiency wage hypothesis, surplus labor and the distribution of income in LDCs," 28 *Oxford Economic Papers* 185–207.

2002. "Information and the change in the paradigm in economics," 92 *American Economic Review* 460–501.

Strazzella, James A. 1997. "The relationship of double jeopardy to prosecution appeals," 73 *Notre Dame Law Review* 1–30.

Stremitzer, Alexander, and Avraham Tabbach. 2009. "Insolvency and biased standards: the case for proportional liability," Faculty Scholarship. Paper no. 24, Yale Law School, New Haven, CT.

Stuntz, William J. 2000. "Self-defeating crimes," 86 *Virginia Law Review* 1871–99.

Sunstein, Cass R. 1996. "Social norms and social roles," 96 *Columbia Law Review* 903–68.

Sunstein, Cass R. (ed.). 2000. *Behavioral Law and Economics*. Cambridge University Press.

Takenaka, Toshiko. 2008. *Patent Law and Theory: A Handbook of Contemporary Research*. Northampton, MA: Edward Elgar.

Taylor, Shelley E., and Jonathon D. Brown. 1988. "Illusion and well-being: a social psychological perspective on mental health," 103 *Psychological Bulletin* 193–210.

Taylor, Timothy. 2011. *Principles of Economics*, 2nd edn. Minneapolis: Textbook Media Press.

Thaler, Richard. 1980. "Toward a positive theory of consumer choice," 1 *Journal of Economic Behavior and Organization* 39–60.

Tiebout, Charles. 1956. "A pure theory of local expenditures," 64 *Journal of Political Economy* 416–24.

Tirole, Jean, and Roland Benabou. 2006. "Incentives and prosocial behavior," 96 *American Economic Review* 1652–78.

Tobin, James. 1974. "Prospects for macro-economic policy," in *The New Economics, One Decade Older*, 71–96. Princeton University Press.

Tollison, Robert D. 1982. "Rent seeking: a survey," 35 *Kyklos* 575–602.

Trebilcock, Michael J. 1993. *The Limits of Freedom of Contract*. Cambridge, MA: Harvard University Press.

Trimarchi, Pietro. 2003. "Transfers, uncertainty and the cost of disruption," 23 *International Review of Law and Economics* 49–62.

Tucker, Albert W. 1950. "A two-person dilemma," unpublished notes, Stanford University, CA.

Tullock, Gordon. 1967. "The welfare costs of monopolies, tariffs, and theft," 5 *Western Economic Journal* 224–32.

1971a. "The charity of the uncharitable," 9 *Western Economic Journal* 379–92.

1971b. *The Logic of the Law*. New York: Basic Books.

1980. *Trials on Trial: The Pure Theory of Legal Procedure*. New York: Columbia University Press.

1993. *Rent Seeking*. Brookfield, VT: Edward Elgar.

1980. "Efficient rent-seeking," in James M. Buchanan, Robert D. Tollison, and Gordon Tullock, *Toward a Theory of the Rent-Seeking Society*, 97–112. College Station: Texas A&M University Press.

Tversky, Amos, and Daniel Kahneman. 1974. "Judgment under uncertainty: heuristics and biases," 185 *Science* 1124–31.

1991. "Loss aversion in riskless choice: a reference-dependent model." 106 *Quarterly Journal of Economics* 1039–61.

Tyler, Tom R. 1990. *Why People Obey the Law*. New Haven, CT: Yale University Press.

Van den Hauwe, Ludwig. 2005. "Public choice, constitutional political economy and law and economics," in Boudemijn Bouckaert and Gerrit De Geest (eds.), *Encyclopedia of Law and Economics*, vol. I, *The History and Methodology of Low and Economics*, 603–59. Cheltenham: Edward Elgar.

Vickrey, William. 1945. "Measuring marginal utility by reactions to risk," 13 *Econometrica* 319–33.

1961. "Counterspeculation, auctions, and competitive sealed tenders," 16 *Journal of Finance* 8–37.

Volokh, Alexander. 1997. "N guilty men," 146 *University of Pennsylvania Law Review* 173–216.

Von Neumann, John, and Oskar Morgenstern. 1944. *Theory of Games and Economic Behavior*. Princeton University Press.

Von Stackelberg, Heinrich 1934. *Marktform und Gleichgewicht [Market Structure and Equilibrium]*. Vienna: Julius Springer.

Wagner, Richard E. 2004. "Meddlesome preferences and rent extraction: the tobacco shakedown," in Charles K. Rowley and Friedrich Schneider (eds.), *The Encyclopedia of Public Choice*, 378–80. Dordrecht: Kluwer Academic.

Wanniski, Jude. 1978. "Taxes, revenues, and the 'Laffer curve,'" 50 *The Public Interest* 3–16.

Wayburn, Laurie A., and Anton Chiono. 2010. "The role of federal policy in establishing ecosystem service markets," 20 *Duke Environmental Law and Policy Forum* 385–415.

Weisbach, David A. 2008. "What does happiness research tell us about taxation?," 37 *Journal of Legal Studies* 293–324.

Williamson, Oliver E. 1964. *The Economics of Discretionary Behavior: Managerial Objectives in a Theory of the Firm*. Englewood Cliffs, NJ: Prentice Hall.

1968. "Economies as an antitrust defense: the welfare trade-offs," 58 *American Economic Review* 18–36.

1970. *Corporate Control and Business Behavior: An Inquiry into the Effects of Organization Form on Enterprise Behavior*. Englewood Cliffs, NJ: Prentice Hall.

1975. *Markets and Hierarchies: Analysis and Antitrust Implications*. New York: Free Press.

1979. "Transaction-cost economics: the governance of contractual relations," 22 *Journal of Law and Economics* 233–61.

1983. "Credible commitments: using hostages to support exchange," 73 *American Economics Review* 519–40.

1985. *The Economic Institutions of Capitalism: Firms, Markets, Relational Contracting*. New York: Free Press.

1991. "Comparative economic organization: the analysis of discrete structural alternatives," 36 *Administrative Science Quarterly* 269–96.

1996. *The Mechanisms of Governance*. Oxford University Press.

2002. "The theory of the firm as governance structure: from choice to contract," 16 *Journal of Economic Perspectives* 171–95.

2005. "The economics of governance," 95 *American Economic Review* 1–18.

Wittman, Donald A. 1984. "Liability for harm or restitution of benefit?" 13 *Journal of Legal Studies* 57–80.

Yablon, Charles M. 2007. "The historical race: competition for corporate charters and the rise and decline of New Jersey: 1880–1910," 32 *Journal of Corporation Law* 323–80.

Zermelo, Ernst. 1913. "Uber eine Anwendung der Mengenlehre auf die Theorie des Schachspiels," in E. W. Hobson and A. E. H. Love (eds.), *Proceedings of the Fifth International Congress of Mathematicians*, vol. II, 501–4. Cambridge University Press.

SUBJECT INDEX

(1) History of law and economics

Biographies

Akerlof, George Arthur
Arrow, Kenneth Joseph
Ayres, Ian
Beccaria, Cesare
Becker, Gary Stanley
Bentham, Jeremy
Buchanan, James McGill
Calabresi, Guido
Coase, Ronald Harry
Cooter, Robert D.
Demsetz, Harold
Director, Aaron
Epstein, Richard Allen
Friedman, Milton
Hayek, Friedrich August von
Kahneman, Daniel
Landes, William M.
Manne, Henry G.
Nash, John Forbes
North, Douglass Cecil
Ostrom, Elinor
Polinsky, A. Mitchell
Posner, Richard Allen
Priest, George L.
Rawls, John Bordley
Romano, Roberta
Rubin, Paul H.
Rubinfeld, Daniel L.
Sen, Amartya
Shavell, Steven M.
Simons, Henry Calvert
Smith, Vernon Lomax
Stigler, George Joseph
Trebilcock, Michael J.
Tullock, Gordon
Williamson, Oliver Eaton

Schools and approaches

Austrian law and economics
behavioral law and economics
Chicago school
comparative law and economics
constitutional political economy
experimental law and economics
functional law and economics
law and economics
law and economics 2.0
neuroeconomics
new institutional economics
Ordoliberalism
positive versus normative law and economics
public choice theory
social choice theory
transaction-cost economics
Virginia school
Yale school

Academic journals

American Law and Economics Review
Constitutional Political Economy
European Journal of Law and Economics
International Review of Law and Economics
Journal of Law and Economics
Journal of Competition Law and Economics
Journal of Empirical Legal Studies
Journal of Law, Economics, and Organization
Journal of Legal Analysis
Journal of Legal Studies
law and economics journals
Papers on Non-Market Decision Making
Public Choice
Review of Law and Economics
Supreme Court Economic Review

Professional associations and programs

ALACDE
ALEA
ASLEA
CLEA
EALE
economic institutes for judges
EDLE
EMLE
Erasmus program in law and economics
ISNIE
Mundus!

Ronald H. Coase medal
Vanderbilt Ph.D. in law and economics

(2) **Methodology and welfare analysis**

Welfare analysis

aggregation problem
allocative efficiency
Bastiat's unseen costs
Bentham's imperative
discounting
disappointment prevention principle
efficiency
exponential discounting
first best versus second best
fundamental theorems of welfare
impartial observer theorem
Kaldor–Hicks criterion
maximand
maximize the pie
Nash criterion of welfare
opportunity cost
Pareto efficiency
Pareto non-comparability
potential compensation
social benefit
social discount rate
social time preference
social welfare
two-step optimization
utility maximization
wealth maximization
welfare analysis

Fairness and distribution

capability approach
dependency theory
difference principle
entitlement principle
Hotelling's rule
Human Development Index
interdependent utility functions
intergenerational equity
other-regarding preferences
Pareto distribution
Pareto index
Pareto-optimal redistribution
procedural preferences
Rawlsian justice
Rawlsian maximin
relative preferences
taste for discrimination
taste for fairness
veil of ignorance
veil of uncertainty

Modeling tools

calibration
comparative dynamics
comparative statics
constrained optimization
corner solution versus interior solution
cost–benefit analysis
cost-effectiveness analysis
decision theory
demand-revealing processes
dynamic models
endogenous variables
ex ante versus ex post
incentive alignment
incentives
input–output analysis
information harnessing
qualitative versus quantitative models
regulatory impact analysis
risk management
robustness
simulations

Methodological debates

Bastiat's unseen costs
cardinalism
carrots versus sticks
contractarianism
demand-side versus supply-side economics
efficiency of democracy
efficiency of the common law hypothesis
falsifiability
interpersonal utility comparisons
invisible hand
laissez-faire
legal origins
marginalism
ordinalism
sanctions as prices
survivor theory of efficiency
utilitarianism
utility monster

(3) **Preferences and choice**

Utility and preferences

axioms of preference
bliss point
cardinal preferences
certainty equivalence
diminishing marginal utility
endogenous versus exogenous preferences
Euclidean preferences
expected utility
exponential discounting

Concepts

(13) Monopoly and competition

(14) Theory of market failures

Asymmetric information

(16) Contract theory and mechanism design

(17) New institutional economics

Biographies

Specialized journals

Concepts

AUTHOR INDEX